BLACK WORDS, WHITE PAGE

Adam Shoemaker came to Australia from Canada in 1980 to take up postgraduate studies at the Australian National University. *Black Words, White Page* has developed from his doctoral research. He is widely published on Black literature and, with Jack Davis, Mudrooroo Narogin (Colin Johnson) and Stephen Muecke, has edited *Paperbark*, the first national anthology of Black Australian writing (UQP, 1989).

UQP STUDIES IN AUSTRALIAN LITERATURE

General Editor: Professor Tony Hassall
Department of English
James Cook University of North Queensland

Also in this series:

J.J. Healy, *Literature and the Aborigine in Australia*

BLACK WORDS, WHITE PAGE

ABORIGINAL LITERATURE 1929-1988

Adam Shoemaker

University of Queensland Press

First published 1989 by University of Queensland Press
Box 42, St Lucia, Queensland, Australia

© Adam Shoemaker 1989

Printed in Australia by Australian Print Group

Cataloguing in Publication Data

National Library of Australia

Shoemaker, Adam, 1957–   .
  Black words white page : Aboriginal literature
  1929 to 1988.

  Bibliography.
  Includes index.

  (1). Australian literature — Aboriginal
  authors — History and criticism. I. Title.
  (Series : Studies in Australian literature).

A820′.9′89915

ISBN 0 7022 2149 X

To Johanna Dykgraaf,
for her time and care

Contents

Acknowledgments

Every writing project starts with an idea and ends with a sigh of relief. *Black Words, White Page* is no exception.

In this case the original idea was especially important since the subject had never really been explored in depth. For his suggestion that I should research Aboriginal literature I will always be indebted to Bob Brissenden, former Reader in English at the Australian National University.

Two of my first interviewees have become both friends and collaborators on other projects. Mudrooroo Narogin (formerly Colin Johnson) and Jack Davis are two of the many Black Australian authors whose talent and openness have made this book possible. I would also like to offer special thanks to Mona Tur, Cliff Watego, Maureen Watson and Archie Weller for their help.

Many non-Aboriginal individuals have encouraged my work in its growth from research to publication: Livio Dobrez, Johanna Dykgraaf, Tony Hassall, Campbell Macknight, Stephen Muecke and Craig Munro have all played an important role. The University of Queensland Press has been supportive throughout, and especially Clare Forster. I also owe thanks to Barry Maher and Miguel Peirano for their computing and typesetting expertise.

Although this manuscript was completely revised and updated in 1987–88 I cannot claim that it is totally comprehensive or up-to-date. Black Australian writing — like Aboriginal politics — is changing and expanding so rapidly that each study becomes like a frame frozen in a point of time.

It is my hope that by providing a socio-historical context for Black Australian literature I have given the subject some of the depth of attention — and respect — it deserves. In this sense the most important acknowledgment will be public recognition that Aboriginal voices tell the unique and vital story of Australia's Fourth World.

Introduction
Australia's Fourth World Literature

As the 1980s progress, modern nation states are increasingly being forced to come to terms with their indigenous minorities. The Laplanders of Finland, the Indians of Peru, and the Inuit of Canada are no longer articulating their aims and grievances solely through appeals to their respective national governments. In a process hastened by the constant improvements in electronic and satellite communications, there is a trend towards indigenous collectivity on a global scale. A clear example of this was the creation in 1975 of the World Council of Indigenous Peoples (WCIP), officially sanctioned by the United Nations as a non-governmental organisation. At the inaugural meeting of the WCIP, George Manuel introduced the concept of The Fourth World, a phrase employed to describe indigenous minorities throughout the earth.

Australia is no exception to this trend. How the nation is perceived internationally depends, in part, on its own Fourth World: the Aboriginal people. In May 1981, Australia's situation was highlighted when it hosted in Canberra the Third General Assembly of the WCIP. It became evident that Australia was at least temporarily positioned at the intersection of what might be termed the First and the Fourth Worlds, especially when the Queen's representative, Governor-General Sir Zelman Cowan, delivered his welcoming address to—and was heckled by—the assembled indigenous delegates. Just a few months later in September 1981, Australia played host to another international gathering: the Commonwealth Heads of Government meeting in Melbourne. During this conference it was possible to describe the country as being at the convergence of, perhaps, *three* different worlds. Aboriginal political spokespersons, denied official access to the conference forum, endeavoured to make private contact with Third World Commonwealth government officials who, in turn, pressed their own cases in the presence of the established First World Commonwealth delegations.

A year later, during the Brisbane Commonwealth Games of 1982, Australian Aborigines made a strong impression upon representatives of the international media who were gathered to cover the sporting events. The rapidly quelled demonstrations of the Aborigines highlighted the plight of Australia's Fourth World most succinctly, and the foreign coverage of their protests illustrated the sympathetic international interest in Australian Aboriginal affairs.[1] Events of 1987, such as the furore over Michael Mansell's attendance at a conference in Libya and Black Australian protests in Portsmouth, UK (over the use of the Aboriginal flag on board the "First Fleet" replica ships) again thrust Black Australian issues onto the world stage. Then, on 26 January 1988 television news crews from around the globe filmed and interviewed while thousands of Black Australians marched in the streets of Sydney to voice their opposition to the Bicentenary. In Hyde Park, over 15,000 Aborigines and their supporters attended the largest protest rally since the days of the Vietnam moratoria. The positive and non-violent focus of the events not only impressed foreign correspondents but also served to unify Aboriginal groups from all parts of Australia.[2] It is therefore clear that within the network of international political opinion and influence, the Aboriginal people are at a crucial stage in their development. As Ribnga Kenneth Green wrote in 1979:

> The concept of the Fourth World is still very much in its early formative stage. Australian Aborigines still have the important opportunity of determining the paradigm of such a movement. The weakness of a minority can be turned into its very source of strength.[3]

These factors, and the accelerating politicisation of many Black Australians over the past two decades, led Bernard Smith to comment in 1980 that:

> During the past twenty years or so a spirit of nationalism which is uniting people of Aboriginal descent has arisen throughout the Commonwealth ... Whether the Aboriginal people constitute today a nation within a nation is arguable; but there can be little doubt that it is now the most important and vocal national minority in the country, is growing in strength and confidence daily, and is developing widespread international connections.[4]

It has not simply been a matter of the rest of the world taking a greater interest in the lot of Black Australians; Aborigines have themselves been reaching out internationally more so than ever before. For example, during the past ten years, Aboriginal delegations have visited the Peoples' Republic of China, the United States, Europe, Nigeria, Canada, and the United Nations. Not all of these overseas contacts have been primarily of a political nature for, over the same period of time, Aboriginal dancers (both tribal and modern) have attended cultural festivals in Papua New Guinea, New Zealand, Tahiti, Nigeria and Canada.

The vibrancy of Aboriginal culture has elicited much overseas interest: to cite one example, a French Society for the Promotion of the Culture of Australian Aborigines has been in existence since 1980. The Western world of the performing arts is increasingly taking note of both traditional and contemporary Aboriginal culture: in 1978, New York drama scout, Elaine Gold, visited Australia with a view to securing scripts of plays written by Aborigines, for possible presentation at Joseph Papp's Shakespearean Summer Festival in Central Park, New York. Four years later, Robert Merritt's play *The Cake Man* was invited to the World Theatre Festival in Denver, Colorado, where it was so enthusiastically received that its two week season was sold out in advance of the first performance. Two years later Jack Davis's *No Sugar* was Australia's representative at the same festival, held in conjunction with Expo 86 in Vancouver, Canada—and again won both popular and critical acclaim. In May 1987, Davis's play *The Dreamers* was revived for a four week season in Portsmouth, providing a most ironic counterpoint to the re-enactment of the launching of the First Fleet to Australia. Finally, at the 1988 Festival of Perth, the third stage of Davis's dramatic trilogy, *Barungin (Smell the Wind)*, had its world premiere prior to a national and international tour.

Had Elaine Gold come to Australia only ten years earlier her quest would have been fruitless, for it was not until 1971 that the first play written by an Aborigine was performed. By 1988, twelve plays and a number of revues written by Black Australians had been staged in various cities and many more were being workshopped. This is just one index of the growing confidence and fluency of Aborigines operating within the constraints of White Australian culture. Indeed, there appears to be some relationship between the fact that as Black Australians have made political and social advances over the past twenty-five years in Australia, they have embarked far more frequently upon projects of creative writing in English. This question will be addressed more fully at a later stage; what is noteworthy here is that, in 1961, no Black Australian had published any works of creative writing for approximately thirty years. By 1988, in addition to the twelve plays already mentioned, eighteen collections of poetry (and many more individual poems) and seven novels—all written by Black Australians—had appeared. One Aboriginal author, Oodgeroo Noonuccal (Kath Walker), claims to have outsold all other living Australian poets, and her works have been widely translated.[5] One branch of the Australia Council, the Aboriginal Arts Board, is directly involved with the funding of Aboriginal literature, and welcomes manuscripts for possible publication. In Sydney an autonomous Aboriginal publishing house, Black Books, became a reality in 1986 with the release of its first publication. Then in early 1988 Magabala Books of Broome, Western Australia—another independent Black Australian publisher—launched its first major title, Glenyse Ward's autobiographical story, *Wandering Girl*. The vast majority of Australians are, however, unaware of these achievements and, more importantly, do not yet appreciate their significance.

I intend to discuss in detail both the nature and the extent of Aboriginal writing in English. It should be stated at the outset that, throughout this study the descriptive term "Black Australian" has been deliberately used, in addition to "Aboriginal", for it embraces the published work of other oppressed, dark-skinned minorities in Australia, such as the Torres Strait Islanders. In the following chapters, a number of specific issues will be addressed: the manner in which this new literature represents the social world around it; the role which it plays in articulating the black past and the contemporary Aboriginal identity; and the relationship between Aboriginal writing and other forms of Australian literature. I will demonstrate that Aboriginal authors have produced literary works which merit thorough analysis as well as public recognition. This will involve describing and evaluating Black Australian literature within both literary and socio-political contexts. Above all, the function of the Black Australian novel as a meaningful and often impassioned form of cultural communication will be emphasised throughout.

One of the most important dimensions of this cross-cultural communication is the fact that the present generation of Australians now have the opportunity to obtain a glimpse of Aborigines as they see themselves, rather than as they are seen by others. Ever since the first Dutch reports in the seventeenth century, Black Australians have been assessed in the writings of Europeans. They have been placed under the figurative microscope of the visual and literary arts, initially for overseas and, later, for domestic consumption. However laudable the motives for this work might have been, it was inevitably affected by the preconceptions and limitations of the artists and authors involved—who were all culturally foreign to their subject matter. Some authors were curious, some were sympathetic, some were bigots, and some were genuinely concerned, but not one was an Aborigine.

Hence, when Oodgeroo Noonuccal's first collection of poetry appeared in print in 1964, a new phase of cultural communication began in Australia. Not only the content, but the very fact of Noonuccal's *We Are Going* was important as, effectively for the first time,[6] one of those best qualified to do so was commenting creatively upon her own race, its aspirations and fears. But this was not all. Noonuccal's book ushered in an era of self-reflective literary examination by Black Australians; it also completely changed the specimen on the slide under the microscope. Aborigines had now begun to analyse, pass judgement upon, criticise, and occasionally praise White Australians.

At the same time that Noonuccal was preparing her first books of poetry, important socio-political changes were altering the status of Aboriginal Australians. Throughout the 1960s, the Federal Council for the Advancement of Aborigines and Torres Strait Islanders (FCAATSI) gained importance as the most influential and nationally representative black pressure group. In 1961, Aborigines were finally granted the franchise throughout Australia and, in 1965, Charles Perkins and others organised the widely reported "Freedom Rides" throughout country towns of New South Wales. In 1965, the federal Arbitration Commission ruled that Northern Territory Aborigines should receive equal wages in the pastoral industry, this parity to be achieved gradually over a three year period. Importantly, in 1966, the Gurindji people at Wave Hill station in the Northern Territory resorted to strike action, initially for improved wages, but ultimately for their tribal land. The following year the Commonwealth government held a national referendum in which an unprecedented majority of Australians (almost ninety per cent) voted in favour of transferring to the Commonwealth paramount legislative and jurisdictional power in the area of Aboriginal affairs. In 1968, FCAATSI accelerated and reinforced its campaign to achieve Aboriginal land rights.

As this brief catalogue of political and legislative measures indicates, the decade beginning in 1960 was one of protest, publicity and, in some cases, significant change in the realm of Aboriginal affairs. This is not to say that the autonomy or the political influence of Black Australians increased evenly throughout the entire country. There were during the same decade clear examples of the continued powerlessness of Aborigines in the face of governmental and industrial economic aims. In 1965, the Commonwealth's grant to the Nabalco consortium of mining leases on Gove Peninsula in Arnhem Land, expressly against the wishes and desires of the Aboriginal people there, was an excellent case in point. So much, of course, depends upon perspective. While one commentator can wax enthusiastic over the unparalleled support for the referendum of 1967, another can throw quite a different light on the same event by noting that it took almost two hundred years for the British settlers of Australia to grant full citizenship rights to Aborigines and to recognise them officially for census purposes.

It is likely that the 1960s brought more important and lasting socio-political changes to the lives of Aborigines than any previous decade since the arrival of Europeans in Australia. One salient indication of the alteration in the Aboriginal socio-political situation was the increasing publication of Black Australian authors. Dramatic—and overdue—changes in the legislative status of Aborigines paralleled the experiments of Black Australian literature during those years. I contend that a fundamental relationship exists between the socio-political milieu and Aboriginal creative writing in English. It is a complex relationship. It is not one in which the literature demonstrably operates as a direct reaction to socio-political events (although this is occasionally the case); nor is it a relationship in which literature observably influences Aboriginal behaviour or political action. But in the case of Aboriginal creative writing, the literature and actual events are very proximate: novels are extremely naturalistic, the inspiration for plays comes largely from the personal experiences of the playwrights, characters are modelled to a great extent upon individuals the author has personally known, and socio-political issues are faced squarely. In short, black creative writing in Australia cannot be studied in isolation: it must be examined and evaluated in terms of the social environment which surrounds it and the historical events which precede it.

It is essential to note, however, that while the approach to the literature of black/white race relations to be taken here is explicitly historical, cultural, and sociological, it is not deterministic or Marxist.

Novels, poems and plays concerning Aboriginal/white relations in Australia are seen as aesthetically significant in terms of both their style and content. In a literature which frequently focuses upon violence and cultural clash, what is said is assuredly crucial, but how it is said also undoubtedly contributes to, or detracts from, the aesthetic impact of the work. This aesthetic criterion cannot be ignored in an examination of Black Australian literature. In fact, such an examination demonstrates that Aboriginal creative writing in English is a phenomenon worthy of serious critical, cultural, and academic consideration: that it is a rapidly developing literature in its own right.

Many White Australian authors have dealt with Aboriginal themes, with varying degrees of success. Certain of Australia's finest writers have derived the inspiration for some of their best work from an observation of Aboriginal situations. On the other hand, it is worth emphasising that talent is by no means an assurance of popularity in the marketplace and, for this reason, the works of several less artistically skilled European writers who have written "best sellers" concerning Aboriginal/white race relations will also be examined. For the concerns of this study, popular literature is just as important, and deserves as much critical attention, as the literature of the educated elite. This is not so much a theoretical as a practical issue: if over 100,000 Australians have read a book written by Douglas Lockwood, it would be both irresponsible and misleading not to discuss his work in relation to the literary perception of Australian Aborigines in White Australian writing. There is a further cogent reason for an examination of the more popular literature of Aboriginal/white race relations: the imagery which Ion L. Idriess employs in his novels may not be as striking and metaphysical as that of Patrick White, but it is, nevertheless, just as important in terms of the articulation of the author's themes and his racial attitudes. In short, I make no claims for the pre-eminence of certain types of literature, but I do assert that many varying types and standards of writing must be treated in a topic as socio-political as this one.

If one believes that the individual reader is affected by what she or he reads, considerations such as the volume of book sales and the choice of certain works of literature for educational syllabuses cannot be ignored. Some tentative propositions can be advanced: for example, as soon as a book is prescribed or recommended for study in schools (especially secondary schools) it gains a degree of legitimacy that increases the longer it remains a set text; if public opposition to its inclusion is strong enough, it will soon be removed.

Similarly, if a book is poorly marketed and distributed by its publisher, then its impact upon the public will be limited, regardless of the talent of the author. Although an analysis of the book publishing industry in Australia is beyond the scope of this study, some reference to such factors as reprint publishing, the volume of sales, and the selection of literature for educational purposes will be made where relevant.

Such relevance can often be viewed in so far as it is part of the entire social milieu in which a work of literature is created. Again, this is not to say that the socio-political situation dictates the form of a literary work. It must be remembered, though, that in the case of Aboriginal literature in English and creative writing by White Australians on Aboriginal themes, literature is frequently so proximate to reality and to social events that these must be surveyed prior to a consideration of the works themselves, if they are to be fully understood and appreciated.

This study is concerned with cross-cultural communication. It begins by describing an historical period during which such communication was minimal. The onset of the Depression provided the impetus for social questioning, and many of the questions—asked by politicians, missionaries, pastoralists and authors—concerned the Aboriginal people. The same period also saw the publication of the work of David Unaipon, the first Black Australian author in English, whose writings are discussed in Chapter Two. It is therefore appropriate to begin the study of black/white literary and socio-political relations in 1929.

During the Depression, relatively few Europeans wrote about Aborigines. Those authors who did so passed comment, not only on Black Australians, but also, to differing degrees, on their own dominant white society. Through this they revealed—sometimes unwittingly—information about themselves. Two such writers were Katharine Susannah Prichard and Xavier Herbert. In the years of the Depression, they rescued the Aborigine from literary invisibility and boldly addressed the embarrassing issue of miscegenation. There is a strong social dimension to their novels—especially Herbert's *Capricornia*—which reflects the general unrest and questioning of those years.

In the 1930s, there were important alterations in the scientific, anthropological, and official views of Aboriginal people; these changes will be discussed in Chapter One. Yet not all authors of the 1930s and early 1940s adopted the sympathetic stance of Prichard and Herbert.

One who did not was Ion L. Idriess, whose first novel dealing in part with Aborigines, *Lasseter's Last Ride*, appeared in 1931. Another was Arthur Upfield, who wrote an entire series of popular but highly stereotyped books concerning the fictional Aboriginal detective Napoleon Bonaparte (or Boney, as Upfield called him). In the fifteen years following 1930, changes in the socio-political climate in Australia paralleled in an intriguing way changes in the literary perception of Aborigines by whites; changes which will also be discussed in the second chapter.

The end of World War II in 1945 marks a turning point in black/white relations in Australia. The returning servicemen had fought against tyranny, discrimination, and oppression in various theatres of war around the globe. The Aboriginal soldiers among them were often prepared to fight these same afflictions in the domestic arena upon their return. In addition, the Black Australians who saw action in World War II sometimes developed uniquely egalitarian relationships with their white fellow-soldiers in the heat of battle, so that both white and black attitudes underwent a radical—if usually temporary—change.[7] Other blacks who had obtained employment in Australia due to the exigencies of wartime production had been absorbed into the trade union movement, a factor which was to become of considerable importance in the genesis of Aboriginal political protest, as the Pilbara strike of 1946 was to illustrate.

The fifteen years following 1945 also saw the emergence of a new generation of White Australian authors, one of whom was Judith Wright. *The Moving Image*, published in 1946 included a number of poems in which her understanding of Black Australians was both original and strikingly symbolic. Over the same period, various writers—almost exclusively novelists who had themselves lived and worked with Aboriginal people—released important works, among them Randolph Stow, Donald Stuart, and the popular authors Bill Harney and Douglas Lockwood. Towards the end of this period Patrick White wrote *Voss*, the first of his three novels which include Aboriginal characters, and a book which offers a singular, metaphysical insight into the culture of Aboriginal Australians. The third chapter of this study will highlight the most noteworthy socio-political events in the area of Aboriginal/white relations in Australia until 1961; the fourth will assess the black/white race relations literature of that same era, with regard to its creative merits and its social commentary and ideological content.

It is in the twenty-five years up to 1988 that the other side of black/white cultural communication in Australia finally found expression. As Aboriginal writers began to respond to the themes which they considered to be of importance, they presented a long delayed reply to the dominant White Australian culture. When they write, Black Australians are not solely responding to the surrounding white society. Although a treatment of the relations between blacks and whites is definitely an important element in their works, perhaps even more significant is the exploration of the nature of "Aboriginality" itself: what it means to be black in Australia. Thus, there are two main tributaries which must be explored in an examination of Aboriginal literature in English. These two streams do flow together in places but they are distinct, if related, concerns. As J.J. Healy puts it, "the volatile pictures that are now emerging in Aboriginal matters ... give us, very starkly, Black on White; very poignantly and angrily, Black on Black".[8]

The self-reflective examination of Aboriginality is a major, but not the only, theme in black creative writing in English. Following a socio-political survey of Aboriginal/white relations from the 1960s to the present, further chapters deal with some of these other related themes: views and varieties of history as expressed in Black Australian writing; sex and violence, as dealt with in the Black Australian novel; the emphasis upon political protest in Aboriginal poetry; and the fascinating position of Aboriginal drama as both critique and often humorous creative expression.

Naturally whites and blacks do not always choose to write about precisely the same topics, but there are cases in which a parallel approach is evident—for example, in two novels concerning the Aboriginal guerilla rebel, Sandamara—and, in such cases, the two approaches will be compared and contrasted at some length. Throughout, an historical and socio-cultural analysis prefaces the thematic and artistic treatment of the works. White Australian writing is discussed here only in so far as it illuminates aspects of Black Australian literature and historical activity. I have been intentionally selective in order to highlight the most distinctive aspects of Aboriginal writing. It is equally important to bear in mind that, while arbitrary dates have been selected to delimit, for example, the assimilation era, the situation was in reality far more fluid. In this study I have deliberately restricted both the White Australian authors and the genres discussed, as well as the boundaries of the periods selected for examination, in order to throw into relief Aboriginal socio-political action and literary achievement.

It is essential to appreciate the social environment which surrounds black/white race relations literature in Australia and, in particular, that of the 1960s to the present. For example, one might suggest that the acceleration in the output of creative writing by Aboriginal Australians is a result of the creation of a Federal government funding agency for Aboriginal artists and writers in 1973 (the Aboriginal Arts Board), together with a general improvement in the receptivity of White Australians to the black viewpoint. While this may be partially true, it would be naive to claim that higher budgetary allocations to Aboriginal affairs and improvements in the autonomy of Black Australians completely explain an upsurge in Aboriginal creative writing. It must be remembered that the first collections of Aboriginal poetry appeared in print without any government subsidy and, even now, some of the most talented and influential black authors publish without the assistance of the Aboriginal Arts Board. Indeed, as will be noted in later chapters, there have been a number of occasions when official government actions which have been considered repressive by Aboriginal Australians have provided the impetus for the writing of poetry or drama. Clearly the matter is not simple, for both advances and regressions in black autonomy have produced literary responses.

However various and complex the circumstances of the time, the years since 1970 have witnessed the appearance of a great deal of Aboriginal creative writing in English. It is interesting to note, however, that there has not been a corresponding increase in the amount of creative writing by White Australians dealing with Aboriginal themes. In addition, while black authors favour the writing of poetry over any other literary genre, current White Australian poets—far greater in number—for the most part avoid writing poems about Aborigines. This represents a marked shift from the poetic preoccupations of, for example, the Jindyworobaks.

Why do Aborigines so frequently choose the medium of poetry? While it is impossible to offer a conclusive answer, some theories can be advanced. One factor is the poignancy and brevity of Black Australian verse: the medium provides an immediacy which allows the theme to shine through directly. Second, since much Aboriginal creative writing is published in limited editions on a shoestring budget, there is an inherent advantage in working in a genre which is more concise and economical. In addition to these pragmatic considerations it is also arguable that, while the creation of poetry in written English requires many Aboriginal authors to bridge a cultural gap, since they are working in a format of foreign origin, that gap may not be as daunting in the case of poetry as it would be in the case of other literary modes. As anthropologists such as Elkin and Berndt have illustrated, traditional Aboriginal song cycles are venerable, complex, and extremely poetic. Rodney Hall's inclusion of the Wonguri-Mandijigai "Moon-Bone Song", and other Aboriginal songs in translation, in the *Collins Book of Australian Poetry*[9] recognises this fact.

Although Hall is the first white editor to include such songs in a major collection of Australian poetry, he is by no means the first to appreciate the intrinsic lyricism of many Aboriginal languages. As far back as the 1940s, such anthropologists as T.G.H. Strehlow were demonstrating this in published works such as *Aranda Traditions*, which first appeared in 1947. [10] More recently, Carl von Brandenstein and A.P. Thomas's collection of *djabi*—initiation songs of Aboriginal men from the Pilbara region of Western Australia—brought these poetic elements to the fore. These *djabi* "in their use of a few words to evoke a mood, have a kinship with Japanese *haiku*":[11]

Drop, leaves, silvery stars!
Drop, leaves from the spearwood to the east of me!
Drop, leaves, wind-swayed, wind-ruffled.[12]

Given the impressiveness of this poetic tradition, it is not surprising that poetry is the single most popular medium of creative expression in written English for Aboriginal people. Moreover, Aboriginal authors today are fusing traditional languages with English in their poems to achieve a unique phonetic synthesis. More will be said of this innovation in Chapter Eight, but it is important to be aware of the historical dimension and traditional links of much Aboriginal literature in English, particularly Black Australian poetry and drama.

Although this primacy of poetry has not been challenged since 1970, Aboriginal authors have begun to work with other literary genres, drama being one of the most significant. Plays written by Aboriginal Australians have been performed from Sydney to Perth and overseas, have gone on state and national tours, have been published, have been presented at a number of drama festivals, and have been aired nationally on television. Theatre has the advantage over the printed page of providing an immediate and total sensory impact. Given the socio-political preoccupations of Black Australian writers and their desire to achieve just such an impact, it is not surprising that they are writing for the stage. The potential transformation of plays into the media of video and film has not escaped Aboriginal dramatists, which further reinforces the attractiveness of the theatre. I will argue in a later chapter that Aboriginal drama is of both historical and contemporary significance, by examining the influence of traditional Black Australian oral literature upon modern Aboriginal plays.

The point is that, while I am not adopting a literary "genre criticism" approach to race relations literature in Australia and am, rather, examining the subject thematically, the fundamental importance of the medium of communication cannot be ignored. Both white and black authors consciously choose to write in a particular mode or style for a wide variety of reasons, including the influence of mentors, education, economic aims, gender, subject matter, and personal disposition. They may also consciously choose to write for a particular or a general audience—in this case, primarily for an Aboriginal or white readership—or for both simultaneously. The genre and what may be termed the target of a work can be thought of as independent variables affecting both its financial success and its general impact. The task of isolating these variables from the works themselves is not only extremely difficult but extends beyond the ambit of this socio-cultural and literary study.

However, it is valuable to raise this issue because, when Aboriginal and White Australian authors do explicitly state why they choose a particular literary mode, and name the specific target of their writing, the matter becomes very pertinent. Such information is even more relevant when the themes of the literature involve cultural clash, as is the norm in the works discussed here. Since the texts themselves do not provide this information, my research has included as many personal interviews as possible with the authors being studied and, in these and other cases, relevant autobiographical and biographical material has been collected.

There is a further reason for this partly sociological perspective, which can be subsumed under the category of political activism. Over the past twenty-five years in Australia, the debate over Aboriginal rights (to land, to education, to citizenship, and to compensation) has received considerable publicity. Specific issues will be discussed at a later stage; what is presently important is that the group of black activists grew both in numbers and in audibility through the decades of the 1960s, 1970s, and the 1980s, as did the politicisation of many other

Aborigines. The activists made themselves heard through petitions, protests, demonstrations, interviews, and publicity campaigns and, importantly, many of them also began to write. Some produced purely political treatises, but a significant number of them wrote poems, plays, and even novels. Even those who did not demonstrate often wrote works sympathetic to the concerns of those who did.

Amongst today's White Australian community, those with official political power rarely produce creative writing on a political theme, especially one involving the Aboriginal people: the white public spokespersons are, by and large, not authors. However, amongst the Black Australian community, public spokespersons far more frequently are writers, or are influenced by them. What is important here is that Aboriginal authors are very frequently highly motivated in a political sense and are influential both among their own race and, to growing extent, among the larger Australian community. As Bernard Smith writes, "A few black writers ... are playing a leading part in developing a new awareness of nationhood among their own people".[13]

A number of conclusions may be drawn from this. First, the role of these writers means that an analysis of Aboriginal creative writing in English has wider ramifications: one gains a clearer view of Aboriginal socio-political aspirations through interviews with the writers concerned and through reading their works. Second, Aboriginal creative writing illustrates the fact that artistic skill need not be a casualty of political commitment. Third, the contrasting perceptions of White Australian authors who write on similar themes are thrown into even clearer relief, as the majority are not as strongly politically motivated as their black counterparts. Thus, while this study deals with the literature of Australian black/white race relations over the past sixty years and the socio-political milieu in which it emerged, my major concern is the creative writing of the last twenty-five years up to 1988.

As noted at the beginning of this introduction, there are strong indications of a global trend towards a collectivity of indigenous peoples which is theoretically, and, in an increasing fashion, politically expressed. It is probable that a necessary precondition for the full participation of the Australian Aboriginal people in this Fourth World movement will be a unified black collectivity within Australia itself. Although Smith considers it "arguable" at the moment whether or not "the Aboriginal people constitute today a nation within a nation",[14] it does seem both logical and likely that—at least in symbolic terms—this is precisely the direction in which they are presently headed. During his 1986 tour of Australia, the Pope underlined the distinctive resilience and solidarity of Black Australia:

> You have kept your sense of brotherhood. If you stay closely united, you are like a tree standing in the middle of a bush-fire sweeping through the timber. The leaves are scorched and the tough bark is scarred and burned; but inside the tree the sap is still flowing, and under the ground the roots are still strong. Like that tree you have endured the flames, and you still have the power to be reborn.
>
> The time for this rebirth is now![15]

Since it can be argued that the nature of the pontiff's statement was both political and spiritual, the implications of his words for Aboriginal unity are certainly significant. And, as the events of 1988 have already demonstrated, Black Australians have now drawn closer together on a national scale than ever before.

Contemporary Black Australian creative writers have already played a major role in articulating this sense of unity and defining the Aboriginal identity. As the third decade of such writing continues, one can expect to find them growing in numbers, confidence and skill, and increasingly expressing and moulding the Aboriginal nationalism of which Smith speaks. More and more, Australia's Fourth World will define itself and demand both artistic and political recognition through its creative literature.

Notes

1   See, for example, Spencer Reiss and Carl Robinson, "Aborigines vs. Queensland", *Newsweek,* 11 October, 1982, p. 13.

2   See, for example, Tony Hewett and David Monaghan, "Blacks Boo Royal Pair on Barge", the *Sydney Morning Herald* 27 January, 1988, p. 2, and Anne Jamieson, "The Push for an Aboriginal Parliament", the *Weekend Australian,* 6-7 February, 1988, p. 24.

3   Ribnga Kenneth Green, "Aborigines and International Politics", in Berndt and Berndt, eds, *Aborigines of the West,* (Perth, 1979), p. 392.

4   Bernard Smith, *The Spectre of Truganini,* (Sydney, 1980), p. 36.

5   Jim Davidson, "Interview: Kath Walker", *Meanjin,* vol. 36, no. 4, 1977, p. 430.

6   Although, as will be discussed in Chapter Two, David Unaipon was the first published Aboriginal author, his works were never widely distributed.

7   For a fuller treatment of this topic, see Robert Hall's unpublished M.A.(Qual.) thesis, "The Army and the Aborigines, World War II", (Canberra, 1979).

8   J.J. Healy, *Literature and the Aborigine in Australia,* (St. Lucia, 1978), p. 3.

9   Rodney Hall, ed., *The Collins Book of Australian Poetry,* (Sydney, 1981), pp. 13-19.

10   For further examples of traditional Aboriginal poetry, see Strehlow's *Songs of Central Australia,* (Sydney, 1971); Ronald M. Berndt's *Love Songs of Arnhem Land,* (Melbourne, 1976), and *Three Faces of Love,* (Melbourne, 1976); and Tamsin Donaldson's article, "Translating Oral Literature: Aboriginal Song Texts", *Aboriginal History,* vol. 3, 1979, part 1, pp. 62-83.

11   C.G. von Brandenstein and A.P. Thomas, *Taruru: Aboriginal Song Poetry From the Pilbara,* (Adelaide, 1974), Inside Front Cover.

12   *ibid.* p. 38.

13   Smith, *The Spectre of Truganini,* p. 35.

14   Smith, *The Spectre of Truganini,* p. 36.

15   "The address given by his Holiness Pope John Paul II at the meeting with Aboriginal and Torres Strait Islander people at Alice Springs on 20 November 1986", (Canberra, 1986), p. 4.

1

From Depression to War

In 1929, the impact of the American stock market crash was felt all around the world. By 1930, in Australia, as in most other countries, the economy was in the grip of the Depression. Not until the outbreak of the Second World War did Australia's economy truly recover; as the military battles were fought, the economic battle was won.

But there was much more to the Depression than its impact upon Australia's national economic performance. In retrospect, it is far too easy to gloss over the personal suffering of the period, the thwarted aspirations, the dislocation of families. It is even easier for a student of the era to gloss over the severe plight of Aboriginal Australians during the period. The decade between the onset of the Depression and the beginning of the World War II deepened the poverty of a minority group which was already, in 1929, at the bottom of the Australian economic ladder. To cite one example, Aboriginal reserve dwellers in New South Wales received only 41 pence per week throughout the entire Depression, while between 1930 and 1936 dole payments rose from 69 to 108 pence per week.[1]

In fact as Rowley notes, in order to avoid spending dole money on Aborigines during these years, the police coerced significant numbers into returning to live on government reserves.[2] Aboriginal people throughout Australia were invariably hit harder by the Depression, and took longer to recover from its hardships, than the white citizens of Australia.[3] This was just one factor which oppressed Aboriginal people to an inordinate degree during the Depression years. Not only economically, but politically, judicially, socially and culturally, Black Australians suffered at the hands of white politicians, policy-makers, and pastoralists. In Rowley's words, "One of the effects of the great depression, all over Australia, seems to have been a more rigid containment in institutions, where conditions were probably worse than ever before, with enduring effects on Aboriginal attitudes".4

The late 1930s and early 1940s was also an era of ironies. One of the greatest of these was that the 1939-1945 period, which saw the height of legislative restrictiveness, also saw the first tentative moves towards legal equality for Aboriginal Australians. Another was that the framers of Aboriginal policy in the states and territories of Australia devised measures for the "protection" of a race from extinction, just when it was on the brink, in relative terms, of a population explosion. Therefore, the policy-makers had to execute a significant about-face mid way through the era. A third irony was the fact that, while atrocities and massacres of Aboriginal people were still a very recent memory in the early 1930s—especially in the Northern Territory—a greater number of influential philanthropic groups dedicated to the advancement of Black Australians were formed between 1929 and 1939 than ever before. Throughout, it was frequently international pressures and events which acted as a catalyst for the improvement of the lot of Aborigines, rather than domestic policies. This chapter provides an historical overview of this complex period and its effects upon Aboriginal Australians, from the commencement of the Depression to the close of World War II.

It is clear that White Australians held numerous and often conflicting views of Aborigines, ranging from the sympathetic and humanitarian to the violently racist and bigoted. But, as the 1930s began, almost everyone agreed on one point: the Aboriginal people were a race doomed to extinction. Of course, the emphasis at this stage was upon the numerical waning of the full-blooded Aboriginal population, and in this regard, the demographic evidence appeared to be incontrovertible. From a population estimated to be in the vicinity of 300,000 in 1788, only about 60,000 remained in 1930, and this was a generous estimate, according to those such as Stanner.5 More specifically, approximately 8,000 Aborigines remained in New South Wales in 1930 and 1,000 in Victoria: "only about a tenth of the population of these areas in 1788".6 To most of the population which was either professionally or personally concerned with Aboriginal Australians, the fading away of the full-bloods seemed inevitable. It appeared that Aborigines in all of Australia would go the way of the Tasmanian blacks who were commonly believed to have been totally exterminated in the space of some seventy years.

Concern for the plight of the full-bloods was motivated by a number of factors. These included the keenness of anthropologists to preserve for posterity that which might otherwise be lost forever, the desire of the state and Commonwealth governments to avoid the international criticism which would follow the extinction of a unique indigenous people, and the sincere concern of some private citizens for a seemingly doomed ethnic minority. In almost all cases, this anxiety was couched in terms reminiscent of a contemporary campaign to save an endangered animal species. The analogy is an instructive one, for in 1930 the reigning popular view of Aborigines was that they were somehow sub-human, both intellectually and culturally inferior to whites.[7] It is ironic that this same view acted both as a spark for a campaign of protection and as a rationale for many of the massacres and "punitive expeditions" which persisted into the early 1930s.

These allegedly "retaliatory" massacres in themselves focused public attention upon the precariousness of Aboriginal existence as much as they did upon the gross injustice of the frontier vigilante squads involved. Historians have documented at some length such punitive raids of the late 1920s as the Umbali Massacre[8] and the murder of thirty-one Aborigines to avenge the killing of a white dingo-hunter in the vicinity of Alice Springs in 1928.[9] But it is necessary to discuss here the Tuckiar case of 1932-1934, for it threw into relief many of the issues directly involved in the formulation of Aboriginal policy in the 1930s.

The exceptional case of the Arnhem Land Aborigine, Tuckiar, accused of the murder of Constable McColl, is fully documented by Rowley in *The Destruction of Aboriginal Society*.[10] As he notes, the court-room drama involved the church, the state, the judiciary, various pressure groups and even foreign governments. Missionaries, who were often a frustrated minority in Aboriginal policy-making in the 1930s, were involved in the somewhat dubious apprehension of the accused. During the trial, the impartiality of the judiciary was called into question, in particular, the conduct of Judge Wells. Political officials ranging as high as the Prime Minister were directly involved in the aftermath of Tuckiar's conviction, opposed so vehemently by pressure groups such as the Association for the Protection of Native Races, led by Professor Elkin. Even the British government was affected by the publicity surrounding the case. Broome puts it most succinctly:

Within two days the Prime Minister, J.A. Lyons, was on the telephone to Elkin, to inquire about the truth of his allegations, as Lyons had just been approached by the

British Dominions office which had read a report of the Tuckiar protest meeting in the *Times*. Pressure was being exerted in high places.[11]

As Broome goes on to note, Australia was particularly sensitive to international opinion regarding its treatment of native peoples at the time, for its competence to administer a League of Nations mandate over New Guinea (and Nauru) was at stake.[12]

The Tuckiar case was arguably the most visible, the most publicised and the most important of many incidents which worked to the detriment of Aboriginal Australians in the 1930s, particularly in the Northern Territory and Western Australia. It is significant that it occurred in the early 1930s, when concern over the annihilation of full-blooded Aborigines was becoming more pronounced, and that it was foreign intervention which played a noteworthy role in resolving the legal and public debate and prodded the Commonwealth and Australian state governments to revise their Aboriginal policies.

Those policies had to embrace Black Australians with varying degrees of Aboriginal blood, not only the full-bloods ostensibly on the verge of extinction. The demographic situation with regard to mixed-blooded Aborigines was very different: in relative terms, throughout the 1920s and 1930s, part-Aborigines were undergoing a population explosion. For example, in 1938 Stanner quoted current figures concerning the rate of population increase of mixed-blooded Aborigines in the Northern Territory. The estimate of 18 live births/1,000 for the part-Aboriginal group absolutely dwarfed the growth rate of the white population of the Territory, calculated at 0.3 live births/1,000.[13] No demographic training is required to reach the conclusion that miscegenation between blacks and whites was widespread, the typical sexual union being between European men and Aboriginal women. Furthermore, the men involved—most often in the frontier areas of Queensland, Western Australia and the Northern Territory—were hardly motivated by any compassionate desire to aid the "preservation" of the Aboriginal race, and they very seldom accepted and recognised their offspring.

The exponential increase in the part-Aboriginal population created very serious problems for the racist and the humanitarian alike. The former was increasingly cursed with visible examples of his compatriots' predilection for so-called "Black Velvet", and the suspicion that the Aboriginal race might not be as moribund as was officially supposed. The latter viewed with concern the exploitation of black women and the dilemma of the "half-caste": neither fully a traditional Aborigine nor entirely white. Therefore, in the early 1930s, both racists and humanitarians officially requested governmental policies which would segregate blacks and whites; policies which would protect the purity of both races. As one Queensland politician put it:

> We must be careful to see that the half caste is not given the same liberties that are enjoyed by the whiteman. We do not want any further mixing of the population. We want to keep the white race white.14

The operative word is, of course, "officially". One of the ironies of the 1930s was the gulf between the articulated aims of the policy-makers and the conditions in which those for whom the policy was devised actually lived.15 The hope that legislative pronouncements could make Aboriginal women safe from predatory white males was as ill-founded as the belief that the police could be impartial and effective Protectors of Aborigines. The fact that the officially enunciated theory of Aboriginal policy shifted so dramatically in the second half of the 1930s—almost entirely because of a national conference of "experts" in Aboriginal administration—is a further indication of how arbitrary and unresponsive to local events the policy-makers actually were.16

In the early years of the 1930s, the two emphases of Aboriginal policy in the states and territories were the protection and the control of Black Australians. J.W. Bleakley's 1929 report on the Northern Territory situation advocated many of the policies introduced in Queensland17 which were to be adopted in other states throughout the 1930s. Two of the most important of these were the strict control of Aboriginal women (allegedly to prevent miscegenation) and, progressively, the forced removal of mixed-blooded children from their parents and camp life to be raised in orphanages, institutions and foster homes in White Australia. In order to check the rise of the part-Aboriginal population, Black Australians were coerced into and concentrated in reserves during this decade. Various amendments to Aboriginal Acts in the Northern Territory (1933 and 1936), Western Australia (1936), Queensland (1934 and 1939) and South Australia (1939) served to heighten the legislative control of the respective administrations.18

The new publicity which was showered upon the frontier massacres and atrocities which had taken place highlighted the need for safeguards for Aboriginal human rights. Indeed, many philanthropic groups did press for the inviolability of native reserves. But the end result of the legislation which ensued restricted those human rights to a greater extent than ever before. In Rowley's words:

> The general trend of the 1930s was to establish Aboriginal administrations on the basis of even more rigid control, for their 'good' and for their education ... The spectacular injustices of the frontier had produced a real reaction, but the effort was to be channelled into more extensive and more rigid control of individuals.[19]

One of the major shifts during the 1930s was the fact that, while much attention was initially devoted to the dying-out of full-blooded Aborigines and the concomitant necessity for "protection", as the decade wore on, it was the part-Aboriginal problem which began to take precedence in the minds of administrators. The Aboriginal policy of this period had to deal with the apparent extinction of one group and, concurrently, the proliferation of another, closely related group. This presented a serious logical problem: while it was decided that the former group would survive best totally separated from white society, the latter allegedly required total and continuous contact with that society; in a word, assimilation. The uncomfortable mixture of the two concepts was most clearly reflected on a national scale at the Commonwealth and State Authorities Conference in Canberra, in April 1937, which passed the following resolution:

> This Conference believes that the destiny of the natives of aboriginal origin, but not of the full blood, lies in their ultimate absorption by the people of the Commonwealth, and it therefore recommends that all efforts be directed to that end.[20]

This conference was significant perhaps more for the matters it did not address than for those which it did confront.[21] Its importance derives from the following factors: first, it enunciated a principle of Aboriginal administration—that of assimilation—which was not to be consistently applied until a decade later. Second, key words in the statement, such as "destiny" and "absorption", indicate the extent to which coercion was embraced as an administrative concept at the time. Third, it has tended to deflect the attention of many students of Aboriginal history away from other issues which bore more directly upon Aboriginal Australians in 1937. In other words, the Aboriginal policy of the 1930s was certainly significant, but it was not a sufficient factor to entirely explain the behaviour of Black Australians during the period. As a consequence, the historiography of the era generally suffers from an unwarranted emphasis upon matters of policy formulation.[22]

One of the most important questions for students of the era to ask themselves is, "How did Aboriginal people react to the legislative circumscription of their lives?" Here, Aboriginal oral history can provide valuable insights. For example, researching the oral history of the Wiradjuri people of New South Wales, Read has found that during the Depression they responded similarly to a variety of factors. The Wiradjuri

moved less frequently than previously from reserve to reserve or from town to town. Through choice, economic circumstance or legislative action, most people remained on the official or unofficial camps.[23]

Only in the past decade have Australian researchers begun to try to consider Aboriginal history from the black viewpoint. Rather than emphasising what has been done to Black Australians, recent studies have also highlighted Aboriginal reaction and response. For example, Broome details the Aboriginal resistance movements of the 1920s and 1930s, illustrating the fact that black political protest is not a phenomenon which commenced in the 1960s. He describes the genesis of such groups as the Australian Aborigines Progressive Association (1924 to 1927), the Euralian Association of Western Australia (formed in 1934), and the Aboriginal petition to the King of 1937 (which never reached its destination) on behalf of the Australian Aborigines League. [24] The most important Aboriginal protest group of the era was William Ferguson's Aborigines' Progressive Association (APA), formed in 1934. Although its activities and the life of Ferguson himself are both thoroughly described in Horner's *Vote Ferguson For Aboriginal Freedom*,[25] the APA must be at least briefly examined with reference to the contradictions of the 1929-1945 period.

The first of these stemmed from the fact that the APA, and its leading lights Ferguson and John Patten, strongly emphasised the view that Aboriginal people were the equals of the white citizens of Australia. Their conclusion—which would certainly not be embraced by contemporary Aboriginal activists—was that blacks deserved both citizenship and equality via complete absorption into White Australian society. Despite the rhetoric of the 1937 conference, the time was not yet ripe to even attempt the assimilation of Aborigines into the larger Australian community.[26] In the light of later government policy, it is ironic that the views which Ferguson propounded fell upon deaf ears, and he died before any widespread and sincere efforts to promote assimilation had been undertaken in the nation. Just as ironic was the fact that the Commonwealth government saw the need to obtain an Aboriginal blessing of its Sesquicentenary celebrations in Sydney on 26 August 1938, and engaged the services of some tractable blacks from western New South Wales for this purpose. However, it virtually ignored the APA's "Day of Mourning" meeting—held only a short distance away and timed to coincide with the fanfare—which lamented the same event on behalf of the Aboriginal people.

Nevertheless, the symbolic and the actual achievement of the APA should not be belittled. For example, its 1938 manifesto, "Aborigines Claim Citizenship Rights", stated in no uncertain terms that "this festival of 150 years' so called 'progress' in Australia commemorates also 150 years of misery and degradation imposed upon the original native inhabitants by the white invaders of this country".[27] This was one of the first times that Black Australians had publicly submitted their view of the continent's interracial history.[28] Furthermore, Ferguson and Patten made a significant breakthrough when, shortly afterwards, they secured an interview with Prime Minister Lyons—even if the Commonwealth's Aboriginal policy was not dramatically affected by the visit. Finally, such events as the walk-off of the residents of the Cummeragunga Reserve in February 1939, the investigation into the affairs of the Aborigines' Protection Board by the Public Service Board, the New South Wales Aborigines' Welfare Act of 1940, and the eventual appointment of two blacks to the state's Aboriginal Welfare Board (in 1943) are all attributable—at least in part—to the concerted lobbying and protest of Ferguson, Patten and the APA. The call for Aboriginal rights may have altered both in content and in tone over the years but it has not ceased.[29]

Aboriginal protest organisations of the 1930s were, however, neither the most articulate nor the most influential of the pressure groups arguing the Black Australian cause. There were a number of active religious and philanthropic organisations—such as the National Missionary Council—but one of the most effective and successful of these was the Association for the Protection of Native Races (APNR), which has already been noted in connection with the Tuckiar case. Professor A.P. Elkin's 1931 address to the APNR, published in 1933 under the title *A Policy For The Aborigines*, is considered to express "the first notion of a 'positive' policy" in Aboriginal affairs, "unadventurous as it may seem now".[30] This concept affirmed, in Stanner's words, "that a major development of Aboriginal economic, social and political life from its broken down state was a thinkable possibility".[31] If publication of this pamphlet *did* represent "a turning point of Aboriginal affairs in Australia" [32] and it therefore is an important document in the nation's cultural history, it is noteworthy that it was written by an anthropologist. The predominant role of anthropologists from 1929 to 1945 (and indeed, to the present) in interpreting Aboriginal society, analysing its ills, and in recommending ameliorative policies, is remarkable. In fact, the Canadian historian K.A. MacKirdy commented in 1966 that "[Australian] historians generally have been content to leave the study of Aborigines to the anthropologists and then to ignore the anthropologists"![33] Though MacKirdy's observation is an exaggeration, the question remains: "Just how influential were the anthropologists?"

The contribution of anthropologists was major, especially in the realm of academic and policy considerations. For example, the year 1930 saw the publication of the inaugural issue of the anthropological journal *Oceania* and thus, "for the first time Australia maintained an academic journal devoted to the record of native people".[34] In addition, the editorial of this first issue succinctly outlined the pragmatic potential of scientific and anthropological research:

> The general policy of *Oceania* will also be guided by the view that anthropology is no longer to be treated as an academic subject having a purely theoretical interest, but can and should be made a science of immediate practical value, more particularly in relation to the government and education of native peoples.[35]

This decision to embark upon what may be dubbed "applied" rather than "pure" anthropology was itself a conscious theoretical choice. In addition, as Mulvaney illustrates, other scientists were altering their methodological perspective in 1930. In that year Hale and Tindale's excavation report on the Devon Downs shelter also appeared in print. This was "the first systematic attempt, in Australia, to apply stratigraphic, rather than conjectural principles, to the uncovering of aboriginal prehistory". Mulvaney summarises: "[1930 was therefore the year] in which objective studies of the aboriginal past and present reached maturity within Australia".[36]

In themselves, these were primarily theoretical breakthroughs. Like much of the high-flown Aboriginal policy of the 1929-1945 period, such considerations were somewhat removed from the life-and-death issues of poverty, disease, malnutrition and repression which afflicted Aboriginal Australians daily during this era. Nevertheless, it is true that the 1930s did see a number of distinct attitudinal changes in White Australia: in scientific methodology, in protectionist policies, in philanthropic involvement, in press coverage of atrocities, and in government lobbying. Many of these can be traced to the direct influence of anthropologists. But it is open to question to what extent these shifts actually affected the survival conditions of Black Australians at the time.

For example, one officially sanctioned attempt to address the problem of Aboriginal living conditions of the day in the Northern Territory was the policy of assimilation, first enunciated in 1937. However, in 1938 Stanner, always a shrewd and observant commentator, indicated the policy's limitations when he posed the following rhetorical question:

> Can the pioneer fringes of Australia blot out such bitter complications ... suspend all the convictions and attitudes which would be an embarrassment to the new "policy", and on any given morning in 1938 set out, say, to "absorb" their mixed-blood populations?[37]

So, despite the tendency to laud the achievements and influence of the scientific/anthropological group during this period, the lobbying power of these professionals was still circumscribed by other community and institutional factors. Biskup notes that in spite of the exhortations in *Oceania*, "Most Aboriginal administrators ... continued to stress the 'practical' nature of their work, deprecating unsolicited advice from the scientists", and he carries on:

> As late as 1945 ... when urged to appoint an anthropologist to his staff, Neville's successor, F.I. Bray, replied, " ... the welfare of the native is not bound up with the advice and guidance of trained anthropologists, and it is not apparent just what advantage would result to the natives."[38]

If some Aboriginal affairs administrators viewed the work of anthropologists with scepticism during the 1929-1945 era, they were far more frequently critical of missionaries in this period. For example, in Western Australia it was pastoral employers who consistently had the ear and the sympathy of the state's Aboriginal affairs officials.[39] The missionary lobby in the same state was repeatedly ignored and criticised by such influential policy-makers as A.O. Neville, the Chief Protector of Aborigines from 1914 to 1940 and Commissioner of Native Affairs for the last four of those years. Eloquent proof of this pro-pastoralist bias was the fact that, relatively speaking, missions were almost entirely passed over in the Western Australian Department of Native Affairs' budgets of the day. For example, in 1939-1940, they received a mere $3,776 out of a total departmental allocation of $135,550.[40] The financial neglect of the missionary group was not confined to Neville's state, for the Northern Territory presented a very similar case. More than twenty missions had been founded there by the 1920s, yet the work of the

Church Missionary Society in Arnhem Land during this time was voted only 250 pounds per year by the Territory administration.[41] It was not until 1953 that the financial straits of Australian missions were eased in a major way, when the Commonwealth government voted to underwrite and staff the medical and educational services which they provided.[42]

Why were missions so under-financed, and why was there animosity between many administrators, protectors, and pastoralists on the one hand and missionaries on the other? Some government officials involved in Aboriginal affairs at the time were, no doubt, opposed to the "Christianising" which was the policy on many missions. According to Biskup, there were too many reports of irregularities on the missions—including accusations of sexual relations between men of the cloth and their spiritual charges—for them to be ignored.[43] As well, there was evidence of violent corporal punishment on some missions, including chainings and floggings in extreme cases.[44] But perhaps the most important factor was that mission Aborigines were, frequently, Aborigines lost to the droving and farming industries. Therefore, it is no surprise that a coalition between pastoralists and governments often arose (in the Territory, Western Australia, and Queensland), whereby the former agreed to provide for poor blacks on their properties while the latter pegged wages at artificially low levels, and instructed Protectors to discourage Aborigines from leaving their pastoral employers.[45]

In fairness, it must be said that there were also many enlightened and sympathetic missionaries. In addition, there were missionaries and other clergymen, such as A.P. Elkin, who definitely did exert a significant influence upon the formulation of Aboriginal policy in various areas of Australia. They affected domestic policy and practice indirectly—through overseas philanthropic organisations, funding bodies, churches and even newspaper reports—at least as much as they did directly. Missionaries could be instrumental mediators of foreign views of Australia's native affairs policies. By the same token, what gave the missionaries this prominent role in the first place was, to some extent, the existing international interest in the plight of Black Australians.

Although it is difficult to quantify the precise degree of foreign influence upon the Commonwealth and state Aboriginal policies beyond the assertion that it was considerable, it is far easier to highlight common characteristics of those policies. One of the most striking of these was the tendency of Aboriginal affairs administrators to become enamoured of the status quo. During the 1929-1945 period, they often succumbed to an inertia which inhibited enlightened thought and action. The logical corollary of this inertia was that radical new approaches to Aboriginal affairs during this era were confined to an elite of theorists and practitioners. As Stanner honestly and somewhat ruefully admitted in 1968:

> It seems clear to me now that the change of attitude and policy towards the Aborigines which we trace back to the 1930s was confined very largely to a rather small group of people who had special associations with their care, administration or study. Outside that group the changes made very little impact for a long time.[46]

Yet, it is equally true that there were significant changes—if not always improvements—in the lot of Black Australians during the period. For example, Aboriginal people in New South Wales who in 1929 were still being systematically dispersed were methodically concentrated in reserves in the 1930s, only to be dispersed once again in the early 1940s.[47] The judiciary was beginning to take account of customary law in court proceedings and the Commonwealth government did overturn guilty verdicts which had been handed down to Aborigines accused of murder. Many factors—anthropological influence, the protests of philanthropic groups, media coverage of atrocities, and others—played a part, but a common thread running through the events of the era is that the primary motor for change came from forces which were largely external to Australia in origin. These included the Depression, the sanction of world opinion in general terms and that of the British Foreign Office in specific terms, legal cases in other British colonies and former colonies, and the outbreak of World War II. Probably the most influential of these forces were the Depression and the Second World War. The detrimental effects of the former upon Aboriginal people have already been noted, but the varied effects of the latter upon Black Australians deserve further attention.

The accepted historical wisdom in Australia is that for the first time in its history, during World War II the country was under threat of direct foreign invasion by an aggressive, imperialistic power. No Aboriginal Australian has yet written a "black history" of World War II but, when one does appear, it may revise this orthodox view quite dramatically. For example, it may well be based on the premise that, just over one hundred and fifty years after Australia was first invaded—by an aggressive, imperialistic power—it was threatened for a second time by a belligerent imperialism. An Aboriginal history of the conflict would be most welcome because both the military and non-military contributions of Black Australians to the war effort deserve to be more fully investigated. Furthermore, like the first successful invasion of the continent, the second unsuccessful offensive significantly altered Aboriginal roles, perceptions, and (to some extent) powers in Australia.

Historians concur that World War II was one of the most important catalysts for change in Aboriginal affairs in the twentieth century. This consensus cuts across national and ideological boundaries. For example, the Australian social scientist C.D. Rowley, writing in the liberal democratic tradition, states that "The war may be taken as indicating the end of the process of destruction of Aboriginal society",[48] and that after World War II "passive acceptance of the status quo, based on ignorance, could not continue".[49] Hannah Middleton, a British Marxist historian agrees that:

> Fundamental changes in the conditions of the Aborigines and the development of their own organisations were brought about ... by the effects of the Second World War within Australia and internationally.[50]

In his excellent unpublished thesis, "The Army and the Aborigines, World War II", the Australian historian Bob Hall puts the matter very succinctly: "The Second World War is the most significant and influential event in recent Aboriginal history".[51]

As Hall clearly demonstrates, what is still lacking in Australian historiography is a comprehensive assessment of not only what was done to Aborigines during the 1939-1945 period but also of what they themselves achieved. Second, as Middleton relates, the changes in Aboriginal/white relationships which occurred cannot be explained solely by examining the domestic situation. Both during and after the war—and largely because of it—international factors impinged upon Aboriginal policy, protest, and political activity at least as much as they had during the 1930s. Third, a whole range of specific conditions were either initiated or changed by the war experience: among them, missionary activity, and Aboriginal wages, strike action, health, and demographic patterns. Some of these bore fruit in increased Aboriginal self-confidence and defiance; others resulted in excessive exploitation of Aborigines and consequent Black Australian despair.

In Australia, World War II was a crisis, definitely an aberrant state of affairs and, ultimately, a victory. But was it a victory for all Australians? In all the states of Australia, Aborigines were involved in the war effort and "over 1,000 people of Aboriginal descent fought with the second AIF".[52] During the war years, Aboriginal combatants fought in North Africa and New Guinea. One soldier, Reg Saunders, was the first Black Australian to become a commissioned officer. In addition, an equal number of Aborigines—primarily in Northern Australia—were directly involved in the war effort as coastal patrol and reconnaissance personnel, as support staff, and as labourers in war-related construction and development projects.

Many commentators have implied that the ideal of egalitarianism which is imputed to the military extended to all Black Australians involved in the war effort. For example, Broome has observed that "Their [the Aborigines'] work was praised by the army and they reportedly mixed well with the regular troops".[53] However, as Hall's research has conclusively demonstrated, egalitarianism embraced only some Aborigines in some areas for a specified period of time.[54] It is noteworthy that throughout the war years it was only Black Australian *men* who were pressed into military and support service, and this was particularly true in 1942, when the nation was threatened with Japanese invasion. Had there been no direct menace to the Australian mainland, there is no doubt that only a small fraction of those Black Australians who saw military action or were employed by the Army would ever have been allowed to contribute. In short, the Army's resort to Aboriginal manpower was largely the result of a crisis mentality operating within the context of strategic considerations.

The supreme irony is that throughout the entire war, official policy forbade the conscription of Aboriginal Australians, yet their familiarity with the land and their talents of tracking and bushcraft were skills highly prized by the military. Indeed, though it was not officially admitted at the time, the anthropologist Donald Thomson was empowered to mobilise an entire unit of about fifty Aborigines skilled in guerilla tactics, in order to repel a potential Japanese invasion in remote areas of Arnhem Land. In Hall's words:

> This unusual unit was manned almost entirely by full-blood Aborigines at a time when official Army policy was that only people of substantially European origin or descent could be accepted into the Army.[55]

He continues:

> Aborigines could be recruited contrary to official policy so long as they remained out of the public eye and so long as they contributed to the defence of a strategically important area where white manpower was scarce.[56]

The only pay which members of this Northern Territory Special Reconnaissance Unit received was three sticks of tobacco per week.[57]

Similarly contravening published regulations, a separate battalion of approximately 740 Torres Strait Islanders was established, which counted some fifty mainland Aborigines among its numbers. These soldiers gave devoted service until the long enforced separation from their wives and children and the realisation that their wages—which included compulsory payments to the Queensland Government's Protector of Islanders—were only a fraction of those being paid to white soldiers in the islands, caused such unrest that a short-lived strike ensued in January, 1944. It was calculated in that year that the Australian government had underpaid its Torres Strait Battalion by a total of some 30 million dollars.[58] Nearly forty years were to pass before the Commonwealth government partially compensated the Islanders for this deficit.[59] There is no need to go into all of the details of the events recounted by Hall, but the above situations illustrate the major point that the military was just as willing and able as any other element of Australian society to exploit Black Australians—and did so during the war years.

The highly touted atmosphere of brotherhood between black and white no doubt did exist. Reg Saunders's brother Harry also enlisted, and his section commander said:

> We lived with Harry ... as a brother ... Our love for him was such that there could be no place for any colour barrier ... we were *forced together* by events and our comradeship was completely *necessary*.[60]

Yet, even in this testament to racial harmony there is a (perhaps unwitting) undertone implying that Harry's white "brothers" had pragmatically bowed to the force of circumstances. Like the Anzac Legend, the myth of interracial brotherhood was one born of shared experience in the line of fire, between those of roughly similar rank. However, one cannot presume that because a Saunders or a Silas Roberts won the respect and acceptance of his fellow soldiers that an Aboriginal road worker, or a Black Australian toiling in the machine works at Mataranka in 1943, was accepted as a mate by his commanding officer. However inspiring egalitarianism may have been, it was the exception, not the rule. The only certainty was that it never embraced Aboriginal women, who were doubly disqualified by their sex and their skin from equality with White Australia.

How did Aboriginal people involved in the war effort view these changes? How did World War II affect their perspective? One can only theorise, but a number of conclusions seem probable. First, those Aborigines involved no doubt welcomed the higher, stable wages offered by the Armed Forces as well as the provision made for maintenance of their dependants. Thus, they were loath to return to the situation of wage exploitation which had existed in the Northern Territory cattle industry. Second, the taste of near-equality which the Armed Forces provided for some Aboriginal soldiers would not be soon forgotten. Instead, it would serve to heighten the bitterness and anger which would attend a return to the prejudice and inequality of civilian life. Men who had fought for their country would deeply resent the legal restrictions which that country placed upon them. Third, it is very probable that—for at least some Black Australians—a more positive and confident self-perception was a result of their war experience.[61] On the other hand, even those Aborigines who did secure vastly improved living conditions in military camps, including full rations for their dependants, did so at the risk of White Australian (and later White and Black American) sexual depredations upon their women, and with the certainty of vulnerability to exploitation by and for liquor. It is true that Aborigines living on Army settlements did receive excellent, free health care but even in this case there is an element of truth in Middleton's observation that:

> During the war ... it was necessary for black and white to work literally side by side. In this context so long as the Aborigines were diseased, suffered from malnutrition and lived in unhygienic conditions they were a direct threat to the health of the Allied troops in the north ... For the first time since colonisation began the Aborigines received decent food and the same medical care as the whites. But it was not given to them as their right or even as a generous humanitarian gesture but in order to protect the white troops and to maintain their fighting efficiency.[62]

In spite of their valuable contribution to the war effort, the official prejudice against Aborigines was such that many were forcibly removed from coastal areas in both the Northern Territory and Western Australia and were re-located in native settlements, allegedly for their own protection but, in large measure, because they were perceived as a security risk. For example, "In June 1942 a Special Mobile Force stationed at Moora rounded up all unemployed Aborigines from the Midlands and interned them in Moore River as 'possible potential enemies' ".[63] This so-called "nigger hunting", with its coercive treatment of Aborigines as enemy aliens—almost as prisoners of war—offers a sobering contrast to the mythology of wartime egalitarianism.

On balance it is clear that some, but certainly not all, Aborigines did benefit directly from their wartime experience. For example, there is little doubt that Aboriginal contact with Black American soldiers represented a real awakening in ideological terms; in Len Watson's words:

> The Black Americans had a big effect in the coastal areas in Queensland where there were large numbers of them stationed. We met and talked to them. This laid a basis for learning ... All this led to a new attitude in blacks: black Australians started to see white Australians as only human beings, not as people with supernatural gifts, or as people to stand in awe of, the men born to be bosses ... this change in outlook is terribly important—revolutionary in a way. It has laid the basis for all the other changes that have occurred in the post war years.64

It is also clear that the taste of wage justice which Aboriginal Australians obtained in certain places and at certain times was of importance, especially in view of post-war Aboriginal agitation in the pastoral industry. But European Australians still had a long way to go if they were to accept Aborigines in general terms for more than pragmatic, exploitative reasons. At the same time, Black Australians had cause to be deeply disillusioned in the face of the evaporation of wartime promises of equality and fulfillment. For example, Hall notes the heartfelt disappointment of Torres Strait Island soldiers who did not receive improved accommodation after the victory over Japan, despite having been repeatedly promised new housing throughout the war years.65 In many ways coercion was still to be the norm in Aboriginal affairs, at least until the 1960s.

It is possible only to guess at the nature of the Black Australian perception of Europeans in 1945. However, it is likely that the events of the war did not dramatically improve the views which *most* Aboriginal people held of White Australians. After all, for every fortunate Aboriginal soldier there was also a black person in a fringe camp, in jail, unemployed, and in an inner-city slum, in all the states of Australia. In short, while it is tempting to laud wartime achievements in the field of Australian black/white race relations one should not be overly enthusiastic. After all, the war experience was an aberrant state of affairs; solutions to the dilemmas faced by Aboriginal Australians had to come in peace-time if they were to be of permanent value. Similarly, it is probable that in the period before, during, and after the conflict, the majority of Australians were at most ambivalent about the Aboriginal cause.

However, the role of World War II as a catalyst for policy change is undeniable. For example, in the field of legislation, Aboriginal soldiers were given a voluntary wartime vote under the *Federal*

Electoral Act of 1940 though again, by definition, black women were excluded from this privilege.[66] Further legislation of the early 1940s provided social services (such as child endowments, old age pensions, and invalid benefits) to certain categories of Aboriginal people.[67] During the war, various "Exemption Acts" passed in the states enabled some Black Australians to obtain certificates which substantially entitled them to citizenship rights, if they were prepared to, effectively, renounce their Aboriginality. Despite the distasteful circumstances of the offer, these were rights which McEwen had in 1939 not envisaged Aborigines possessing for generations to come.[68] Therefore the 1929-1945 era saw both the summit of legal control and legislative repression of Aboriginal Australians and the first halting steps towards equality and citizenship for that oppressed minority. Unfortunately, this marginally more enlightened legislation often did not mirror (and was frequently subverted by) popular Australian views and attitudes.

Finally, World War II, like so many other catalysts for change in Aboriginal/white relations, was international in origin. From the outset of the Depression until the victory over Japan, foreign forces impinged both directly and indirectly upon Aboriginal Australians, whether for good or ill. Perhaps the final contradiction of this era of ironies is the fact that so many Australians have been unaware of the extent to which the domestic issue of Aboriginal Affairs has been (and still is) viewed, outside its shores, as an international one. Again, perspective is the key. It is also fascinating to observe the number of different perspectives on the Aboriginal theme in the literature of the same 1929-1945 era, to be discussed in the next chapter.

Some observers have alleged that, just as certain conferences or pieces of legislation reflect a turning point in the black/white race relations of the Depression and war years, some literary works are also representative of the same phenomenon. In both cases, many commentators have fallen into the trap of being both overly enthusiastic and premature with their praise. As Stanner has remarked, these so-called turning points during the 1929-1945 era resulted from the labour of a small, enlightened, and progressive elite of individuals and were well received during the period only by like-minded Australians: "It was a case of the faithful preaching to the converted about a 'revolution' which in fact had arrived only for them".[69] It was to be many years before the majority of Australians became aware of this revolution; even longer before they gave it their support.

Notes

1   Jack Horner, *Vote Ferguson for Aboriginal Freedom*, (Sydney, 1974), p. 29.

2   C.D. Rowley, *Outcasts in White Australia*, (Ringwood, Vic., 1972), p. 81.

3   In fairness it must be noted that, in relative terms, some White Australians had "further to fall" economically during the Depression and therefore suffered greatly during those years. But this does not negate the fact that Black Australians remained the poorest group of the Australian populace during the period.

4   Rowley, *The Destruction of Aboriginal Society*, (Canberra, 1970), p. 281.

5   W.E.H. Stanner, "The Aborigines (1938)", in *White Man Got No Dreaming*, (Canberra, 1979), p. 19.

6   Richard Broome, *Aboriginal Australians: Black Response to White Dominance, 1788-1980*, (Sydney, 1982), p. 143. The estimates of 1788 population have since been challenged by N.G. Butlin in his *Our Original Aggression*, (Sydney, 1983), who suggested substantially higher figures. Whatever the truth of Butlin's claims, the figures quoted here derive from the estimate of A.R. Radcliffe-Brown in *The Official Yearbook of the Commonwealth of Australia*, (Canberra, 1930), and represent the best opinion of that period.

7   Peter Biskup, *Not Slaves, Not Citizens*, (St. Lucia, 1973), p. 66; Broome, *Aboriginal Australians*, p. 160.

8   See, for example, Biskup, *Not Slaves*, p. 84.

9   Broome, *Aboriginal Australians*, p. 164.

10 See Rowley, *The Destruction*, pp. 290-297. R.M. and C.H. Berndt also examine the Tuckiar episode in detail in their *Arnhem Land: Its History and Its People*, (Melbourne, 1954), pp. 134-152. See also A.P. Elkin's "Aboriginal Evidence and Justice in North Australia", *Oceania*, vol. 17, no. 3, March 1947, pp. 173-210, especially pp. 181-182.

11 Broome, *Aboriginal Australians*, p. 165.

12 *ibid.*, p. 165.

13 Stanner, "The Aborigines(1938)", p. 15.

14 Broome, *Aboriginal Australians*, p. 161.

15 Stanner, "The Aborigines (1938)", p. 7ff.

16 ibid., p. 14.

17   Bleakley was the Queensland Chief Protector of Aborigines when he surveyed the Territory in 1929.

18   Broome, *Aboriginal Australians*, p. 162.

19   Rowley, *The Destruction*, p. 304.

20   Resolution passed in the proceedings of *Aboriginal Welfare—Initial Conference of Commonwealth and State Aboriginal Authorities*, (Canberra, 1937), p. 2.

21   Stanner raises this point in "The Aborigines (1938)", p. 14.

22   Biskup, Rowley, and Paul Hasluck,in his *Black Australians*, (Melbourne, 1942), are arguably all guilty of this over-emphasis.

23   Peter Read, "A History of the Wiradjuri People", Ph.D thesis, (Canberra, 1983), p. 167.

24   Broome, *Aboriginal Australians*, p. 166.

25   Jack Horner, *Vote Ferguson for Aboriginal Freedom*, (Sydney, 1973).

26   Broome, *Aboriginal Australians*, p. 167.

27   Quoted in Broome, *Aboriginal Australians*, p. 167.

28   *ibid.*, p. 167.

29   Horner, *Vote Ferguson*, pp. 56-71.

30   W.E.H. Stanner, "After the Dreaming", in *White Man Got No Dreaming*, (Canberra, 1979), p. 206.

31   *ibid.*, p. 205.

32   Biskup, *Not Slaves*, p. 93.

33   K.A. MacKirdy in R.W.Winks, ed., *The Historiography of the British Empire-Commonwealth*, (Durham, N.C., 1966), p. 170(note).

34   D.J. Mulvaney, "The Australian Aborigines 1606-1929: Opinion and Fieldwork", in *Historical Studies: Selected Articles*, Part 2, (Melbourne, 1964), p. 56.

35   "Editorial", *Oceania*, vol. 1, no. 1, April, 1930, p. 2.

36   Mulvaney, "The Australian Aborigines", p. 56.

37   Stanner, "The Aborigines(1938)", p.19.

38   Biskup, *Not Slaves*, p. 92.

39   Biskup, *Not Slaves*, pp. 180-181ff.

40   *ibid.*, p. 179. The figure has been converted from pounds to dollars.

41   Broome, *Aboriginal Australians*, p. 104.

42   *ibid.*, p. 115.

43   Biskup, *Not Slaves*, p. 176.

44   *ibid.*, pp. 175-176; Broome *Aboriginal Australians*, p. 108.

45   Biskup, *Not Slaves*, p. 181.

46   Stanner, "After The Dreaming", in *White Man Got No Dreaming*, p. 211.

47   Read, "A History of the Wiradjuri People", pp. 215-216.

48   C.D. Rowley, *The Destruction*, (Canberra, 1970), p. 337.

49   *ibid.*, p. 339.

50   Hannah Middleton, *But Now We Want the Land Back*, (Sydney, 1977), p. 73.

51   Robert A. Hall, "The Army and the Aborigines, World War II", Unpublished MA(Qual.) thesis, (Canberra, 1979), p. 2.

52   Broome, *Aboriginal Australians*, p. 169.

53   Broome, *Aboriginal Australians*, p. 137.

54   Hall, "The Army and the Aborigines". See, in particular, Chapter Five-"The Determinants of Army Attitudes"—especially pp. 93-94.

55   ibid., p. 32.

56   ibid., p. 108.

57   ibid., p. 32.

58   ibid., p. 24.

59   It was reported in late 1983 that the Australian government had "taken action to rectify underpayments in salaries totalling $7.4 million to about 800 Aboriginal and Torres Strait Islander World War II veterans and their beneficiaries" Department of Aboriginal Affairs, *Aboriginal Newsletter*, no. 130, November, 1983, p. 1.

60   Harry C. Gordon, *The Embarrassing Australian: The Story of An Aboriginal Warrior*, (Melbourne, 1962), p. 47. The emphasis is mine.

61   In his play, *Kullark*, Jack Davis explores some of the options open to Western Australian Aborigines immediately following World War II, and particularly emphasises the Aboriginal ex-serviceman, Alec Yorlah, who asserts his opposition to unjust white authority. See, for example, Act Two, Scene Five, of *Kullark* in *Kullark/The Dreamers*, (Sydney, 1982), pp. 57-64. *Kullark* is discussed in detail in Chapter Nine.

62   Middleton, *But Now We Want*, p. 83.

63   Biskup, *Not Slaves*, p. 210.

64   Len Watson, "1945: Enter the Black Radical", *The National Times Magazine*, April 1, 1974, p. 5.

65   See, in particular, the questionnaires completed by Mr S. Gela and Mr J. Mooka in the course of Hall's research for "The Army and the Aborigines, World War II". These are contained in volume two of the thesis, housed in the Australian Institute

of Aboriginal Studies Library, Canberra, ms. 1294.

66   Biskup, *Not Slaves*, p. 196.

67   Broome, *Aboriginal Australians*, pp. 170-171.

68   Rowley, *Destruction*, pp. 328-332.

69   Stanner, "After the Dreaming", in *White Man Got No Dreaming*, p. 211.

2

Popular Perceptions of an Unpopular People, 1929-1945

When the results of the *Bulletin*'s literary competition were announced in August 1928, Katharine Susannah Prichard was awarded joint first prize for her novel, *Coonardoo*. The judges said, "Our first choice is *A House is Built*, an Australian prose epic of marked literary quality. We find, however, such great merit in *Coonardoo*, with its outstanding value for serial publication, that we recommend it also as worthy of a first prize".[1] This official praise gave the impression that the judging party was unanimous in its approval of Prichard's work, but this was not the case. One of the judges, Cecil Mann wrote, "With any other native, from fragrant Zulu girl to fly-kissed Arab maid, she could have done it. But the aboriginal, in Australia, anyway cannot excite any higher feeling than nauseated pity or comical contempt".[2]

This dissension amongst the competition judges was reflected on a wider, public scale when *Coonardoo* was serialised in the *Bulletin* between September and December, 1928. There were those readers who appreciated the book's insight into traditional Aboriginal culture, but the vast majority were outraged by the moral issues addressed in the novel—specifically the author's sanction of a love affair between a white man and an Aboriginal woman. As Healy has noted, the *Bulletin* subsequently refused to publish Vance Palmer's *Men are Human*, (which dealt with similar issues) following the public furore over Prichard's book: "Our disastrous experience with *Coonardoo* shows us that the Australian public will not stand stories based on a white man's relations with an Australian Aborigine".[3] Even when the moral implications of *Coonardoo* were not considered objectionable, the novel was criticised by some for its romantic idealisation of traditional Aboriginal life. For example, in the "Red Page" of the *Bulletin*, one week after the contest results were announced, Prichard's book was damned with ironic praise: "Miss Prichard (Mrs. Throssell) paints a vivid picture of a woman's life and work on a remote run. There are fine incidental glimpses of the life of the aborigines of those parts— *easily the finest type of blacks in Australia*". [4] Whether the slight undertone of incredulity is intentional or otherwise, the point is that Prichard has come under critical fire for the sentimentality and idealisation in *Coonardoo*.[5]

While the novel had a rather tempestuous reception in Australia in 1928-29, in Britain it was soundly praised upon its release by Jonathan Cape. In 1929, the reviewer for *The Times Literary Supplement* wrote:

> The story is a vivid and moving study of the blacks in relation to the whites, and in particular of the lovely and faithful Coonardoo ... Mrs. Prichard has the trick of making her characters come alive ... The north-western life is pictured vividly in all its aspects and seasons with what seems to be an unexaggerated emphasis.[6]

The only criticism levelled at the book was that it contained too many native words which would tend to befuddle the English reader.

The different critical reception of *Coonardoo* in Australia and England is instructive. It once again illustrated the fact that the perception of Aboriginal matters was often quite different overseas. For this reason, one must not over-emphasise the impact of *Coonardoo* upon the Australian reading public at the time of the *Bulletin* serialisation. It is probably correct to say that most Australian readers of the story had a taste of the book in 1928-29—and then promptly rejected it. When it was written, *Coonardoo* was undeniably ahead of its time. But Australian society did not become open to the interracial ideas it espoused for at least another twenty years. Certain "classic" Australian works of literature,—such as *Coonardoo* and Xavier Herbert's *Capricornia*—dealt with Aboriginal/white racial and sexual relations themes in an honest and incisive way which was welcomed, at first, only by a small minority of Australian readers.

It is in some ways unwise to deal with Prichard and Herbert in the same breath, for the two novels for which they are most famous are radically different, in style, tone, construction and content. But, their obvious sympathy for, and admiration of, the Aboriginal way of life requires one to evaluate them here together. In view of the socio-political events which determined the course of race relations in Australia, as outlined in the previous chapter, both books must be seen as precursors of more enlightened white views of Aboriginal

Australians. It is interesting that, while Prichard's novel was viewed with disfavour in this country for many years, Herbert's book was generally approved, in part because his black humour masked the seriousness of his racial critique for many readers. Those who did seriously consider the informing ideas of the book often found it a cosmic comment on the wastefulness, anarchy and violence of human existence as a whole, rather than a particular comment on Aboriginal existence.[7]

The social and political conditions which prevailed between 1929 and 1945 militated against either *Coonardoo* or *Capricornia* having a significant educative impact on racial prejudice and Aboriginal stereotypes, especially before World War II. Such books have more recently been ascribed greater importance as reflections of a changing public opinion of Black Australians than is warranted—even if their influence is still being felt to the present day. For example, in 1959 Vance Palmer enthused, "If a change has come over our attitude to the aboriginals it is largely due to the way Katharine Prichard has brought them near to us. This is a great achievement."[8] The great achievement is that the attitude has changed in many areas of the country, but to distort the case as Palmer does is to ignore a host of factors which have affected White Australian perceptions of Aborigines. Clearly, reading Prichard—or Herbert for that matter—was not a necessary precondition for, nor a definite indication of, increasing black/white racial tolerance.

This chapter underlines several points. First, that there is a tendency to over-emphasise the importance of such works as *Coonardoo* and *Capricornia* as indicators of a supposedly new, enlightened view of the Aboriginal people. Second, by highlighting these so-called beacons of enlightenment, academic criticism has cast into a shadow the significance of the extremely popular works of historical fiction dealing with Aboriginal themes written by Ion L. Idriess, who outsold both Prichard and Herbert in the 1930s with such books as *Flynn of the Inland* and *Lasseter's Last Ride*. Third, a number of other popular works of literature written and published in the 1929-1945 period still exerted some influence on Australian readers as late as the 1960s; for example, Daisy Bates's *The Passing of the Aborigines*. Finally, the achievements of the first Aboriginal writer, David Unaipon, who published in the 1929-1945 period, were almost totally ignored until the 1970s and still deserve far more study than they have received.

Until the past decade, very little research has focussed on the

Aboriginal writers themselves. Very few White Australians would be aware of the fact that the year 1929 saw the publication of the first book by an Aboriginal Australian: David Unaipon's *Native Legends*.[9] More properly termed a booklet, given its diminutive length of fifteen pages, *Native Legends* is a fascinating social and artistic document. One must know something of this singular man's background in order to appreciate the eclectic stylistic synthesis of his work.[10]

Unaipon was born in 1872 at the Point McLeay Mission in South Australia, administered by the interdenominational group, the Aborigines' Friends' Association. The AFA was to become the most important formative influence on his life and career: it made possible his education, it provided him with employment, it sponsored his travels and speaking engagements, and it financed most of his publications. It is little wonder that Unaipon's work is strongly marked by his Christian upbringing and career. But there were other more specific factors which affected his writing. For example, Unaipon had been trained in both Latin and Greek and was extremely fond of reading sermons, especially those of Thomas de Witt Talmage and Henry Drummond, the latter being his favourite. [11] Especially in his recounting of Aboriginal legends, Unaipon emulated the elevated, sermonic prose style which characterised the work of these men.

The analytical and synthetic approach of his more factual writing is indicative of a mind which was both questing and incisive. It therefore comes as no surprise to learn that Unaipon was fascinated by modern scientific books and journals, and himself experimented with many models in an attempt to solve the problem of perpetual motion. These scientific works inspired him to attempt numerous inventions. In 1909 Unaipon obtained a patent for a device which transformed the action of sheep-shears from curvilinear to straight-line motion. As he relates in *My Life Story*, scientific writings, especially those of Newton:

> stimulated my mind and I decided to try and invent something too. I suffered a disadvantage in doing this for I lacked a training in mathematics, but I began by studying the machine used in sheep-shearing for an Adelaide firm with a view to bringing about an improvement in its working. This I succeeded in doing and I obtained a patent for the same, but not being properly protected I lost financially any material gain arising from this discovery, as this was passed to others who made use of my invention without giving me any compensation.[12]

Despite the brilliance of many of his ideas, which ranged from the field of ballistics to that of helicopter flight, Unaipon was unable to secure financial support to develop any of the nineteen patent applications he obtained between 1909 and 1949; in itself, a comment on White Australian ignorance of Aboriginal talent at the time.[13]

As a writer, musician, inventor, and public speaker who was schooled in the classics, Unaipon must have seemed to the AFA a heaven-sent token of the worth of its policies, which were assimilationist many years before the concept became widely accepted throughout Australia. Unaipon became their star pupil and their mouthpiece. As Gordon Rowe enthused in his booklet *Sketches of Outstanding Aborigines* (published in 1956 by the AFA), "He [Unaipon] says that he is everywhere kindly received, and that the acceptance of the aborigine today depends mainly on the aborigine himself. He was among those who received the Coronation Medal".[14] But the question remains: "Was Unaipon so fully indoctrinated into the Western, Christian lifestyle that he renounced his independence and his Aboriginality?"

In the first critical analysis of Unaipon's work, which appeared in 1979, John Beston asserts that "Unaipon was by no means a white man's puppet".[15] Beston concentrates upon the symbolic Aboriginal development which he perceives in four of Unaipon's legends, which underlies the Christian idiom of expression. One can take issue with Beston's conclusion, both because it proceeds from false premises and because it is derived from research which was not comprehensive. In fact, Beston ignores the clear evidence of one of Unaipon's published addresses, "An Aboriginal Pleads For His Race", which he cites in his bibliography but does not discuss in his article. The essence of Unaipon's brief speech is its implied endorsement of Aboriginal assimilation into White Australian society. He says:

> The white man must not leave the aborigine alone. We cannot stand in the way of progress. The aborigines must not be left alone in the middle of civilization. That would be like an aborigine leaving a white man alone in the middle of the bush.

And he continues:

> If some sort of reserve were possible, in which only the good influence of civilization could be felt, a new civilized race could be built up. With a gradual process of introducing Christianity and all the best civilization can give, the aborigine would come up fully developed. It might take two generations, perhaps more, but eventually we would be able to take our stand among the civilized peoples.[16]

As these quotations indicate, Unaipon may be a full-blooded Black Australian, but he does not view himself as being the same as other Aborigines. If anything, he comes across as something akin to a self-professed black prophet or seer, who has managed to cast off his "uncivilised nature" (read Aboriginality) and has adopted the lifestyle and attitudes of "civilisation" (read Christian white society). In this light, Beston's contention that "his Christianizing of the legends somewhat obscures his strong underlying sense of Aboriginal identity and allegiance"[17] is difficult to accept. Beston implies that, at base, Unaipon was faithful to his Aboriginal heritage above all else, whereas the evidence seems to indicate that he was so fully indoctrinated by the AFA that an Aboriginal world view was encouraged and permitted only so long as it did not conflict with Christian religious tenets.

Unfortunately, Beston is even more misleading when he claims that "Unaipon's output was not large ... [he] recounted only four legends altogether".[18] Obviously Beston had not consulted the substantial original manuscript and typescript of Unaipon's writing—held by the Mitchell Library—which includes some thirty Christianised legends, religious fables and anthropological notes, under the title, "Legendary Tales of the Australian Aborigines",[19] let alone the five of these legends which were subsequently published in *Dawn* magazine. In turn, this leads Beston to his most unfortunate conclusion:

> Perhaps that is why Unaipon told no more legends: within their small framework, his four legends encompass his view of the present situation and the ultimate role of the Aboriginal people.[20]

One cannot be overly critical of Beston's paper as it did serve a useful function: it was the first example of scholarship to draw serious attention to Unaipon's work; it describes salient aspects of his writing style accurately; it provides enlightening biographical information; and it helpfully reprints one of Unaipon's legends ("The Story of the Mungingee"). However, because the author has neglected to examine some of Unaipon's published work and all of his unpublished writings, many of his conclusions are either dubious or are simply incorrect.

One is left with the question: "What does an examination of Unaipon's entire known corpus of literature tell us about the first Aboriginal writer and his work?". All of Unaipon's writing is fascinating, complex and almost defies classification, for he did not simply write one type of story nor did his style remain constant—even within the confines of one tale. In fact, the atmosphere of his stories occasionally borders upon the schizophrenic, for the Christian/

Aboriginal synthesis which he repeatedly sought is not always achieved without considerable effort and is sometimes realised at the expense of logic. Despite these difficulties and qualifications, it is possible to place Unaipon's writing broadly within four categories: the historical/mythological, the Christian/Aboriginal spiritual exempla, the practical/anthropological, and the fairy tale/fable.

A good example of the first is the short piece entitled "Totemism", which appears in the pages of *Native Legends*. Unaipon initially sets out to explain the concept, writing in an academic and authoritative tone:

> Totemism is one of the most ancient customs instituted by the Primitive Man. The practice of it among the Australian Aborigines and its adoption owes its origin to a Mythological conception during the Neolithic Age.

Gradually, the tone shifts until the author begins to recount his interpretation of the myth which led to Aboriginal totemic belief, complete with philosophical concepts which are striking:

> And when the appointed period arrived Spirit Man made the Great Decision and adventure [sic] to be clothed with earthly body of flesh and blood, his Spirit Consciousness experienced a great change, for he was overshadowed by another self, the Subjective Consciousness, which entirely belongs to the Earth and not to the Sacred Realm of Spirit.[21]

Unaipon relates how the baser "Subjective Consciousness" tied man to the torments of the earth and flesh and caused his corresponding "Spirit Consciousness" to "pine for its Heavenly Home". This spiritual dichotomy is not resolved by the benign intervention of a deity nor by a sudden revelation but by the animals of the earth, who take pity on man and impart all their knowledge and instinct for survival to him. Unaipon concludes:

> Thus the Aborigines of Australia have from time immemorial ... selected these living creatures for companions and guides.[22]

The assumption is that when they have reached the stage described at the end of "Totemism", the Aboriginal people are ripe for a reawakening of that spiritual consciousness which since time began had been yearning for its home—via Christianity.

The unpublished introduction to "Legendary Tales of the Australian Aborigines", entitled "Aboriginal Folk Lore", reflects once again an emphasis upon first causes in Unaipon's historical/mythological mode of writing. From a preliminary discussion of the value and longevity of Aboriginal myths and story-telling, the author proceeds to relate the flight of the Aborigines "from a land in the Nor'-West, beyond the sea, into Australia". In Unaipon's re-telling, the obvious aim is to achieve a synthesis with Christian—specifically Old Testament—narrative:

> The traditions also relate that the aboriginals were driven into Australia by a plague of fierce ants, or by a prehistoric race as fierce and innumerable as ants ... Like the Israelites, the aboriginals seem to have had a Moses, a law-giver, a leader, who guided them in their Exodus from Lemuria. His name is Nar-ran-darrie.

This Nar-ran-darrie is a being now living in the heavens who gave both laws and customs to the Aborigines (all that is lacking is the Ten Commandments). Equally important is the fact that Unaipon relates this tale from the point of view of a civilised European, as his idiom and his attitude illustrate:

> Aboriginal myths, legends and stories were told to laughing and open-eyed children centuries before *our* present-day European culture began; stories that stand to-day as a link between the dawn of the world and *our latest civilization*.23

This brief article leads to a number of important observations concerning Unaipon's work. First, the story is clearly directed at a white audience—as were all of the author's legendary tales. Second, it is implicit here and elsewhere in Unaipon's work, that Aboriginal myth, while ancient and meaningful, is not of the same stature as Christian Scripture: the Aborigines, despite their good points, were a primitive people. Their spirituality and their mythology is accorded stature in retrospect by Unaipon because he sees these as being proto-Christian. Christian belief gives Aboriginal belief the grandeur of incipient enlightenment.

The scriptural influence upon Unaipon's writing is even more evident in the second broad class of stories, which I have termed the Christian/Aboriginal spiritual exempla. The prose style of the historical/mythological tales is relatively plain and descriptive but the style of this second class of stories is unashamedly Biblical. For example, in "Release of the Dragon Flies, by the Fairy, Sun Beam", published in *Native Legends*, frogs stand guard over imprisoned water grubs in a place which is so "beautiful and enchanting" that it will

> arouse feelings and emotions of sacred fear, and in reverence [anyone intruding will] retrace their steps, lest they trespass upon holy ground.24

When the malicious frogs are finally conquered and the water grubs are liberated, the descriptive tone is derived directly from the Old Testament, complete with pyrotechnics:

> Above the whirlwind there formed a cloud like mid-night, suddenly lightning flashed, then a terrible thunder peal that seemed to roll around the meadow a score of times.

This is immediately preceded by a cogent moral exemplum:

> Then a guilty conscience smote them one and all; for the wrong they did unto the helpless, harmless water grubs who did need the help; the strong should give.[25]

Beston quite correctly describes Unaipon's style in such stories as "seventeenth-century, suggestive of the King James Bible, Bunyan, and Milton".[26] Unfortunately, his sample of Unaipon's writing was so small that he failed to appreciate the author's stylistic diversity. For Unaipon's mode of expression is, in contemporary Western terms, the most archaic when he is relating the speech of spirit characters in his stories. For example, in "Youn Goona the Cockatoo" (also printed in *Native Legends*) the spirit bird Youn Goona asks his wife, "Well, dear, what shall we do, are we to continue to exist in Spirit or shall we decide to take a body of flesh and blood? Choose ye, my dear".[27] On other occasions, Unaipon abandons any pretence of paraphrasing Scripture and quotes from it directly. For example, in the unpublished "Nhung e Umpie", a story concerning the universality of human nature (regardless of race and skin colour) he writes, exactly as follows:

> I would like to call your attention to the Christian faith ... of the Gospel Luke I chapter verse 42, you will these [sic] words. Blessed art thou among women and Blessed is the fruit of thy womb verse 46 and Mary said My soul doth magnify the Lord 47 verse, and my spirit hath rejoiced in God my saviour, 48 verse. For he hath regarded the low estate of his hand maiden for behold from henceforth all generations shall call me blessed.

Then, in the very next line Unaipon writes "Now the gut or part of the intestine of mother and child has a great significance to us"[28]—a fine example of the stylistic schizoprenia of some of the author's work. Yet another of Unaipon's experiments with style—in this case a successful one—is his emulation of the Biblical psalm, as in "The Song of Hungarrda" (published in *Native Legends*), essentially a hymn to the potency of fire:

> As I roam from place to place for enjoyment
> or search of food,
> My soul is filled with gratitude and love
> for thee.[29]

Whereas both the historical/mythological and Christian/

Aboriginal spiritual exempla stories of Unaipon are indebted to Scripture to some degree, the third general form, which I have termed the practical/anthropological, is not. To cite one example, his unpublished tale simply entitled "Hunting" is solely concerned with techniques of tracking and taking various wild birds and animals: "A few furs amongst the rocks leading to a hole indicates that Mr. and Mrs. Possum are having their daily nap".[30] The only exception to this statement is Unaipon's preliminary overview of Aboriginal hunting talent:

> I may say with confidence that in bushcraft and hunting the aborigines excel, and are undoubtedly second to no other of the primitive races in this respect.[31]

Other stories in "Legendary Tales" written in this informative format include "Sport" and "Fishing", although this last is bolstered by a legend in the explanatory tradition concerning a huge fish which was responsible for excavating the river beds of Australia.[32] Unaipon employs a plain style of expression here which avoids imagery and literary flourishes and is very like the concise explication in "An Aboriginal Pleads For His Race".

The final stylistic category which I have proposed, the fairy tale/fable, is typical of many of Unaipon's stories which explain how particular animals came to possess—or lose—certain physical characteristics, such as "How the Tortoise Got His Shell"[33] and "Why Frogs Jump Into the Water".[34] Beston notes that the author occasionally writes in the "mould of the Germanic *Maarchen* or fairy tale",[35] but Unaipon's more juvenile stories often owe as much to Aesop and Kipling's "just so" stories as they do to the Brothers Grimm. His wide-ranging personification, his frequent targets of proud or foolish animal characters, and his propensity to indulge in moralising characterise many of the tales; for example, "Why All The Animals Peck at the Selfish Owl".[36] But, the classic example of Unaipon's fairy tale/fable mode is the final story in "Legendary Tales", "How Teddy Lost His Tail".

The story begins with the customary fairy tale opening familiar to European readers:

> Once upon a time, long long ago, before the animal, bird, reptile and insect life came to Australia, they occupied the many islands that existed in the ocean Kar ra mia, a place of the beginning of day, where all is peace and rest.

The story is definitely stamped in Unaipon's eccentric and—in this atypical case—humorous mould, for the islands are inhabited by Teddy Bears so wise that the elders take their young to mountaintops to teach them astronomy! During their astronomical observations the Elders note streaks of light on the distant horizon, which they ultimately realise are the fires of other species of life. The Philosopher Bear reports:

> Children ... there are other lands like ours all around us, which are occupied by strange and queer people I am not prepared to describe, as I have never seen them; but I do say that there are other forms of life.

This sets the stage for the bears' voyage to the land of these mysterious fires—Australia—and their exploration of precise geographical locations in New South Wales. It is after returning to their original islands to invite the other animals "to come down and share this wonderful country" that the bear tribe comes to grief. Their canoes are swamped in heavy surf off the Australian coast on the journey back to their new home and, while swimming ashore, "the hungry sharks followed them and bit their tails off, and that accident completely subdued the adventurous spirit of the Teddy Bears".[37]

In many respects this is whimsical, humorous fantasy, but is Unaipon's work purely a curio—a rambling, inconsistent mixture of Christian and Aboriginal influences? Or is his work both talented and important? Is his *Native Legends*, as John Beston has claimed, the best collection of legends written by an Aborigine "in its stylistic elegance, in the organisation of the material, and in its evenness and fullness of development"?[38]

Beston's assessment is limited and too forgiving. When one examines Unaipon's entire corpus of work, it becomes clear that his story-telling is uneven, inconsistent, and is frequently fraught with tension between the Aboriginal and white Christian worlds. One receives the impression that Unaipon did not have a very great knowledge of traditional Aboriginal matters, and this might partly explain why his legendary stories often take such a sanitised, European form. Second, the very marked stylistic variance which I have illustrated makes it impossible to consider many of his stories as "legends": the term does not adequately embrace some of the eclectic elements which Unaipon incorporates into his narratives. This is not to dismiss his work. In fact, some of the author's more lyrical writing, such as "The Song of Hungarrda" and "The Voice of the Great Spirit"[39] impresses through its vivid imagery and fresh cadences.

It seems that Unaipon tried to tailor the Aboriginal traditions of which he was aware to his newly-acquired and fervent Christianity. The two do not always sit well together, but the confusion and inconsistency of much of his work is both intriguing and revealing. Especially in terms of the socio-political climate at the time he wrote, his work *is* important. It illustrates the honest response of a brilliant Aboriginal man to the pressures and expectations of the mission system. It portrays the paradox of a man moving away from traditional Aboriginal society while he ostensibly celebrates narrative and mythical elements of that society in his writing. It shows in a very clear and telling way the potential of the assimilation doctrine (especially when bolstered with the allure of Christianity), which was to be so comprehensively applied in Australia many years after Unaipon had written *Native Legends*. His literary shortcomings presage some of the successes and destructive consequences of assimilation. Finally, at the time when full-blooded Aborigines were commonly believed to be dying out, Unaipon's work exemplified an inventiveness, a vigour and a vibrancy which paralleled those qualities in his personal life. For all these reasons, the writings of David Unaipon deserve to be collected and re-published *in toto*.

Though Unaipon's literary works had a negligible impact during the 1929-1945 era, having been published so incompletely and obscurely, the writings of many white authors who dealt with Aboriginal themes were more influential during that same period—and for many years afterwards. One of the best-known of these was Daisy Bates's *The Passing of the Aborigines*,[40] often considered to be the crystallisation in print of the doctrine that Aboriginal people were irredeemably primitive and moribund.

There is little doubt that Bates's book, first published in 1938, had a significant impact upon the perception of Aborigines by European Australians and overseas readers. *The Passing of the Aborigines* is a prime example of a work published in the 1929-1945 period which still exerted some influence upon Australian readers as late as the 1970s. Despite the changes of the intervening years, *The Passing of the Aborigines* was reprinted five times up to 1948 and a second edition, issued in in 1966, was reprinted three times to 1972. As recently as 1979, Virago Press of London was considering re-issuing the book as an example of feminist literature, until dissuaded by protests concerning its racial viewpoint![41] The popularity of the book indicates the continuity and longevity of interest in Aboriginal themes and issues among both Australian and British readers. Unfortunately, it also illustrates the continuance of misinformation and Aboriginal stereotypes in Australian literature, even to the present day. The following passage is taken from a book, published in 1980 and directed at primary school children, entitled *From Many Lands—Australians of the Past*:

> Daisy went to Eucla on the edge of the Nullarbor Plain. The desert was hot and dry. At first Daisy stayed with friends, but later she lived in her tent. She again helped the Aboriginals. She fed them, nursed the sick and looked after the babies.
>
> Daisy learnt languages easily. She could talk to the Aboriginals in 188 dialects. She collected legends, languages and customs. The Aboriginals loved and trusted her and told her many tribal secrets.
>
> Once she witnessed an initiation ceremony. This was when the young men were tested for their manhood and then taken into the tribe. Normally no women were allowed to watch the ceremony.[42]

What is implicit in this simply descriptive and approving treatment of the Daisy Bates myth is important, for it is aimed at probably the most impressionable and uncritical of all audiences. Yet it takes no account of many commentators' ambivalent—and openly critical—view of Bates's life and career. For example, Ken Hampton, a Black Australian working for the Department of Aboriginal Affairs in Adelaide, writes:

> To say she was eccentric is to be ridiculously soft-hearted. She began camp life in the early 1900s and her book ... has been described by the Professor of Australian Linguistics at the University of Adelaide as "the most destructive book written on Aborigines. If anybody other than Daisy Bates had written that book they would have been condemned as a racist. White people regarded her as a heroine but she never was as she claimed to be a blood brother of the Aborigines. It is nonsense. There is no such thing. In her book she alleges the women killed their children and ate them. She sent the bones of these alleged dead children to the Adelaide University for investigation. The late Professor J.B. Cleland examined them and found them to be those of a wild cat. She claimed she could speak 188 Aboriginal dialects, but in fact, she couldn't even speak the language of the Aborigines at Ooldea where she spent 16 years".
>
> If possible, she was even more maternalistic than Mrs. Gunn and far more destructive of Aboriginal dignity. Poor little woman. [43]

Given the widespread criticism of the Bates fables it seems incredible that, as recently as 1980, a book could be published which blithely imparts the misinformation contained in Kohler and Kohn's *From Many Lands*. For the purposes of this study, what is noteworthy is that a popular book of the 1929-1945 era could still be exerting some influence on the Australian reading public of the present day. *The Passing of the Aborigines* is not alone in this regard. Certain classic examples of Australian black/white race relations literature—such as *Coonardoo* and *Capricornia*—have been continuously available since World War II. Moreover, both have very frequently been chosen as set texts at the high school and university levels during those years.

With reference to *Coonardoo*, in 1980 the critic Kay Iseman wrote that *"for its time* the novel had immense significance, both literary and political",[44] and she concludes "it paved the way for a complete reassessment of aboriginal culture".[45] Such generalisations are open to question, and critics such as Vance Palmer and Kay Iseman overstate the case. Certainly, in artistic terms *Coonardoo* broke new ground. In stylistic terms, it evokes station life minutely and brilliantly, and the harshness and oppressiveness of the Australian environment are captured with imagistic precision:

> The air, at a little distance, palpitated, thrown off from the stones in minute atoms, visible one moment, flown to invisibility the next. Weaving, with the sun for shuttle, the air spun heat which was suffocating. The sun, an incandescence somewhere above and beyond the earth, moved electric, annihilating. And stillness, a breathless heaviness, drowsed the senses, brain and body, as if that mythological great snake the blacks believed in, a rock python, silvery-grey, black and brown, sliding down from hills of the sky, were putting the opiate of his breath into the air, folding you round and round, squeezing the life out of you.[46]

But how can one state that a novel "paved the way for a complete reassessment of Aboriginal culture"? It appears that numerous commentators have fallen into the trap of mythologising in retrospect. In other words, novels like *Coonardoo* and *Capricornia* have been ascribed more importance than they deserve—especially when one is speaking of the time when they were written. As was demonstrated in the previous chapter, changes in Aboriginal policy in the 1929-1945 period came about as much because of the workings of international factors as in response to domestic forces. Novels such as *Coonardoo* and *Capricornia* are taken as evidence of greater sensitivity to the value of Aboriginal culture during that time. But, just as social reforms in race relations were advocated during these fifteen years only by and for an educated elite, so too did the revolutionary ideas imputed to these novels have an impact only upon a very select minority of Australian readers. One can contend that these books had a negligible impact upon the average Australian reader—in terms of altering ideas concerning the Aboriginal people—until the socio-political environment *facilitated* those changes.

What, then, did Prichard and Herbert achieve? In their written work both provided an honest and direct appraisal of interracial sexual relations, which one can consider an accurate historical index of the state of affairs at the time. For example, in the following excerpt from *Capricornia*—which illustrates Herbert's mastery of the vernacular—the aptly-named Andy McRandy tells Norman:

> In the case of lubras it certainly aint [sic] a matter of mere taste that sends the boys after 'em. I reckon any normal healthy man'll fall for 'em if he'll expose himself to the risk. I don't care what anybody says. Even parsons have done it; and they aint what you'd call normal and healthy. I've seen comboes of all sorts—as smart fellers as you'd wish to find, and dunces, and fine lookin' fellers, and others with faces like fried grummets, and even married men. They're all the same. It's only a question of gettin' used to the colour and the different kind of countenance.[47]

Both Prichard and Herbert captured the deep-seated prejudice and loathing which whites associated with "half-castes" during the period. It is Hugh Watt's inability to accept his love for the Aboriginal woman Coonardoo (at least in part because of the stigma surrounding the visible presence of his "half-caste" son) which causes the tragic decline, banishment, and eventual death of the heroine. Similarly, it is the treatment of the part-Aboriginal Norman; his misconceptions concerning his ancestry and his futile attempts at disassociation from other "half-castes" (including Tocky, the mother of his child) which are bleakly driven home in the pages of *Capricornia*. The final words of the novel present—in stark, spare, and powerful language—what seems to be a profoundly pessimistic view of the future for part-Aboriginal people. The only prospects are of disregard, neglect, and death:

> Dry grass rattled against the iron. Dry wind moaned through rust-eaten holes. He stepped up to the tank and peeped through a hole. Nothing to see but the rusty wall beyond. He climbed the ladder, looked inside, saw a skull and a litter of bones. He gasped. A human skull—no—two—a small one and a tiny one. And human hair and rags of clothes and a pair of bone-filled boots. Two skulls, a small one and tiny one. Tocky and her baby!
>
> The crows alighted in a gnarled dead coolibah near by and cried dismally, "Kah!—Kah!—Kaaaaah!"[48]

It is vital to realise that, widely read as novels like *Capricornia* were during the 1929-1945 period, they were not the most popular works of fiction on Aboriginal themes sold during those sixteen years. Two individual award-winning novels have been exalted as literary signposts to interracial understanding when there were a number of other novels published during the same period, also dealing with

Aboriginal/white relations, which offered diametrically-opposed conclusions and attitudes. If these had been execrable pieces of writing which were ignored by the reading public the point would hardly be worth making, but they were not. They were best-sellers, promoted personally throughout country towns the length and breadth of Australia,[49] and they were written by a raconteur who is still the highest-selling author published by Angus and Robertson: Ion L. Idriess.[50]

To give some indication of Idriess's phenomenal popularity, "by the time he finished, this bushman-turned author had his name on 55 books with total sales of more than three million copies".[51] In comparison, *Capricornia*, first published in 1938, was reprinted in 1939, 1941, 1943 and 1945. By 1980 it was termed a "best-selling epic novel" and had sold over 75,000 copies in Australia.[52] These are impressive figures, but they are easily eclipsed when one compares them with the sales totals of Idriess's earliest books, such as *Lasseter's Last Ride*, first published in 1931. It was reprinted every year until 1939, then again in 1941, 1942, 1943 and 1945. By 1980 it had sold some 120,000 copies and was "still going strong".[53]

What do these figures reveal? First, that the books of Idriess must be discussed when one is considering Australian literary perceptions by, and about, Aborigines. Yet in D.L.M. Jones's 1960 M.A. thesis, "The Treatment of the Australian Aborigine in Australian Fiction" and J.J. Healy's 1978 study, *Literature and the Aborigine in Australia, 1770-1975*, Idriess does not rate a mention. This cannot be because some of his books are not strictly novels and involve adventure reportage; Healy, for example, devotes three pages to a discussion of Daisy Bates and her self-aggrandising pseudo-history.[54] The exclusion of an immensely popular writer like Idriess probably results from two factors. First, his writing is not considered by many to be artistically skilled. Second, the attitudes and honest prejudices both implicit and explicit in his writings are incompatible with the theory that the major Australian writers were beginning to understand Aboriginal people more sympathetically during the 1929-1945 period.

But what is a "major writer"? Certainly talent is a crucial factor but it is arguable that popularity is an important consideration as well. One cannot argue that Idriess was a writer who enjoyed transient popularity, only to sink from sight a decade later. In fact, there are more of his books in print today than there were in 1976.[55] In addition, he has received numerous accolades for his work. For example, in the May, 1954 issue of *Fragment*, he was praised as follows: "Among our contemporaries, no man has done more to make Australian literature genuinely popular than Idriess".[56] In the same vein, Julian Croft has written:

> Idriess's contribution to Australian publishing and literature was profound. His combination of the bush yarn and historical or geographical subjects brought a new vision of Australia to its city-bound readers ... Idriess was no stylist, but his writing was immediate, colourful, well-paced and, despite the speed at which it was written, always well structured. The combination of an optimistic view of Australia's progress and the romance of the past with a style drawn from the spoken language ensured his popularity.[57]

Idriess is, then, an influential writer, and his attitudes towards the Aboriginal people must be taken into account.

Lasseter's Last Ride provides an excellent starting point. Subtitled "An Epic of Central Australian Gold Discovery", the novel emphasises the thwarted explorations of white men, especially Lasseter, in the search for a mythical reef of Centralian gold. The Aboriginal people are everywhere in the novel, but they are never individualised as real characters. One encounters a number of stereotypes of Black Australians in the book: the "jovial Aboriginal comic", the "childlike father", the "venerable tracker" and the "evil witch doctor". The first is clearly exemplified in the character of Micky, a tracker directing the explorers to water holes. For their own amusement, the whites put the wireless earphones on Micky in order to observe his reaction:

> Seated on a box, he submitted with a grin, anticipating anything might happen. Something did. Statics! Micky bolted. When they caught him they held him down, patting him as they would a horse. They hung on until he got the music which "soothes the savage beast". The glare faded from his eyes; his breast heaved less riotously; the frightened gash that was his mouth expanded into a grin that spread from ear to ear; his eyes grew normal, then sparkled.[58]

The lowering of the character of Micky to the level of a simpleton—and a wild simpleton at that—is all too clear in this extract.

The stereotype of the malicious witch-doctor is equally obvious in the following:

> With skinny claw the witch-doctor pulled out a dried lizard, laid it down and stared at it for minutes. Then his lips moved sibilantly and Lasseter could have sworn that the lizard hissed in reply ... over each article he pored as if actually conversing with it, as if it possessed some power of evil.[59]

Though one may cringe to read these descriptions today, one might ask how many thousands of readers have accepted the implicit prejudices contained in these passages in the past, as merely a legitimate component of the adventure story-line. The distancing of Black Australian people in literature, either as mindless though amusing imbeciles, or as cunning animalistic savages, arguably reflects the condescension and disdain which many Australians of the 1929-1945 period felt for Aborigines.

Prichard and Herbert have both been praised for highlighting Aboriginal characters in their books. Idriess cannot be excluded from consideration by this criterion, for his 1941 novel *Nemarluk: King of the Wilds* (which had sold some 36,000 copies by 1980)[60] highlights the exploits of this Northern Territory rebel. As is so often the case, the author reduces his Aboriginal characters to a brutal, bestial level. For example:

> They caught Tiger and Wadawarry in their full war paint dancing in the madness of a war corroboree. Tiger fought like the tiger he was, but they bore him to earth and snapped the steel upon his wrists. Screaming his fury he bit up into the panting face of Bul-bul. Bul-bul held his throat just out of reach and laughed while Tiger writhed and spat up at him.[61]

The undertone of white supremacy is ever-present and surfaces in the most unlikely places. Even the incomparable Aboriginal trackers have to defer to their employers, as follows:

> Again and again, however, some exceptionally clever native outlaw has beaten a persistent and clever tracker. What has then caught the outlaw has been the thinking power behind the tracker—the deduction of the policeman. His brain is constantly working far ahead of and many miles around his own tracker.[62]

The condescending conception of Aboriginal people which underlies Idriess's novels was one which was shared by the majority of Australians in the 1929-1945 period. His writings probably reflect the European view of Black Australians at the time far more accurately than the sentimental idealism of Prichard or the cosmic black humour of Herbert.

Moreover, reading the books of Idriess could be a painful and degrading experience for Black Australians during those years. Faith Bandler remembers their impact:

Bandler:	Well, I can recall my days—I think still in primary school and we were reading Idriess's books then, and the terrible effect that those books had on me as a black child in a classroom.
Interviewer:	Really?

Bandler:	Devastating, devastating. Yes. And I think that if it were not for the fact that we—my family—had a pretty good friendship and relationship with teachers, perhaps I would have dropped out.
Interviewer:	Really?
Bandler:	And, yes. And *Drums of Mer*: practically every one of the thirteen books at that time were considered by—were felt by me as a child as—I can't explain it. It was just so *dreadful*, it …
Interviewer:	Were they actually taught as course books in school?
Bandler:	Yes, yes. And it made me feel that we had absolutely nothing. Absolutely nothing to give. All that was black was bad. You know: they were beggars and they were thieves in *Lasseter's Last Ride*.[63]

In view of Idriess's popularity, and given the potentially damaging impact of his work which Bandler has emphasised, it is remarkable that his writing has not been considered in the existing studies—both published and unpublished—of the Aboriginal theme in Australian literature. Without doubt, the novels of Idriess must be evaluated if one is to gain an accurate picture of the literary treatment of Aboriginal Australians yet, until now, there has been little research on either Idriess or Unaipon.

It is not only the work of Prichard and Herbert which has been over-emphasised in studies dealing with the Aboriginal theme in Australian literature. In my view, the poetry and prose of the Jindyworobak writers has also been ascribed too much significance, despite the claims of Brian Elliott in his comprehensive treatment of the movement.[64] Officially inaugurated in 1938 with the publication of Rex Ingamells's and Ian Tilbrook's *Conditional Culture*, the Jindyworobak group was described as "probably the most important literary movement in Australia today"[65] —but it is noteworthy that this was by one of its members. D.L.M. Jones has perceptively illustrated how these men sought to develop a truly indigenous White Australian culture, using Aboriginal culture—or rather, their superficial understanding of it—as the theoretical key. And to what end? Primarily, to establish the autonomy of Australian culture from that of European countries, particularly England.[66] Without belittling the efforts of those White Australians who have subsequently attempted to explore the Aboriginal theme more sensitively, most of the original Jindyworobaks told their readers next to nothing about Aboriginal people. Rather, their usage of the ostensible trappings of Black Australian languages was indicative of a kind of souvenir mentality. As Judith Wright succinctly put it, "The movement was a matter of white art theory".[67]

Therefore, I believe that there is a clear and cogent case for de-emphasising certain forms of Australian literature of the 1929-1945 period which deal with the Black Australian theme. The novels of Prichard and Herbert were, indeed, ahead of their time, but it is wrong to suggest that they actually changed their times, or even the ideas of a sizeable number of Australian readers during those years. On the other hand the consistent and pervasive attempts of certain fringe missionary groups to control the lives (including the creative lives) of their Aboriginal charges deserve to be far more fully-researched. The life and work of Unaipon provides a particularly fascinating example of such control. Third, the popular literature of the 1929-1945 era must be rescued from the shadow of critical neglect which, up to now, has fallen across it: an analysis of the complete works of Idriess is long overdue.

Stanner's observation concerning socio-political attitudes embodied in the governmental Aboriginal policy of the 1929-1945 era applies equally accurately to the racial attitudes and ideas housed in its literature. He wrote:

> The change of attitude and policy which we trace back to the 1930s was confined very largely to a rather small group of people who had special associations with their [Aborigines'] care, administration or study. Outside that group the changes made very little impact for a long time.[68]

In many ways, if it was anyone's, the 1929-1945 period was the age of Idriess. The coalescence of real sensitivity to the Aboriginal people—literary, social and political—had not really begun to occur during that era and did not crystallise for many years afterwards.

Notes

1   "Judges' Report", The *Bulletin*, vol. 49, no. 2532, 22 August, 1928, p. 9.

2   Quoted in Ric Throssell, *Wild Weeds and Wind Flowers*, (Sydney, 1975), p. 54.

3   Letter from S.H. Prior to Vance Palmer, dated 9 June, 1929; Palmer Letters, National Library of Australia. (Quoted in Healy, *Literature and the Aborigine in Australia, 1770-1975*, (St. Lucia, 1978), p. 140.

4   "The Red Page", The *Bulletin*, vol. 49, no. 2533, 29 August, 1928, p. 5. The emphasis is mine.

5   See, for example, Dianne Schwerdt, "A Changing Black Image in Australian Fiction", in W. Menary, ed., *Aborigines and Schooling: Essays in Honour of Max Hart*, (Adelaide, 1981), pp. 84-88.

6   "New Novels", *The Times Literary Supplement*, no. 1433, 18 July, 1929, p. 574.

7   The classic exposition of this viewpoint is Vincent Buckley's article *"Capricornia"*, *Meanjin*, vol. XIX, no. 1, 1960, pp. 13-30.

8   Vance Palmer's Foreword to *N'goola and Other Stories*, (Melbourne, 1959), p. 8.

9   David Unaipon, *Native Legends*, (Adelaide, 1929[?]). There is some uncertainty over the precise publication date of this booklet, but it definitely appears to be earlier than the National Library's estimate of 1932. I follow Beston's conclusion that 1929 is the most likely date.

10   Biographical details are taken from David Unaipon, *My Life Story*, (Adelaide, 1951), and from Gordon Rowe, *Sketches of Outstanding Aborigines*, (Adelaide, 1956).

11   Unaipon, *My Life Story*, p. 2.

12   *ibid.*, p. 3. (Quoted in John Beston, *"David Unaipon: The First Aboriginal Writer, [1873-1967]"*, *Southerly*, no. 3, 1979, pp. 335-336.)

13   Australian Institute of Aboriginal Studies, *40,000 Years of Technology*, (Canberra, 1982), p. 11.

14   Rowe, *Sketches*, p. 8.

15   Beston, "David Unaipon", p. 345.

16   Unaipon, "An Aboriginal Pleads for His Race", in *Australian Aborigines, Photographs of Natives and Address*, (Adelaide, 1928[?]), p. 9. Again, the National Library's publication estimate of 1930 appears to be slightly late.

17   Beston, "David Unaipon", p. 345.

18   Beston, "David Unaipon", p. 337.

19   David Unaipon, "Legendary Tales of the Australian Aborigines", manuscript and typescript, (Sydney, 1924-1925). The Mitchell Library ms. nos A1929-A1930.

20   Beston, "David Unaipon", p. 345.

21   Unaipon, "Totemism", in *Native Legends*, p. 4.

22   *ibid*, p. 5.

23   Unaipon, "Aboriginal Folk Lore", in "Legendary Tales", p. XII. The emphasis is mine.

24   Unaipon, "Release of the Dragon Flies, by the Fairy, Sun Beam", in *Native Legends*, p. 1.

25   ibid., p. 3.

26   Beston, "David Unaipon", p. 345.

27   Unaipon, "Youn Goona the Cockatoo", in *Native Legends*, p. 8.

28   Unaipon, "Nhung e Umpie", in "Legendary Tales", Story 17, p. 4.

29   Unaipon, "The Song of Hungarrda", in *Native Legends*, p. 14.

30   Unaipon, "Hunting", in "Legendary Tales", Story 9, p. 17.

31   ibid., p. 1.

32   Unaipon, "Fishing", in "Legendary Tales", Story 5.

33   Unaipon, "How the Tortoise Got His Shell", in "Legendary Tales", Story 10. Also published in *Dawn*, vol. 3, no. 11, November, 1954, p. 9.

34   Unaipon, "Why Frogs Jump Into the Water", in "Legendary Tales", Story 25.

35   Beston, "David Unaipon", p. 342.

36   Unaipon, "Why All the Animals Peck at the Selfish Owl", in 'Legendary Tales", Story 24. Also published in *Dawn*, vol. 4, no. 4, 1955, pp. 16-17.

37   Unaipon, "How Teddy Lost His Tail", in "Legendary Tales", Story 30, p. 1.

38   Beston, "David Unaipon", p. 338.

39   Unaipon, "The Voice of the Great Spirit", in "Legendary Tales", Story 21. Also published in *Dawn*, vol. 8, no. 7, 1959, p. 19.

40   Daisy Bates, *The Passing of the Aborigines*, (London, 1938).

41   This information provided by Dr. Isobel White during a seminar at the Australian Institute of Aboriginal Studies, Canberra, November, 1982.

42   Ann Kohler and Janette Kohn, eds, *From Many Lands: Australians of the Past*, (Richmond, 1980), p. 65.

43   Ken Hampton, "The Aborigine in Australian Literature", Unpublished DAA paper, (Adelaide, 1976), pp. 7-8.

44   Kay Iseman, "Katharine Susannah Prichard, *Coonardoo* and the Aboriginal

Presence in Australian Fiction", Unpublished conference paper, (Sydney, 1980), p. 1.

45 ibid., p. 15.

46 Katharine Susannah Prichard, *Coonardoo*, (Sydney, 1982), p. 116.

47 Xavier Herbert, *Capricornia*, (Sydney, 1979), p. 314.

48 Xavier Herbert, *Capricornia*, p. 510.

49 In a personal letter from Josie Hilliger, Editorial Administrator, Angus and Robertson Publishers, dated 8 September, 1982, she states, "Ion Idriess ... toured country towns selling [his] books and at the same time gathering background material. These personal tours helped tremendously to make ... [Idriess] ... and the books better known".

50 Information provided in a telephone interview with Mr. R. Shankland, Royalties Department, Angus and Robertson Publishers, July, 1980.

51 "Empty Stomach Turned Bushman Into Great Author", The *Sydney Daily Mirror*, 22 August, 1979, p. 73.

52 Information quoted from the front cover of the 1979 paperback edition, published by Angus and Robertson.

53 Information provided by Mr. R. Shankland, July, 1980.

54 Healy, *Literature and the Aborigine in Australia*, pp. 132-135.

55 Information provided by Mr. R. Shankland, July, 1980.

56 C.R., Untitled tribute to Idriess, *Fragment*, (May, 1954), Unnumbered. Contained in the file of news clippings pertaining to Idriess held by the Mitchell Library, Sydney.

57 Julian Croft, Entry on Ion Llewellyn Idriess in *The Australian Dictionary of Biography*, vol. 9, 1891-1939, (Melbourne, 1983), p. 426.

58 Ion L. Idriess, *Lasseter's Last Ride*, (Sydney, 1959), pp. 24-25.

59 *ibid.*, p. 142.

60 Information provided by Mr. R. Shankland, July, 1980.

61 Idriess, *Nemarluk: King of the Wilds*, (Sydney, 1941), p. 138.

62 *ibid.*, p. 9.

63 Personal interview with Faith Bandler, Perth, February, 1983.

64 Brian Elliott, ed., *The Jindyworobaks*, (St. Lucia, 1979).

65 Kenneth Gifford, *Jindyworobak; Towards An Australian Culture*, (Melbourne, 1944), p. 1. Quoted in D.L.M. Jones, "The Treatment of the Aborigine in Australian Fiction", Unpublished M.A. Thesis (Adelaide, 1960), p. 164.

66 Jones, "The Treatment of the Aborigine", pp. 163-164.

67   Personal interview with Judith Wright, Canberra, July, 1982.

68   W.E.H. Stanner, "After the Dreaming", *White Man Got No Dreaming* , (Canberra, 1979), p. 211.

3

World War II and the Assimilation Era: A Self-Destructive Doctrine

The end of World War II marked a time of celebration and relief for most Australians. For Aboriginal Australians in many parts of the nation, the celebration was short-lived. While the post-war years ushered in an era of tremendous economic expansion and increased prosperity, the experience of many Aborigines belied the optimistic statistics. In the midst of the upward economic spiral, the Aboriginal people remained at the bottom end of the socio-economic scale, and their poverty only accentuated severe health problems, which particularly afflicted the young. Though it did not provide the impetus for prosperity for most Aborigines, the end of World War II did, however, provide the spark for increased Black Australian urbanisation, activism and self-determination.

It is significant that in almost all cases these trends ran counter to the enunciated aims of the Commonwealth and state governments' official Aboriginal policies of the 1945-1961 period. These policies, especially after 1951, became fervently directed towards the goal of assimilation, first introduced theoretically during the 1930s although not implemented until two decades later. This chapter examines the gulf between policy and practice during the 1945-1961 period. It emphasises the inherent contradictions of a era of attempted assimilation by highlighting Aboriginal activity which, to a great extent, traces its roots to the experiences of World War II.

In the year following the cessation of hostilities, the first concerted Aboriginal labour protest took place, in the Pilbara region of Western Australia. Cynics may argue that the Pilbara Strike of 1946 was fomented by a white man and was, moreover, a Communist plot. Apologists may laud it as the most important example of Aboriginal self-determination and protest action in post-war Australia. No doubt the truth lies somewhere between these two extremes, but it is indisputable that the strike provided, and still does provide, fertile ground for ideological assertions. For example, in 1972 Don Atkinson wrote in *Arena*:

> Pindan was for years *the* example of aboriginals taking survival into their own hands … The real history of these years and their outcome for the Nomads, has yet to be seen as part of the worldwide anti-colonial struggle, although Nkrumahas's Ghana petitioned the United Nations organisation on their behalf.[1]

Perhaps Atkinson exaggerates the international anti-colonial significance of the Pindan Movement, but he does not overstate the significance for Aboriginal people of the strike and its aftermath. As Allan Muriwulla Barker stated in interview with Kevin Gilbert:

> I am a revolutionary. Now to me a revolution is when I picked up a pick and shovel and starved in the strike of '46 … When you're completely revolutionary you're one, you're together, you [sic] one for all and all for one … I think we still have a chance, the blacks. We still have a chance to turn around, where gubbahs [whites] don't. We can still change, no matter how … Aboriginals *are* standing up. Look at that strike.[2]

And this strike, which was both symbolically and actually of great importance for the Aboriginal people, was in a number of ways a direct legacy and logical result of their experiences during World War II.

Even prior to the war, the Pilbara Aborigines had a venerable tradition of opposition to white incursions in their region.[3] Moreover, the Port Hedland area had for some years before 1946 been a focus for part-Aboriginal political activity, as the formation there in 1934 of the Euralian Association exemplified. World War II brought together the tradition of resistance and this political awareness because, especially with the evacuation of whites from the area, part-Aboriginal labour became even more essential to war operations and preparations. Yet, in an extremely ill-considered move, the Port Hedland district was in October, 1942 declared a prohibited area for Aborigines, with the exception of those who had been granted exemption passes. Clearly this measure was prompted by the pastoral lobby of the region, which sought to stem the flow of Aboriginal workers to more highly paid jobs in Port Hedland. This restriction on both wages and physical movement caused tremendous resentment among the Pilbara Aborigines. Added to their long-standing grievances over working conditions, these factors go a long way towards explaining their support for the strike of May,

1946, led by Don McLeod and his Aboriginal "lieutenants", Clancy McKenna and Dooley Bin-Bin.

The genesis of the strike and its aftermath have been described thoroughly by a number of commentators[4] so there is no need to re-examine the course of events. However, a number of general observations are pertinent: first, that the Pilbara Strike was strongly influenced by international factors aside from the war itself, such as the rise of Communism, the growth of the trade union movement, and overseas charitable organisations' increased interest in oppressed minorities. Specifically, Don McLeod was a member of the Communist Party at the time he initiated the idea of the strike. Commentators differ on this point: Broome views it as a sincere, if implicitly unfortunate, conversion ("McLeod had come under radical and communist influence in the 1940s"[5]) while Wilson describes it as opportunistic manipulation ("In order to gain support for the strike venture ... Mcleod took out a three-year membership with the Australian Communist Party"[6]). The fact was that, together with non-conformist church groups, the Communist Party represented an important element of support for the Pilbara Aborigines.

The trade union movement, too, played its part. The Port Hedland wharf workers of the International Workers' Union briefly banned wool from a number of "struck" stations in order to demonstrate their solidarity with the Pilbara strikers. When the three strike leaders were jailed, charitable interest in the case in Perth was so great that a Committee for the Defence of Native Rights was formed to lobby on their behalf, which included clergymen, academics, and many other prominent citizens, notably Katharine Susannah Prichard among them. This group was responsible for bringing the plight of the Pilbara strikers to the attention of the World Federation of Trade Unions and ultimately to the United Nations, which underlines yet again the international perspective of the events.

Yet despite White Australian collaboration and support, it must be emphasised that this was an Aboriginal strike. Those stockmen who left their jobs in early May, 1946 did so freely and because they believed in their cause; the fact that the momentum of the strike actually grew after the incarceration of its leaders supports this point. More important, although it was a Western economic weapon, the strike cannot be cast solely in Western economic terms. For even when in 1949 the pastoralists offered the strikers twice their original wage demand, many refused the enticement. Clearly, the Pilbara walk-out was for more than wages. It was eventually aimed at self-determination and autonomy; in Broome's words, "freedom from wage labour".[7] Despite the vicissitudes which the strikers endured and the troubles and divisions of the later Pindan movement, this Aboriginal ideal has persisted until the present day, and the Pilbara Aborigines did fight "the longest strike action in Australia's industrial history".[8]

Although those involved in the Pindan movement could not be termed traditional Aborigines, they did retain significant and distinctive elements of Aboriginal culture in spite of their involvement with the cash economy. It is ironic that, as the ideology of assimilation developed, so did a conviction amongst the administrators of Aboriginal "welfare" departments that Black Australians had to learn to appreciate the value and usage of money. Yet, when the Pilbara Aborigines demonstrated that they had an independent economic power base (and had "assimilated" an awareness of how to make the capitalist system work in their favour), numerous impediments were placed in their path. It is difficult to find a more lucid example of the internal contradictions of the assimilation doctrine. This policy was doomed to failure because it presumed that Aborigines had to absorb a white lifestyle totally in European terms. There was an inability to contemplate the capacity of Black Australians to assimilate some elements of White Australian society—and to resist others—*within* an Aboriginal framework, and this inability has in fact persisted in many areas until the present day.

The Pilbara strike was the first major example of an Aboriginal labour protest, but it was by no means the only case of what has come to be known as industrial action. For example, Middleton has detailed the strike of black workers at the Bagot Aboriginal Reserve in Darwin in 1950 and 1951, emphasising the support of the North Australian Workers' Union for their cause.[9] Further assertive action was demonstrated in the creation of Half-Caste Progressive Associations in Alice Springs and Darwin in 1949 and 1950. Hence, although the Northern Territory was not strictly comparable to the north-west of Western Australia, this was a time of change in Northern Australia generally, again stemming largely from Aboriginal wartime experiences.

This atmosphere of change in the Northern Territory had a number of constituent elements: the desire of pastoralists to maintain at an artificially low level the wages of their essential Aboriginal work force, the new emphasis upon Aboriginal health problems which emerged in the wake of the war, and the redoubled involvement of missionaries in the area, particularly as the 1950s progressed. There is no need to examine in detail the Northern Territory cattle industry as there is already a comprehensive study of the subject,[10] but the conclusion has to be drawn that coercion, exploitation and wage injustice persisted in the industry throughout the era of assimilation.

For the sixteen years between 1933 and 1949, the Aboriginal minimum wage in the Northern Territory pastoral industry was pegged at the lamentably low level of five shillings per week (along with some allowance for food, tobacco, and clothing).[11] In 1949, that minimum payment was raised to one pound per week—but only for male Aborigines with at least three years' experience. The labour of female Black Australians continued to be exploited as it had always been and female Aborigines languished at the bottom of the Territory's socio-economic ladder. Furthermore, equally damaging to all indigenous Territorians was the fact that the minimum payment covenant was not fully honoured. As Stevens points out, pastoralists "openly broke the agreement entered into on their behalf in 1949 concerning the provision of rudimentary accommodation for Aboriginal employees". It was to be another eight years before any further improvements in wages or working and living conditions were to be made in the industry. It is little wonder that in 1981 Stevens summarised, "Since the end of World War II the larger pastoral organisations have fought the introduction of even the smallest vestige of civilised conditions for their Aboriginal employees".[12]

The pastoral lobby in the Northern Territory was so powerful and influential a pressure group that it could virtually dictate to the government the Aboriginal wages it was prepared to pay. Given that during the 1950s an increasing amount of foreign capital—primarily British and American—was invested in the Territory cattle industry, it is arguable that a growing amount of international exploitation of Black Australian labour was taking place in the region as the decade progressed. In this sense, international connections did not always benefit Aboriginal Australians. For a people who had in some cases experienced the vastly improved living conditions and relative wage justice of the wartime period, this oppression must have been infuriating. But the question was, "What choice did they have?"

One alternative was to live on one of the many missions which were founded or revived in the Territory during the post-war era. This trend accelerated after 1953 when, for the first time, the federal government agreed to finance and provide staff for the missions' medical facilities and educational programmes.[13] This had numerous effects, one of which was the beginning of concerted attempts to combat the incidence of diseases such as leprosy, which was rife among the area's Aboriginal population.[14] The motive for this financial underwriting of mission services was hardly pure philanthropy: the various governments concerned with Aboriginal "welfare" had determined that the Black Australians were to be assimilated and missions were considered to be "indispensable agents in implementing this new policy". As early as February 1947, A.P. Elkin had informed a conference of mission officials that it was essential for their institutions to:

> have a positive economic and welfare policy. In addition to the spiritual ... [they] should set out to teach the native to meet the new era of civilisation, which must, of necessity, make its impact on him in the future.[15]

As Minister for Territories, Paul Hasluck convened a nationally representative Native Welfare Conference in 1951. This conference of Commonwealth and state officials and Aboriginal affairs administrators was inconclusive, for not all states were represented: Victoria argued that it had no need to attend as, in effect, its Aboriginal problems had been solved![16] Nevertheless, in the proceedings Hasluck did enunciate the clearest definition of the doctrine of assimilation up to that point in time: that, after generations of "cultural adjustment", "in practical terms ... it is expected that all persons of aboriginal blood or mixed blood in Australia will live like white Australians do".[17] Missions were to be an integral component of this endeavour, as the vehicles of assimilation. The Northern Territory Welfare Ordinance of 1953 was based on this very principle: if Aborigines were encouraged to develop occupational skills, to care for their own health and hygiene, and to live in settled communities such as missions, assimilation would be the logical ultimate result.

But what appears logical on paper in a Canberra office does not necessarily operate "logically" in Oenpelli or Maningrida. Even those welfare officials and missionaries with the best of intentions could easily interpret their mandate over-zealously and attempt to force Aborigines to become pseudo-Europeans as quickly as possible, rather than encourage them to adopt European ways gradually. This was another of the inherent flaws in the theory of assimilation: that it could so easily be perverted into a campaign of absorption, bordering upon cultural genocide, by those individuals just slightly too eager to make it a success. Despite the attractions which missions and settlements offered in terms of food, accommodation, and health care, many—if not most—Aborigines failed to assimilate. Ironically, the effort which was put into the process was often inversely proportional to the success derived from it.

At its best, the policy of assimilation was charitable, though tainted by a strong streak of paternalism. At its worst, it offered little more than an empty cultural shell to Black Australians. In Northern Territory missions and settlements, as in Australia as a whole, the application of this theoretical policy throughout the 1950s implied the actual policy of coercion at the personal level, in many cases hardly less oppressive than the "protection" policies of the 1930s. The question then arises, "If assimilation was fated to failure in northern Australia, was it any more successful in the south, in urban areas, or among people of part-Aboriginal ancestry?" Again, World War II surfaces as an influential factor.

The war radically altered the demographic pattern for both White and Black Australians in the Northern Territory. For example, tribal boundaries were effectively ignored by the military authorities in their relocation of Aborigines. In southern Australia, the war also wrought striking economic and demographic changes. In the north it was the presence of troops which was the determinant factor. In the south it was the absence of troops, translated into a vacuum in the urban work-force, which was the crucial element—and it produced quite a different type of Aboriginal/white relationship. The first observable demographic trend of Aborigines moving to major urban areas had its inception during the war years, as the demand for labour—especially in military-allied industries—became intense. Steady employment and reasonable cash wages would have been a new experience for many Aborigines but again, the bubble burst when Japan surrendered and the feverish industrial pitch died down.

Rowley has noted the presence of identifiable sub-groups of Aborigines in all major Australian coastal cities in the immediate post-war years.[18] The promise of permanent employment, though seldom fulfilled, motivated many Black Australians to try their luck in the big cities. Once there, the sense of Aboriginal solidarity, as well as economic necessity, caused many to congregate in particular suburbs or metropolitan areas: Redfern and Surry Hills in Sydney, South Guildford and East Perth in the Western Australian capital, and South Brisbane where, significantly, Black American troops had been housed during the war.[19] Rowley quotes Adelaide press reports of Aborigines allegedly guilty of drunken and disorderly behaviour in that city in 1946, and of black prostitutes soliciting in the centre of Perth in 1950.[20] Clearly, once the honeymoon of wartime collaboration was over, civic officials considered that the vices of Aborigines—especially their supposed weakness for (illegal) liquor—made them unwelcome in the cities.

Yet as Rowley perceptively illustrates, "the basis for the unrest seems to have been the discharge of numbers of Aborigines from the war-time industries, a practice which seems to have been common to all capital cities". He also notes Duguid's justified sympathy for urban Aborigines caught in the double predicament of unemployment and official attempts to expel them from urban areas.[21] However, despite the difficulty of securing work, once Black Australians had made the initial move to large city areas they were there to stay, as their increasing urbanisation throughout the 1950s attested. Perhaps no better index of the sincerity of the White Australian population's belief in the worth of assimilation—or lack thereof—was its frequent rejection of Aborigines in these urban areas.

This rejection was many-sided. It was sometimes overt, as in the case of preferential hiring procedures of the "Aborigines need not apply" variety, but it was more often covert and related to what numerous commentators have termed a caste barrier. Considerable research has been undertaken concerning the unofficial caste barrier in the state of New South Wales[22] and all these studies arrive—at least implicitly—at the same conclusion: such a barrier is the function of ignorance and racism and always necessitates the separation of Aboriginal and White Australians. Regardless of the official governmental policy of assimilation, the unofficial policy—that is, the reality of caste prejudice—worked to drive a wedge between the two races and militated against any more than token assimilation. In short, this period saw just as much distancing of Aboriginal and White Australians as the "protection" era of the 1930s.[23] The importance of this concept is such that it is worth examining in greater detail.

If it can be accepted that "the conditions affecting New South Wales affected the whole country" in the post-war period and that "Aborigines everywhere were in great economic difficulties",[24] then the circumstances encountered in two communities of Aboriginal fringe-dwellers in New South Wales in the mid-1950s can be considered fairly representative of those which applied throughout the settled areas of Australia at the height of the assimilation period. Two such areas, populated by part-Aborigines, were exhaustively researched by James H. Bell and Malcolm Calley in 1954-1955,[25] and their conclusions are fascinating.

Focussing upon the Nowra/Jervis Bay district of the south coast of the state, Bell found conditions which negated the aspirations of the assimilation policy. For example, the Aborigines of the region possessed a fundamental and distinctive conception of security which meant for them, above all, their kin-group affiliations—not the accumulation of earnings or material wealth, as in White Australian society. Second, racial prejudice began at the public school level ("some teachers on the South Coast believe that the Aboriginal children are congenitally handicapped"[26]) and extended into adulthood and into the marketplace ("White employers on the South Coast, whether they have ever employed Aborigines or not, are highly critical of them as workers"[27]). This made it next to impossible for Aborigines who aspired to steady employment (which might lead to some degree of assimilation) to realise this goal. In other words, Black and White Australians were isolated from each other by institutionalised prejudice and rejection which permitted the former only very marginal, seasonal employment. Third, Aborigines themselves would have perceived the assimilation policy as punitive for, in order to educate them in the "responsible" ways of white society, rations on Aboriginal reserves were to be lessened and legal action to recover unpaid rent was to be undertaken.[28] Fourth, the stations on which Aborigines were living on the South Coast were all located a "safe" distance from towns—a legacy of the protection era—so that life and employment proximate to whites was a geographical impossibility.[29] Finally, it was clear that theoretical assimilation did not imply any Black Australian self-determination, for even the Aboriginal returned serviceman in the district was deemed unable to manage his own war pension. This was administered by the local Aborigines Welfare Officer, in spite of the fact that the veteran had been competent to fight for his country![30]

The picture which Calley paints of Aboriginal station life in northern New South Wales is remarkably similar. For example, wage exploitation of Black Australians was ubiquitous:

> During 1954, rates of pay for Aboriginal workers in the ... area were about half of those demanded and received by white employees doing the same work ... Frequently Aboriginal employees were persuaded to take cheap wine (sweet sherry or muscat) in lieu of part of the wage due to them.

Almost identical racial stereotypes are invoked by the Europeans ("the mixed blood is not worth as much as a white employee ... he does not work as hard and is 'unpunctual' "[31]) and there is a similar Aboriginal attitude to paid labour ("work is undertaken to gain leisure ... leisure is regarded as the normal state, and work, something which regrettably interferes with it"[32]). It is obvious that as in the case of the South Coast part-Aboriginal communities, those in northern New South Wales and indeed, fringe-dwelling groups throughout Australia, adhered to a lifestyle which was in so many ways inimical to both the theoretical possibility, and the actual policy, of assimilation.

It is natural that the widespread poverty of these communities and the racial rejection of their inhabitants caused many health problems, numerous hardships and much unhappiness. What is perhaps more surprising is to find the pride, solidarity and defiance which survived alongside this despair and alienation. The Pilbara and Darwin strikes exemplified one form of committed defiance, but there were many other forms of rebellion and assertion, often of a personal nature. For example, a number of commentators have noted the prominence of Aboriginal boxers in the sporting world of the 1940s and 1950s.[33] The successes of fighters like Ron Richards and Dave Sands were an inspiration for hundreds of young Aborigines who entered the ring in the post-war era. Even Calley noted the distinctive ethic of the fringe-dwellers of northern New South Wales, many of whom considered themselves "first and foremost to be boxers".[34]

Significantly, success in this sport conferred prestige in White Australian society as well; it was one way of vaulting over the caste barrier. Champions in the ring were heroes to both White and Black Australians, as Corris has noted:

> The crowds roared for them—Bennett, Hassen and Sands—as they had roared for Ron Richards. Their exploitation went unnoticed in the days of their success for they were part of a new boom in Australian boxing which began during World War II and rolled on into the 1950s.[35]

There were numerous other Aboriginal achievers as well; for example, Pastor Douglas Nicholls, who also originally made a name for himself in sport but became even better known as a public speaker by the close of the war. The popularity of Albert Namatjira's painting was widespread and he was at the height of his fame in 1954, the year in which Bell commenced his study of the South Coast Aborigines. In 1951, Harold Blair made his international operatic debut in New York. In 1955, Robert Tudawali and Ngarla [Rosie] Kunoth starred in the first Australian colour feature film, *Jedda*, directed by Charles Chauvel.

But there is another unfortunate side to these achievements. The fact that they took place in the era of assimilation is extremely significant for, in almost all cases, these Aborigines were held up as models for their race. They were models, not solely because of their talents and skills, but because they had succeeded according to the standards of the White Australian world. They were, allegedly, assimilation personified. But this tokenism had disastrous consequences, which illustrate the inherent flaws of the doctrine yet again. In an attempt to shower fame and recognition upon these Aborigines and to set them upon an assimilationist pedestal, White Australians also—if unwittingly—endeavoured to cut them from their Aboriginal roots. In short, White Australia tried to deny their Aboriginality, except as a somewhat romantic creative impulse. The sorry consequences of this pressure on those such as Namatjira and Tudawali have been documented elsewhere,[36] but the point remains that assimilation was a potentially and actively destructive doctrine and, above all, this explains why it was doomed to fail.[37] But only in the 1960s did Australians begin to realise the magnitude of that failure and the folly of the original attempt.

That most perceptive of commentators, W.E.H. Stanner, has put it this way:

> To rely on "education" to bridge the gap between the old way of life and a new way independent of it, was our policy from 1954 onward. The Aboriginal future was to be one of "development through individualism". The new Aboriginal was to be made into an "independent unit" in a life-system like ours. It did not matter if Aboriginal society and culture fell to pieces. We could fit them together again in a better way. Yes, there would be inevitable human costs but we would have to brace ourselves to be equal to the burdens carried on Aboriginal shoulders.[38]

But, as he continues, this was a gross delusion:

> Since the 1950s we have known that it is a false assumption, but we have often persisted with substantially the same outlook and new methods. There was already pretty plain evidence in the 1950s that what we were requiring the Aborigines to do was radically maladaptive for them. What clearer meaning could sickness, drunkenness, alcoholism, criminality, prostitution and psychic disorders have?[39]

It is unfortunate that contemporary governmental policies are rarely as perceptive as those which could have been devised with the benefit of hindsight. The signs were there in the Australia of the 1950s that the policy of assimilation was fated to failure, but it was only in the decade after 1961 that a more enlightened alternative was promoted. Significantly, in that later era the voices of Aboriginal representatives became far more audible. New, nationally-based Black Australian organisations emerged, to state their own cases forcefully and effectively—a process which largely traces its roots to the formation of the Federal Council for the Advancement of Aborigines in 1958.

I have emphasised that the tenor of the 1945-1961 period was to a great extent determined by international forces and that one of these, World War II, had repercussions which dictated the nature of the most important developments in Australian Aboriginal affairs over that sixteen-year span. To cite yet another example of foreign influence, while a back-bencher in the House of Representatives Paul Hasluck rose to claim that in the international sphere, Australia's position *vis-à-vis* human rights was:

> mocked by the thousands of degraded and depressed [Aboriginal] people who crouch on rubbish heaps throughout the whole of this continent.[40]

But the key point was that the solution to the inequalities suffered by Aborigines had to come domestically. During the years of the assimilation doctrine, few Australians perceived the importance of Aborigines *as Aborigines* to Australian society as a whole, or saw them in either symbolic or real terms as an integral part of the nation. Some of these perceptive observers were authors, whose works will be discussed in the following chapter. They indicated that the forces impinging upon Aborigines had to have an Australian solution. In this connection, Stanner once again deserves the final word:

> My impression is that we are watching within Australia something with a family-likeness to the movement which became overt in scores of colonies after 1945. In their case it led finally to the liberation of hundreds of millions of non-European people from imperial colonial rule. The tension found its relief, so to speak, outwards. There can be no such solution for Europeans or Aborigines in Australia. The tension must find its relief inwards.[41]

Notes

1   Don Atkinson, "Aboriginal Project", *Arena*, no. 30, 1972, pp. 3-4.

2   Kevin Gilbert, *Living Black: Blacks Talk to Kevin Gilbert*, (Melbourne, 1977), p. 163.

3   Peter Biskup, *Not Slaves, Not Citizens: The Aboriginal Problem in Western Australia 1898-1954*, (St. Lucia, 1973), p. 210.

4   John Wilson's unpublished M.A. Thesis, "Authority and Leadership in a 'New-Style' Aboriginal Community: Pindan, Western Australia", (Perth, 1961) is the most comprehensive treatment. His article "The Pilbara Aboriginal Social Movement: An Outline of its Background and Significance", in R.M. and C.H. Berndt, eds, *Aborigines of the West; Their Past and Present*, (Perth, 1979), pp. 151-168, is more than adequate for most purposes. See also Biskup, *Not Slaves*, especially pp. 219-222 and pp. 235-240, and K. Wilson, "Pindan: A Preliminary Comment", in A.R. Pilling and R.A. Waterman, eds, *Diprotodon to Detribalization*, (East Lansing, 1970). The best source for Aboriginal views of the events is the biography of one of the participants, Clancy McKenna: Kingsley Palmer and Clancy McKenna, *Somewhere Between Black and White*, (Melbourne, 1978).

5   Broome, *Aboriginal Australians*, p. 138.

6   Wilson, "The Pilbara Aboriginal Social Movement", p. 167 (Footnote 8).

7   Broome, *Aboriginal Australians*, p. 139.

8   Hannah Middleton, *But Now We Want the Land Back*, (Sydney, 1977), p. 97.

9   *ibid.*, pp. 99-100.

10 F.S. Stevens, *Aborigines in the Northern Territory Cattle Industry*, (Canberra, 1974).

11 W.E.H. Stanner, "Industrial Justice in the Never-Never", in *White Man Got No Dreaming*, (Canberra, 1979), p. 252.

12 F.S. Stevens, *Black Australia*, (Sydney, 1981), p. 90.

13 Broome, *Aboriginal Australians*, p. 115.

14 Keith Cole, *The Aborigines of Arnhem Land*, (Adelaide, 1979), p. 230.

15 *ibid.*, p. 92.

16 C.D. Rowley, *Outcasts in White Australia*, (Canberra, 1971), p. 89.

17 Quoted in Broome, *Aboriginal Australians*, p. 171.

18 Rowley, *Outcasts*, pp. 362-379.

19   *ibid.*, p. 371.

20   *ibid.*, pp. 373, 377.

21   *ibid.*, p. 373.

22   This situation is described in much of Rowley's work, especially *Outcasts* and *The Remote Aborigines*, (Canberra, 1971). See also Broome, *Aboriginal Australians*, particularly chapters eight and nine (pp. 143-183). A number of anthropological studies published in *Oceania* are also relevant; for example, Mary Reay, "A Half-caste Aboriginal Community in North-Western New South Wales", *Oceania*, vol. 15, no. 4, June, 1945.

23   For a specific illustration of this point in the context of rural New South Wales, see Peter Read, "A Double Headed Coin: Protection and Assimilation in Yass 1900-1960", in Gammage and Markus, eds, *All That Dirt; Aborigines 1938*, (Canberra, 1982).

24   Rowley, *Outcasts*, p. 85.

25   James H. Bell, "The Economic Life of Mixed-Blood Aborigines on the South Coast of New South Wales", *Oceania*, vol. 26, no. 3, March, 1956, pp. 181-199; Malcolm Calley, "Economic Life of Mixed-Blood Communities in Northern New South Wales", *Oceania*, vol. 26, no. 3, March, 1956, pp. 200-213.

26   Bell, "The South Coast", p. 191.

27   ibid., p. 196.

28   ibid., p. 196.

29   ibid., p. 194.

30   ibid., p. 198.

31   Calley, "Northern New South Wales", p. 201.

32   ibid., p. 207.

33   See, for example, Peter Corris, *Lords of the Ring*, (Sydney, 1980), and Richard Broome, "Professional Aboriginal Boxers in Eastern Australia 1930-1979", *Aboriginal History*, vol. 4, 1980, pp. 48-71.

34   Calley, "Northern New South Wales", p. 209.

35   Corris, *Lords of the Ring*, p. 144.

36   See, for example, Joyce D. Batty, *Namatjira: Wanderer Between Two Worlds*, (Melbourne, 1963).

37   It must be emphasised that it was not only prominent Black Australians who suffered under the assimilation policy. As Peter Read has lucidly illustrated, Aboriginal children often bore the brunt of this dictatorial doctrine, enduring forced removal from their families, institutionalisation, and menial labour in white households: "Missionaries, teachers, government officials, have believed that the best way to make black people behave like white was to get hold of the children who had not yet learned Aboriginal lifeways. They thought that

children's minds were like a kind of blackboard on which the European secrets could be written"(*The Stolen Generations*, [Sydney, 1982], p. 2.). Read expands upon this theme in his Ph.D. thesis, "A History of the Wiradjuri People of New South Wales, 1883-1969", (Canberra, 1983), especially in Chapter Eight, pp. 315-355.

38   W.E.H. Stanner, "Aborigines and Australian Society", in *White Man Got No Dreaming*, p. 352.

39   Stanner, "After the Dreaming—Whither?", in *ibid.*, p. 335.

40   Quoted in Sharman Stone, ed., *Aborigines in White Australia*, (Melbourne, 1974), p. 192.

41   Stanner, "After the Dreaming—Whither?", in *White Man Got No Dreaming*, p. 333.

4

The Literary Perception, 1945-1961

In the years following 1945, whether they despised Aborigines or felt genuine compassion for them, most Australians continued to believe that Black Australians were basically incapable of looking after themselves. Despite evidence to the contrary provided by incidents such as the Pilbara strike, the attitude that Aborigines were a people who for their own good had to be coerced into "correct" modes of behaviour was manifested in almost all governmental Aboriginal policy until the early 1960s. Even those Aborigines who had accepted the ideal of assimilation were denied the rights held by all Australian citizens—including access to liquor, the franchise, and enumeration in the census—and faced social and legal obstacles to that citizenship.

The concept of Aborigines needing things done for them is a significant one. When they were viewed as objects of derision this naturally led to prejudice, discrimination, and the invoking of pejorative stereotypes. When they were viewed as objects of praise this could easily develop into idealisation, most frequently of traditional Aboriginal ceremonies and beliefs. Both responses were damaging because they necessitated an ideological distancing of White and Black Australians. Neither provided the means by which men and women could see the other race solely as human beings, to whom skin colour was of secondary importance. This ideological gap was just as difficult for members of either race to bridge as the physical, political and socio-economic gulf between Europeans and Aboriginal Australians. This concept was, of course, in direct conflict with the avowed aims of the assimilation policy and buttressed a host of more overt and institutionalised racial barriers. It was true that Aborigines were no longer effectively invisible in Australian society, but they were often treated as if their existence—certainly their autonomous existence—was meaningless.

Similar perceptions of Aboriginal people can be identified in the poetry and prose of the 1945-1961 period. As in the preceding fifteen year span, popular literature—which still often characterised Aborigines according to damaging and degrading stereotypes—continued to be absorbed by the reading public. On the other hand, anthropologists such as Berndt and Strehlow promoted the notion that Black Australians in their traditional culture were worthy of praise. These anthropologists' translations of traditional songs and poetry may have enhanced the reputation of tribal Aborigines, but this process concurrently denigrated the popular perception of the culture of the growing numbers of fringe-dwelling and urban Aborigines.[1] Through their emphasis upon traditional Aboriginal culture as the only authentic Black Australian voice, both the popular and the scientific literature of the period harmonised in a disturbing way with the prevailing governmental policies aimed at assimilation, for all non-traditional blacks were considered to be ripe material for cultural absorption.

Fortunately, other writers during the period saw far more intrinsic value in *all* Aboriginal culture. The poet Judith Wright set the literary stage for a period in which major writers concerned themselves with Aborigines as members of a wronged race, as symbols of indigenous and environmental values, and as subjects—not objects—worthy of sensitive compassion. Yet even in the culmination of the literature of that period, represented by the seminal works of Patrick White (*Voss* and *Riders in the Chariot*), the Aborigine continued to be one step removed from humanness and humanity. In *Riders in the Chariot* the Black Australian remains a symbol of an Aboriginal pariah, and does not have significance solely as a human being. Despite the fact that these writers progressed much further than their predecessors towards a picture of the unrepresentative Aborigine and appreciated far more completely the environmental identification of Black Australians as well as their deeply spiritual nature, they still used Aborigines to exemplify their own aesthetic and philosophical convictions. In other words, while they could outline the need for just compensation for past wrongs, they were still distanced from Black Australians as living and breathing women and men.[2]

There are exceptions to this: the author of *Yandy*, Donald Stuart, probably comes the closest of any White Australian writer during this period to a sensitive depiction of the Aboriginal people as Aboriginal human beings. It is important to note that during the 1945-1961 period certain White Australian authors foreshadowed an increased sensitivity amongst the larger Australian population to the symbolic and environmental value of Aboriginal culture, a sensitivity which was non-assimilationist in perspective.

In this chapter, four literary views of Aboriginal Australians will be isolated and discussed: the poetic and symbolic approach; that of the anthropologist as translator; the perpetuation of popular stereotypes; and the sensitive, naturalistic stance. While the four sometimes intermingle, each view can be linked very directly with the work of one or more influential White Australian writers who published during the 1945-1961 period.

The decades of physical and psychological violence suffered by Australian Aborigines had to take their toll, but this was not exacted only from the victims. It was impossible for a sensitive conscience to remain untouched by the exploitation, murder, and dispossession of Aboriginal people—especially if one's own ancestors had been directly involved in the process. In some parts of Australian society there was, beneath the surface, an element of guilt which was routinely sublimated by charity, and more often by distancing and ignorance. It is not surprising that, following the stresses of World War II, this latent guilt would find its way to the surface through the workings of a hyper-sensitive mind. In this case, it was the mind of a poet keenly attuned to suffering and injustice; the mind of Judith Wright.

Wright's work ushered in a phase of guilt investigation and symbolic expiation which has persisted in White Australian literature until the present day. In the period between 1945 and 1961 she was one of the most perceptive of Australian writers to come to terms with the fact of an Aboriginal Australia which had been both physically and psychologically invaded. Wright transformed her understanding into a treatment of the theme of that violation expressed in environmental and humanistic terms.

Wright's first volume of poetry, *The Moving Image*, was published in 1946. Just as the experience of the war years strongly affected the world-view of many Aborigines, the horrors of that period had a strong impact upon Wright's sensibilities. Those sensibilities were given voice in her verse, for it was during those years that she "began writing some poetry, largely because the country seemed to be very beautiful and very threatened".[3] Wright's poetry has justifiably received considerable critical attention and acclaim and I do not intend to summarise the significance of the entire corpus of her work here.[4] With regard to her poetic perception of Aboriginal Australians,

The Moving Image still remains one of her most impressive achievements.

Three of the poems published in that volume, "Bora Ring", "Nigger's Leap, New England" and "Half-Caste Girl", attempt and achieve a striking reappraisal of Aboriginal culture. When compared with virtually any preceding Australian poem, their distinctiveness becomes obvious. All three exhibit a profound sense of history as the agent of malevolent time, a marked sense of place, and a singular appreciation of the symbolic and environmental importance of Aboriginal culture. Above all, a keen awareness of historical guilt "not only racial, but explicitly familial"[5] surfaces in these poems. For example, in "Bora Ring":

> The song is gone; the dance
> is secret with the dancers in the earth,
> the ritual useless, and the tribal story
> lost in an alien tale ...
>
> Only the rider's heart
> halts at a sightless shadow, an unsaid word
> that fastens in the blood the ancient curse,
> the fear as old as Cain.[6]

The fear and guilt is both collective—pertaining to all of White Australia's history—and individual, referring to the participation of Wright's own ancestors in massacres of the past. The specific inheres in the universal most impressively in her "Nigger's Leap: New England" with its disconcertingly direct and alliterative imagery:

> Be dark, O lonely air.
> Make a cold quilt across the bone and skull
> that screamed falling in flesh from the lipped cliff
> and then were silent, waiting for the flies.

Then Wright vaults the memory of this particular massacre into a larger sphere:

> Did we not know their blood channelled our rivers,
> and the black dust our crops ate was their dust?
> O all men are one man at last.[7]

Thus, her observation on the violence and precariousness of the Aboriginal post-conquest past expands outwards to embrace all humanity. In Brennan's words, this "reminds us that the cry of the falling aboriginal is not only the cry of his passing culture, but of ours too. His death, and the death of his people are an ominous reminder of our own ephemerality".[8]

This raises a critical question: "Did Judith Wright in 1946 use the Aborigine purely as a poetic symbol of historical injustice and of repressed Australian fear and guilt, rather than to signify a specific and continuing social problem?" Was her engagement with the theme more philosophical and artistic than socially conscious, and are the two incompatible? Regarding her poem "Half-Caste Girl", Wright stated in 1982 that "The little girl in the poem is based upon a person still alive ... But a poem is very seldom real—the literal becomes transformed". Further, she has admitted very little direct contact with Aborigines during her youth, and certainly not during the time the poems in *The Moving Image* were composed:

> There were very few Aborigines around us at the time, though some passed through and some worked for us. The Bora ring of the poem was on my uncle's place ... But, we were *not allowed* to know Aborigines in ... terms of friendship ... The first Aboriginal friend I had was Kath Walker.

There were on a large pastoral property such as Wright's well-established conventions and institutions which separated black from white. Yet, this did not prevent the seepage of guilt into the atmosphere:

> To say that we had been the murderers was not a popular view at the time! Nobody mentioned Aborigines at all in my youth. I didn't even know there *was* a dying pillow ... Quite certainly there was guilt. That's why there was so little said.[9]

In view of these admissions, it would be misleading to ascribe to Wright's poetry an explicitly sociological dimension. Her verse is far too complex to be termed overtly propagandist, and she herself rejects such a description. Rather, the Black Australian characters she creates in her poetry can be more appropriately interpreted as symbols of the Aboriginal people's unity with the environment as well as of the invasion which they had been forced to endure. It is significant that for Wright, Europeans have never atoned for that invasion and atonement is essential if there is to be harmony between black and white in Australia. In symbolic terms, it is as if the souls of the murdered blacks are in limbo, or the perpetual rootlessness and torment of Purgatory awaiting, in Healy's words, the "new recognition, and fresh syntheses"[10] that can liberate them. For example, Josie in "Half-Caste Girl".

is restless still under her rootwarm cover,
hearing the noise of living,
forgetting the pain of dying.[11]

But how are these "fresh syntheses" to be achieved? Wright outlines the problem most succinctly in the final stanza of her poem, "At Cooloola", published in the 1955 collection, *The Two Fires*. It is one of coming to terms with the past and with the guilt spawned by that past:

And walking on clean sand among the prints
of bird and animal, I am challenged by a driftwood spear
thrust from the water; and, like my grandfather,
must quiet a heart accused by its own fear.[12]

This dilemma of ingrained historical guilt is repeatedly addressed in Wright's poetry, but she actually argues the potential solution most cogently in her prose. For, in *The Generations of Men* (1959) she writes:

To forgive oneself—that was the hardest task. Until the white men could recognise and forgive that deep and festering consciousness of guilt in themselves, they would not forgive the blacks for setting it there. The murder would go on—open or concealed—until the blacks were all gone, the whites forever crippled.

Is this the solution or sophistry? For immediately preceding this passage, Wright emphasises in clear terms the fundamental disjunction between White and Black Australians, a gulf which is described as being nearly impossible to bridge:

Why should the blacks, with that soft obstinacy that was almost gaiety, thus invite their own murder? They refused the conditions his people had imposed; they preferred their own stubbornness. It was unfair, unfair, that such a choice should be given, such an invitation made. "Kill us, for we can never accept you" the blacks said; "kill us, or forget your own ambitions".[13]

There are two plausible alternatives open to the critic attempting to clarify this ambivalent view of the Aboriginal people. The first is to concur with Shirley Walker that "Despite the strength of the presentation of evil and guilt in these poems ... the possibility of reconciliation through love is present. Indeed, each of the poems ... is an act of atonement in itself".[14] According to this interpretation, lines such as the following, taken from "The Dust in the Township" section of "The Blind Man", in themselves and through their tender evocation of Aboriginal oneness with the land serve to erase at least some of the sense of historical guilt under which Wright laboured:

Under the Moreton Bay fig by the war memorial

blind Jimmy Delaney sits alone and sings
in the pollen-coloured dust, is of that dust
three generations made.[15]

I find this interpretation less than totally convincing, largely because of the primarily symbolic rather than individualised use of Aboriginal character and place which Wright adopts in her poetry. It is true that in her verse she introduced a new sensibility to an examination of the Aboriginal theme, but that theme was itself adopted because it facilitated an examination of larger aesthetic, moral, and philosophical issues. Her verse has had such an impact because of the considerable power of her poetic and creative imagination; not exclusively because of its expiatory qualities.

The second explanation for the ambivalence which one senses in *The Generations of Men* is twofold and, I feel, more persuasive. It is that Wright's own views concerning Black Australians have not remained constant and, as she has become more actively committed to the cause, her writing has reflected this increased engagement. For example, in 1982 Wright delivered a speech at the Adelaide Festival Writers' Week in which she asserted that the dispossession of the Aborigines and their "tragic situation"

have been my own chief social concerns, but I don't think they have done my work as a poet any harm whatever. Indeed, both have provided a spur to writing, and deepened my own knowledge and perceptions in many ways.[16]

The point is not that Wright has been inconsistent. The point is that in the 1945-1961 period her engagement with the Aboriginal people was almost entirely limited to detached—if extremely empathic and sensitive—poetic observation, in which Black Australian themes were the springboard for profound moral questioning. In the post-1961 era, her writing—particularly her prose—becomes far more committed to a conception of Aborigines as Aboriginal human beings, rather than as metaphysical symbols. During the period under consideration here, her work exemplifies the symbolic treatment of Aborigines in Australian literature extremely well.

However, it should be emphasised that personal contact with Black Australians was no guarantee of authorial integrity in the post-World War II period. It is intriguing and ironic that during the entire assimilation era, when Aborigines were in theory being gradually absorbed into the mainstream of Australian society, not a single Aboriginal writer's work was published. One can only speculate upon the reasons for the hiatus in the production of Aboriginal literature between Unaipon's work in the 1920s and 1930s and Oodgeroo Noonuccal's in the 1960s. There seems to be little doubt that there would have been a market for such literature if it conformed to expectations; in short, if it looked like material derived from traditional sources. For the late 1940s and early 1950s were years in which what may be termed "traditional Aboriginal literature not written by Aborigines" came into vogue. This was largely due to the stalwart efforts of anthropologists such as T.G.H. Strehlow and Ronald M. and Catherine H. Berndt, who sought out traditional Aboriginal myths during their field work with such groups as the Aranda and the people of Arnhem Land. These poetic renderings of the source material were invariably published and were frequently highly acclaimed. For example, R.M. Berndt's translation of "The Wonguri-Mandijigai Song Cycle of the Moon-Bone" (which was first published in the anthropological journal *Oceania* in 1948[17]) has been reprinted in magazines, journals and books on numerous occasions, and most recently was given pride of place as the opening poem in Rodney Hall's *The Collins Book Of Australian Poetry*. In 1977, the respected poet and critic Les A. Murray commented that "It stunned me when I first read it, and it may well be the greatest poem composed in Australia".[18]

Setting aside a consideration of Murray's evaluation, my point here is that the publication of "traditional Aboriginal literature" occasioned considerable interest in the late 1940s and has continued to do so until the present day. A representative example of the genre was Strehlow's *Aranda Traditions*, which first appeared in print in 1947. The book contains more conventional anthropological analysis as well as a forty-page section devoted to "Northern Aranda Myths", which comprises traditional stories ranging from a description of the bandicoot ancestor (*gurra*) to raw meat-eating habits. It also contains a number of chants which Strehlow translates in what can only be described as poetic fashion, as in the Ulamba Chant:

> Enfolded by plains lies Ljaba;
> Beyond the far horizon lies Ljaba.
>
> Enfolded by plains lies Ljaba,
> Dimmed by the enveloping mists ...
>
> High in the heavens shines the afternoon sun:
> His heart is filled with yearning to turn home.

My own home, my own dear home—
O Ulamba, rugged, chasm-cleft.

The birds are speaking with many voices
At Ulamba, chasm-cleft Ulamba.

My own dear home,—
Whose feet have disfigured it?

The mulga parrots have disfigured it;
Their feet have scratched the deserted hollow.[19]

Without questioning either the sincerity or the integrity of Strehlow's translations, it must be conceded that they represented a daunting task. Strehlow himself has admitted that "the difficulties of translation from Aranda to English are considerable" and that "he [the translator] has to use inversion and certain poetical turns in an attempt to capture some of the dramatic effect of the original".[20] The mediating effect of the translator upon the text is obviously important and in such cases the English version becomes very much the anthropologist's interpretation of the intent of the original, filtered through his preconceptions concerning the nature of poetry in English.[21]

This mediating role is made even more explicit in the case of the "Song Cycle of the Moon-Bone". Berndt confesses in the notes accompanying the text that "the general translation is a poetic rendering of the song and … as in most translations, the euphony of the verse, the play of words, and the native subtlety of expression, have to some extent been lost". Rodney Hall's accompanying notes are even more revealing:

> The translator, a distinguished anthropologist, has tackled the problem, *boldly preferring a firmly European metre*, sufficiently derived from the King James version of *The Book of Numbers* to convey a sense of ritual and sacredness adequate for the tone of this magnificent song. [22]

Is it quibbling to suggest that, in view of the above, Berndt's role in the production of the English version of the text was more than that of a translator: that he was, in effect, also an editor and nearly a co-author? It can be argued that this suggestion is irrelevant, for the song cycle *is* beautifully lyrical and poetic in translation:

> Blown backwards and forwards as they lie, there
> at the place of the Dugong.
> Always there, with their hanging grapes, in
> the clay pan of the Moonlight …

> Vine plants and roots and jointed limbs, with
> berry food, spreading
> over the water.[23]

While the Moon-Bone song has been significantly altered by Berndt, the greatness which does shine through resides primarily in the original oral version.

But even if one ignores the anthropologist's very significant role in the production of this poetry, there is another sense in which the translation of this song cycle—in fact, all anthropological "poeticising" of traditional material—was and is significant, for two main reasons. First, the conviction that tribal Aborigines of Northern Australia had a venerable culture worth preserving motivated these experts to protect whatever elements of that culture they could secure for "posterity" or for "the good of the tribe". However, the formalisation of tradition can lead to a denigration of the present. All that is worthwhile belongs to the traditional realm rather than to the ongoing, adaptive life of the people. Second, a corollary of the elevation of the status of northern Australian Aborigines (even in retrospect) could have been a lowering of the perceived status of non-traditional Black Australians in the remainder of the country. It was a small step from this conviction to the belief that the latter group had entirely lost their culture—that they in fact had *no* culture—a viewpoint which was to have negative ramifications for many years. Therefore, the translations of anthropologists were, both in literary and in social terms, important factors which influenced the perceptions and opinions of those Australians either associated with, or interested in, the Aboriginal people.

In the late 1940s and early 1950s relatively few Australian novelists demonstrated either this interest or this association in their works. Of those who did (almost exclusively Western Australian writers) none fully resolved what Stow has described as "a rather uneasy teetering between the demands of sociology on the one hand and art on the other".[24] Two novels, both published in 1955, illustrate this inherent tension: Mary Durack's *Keep Him My Country* and Frederick B. Vickers's *The Mirage*. Contrary to Stow's appraisal that in the former the sociological/artistic conflict is satisfactorily resolved, Durack's book, though obviously sympathetic and well-informed, suffers from melodramatic and romantic excesses similar to those which over twenty-five years earlier had flawed Katharine Susannah Prichard's *Coonardoo*. For example, there is the same quasi-magical association of the Aboriginal woman (as lover) with the land (as possessor):

A man can break with the black women right enough, but to leave the country after—that's not so easily done. It's like something gets into the blood. Some of 'em
reckon it's sorcery.[25]

The attempt to symbolise the Aboriginal woman as the mystically
enthralling and fecund life source wears a bit thin in artistic terms.
Vickers errs in just as well-intentioned a fashion in a novel which reveals more about White Australian perceptions of Aboriginal people
than about Black Australian attitudes. Vickers's failing springs, above
all, from a lack of empathy with Black Australians and one can only
agree with Healy that as a novelist he was "stronger on social conscience than on the Aborigine".[26] In effect, no truly new novelistic
ground was broken by White Australians dealing with the Aboriginal
theme between the publication of *Capricornia* in 1938 and the appearance of *Voss* in 1957.

In any discussion of contemporary Australian literature, the work
of Patrick White cannot be ignored. The novel *Voss* is a marvellous
and resonant achievement. White's exploration of the landscape of
memory and the terrain of the mind parallels Voss's own exploration
of one of the harshest physical landscapes on earth—in which the
Aborigines move with ease and efficiency. *Voss* is hardly an
anthropological novel, although it does detail the actions of tribal
blacks in their extremely demanding local environment. The
Aboriginal servants Dugald and Jackie and the entire mass of face-
less, undifferentiated blacks are significant, not so much because of
the specific traditional customs of the people, but because of their
profound spiritual—and actual—affinity with the land and its crea-
tures. Voss's attempt to dominate the Black Australians with whom
he comes in contact is as impossible as his endeavour to tame the
harshness of the desert itself.

This is not a new observation, nor was White's spiritual and almost sacramental use of the Black Australian theme a radical departure from the poetic approach of, for example, Judith Wright. What
was particularly impressive was White's employment of the
Aboriginal people as a form of tragic chorus which lamented the folly
and presumption of Voss (and European exploration and civilisation
writ large) and the magnificence of his poetic sensibility in so doing.
The theme of religious self-sacrifice runs through much of the novel;
as Boyle of Jildra puts it:

Why, anyone who is disposed can celebrate a high old Mass, I promise, with the
skull of a blackfeller and his own blood, in Central Australia.[27]

This is what Voss does willingly and purposefully, because the novel is based upon the belief that "to make yourself, it is also necessary to destroy yourself".[28] Healy has shown convincingly that White's Aborigines are unified in the novel with the rocks, trees, and sand which are their habitat, as in the following passage:

> During the morning a party of blacks appeared, first as shreds of shy bark glimpsed between the trunks of trees, but always drifting, until, finally, they halted in human form upon the outskirts of the camp.[29]

To draw a further point from this observation: even though the white explorers become themselves blackened by the sun, withered by the heat and increasingly moulded by their surroundings, there always remains an essential gulf between the races. As the expedition progresses, the blacks come to accept the presence of the whites in their terrain and no longer fear them, for they both now share the same environment:

> Such meetings had come to be accepted by all. The blacks squatted on their haunches, and stared up at the men that were passing, of whom they had heard, or whom they had even seen before. Once, the women would have run screaming. Now they scratched their long breasts, and squinted from under their bat's-skin hands. Unafraid of bark or mud, they examined these caked and matted men, whose smell issued less from their glands than from the dust they were wearing, and whose eyes were dried pools.[30]

The shared environment does *not* produce a spiritual rapport. In the critical episode in which Voss attempts to placate Jackie and his adopted tribe with the words, "Tell your people we are necessary to one another. Blackfellow white man friend together", the attempt at conciliation is doomed. Clearly, the Aborigines did not consider the whites to be necessary to them. The lesson learned from contact between the races was a very different one, and Jackie's "Blackfeller dead by white man"[31] is a simple but eloquent rebuttal. The fundamental dichotomy between black and white is beautifully, consistently, and strikingly evoked by the author in this novel.

A similar gulf in Aboriginal/white spirituality is illustrated by Randolph Stow in *To the Islands*, but the logic of the novel's plot is ultimately lacking. Stow's is a fascinating and often moving book which can be compared with *Voss* in certain respects. Both novels deal with egotistical men who wish to dominate the Aborigine as overlords; both men therefore suffer delusions of grandeur by believing that they can communicate with the blacks on the same plane; and both journey through harsh, unforgiving country in a Lear-like endeavour to divest themselves of all the accretions of western civilisation. But Heriot cannot be equated fully with Voss, nor can Justin be paralleled with Jackie. For Stephen Heriot, a mission administrator of the old "stock-whip" school, persuades himself that he can *become* Aboriginal if he undergoes enough self-denial on his journey to the islands. He has a profound desire to be accepted by the blacks as an equal. Hence, he speaks the native language to Justin and asserts, "No more white man. I'm a blackfellow, son of the sun",[32] and a short while later he implores the tribal man Alunggu to treat him as such: "I am one of you", he said. "*Ngaia bendjin*".[33] Heriot's self-effacement is touching, but his belief that he is Aboriginal is pure self-deception, if not also pathetic. As a man lives, so will he be judged, and Heriot must logically purge many past sins before he will be accepted on equal terms by the Aborigines. Even then he will never actually *be* a Black Australian, even in world-view. This is grandiose self-delusion of the order of Voss's pseudo-royal treatment of his black "subjects".

Hence, the forgiveness and spiritual reconciliation between Rex and Heriot is illogical and over-sentimentalised. Heriot's inflated sense of his own importance is never fully purged during the time he craves absolution; in fact, his monomania concerning forgiveness acts to reinforce his self-centredness. Stow's desire to act as an apologist for the mission system thus produces a lack of internal consistency in his novel—despite its imagistic strengths—especially as it draws to a close. Dorothy Jones is therefore justified when she observes:

> *To The Islands* is a beautiful and moving novel, but its aboriginal characters are abstractions rather than real people. This can be justified when the novelist makes a symbol of the natives as does Patrick White in *Voss*. I feel it is scarcely permissible, however, for a writer who makes race relationships a major theme.[34]

Despite Stow's symbolic and poetic approach to the Aboriginal theme, the different internal dynamic of his novel sets it very definitely apart from *Voss* and, ultimately, determines its lack of persuasiveness.

Although also a West Australian by birth, Donald Stuart is a very different type of writer. Stuart lived nearly all his life in the state, with the exception of three years from 1941 to 1944 when he was interned in Southeast Asia as a Japanese prisoner-of-war. Stuart spent much of that career in direct contact with Aboriginal people on the land, swag-carrying, cattle-droving, sinking wells, prospecting, mining and working on the wharves. In many respects he was the archetypal itinerant bushman, but he saw Black Australians with a far more perceptive and empathic eye than did other travelling raconteurs such as Idriess. Moreover, he was directly and intimately involved with the aftermath of the Pilbara strike and later, with the Pindan Co-operative. The genesis of the strike provided the source material for his first—and one of his finest—novels, *Yandy*.

Whereas White is an unparalleled imagist and symbolist, Stuart is a naturalist. He admitted that one of his primary aims in writing was "to see completely from the Aboriginal point of view" but he was enough of a realist to concede:

> Whether I've succeeded or not I don't make any claims ... I think *Yandy* to a great extent is written from the Aboriginal point of view ... *But* it is not for you, it is not for me, it is not for *any* white man to say, "Yes, that is from the Aboriginal point of view". I say that I have tried. I say that in some books I have succeeded. But the only one who can give an opinion thoroughly on that is ... what Elkin calls "the man of high degree"—an Aboriginal proper man, fully initiated, experienced and of high degree.

He has scoffed at the suggestion that a European critic could judge his writing by this criterion:

> I'll defy any white man to say, "Ah, that's all balls; he's got that all wrong". I don't care whether they're anthropologists or who they are. I've seen too many anthropologists who've got it all the wrong way 'round ... I refuse to give them any hearing.[35]

For Stuart, the Pilbara movement was motivated and sustained by traditional Aboriginal ways and beliefs, operating successfully in a modern context. It then becomes clear why in *Yandy* he emphasises the eligibility of part-Aborigines to learn the traditional law:

> Nobody wants a halfcaste. Whites and blacks alike refuse to have him. What a lie! He knew well that a halfcaste who stayed true to his mother's people could be as high in the Law as any fullblood man from the furthest reaches of the Desert country. But then, whitefellers always lied.[36]

It seems that a certain amount of wish-fulfillment is operative here. Stuart falls into a way of thinking which is, in its own way, remarkably similar to that which circumscribed the anthropologists Strehlow and Berndt. As Stuart possesses such a sincere and heartfelt respect for traditional Aboriginal culture, he must attempt to show that it was vibrant in 1946 and that it harmonised with modern techniques of industrial action. But, Clancy McKenna and Dooley Bin-Bin were not "men of high degree", even if they did identify totally as Black Australians. They possessed an Aboriginal culture which was not strictly traditional but was adaptive, and which was as authentic in its own terms as the Aboriginal culture of, say, 20,000 years earlier. Stuart's own admiration for the "true" Black Australian culture blinds him to the fact that fringe-dwelling and urban Aborigines possess to this day a distinctive world-view.

Stuart's eye for detail and perceptive ear for direct speech are exemplified in *Yandy*, which is factual, economically written, measured and restrained. The novel is Stuart's affectionate celebration of the Black Australian world-view and an exploration of the positive possibilities for communally-oriented Aborigines in a contemporary environment. Underlying all of this is an idealistic optimism:

> There were days and sometimes weeks when the tucker was not enough to go around and all hands downed tools and lived on the country ... there was strife, and always the old hands carried the burden, till slowly, ever so slowly, but surely as the sun and stars, men and women came forward to match the old hands, men and women who were willing to sweat and thirst and hunger, men and women who wanted their hard times to lead to better things for their hungry ragged children, and gradually the scales tipped.[37]

Of all the White Australian writers who have treated Black Australian themes in their works, Stuart probably comes the closest to an appreciation of Aboriginal people as human beings. However, his belief in the exclusively genuine nature of traditional Aboriginal society ensured that he would always fail to appreciate fully the worth of contemporary Aboriginal culture.

Despite Stuart's limitations, his natural and unfeigned empathy with Black Australians is preferable to the approach which one finds in the books of a writer such as Douglas Lockwood. Stuart was frank in his criticism of Lockwood's writing, and contended that his work should be ignored in any study of the literary treatment of the Black Australian theme. In Stuart's words:

> He's a journalist; he's not a man of letters ... Douglas Lockwood is not a writer. Douglas Lockwood ... like all good journos gets an idea and he's out for a quick quid. I don't think he's of any consequence.[38]

However, in terms of the perpetuation of popular stereotypes of Black Australians in literature, Lockwood *is* of consequence and his work cannot be overlooked. Though his popularity was not of the same order as that of Idriess, Lockwood's books were certainly not ignored by the Australian reading public. For example, by May 1982, over 85,000 copies of his biography of Waipuldanya [Phillip Roberts] entitled *I, The Aboriginal* had been sold in Australia in various editions. Other titles did not penetrate the market to this extent but a book such as *Fair Dinkum*, first published in 1960, sold over 20,000 copies consistently enough to be in print for almost exactly twenty years.[39] By contrast, Stuart's *Yandy* never sold more than half this number of copies, however worthy a novel it might have been.[40] The point is that whether or not one approves of Lockwood's subject matter, his style, or his attitude to Aboriginal people, he was a writer whose work dealing with Black Australians must be at least briefly examined.

Fair Dinkum is a typical example of Lockwood's writing. It comprises a number of tales—perhaps most appropriately termed yarns—which describe various events in the Northern Territory in the 1940s, and in all cases Aboriginal characters loom large. This is not to say that these characters are described with universal admiration and respect. Some are lauded for their supposedly "instinctual" skills of tracking and telepathy, but the general pattern is one in which Black Australians are damned with faint praise:

> I have lived much of my life in the bush in close touch with black men like Oondabund and Narleeba, two of the pleasantest primitives ever to hurl murderous spears, and the more I see of them the greater is my conviction that they are underrated and much maligned people.[41]

In the pages of *Fair Dinkum* one learns that in 1950 "wild and primitive natives still roam"(p. 9) in The Granites region of the Territory and that the Aborigines were as terrified as children by the Japanese bombing of Darwin: "Me go walkabout now, quick time I think. Flesh belong me, him got pimple all-the-same goose"(p. 33). Lockwood also tells the reader that Black Australians have "an obsessive interest in the spiritual and the mythical"(p. 58), that their religion is "paganism, to be sure"(p. 67), that the "natives" have an "absolute addiction to films"(p. 72), and that the traditional people of the area still possess "primitive harems"(p. 107) threatened by "primitive wolves"(p. 109). In perhaps his most audacious and inappropriate claim, the author describes his affinity with the Northern Territory in Black Australian terms: "Immediately I felt the old muscle-twitch, and I knew I was being called back from the Dreamtime to my own tribal land"(p. 185). Lockwood does profess respect and admiration for his Aboriginal "friends" in *Fair Dinkum*, but his racism—and sexism—are so deeply entrenched that he blithely perjures himself throughout his book. It is possible only to speculate on the extent to which his racial opinions would have struck a responsive chord in Australia when the book first appeared in print, but its popularity suggests that even as late as the early 1960s such attitudes were not considered to be totally unacceptable—let alone unpublishable—by at least a significant proportion of the population. What is beyond doubt is that Lockwood's work epitomises the perpetuation of Black Australian stereotypes in Australian literature.

It is worth noting that in 1961 a number of other Australian works of fiction dealing with Aboriginal themes were also published, including Stuart's *The Driven*, Gavin Casey's *Snowball*, and Nene Gare's *The Fringe Dwellers*. Although space permits only a cursory mention of these novels, a number of points are pertinent. First, all of these authors can be categorised as sensitive to Aboriginal Australians. Second, one novel in particular was very popular: *The Driven*, Stuart's somewhat idealised treatment of interracial harmony amongst a cattle-droving team, was selected as a secondary school text in New South Wales and Victoria during the 1960s. Thereby, some 50,000 copies of the novel were sold and, in addition, the Readers' Digest company included a condensed version of *The Driven* in a three-book Australian volume which sold in excess of 100,000 copies.[42] Third, although the distribution of *Snowball* and *The Fringe Dwellers* was initially not of the same order,[43] both Casey and Gare did attempt to come to terms with the problems afflicting part-Aboriginal families in urban fringe areas and, in the latter's case, did so upon the basis of substantial first-hand knowledge and field-work. The shift to an urban focus was a welcome one, which represented an overdue response of White Australian authors to the changing demographic realities of the Aboriginal situation.

Appropriately, in Patrick White's striking novel, *Riders in the Chariot* (also first published in 1961) it is a part-Aboriginal city-dweller who becomes one of the four primary foci of the book. Many critics have concentrated upon the spiritual communion between the four "riders" in this novel,[44] of whom Alf Dubbo is, arguably, the most persuasively drawn.[45] The portrayal of Dubbo again evinces White's singular imaginative power, for the character is, according to the author, entirely an imaginative creation. When asked in interview if the persona of Alf Dubbo was based in any sense upon a living individual, White replied, "No, not at all. I've only known one or two Aborigines in my life. The inspiration came purely from my own head ... I don't know what Aborigines think of my books".[46] All the more impressive then is White's consummate identification with the character whom Kiernan has justifiably termed "a triumph".[47]

In *Riders in the Chariot* White captures the metaphysical dilemma of a part-Aboriginal: the pressures exerted by both the Black and White Australian cultures on him; the weight of unsuccessful assimilation which lies so heavily upon his shoulders:

> He avoided his own people, whatever the degree of colour, because of a certain delicacy with cutlery, acquired from the parson's sister, together with a general niceness or squeamishness of behaviour, which he could sink recklessly enough when forced, as he had throughout the reign of Mrs Spice, but which haunted him in its absence like some indefinable misery.[48]

It is true that Dubbo is one of the elect in this novel, by virtue of his finely-honed intuitive and spiritual perceptions and because of his status as a rejected outcast. But he is more than an untouchable; he is an *Aboriginal* untouchable, divorced from both the larger white and his traditional black society. In a real sense, then, he is not relegated to the shadow of western society so much as trapped between two conflicting world-views. The pressure and pain are immense, and are commensurate with the vivid hues of tortured paint which virtually leap on to his canvasses. The merging of the internal pain and the external expression of that torment in his paintings is made explicit by White:

> The sharp pain poured in crimson tones into the limited space of room, and overflowed. It poured and overflowed his hands. These were gilded, he was forced to observe, with his own gold.[49]

Healy has written very perceptively that:

> The fact that Alf is an Aborigine is not superfluous for White ... Alf was destined to be Aboriginal. He was a logical successor to Jackie, with whom he joined in providing a removed but indigenous view of the society raised by Europeans in Australia over the bones and rights of the Aborigines.[50]

However, I feel it is wrong to contend, as Healy does, that Alf Dubbo represents "the vehicle for an integrated conception of man in Australia, embracing black and white"; even less valid to claim that the character symbolises "Patrick White's peace with Australia, with himself in Australia".[51] Healy is not alone in his defence of this position, for Michael Cotter also maintains that:

> As in Voss's acceptance of a "eucharistic" witchetty grub ... the relocation of cultural values that is imaged in Alf's painting is White's most significant way of projecting the notion of intercultural harmony.[52]

This is a tidy and idealistic stance, but I also believe it to be an incorrect one. Alf Dubbo, caught between conflicting black and white worlds, achieves a spiritual communion with three other isolates rejected by conventional society. His vision unifies the outcasts but does not and cannot alter the prevailing mores which brought about the rejection of these unconventional individuals in the first place. To see the potential for intercultural harmony in Dubbo's artwork is to ignore its ignominious fate on the auction room floor. The vision is only meaningful if it is seen and understood by others, and in his case it is not.

I believe that White courageously shows the essential differences between Black and White Australians and highlights the societal forces which separate the two groups, but his vision of spiritual unity between the four "riders" does not imply or reflect increasing harmony between Europeans and Aborigines in the general sphere. It acts instead to give succour and strength to those individuals whom society metaphorically crucifies through its rigidity and intolerance. The Aboriginal theme is subsumed by White's exploration of cosmic illumination through isolation and rejection. The experience the author describes is a poetic and symbolic one: he addresses the dilemma of outcast humankind.

The boundaries of the 1945-1961 period are in fact delimited by the writings of those who are still two of Australia's finest authors. It is interesting that both Judith Wright and Patrick White shared a poetic, symbolic and metaphysical appreciation of Aboriginal culture, although the latter's career—unlike Wright's—did not develop in a direction which brought him into fruitful collaboration with Black Australians. The poetic/symbolic approach to the Aboriginal theme of Wright, White and Stow ensured that all three would not succumb to the prevailing view of Black Australians at the time in which they wrote. This view characterised the "Native Affairs" policy of the assimilation period and resulted in the depiction of Aboriginal people as mindless objects of white condescension. It also predominated in the stereotypical writings of those such as Douglas Lockwood. The empathic and naturalistic perspective of Donald Stuart was a third literary option and was one which, along with the poetic/symbolic approach, granted Black Australians at least a measure of the dignity and autonomy that they deserved. Unfortunately, Stuart's belief in the singular authenticity of traditional Aboriginal culture mirrored the viewpoint of a number of prominent and influential anthropologists. Their interpretation of Black Australian society prompted poetic translations of tribal material and, ironically, acted to retard White

Australian awareness of the fact that non-traditional Aborigines also possessed a viable and distinctive culture.

Although none of these four literary options succeeded in presenting an Aboriginal person as a fully sentient and realistic individual, Black Australians were now no longer viewed solely as objects. They were treated by some Australian authors, at least, as creative subjects, even if they were not yet portrayed simply as men and women. This conceptual failure persisted during the 1960s and 1970s and even marred the first Aboriginal novelist's attempt to portray his own people. Only very recently has the barrier been surmounted; only in the past fifteen years have Aboriginal people been fully fleshed and clothed with individualised humanity in Australian literature. This has been one of the salient achievements of contemporary Black Australian writers.

Notes

1   As Stanner has noted, this process logically led to a "romantic cult of the past" which implied a demand solely for "traditional things" and persisted even after 1961. He rightly questions "whether we would be right in reading from the fact of its existence to a proof of any deep-seated change of heart or mind towards the living aborigines". He makes this point in "The Appreciation of Difference", in *The 1968 Boyer Lectures; After the Dreaming*, (Sydney, 1969), p. 39.

2   In his paper, "Painting and the Manufacture of Myth", *Meanjin*, vol. 43, no. 4, December, 1984, George Petelin illustrates how some of Australia's best-known painters of the 1945-1961 period, such as Russell Drysdale, also portrayed this detachment from living Black Australians in their work: "The aboriginal is cast as the mystical 'other' exotic and inscrutable—unknowable except as an erotic or aesthetic commodity, and relegated to a spiritual dreamtime conveniently transcendent of the other fictions of our time"(p. 548).

3   Quoted from "The Poets" section of Rodney Hall, ed., *The Collins Book of Australian Poetry*, (Sydney, 1981), p. 445.

4   One of the best and most comprehensive critical studies of Wright's poetry is Shirley Walker's *The Poetry of Judith Wright: A Search for Unity*, (Melbourne, 1980).

5   *ibid.*, p. 21.

6   Judith Wright, "Bora Ring", in *The Moving Image*, (Melbourne, 1946), p. 12.

7   *ibid.*, p. 23.

8   G.A. Brennan, "The Aborigine in the Works of Judith Wright", *Westerly*, no. 4, December, 1972, p. 48.

9   Personal interview with Judith Wright, Canberra, July, 1982.

10   J.J. Healy, *Literature and the Aborigine in Australia, 1770-1975*, (St. Lucia, 1978), p. 186.

11   Wright, *The Moving Image*, p. 27.

12   Judith Wright, *Collected Poems, 1942-1970*, (Sydney, 1971), p. 140.

13   Judith Wright, *The Generations of Men*, (Melbourne, 1959), p. 156.

14   Walker, *The Poetry of Judith Wright*, p. 22.

15   Wright, *Collected Poems*, p. 64.

16   Judith Wright, "The Writer as Social Conscience", Address at The Adelaide

Festival Writers' Week, March, 1982. An edited version of the address appears in *Overland*, no. 89, October, 1982, pp. 29-31.

17   *Oceania*, vol. xix, September, 1948, pp. 16-50.

18   Les A. Murray, in "The Human-Hair Thread", *Meanjin*, vol. 36, no.4, December, 1977, p. 565.

19   T.G.H. Strehlow, *Aranda Traditions*, (Melbourne, 1947), pp. 32-33.

20   *ibid.*, p. xx.

21   For further discussion of the challenges and issues involved in the translation of traditional Aboriginal song-poetry, see Tamsin Donaldson's article, "Translating Oral Literature: Aboriginal Song Texts", *Aboriginal History*, vol. 3, part 1, 1979, pp. 62-83.

22   Quoted in "The Poets" section of Rodney Hall, ed., *The Collins Book of Australian Poetry*, (Sydney, 1981), p. 444. The emphasis is mine.

23   "Wonguri-Mandijigai Song, the Moon-Bone Song", in *ibid.*, p. 18.

24   Randolph Stow, "Negritude for the White Man", in Marie Reay, ed., *Aborigines Now*, (Sydney, 1964), p. 4.

25   Mary Durack, *Keep Him My Country*, (London, 1955), p. 72.

26   Healy, *Literature and the Aborigine*, p. 216.

27   Patrick White, *Voss*, (Harmondsworth, 1960), p. 168.

28   *ibid.*, p. 34.

29   *ibid.*, p. 204. This point is made in Healy, *Literature and the Aborigine*, p. 194.

30   White, *Voss*, p. 241.

31   *ibid., p. 365.*

32   Randolph Stow, *To the Islands*, (London, 1958), p. 113.

33   *ibid.*, p. 124.

34   Dorothy L.M. Jones, "The Treatment of the Aborigine in Australian Fiction", Unpublished M.A. Thesis, (Adelaide, 1960), p. 152.

35   Personal interview with Donald Stuart, Canberra, May, 1981.

36   Donald Stuart, *Yandy*, (Melbourne, 1959), p. 52.

37   *ibid.*, p. 139.

38   Personal interview with Donald Stuart, Canberra, May, 1981.

39   Figures kindly supplied by Mr. Brian Cook, National Promotions Manager, Rigby Publishers, May, 1982.

40   Information kindly provided in correspondence with Mr. Brian W. Harris, Managing Director, Georgian House Pty. Ltd., August, 1982.

41   Douglas Lockwood, *Fair Dinkum*, (Adelaide, 1969), p. 66. All further quotations will be taken from this edition and page numbers will be given in parentheses in the body of the text, immediately following each citation.

42   Correspondence with Mr. Brian W. Harris, Managing Director, Georgian House Pty. Ltd., August, 1982.

43   The release of the feature film version of *The Fringe Dwellers* in 1987 prompted the re-design and re-issue in paperback of the novel, now set quite extensively throughout Australia as an upper secondary school text.

44   See, for example, John Colmer's *Riders in the Chariot, Patrick White*, (Melbourne, 1978).

45   In support of this view see Brian Kiernan's *Patrick White*, (London, 1980), pp. 75-78.

46   Personal discussion with Patrick White, Canberra, May, 1983.

47   Kiernan, *Patrick White*, p. 75.

48   Patrick White, *Riders in the Chariot*, (London, 1961), p. 383.

49   *ibid.*, p. 515.

50   Healy, *Literature and the Aborigine*, p. 203.

51   *ibid.*, p. 204.

52   Michael Cotter, "The Image of the Aboriginal in Three Modern Australian Novels", *Meanjin* , vol. 36, no. 4, December, 1977, p. 589.

5

Progress and Frustrated Expectations: The Era Since 1961

Just over twenty-five years ago—in 1961—the New South Wales Minister for Health, W.F. Sheehan, announced that his government planned to outlaw the segregation of whites and Aborigines in the state's hospitals. In many areas of the state, European reaction to this news was hostile and indignant. For example, the chairman of the Moree District Hospital Board stated that he and his colleagues would ignore any such directive and that "any attempt to alter the current situation would 'lead to trouble' ".[1] As Rowley has revealed, local segregation of whites and blacks was common throughout New South Wales at the time, and the poor health and hygiene of Aborigines was frequently cited as the reason for allegedly necessary and desirable restrictions upon their freedom. That such explanations often masked patently racist attitudes was obvious. For example, towns such as Moree and Kempsey barred Aboriginal children from swimming in public pools unless they were there as part of a school excursion under the supervision of a teacher.[2] When the end of the lesson arrived a whistle would be blown, signifying that the black children had to leave the water, while their white classmates were permitted to remain.

Such colour barriers were important indications of dominant racial attitudes at the time, and also gave rise to Aboriginal indignation and protest. These local restrictions upon Aborigines were significant for other reasons as well. They reflect an important demographic pattern in Australia: in small country communities with substantial Aboriginal populations and continuous and close levels of contact between the races, interracial disharmony is frequently high. It is no coincidence that Moree, a town which segregated hospital patients and school-children on the basis of race in the early 1960s, was in 1982 the scene of an ugly black/white racial confrontation, which left an Aboriginal man dead and another wounded after a pub brawl. Moree, and other towns like Laverton in Western Australia, have histories of Aboriginal/European conflict and distrust. On the basis of extensive survey work in Western Australia, Ronald Taft reported in 1970 that his respondents who held consistently unfavourable views of Black Australians "have all had a fair amount or a great deal of contact with Aborigines in the course of their life, and they all come from a Western Australian country or an interstate background".[3]

This is not to say that all small-town White Australians are virulent racists, nor the illogical corollary: that all white urbanites are necessarily more tolerant and kindly-disposed towards blacks. The fact is that attitudes towards Aborigines vary widely on a regional and economic basis throughout the country. While advances in Aboriginal autonomy and Black Australian achievements have both been marked over the past two decades, and while there have been signposts of increased white sympathy and understanding over that period of time, it is important to note that prejudice of both overt and covert types has persisted in some areas, particularly those with a history of Aboriginal/European friction. Any evaluation of the socio-political situation of Aborigines from 1961 until the present day must acknowledge that the advances that have occurred have not eradicated many inequalities and repressions.

This chapter briefly surveys the major socio-political developments in Aboriginal affairs over the past twenty-seven years. It was a period of rapid legislative change affecting many Aborigines, and a time of escalating Aboriginal self-confidence and achievement on many fronts. It was also an era of frustrated ambitions for Black Australians, who saw the advances seemingly promised by the referendum of 1967 remain largely unfulfilled, and who witnessed a white backlash to many of those positive developments which did take place. Though the 1961-1988 period was one of success in many fields, it was also one of frustrated expectations and hopes. Perhaps most importantly, the era saw the initiative for protest activity in Aboriginal affairs pass from white-dominated bodies to co-operative organisations, and then to groups controlled administratively—if not financially—by Black Australians.

One of the clearest examples of the shift from European direction to Aboriginal control was that of the Federal Council for the

Advancement of Aborigines. From its inception in 1958, the FCAA had been presided over by three sympathetic whites in succession: Dr Charles Duguid, Doris Blackburn and Don Dunstan. Finally, in 1961, Joe McGuiness was elected as the first Aboriginal president of the organisation, which was to have a very high media profile in the debate leading up to the 1967 referendum and in the publicity surrounding the land rights campaign of the late 1960s. The character of the FCAA as an umbrella organisation attempting for the first time to represent Black Australian views nationally was emphasised when, in 1964, the council changed its name and mandate to articulate the aims and grievances of the Torres Strait Islanders as well. The renamed FCAATSI threatened to approach the United Nations in that same year if the federal government did not heed its demands for changes to the Northern Territory legislation concerning Aborigines. Throughout the years following 1961, FCAATSI was one of the most vocal and visible pressure groups in Australia. With increasing assertiveness, stridency and success, it articulated the Aboriginal viewpoint more and more through Black Australians themselves.

Unfortunately, though the trend towards Aboriginal representation of Aboriginal views was followed in other black organisations, their campaigns did not always succeed. During the early 1960s, the Aborigines' Advancement League led by Pastor Douglas Nicholls was involved in two major campaigns in support of land claims for Victorian Aborigines. In the first, concerning the Cummeragunga Reserve, the debate dragged on for four years: not until 1964 was the leased land returned to the Aboriginal community. In the second case, Nicholls and the AAL fought fruitlessly for many years for local black residents who were attempting to wrest control of the Lake Tyers Reserve from the Victorian Aboriginal Welfare Board. Although the campaign began in 1963, only after seven years of pressure (including a petition sent to the United Nations) was the Reserve finally handed back to the Aboriginal people. While the case illustrated the admirable tenacity and organisation of the Aboriginal claimants, it also reflected the fact that the paternalist and protectionist mentality in some Australian state administrations proved hard to change.

Even when the legitimacy of Aboriginal claims was acknowledged, the federal administration could be just as unwilling as its state counterparts to grant Aboriginal wishes. An excellent case in point was the 1963 bark petition tendered to the House of Representatives in Canberra by the Yirrkala people of Arnhem Land. Using "a political protest of modern content but ... traditional form",[4] the Yirrkala people protested against Canberra's unilateral decision to excise an economically, socially and religiously important section of the Arnhem Land Reserve to permit large-scale aluminium mining at Gove. A parliamentary inquiry refused to cancel the exploration and mining licence, although it did voice the view that the Yirrkala people deserved land and/or monetary compensation. The Yirrkala community were very disappointed with this result, and were even more dejected when their case was lost after it was heard in the Northern Territory Supreme Court in 1971—eight years after the original petition.

For good or ill, and primarily for the latter as far as Black Australians were concerned, set-backs and delays in decision and policy-making were the norm in Aboriginal affairs throughout most of the 1960s. The Northern Territory pastoral wage case of 1965 was a good example of how time-lags could disadvantage Aborigines. In what became the equal wage test-case for the industry, in 1965 the North Australian Workers' Union applied to the Commonwealth Conciliation and Arbitration Commission for the removal of clauses discriminating against Black Australians in the Northern Territory's pastoral award. The proposal met with stiff opposition from owners' and managers' groups, which argued that for the good of the Aboriginal people, a sudden wage rise to parity with whites should be rejected in favour of a gradual, incremental rise—which would ostensibly give the blacks time to "adjust". Obviously, this proposal was far more in the owners' interests than in those of their employees. As Middleton has estimated, the pastoralists were able to save "something in the region of six million dollars"[5] by ensuring that Aboriginal wages rose only gradually over a three-year period. In addition, the power of the managerial lobby was such that it also persuaded the Commission to include a "slow worker" clause in its decision, which would empower the owners to pay Aboriginal employees less than the standard wage if their efficiency was not deemed up to par—a subjective clause which was open to abuse.

Thus, the early 1960s were a time of flux in Aboriginal affairs. Regionally, territorially, and state-by-state, most of the glaring infringements upon Aboriginal personal liberties were removed as the decade progressed. Yet this was an uneven process which varied significantly according to state. For example, in 1961, only in Victoria were Black Australians permitted to drink alcohol and only there and in New South Wales were they free of restrictions on their movement, ownership of property and association with whites. The two most conservative and repressive states then as now, Queensland and Western Australia, still controlled Aboriginal marriages just over twenty-five years ago. Yet in that same year of 1961, the Senate Select Committee on Aboriginal Voting Rights endorsed in principle the proposal that all Aborigines should be given the federal franchise. In short, the door which had for so long been locked shut was now ajar, but it would take the concerted action of Aboriginal people themselves to open it further.

One of the most dramatic door-opening activities of the 1960s in terms of novelty, media interest, and the revelation of injustice was the Freedom Ride campaign of 1965, in which Charles Perkins played such a prominent role. Perkins's autobiography, *A Bastard Like Me* contains an evocative description of the Rides in which he details the personal and collective impact of the events:

> The Freedom Ride was probably the greatest and most exciting event that I have ever been involved in with Aboriginal affairs. It was a new idea and a new way of promoting a rapid change in racial attitudes ... It sowed the seed of concern in the public's thinking across Australia.[6]

In his book Perkins acknowledges that the inspiration for the campaign came from the United States; he also admits that almost all of the riders were sympathetic whites (primarily university students) and that "not one Aborigine from New South Wales eventually went on the trip".[7] Internationally inspired, a product of co-operation between whites and blacks committed to the same ideals, confrontationist but non-violent, the Freedom Rides were a consciousness-raising exercise which was very effective. Awakening media interest in Aboriginal affairs was, for the first time, marshalled in favour of the Black Australian cause, to the severe embarrassment of many white townspeople in rural New South Wales. All of these elements foreshadowed a pattern of protest which was to continue and expand in the 1970s and 1980s.

Perkins's description of the events is fascinating. Not only was this the first Aboriginal experiment of this type but it also produced a violent reaction amongst the ashamed white townsfolk, many of whom became abusive crowds. In his words, in Walgett, "They were swearing viciously in an attempt to provoke the fight they all wanted".[8] Second, primarily due to media coverage and state government interest, the riders were successful in breaking down racial barriers such as the rule which banned Aboriginal children from the public swimming pool in Moree. Third, the events raised awareness of inequalities and injustices, not only amongst whites, but amongst blacks as well. As Perkins relates, some leading Aboriginal activists today, such as Michael Anderson and Lyle Munroe, were children who saw the potential for assertive, non-violent confrontation in aid of Aboriginal rights when the riders visited their towns. For the first time, fringe-dwelling and urbanised blacks witnessed successful opposition to the prejudiced dictates of the small-town whites.

The Freedom Riders fought overt bigotry and helped to awaken Aboriginal self-confidence. The walk-out of the Aboriginal people on Wave Hill station in the Northern Territory in 1966 was equally significant, for it asserted Black Australian rights and established the determination to battle for compensation for past injustices. Originally a response to the unfairness of the Arbitration Commission's pastoral wage decision in 1966, the Gurindji strike soon became far more than a battle for higher wages. With the move of the strikers to Wattie Creek (or Dagu Ragu) in March 1967—an area of traditional and sacred importance to the tribe—the campaign changed into the first clear struggle for traditional land rights in Australia. The genesis of the Gurindji campaign is fully and engagingly documented in Frank Hardy's *The Unlucky Australians*[9]. The story of these Aborigines' nine-year campaign of perseverance, dedication, determination and final victory is a remarkable one. It is significant that the concept of land rights was not one introduced into the minds of the Gurindji by so-called "southern radicals", but was the logical and natural response of traditionally oriented blacks to their dispossession and exploitation by Europeans.

The overwhelming support for Aboriginal Australians indicated by the results of the federal referendum of 1967 suggests that a majority of Australians sympathised with the Gurindji's campaign. For in 1967, nearly 90% of Australians supported the move to include Aborigines in the national census and voted that the Commonwealth should possess "a concurrent power in Aboriginal affairs".[10] However, it is wrong to conclude that general sympathy for Aborigines and a willingness to rectify legal inequalities necessarily implied social or personal approval—or even an acceptance—of Black Australians. There appears little doubt now that many Black Australians (and white commentators as well) became overly hopeful in the wake of the 1967 Referendum, and mistakenly believed that once the overt legal barriers to Aboriginal advancement were removed, more covert personal obstacles would likewise melt away.

The referendum result is often held up as a barometer of cultural *rapprochement* between White and Black Australians. It certainly did signify a general willingness to set blacks upon an equal legal footing, but subsequent events have proven that true social and political equality is still a long way off for most Aborigines. Rowley perceptively de-emphasises the event:

> The result of the referendum ... probably indicates little more than a general view that something has been seriously wrong, that an issue of national importance has remained too long neglected, that it is up to the Commonwealth Government, with its control of taxation, to provide the solution. [11]

Any historical study of Aboriginal affairs reveals that there is frequently a vast gulf between policy and practice: the aftermath of the referendum was no exception to this rule. The very next year, the federal Liberal government asserted that it was unequivocally opposed to the principle of land rights.[12] Its lack of support for the principle disillusioned many Australians both white and black, as Lyndall Ryan put it in 1981:

> We saw the referendum as a recognition by white society that Aborigines were a people who needed recognition by the whole of Australia. It would only be a matter of a few years before the Federal government would take over all involvement in Aboriginal affairs and get on with recognition of Aboriginal rights to land. Well, how green we were.[13]

In the post-1967 period the federal government appeared to be moving, not towards an acceptance of the concept (let alone the reality) of land rights, but in the opposite direction. At this time, the courts were also often examples of conservatism, whose judgements benefited the economic interests both of the Australian government and of multinational corporations, at the expense of Black Australians. For example, Mr Justice Blackburn's decision in the 1971 case of *Milirrpum and others v. Nabalco Pty. Ltd. and The Commonwealth of Australia* was that the "doctrine of communal native title ... does not form, and never has formed, part of the law of any part of Australia".[14] Blackburn agreed that, when it was colonised, New South Wales (which included the Gove Peninsula) was "a colony which consisted of a tract of territory practically unoccupied, without settled inhabitants or settled law" and was "peacefully annexed to the British dominions".[15] Aside from the contentiousness of the claim that Aborigines had no "settled law", Blackburn's ruling that the colony was peacefully annexed represents one of the most glaring fictions in Australian legal history.[16]

The judge then proceeded to disallow contrary evidence, no matter how legitimate:

> Whether or not the Australian Aboriginals living in any part of New South Wales had in 1788 a system of law which was beyond the powers of the settlers at that time to perceive or comprehend, it is beyond the power of this Court to decide otherwise than that New South Wales came into the category of a settled or occupied colony.17

Blackburn therefore concluded that "the attribution of a colony to a particular class is a matter of law, which becomes settled and is not to be questioned upon a reconsideration of the historical facts".18 Ironically, in one sense this all-encompassing denial of legal redress for present and future Aboriginal claimants was the most useful aspect of the 1971 case, however disappointing it might have been for the Gove Aborigines. The decision made it abundantly clear that the only way land rights could be introduced in Australia was via legislation rather than through the courts. Consequently, no federal government could in future temporise by referring this issue to the judiciary for re-examination. It is therefore possible that Blackburn's judgement actually hastened the drafting of what was eventually proclaimed as the *Aboriginal Land Rights (Northern Territory) Act* of 1976.

In the early 1970s, urban Aborigines began to perceive the necessity of having adequate legal representation in the courts in which such a disproportionately high number of their people had to appear every day. Consequently, in Sydney in 1970, a number of young black activists began to agitate for the establishment of an independent legal service which would advise and represent Aborigines. The volunteer operation grew rapidly and successfully. It is significant that, from the beginning, the Aboriginal Legal Service of Sydney—which has since been emulated in centres throughout Australia—was a grass-roots demand on the part of ostensibly radical Black Australians. In the words of MumShirl:

> These young Blacks, Paul [Coe] and Gordon [Briscoe], Gary Williams, Gary Foley—these radicals and militants as they were being called—had started moving around trying to get some lawyers to take some cases of Aboriginal people ... From the first day it opened its doors right up to the present, the ALS has done its best to get justice for Blacks in front of the law.19

Soon afterwards, Briscoe, his wife Norma, Sister Dulcie Flowers, Elsa Dixon, Professor Fred Hollows, MumShirl and others, helped to launch the Aboriginal Medical Service, which became established in Sydney in 1971. Again, the invaluable work—often unpaid—done by this agency provided a model for similar services throughout the country. Since their inception, such organisations have made an indelible mark upon Aboriginal affairs, as they deal with basic issues of welfare which Aborigines encounter daily. Many argue that these services do more for the average Black Australian than some government-initiated advisory groups, such as the National Aboriginal Conference. It is important to reiterate the fact that, originally, the initiators and builders of these programmes were denounced by many Australians as "hot-heads and radical chic ritualists"[20]: clearly such radicalism had a very positive and tangible outcome.

Many of the same denunciations were voiced when, on 26 January, 1972 (Australia Day) a group of young Black Australians erected a tent directly opposite Parliament House in Canberra, calling it the "Aboriginal Embassy". Accusations of Communist sympathy and charges that radical "stirrers" were behind the project increased when, seven months later, the tent was pulled down by the police amid violence. If the Freedom Rides and the Gurindji walk-out were the two most significant events in Aboriginal affairs during the 1960s, the Tent Embassy was one of the most important symbolic gestures of black determination and defiance of the 1970s. Almost all commentators remark upon the simple eloquence of the demonstration; for example, Charles Rowley enthuses, "the idea and location of the Embassy was a piece of political genius".[21] Paul Coe calls it "one of the most brilliant symbolic forms of protest that this country had ever seen".[22] Noel Loos and Jane Thomson comment that "The Aboriginal perspective was communicated very effectively through the media to White and Black Australians all over the country, bringing home to many of them for the first time the justice of the Aboriginal claim for land rights".[23] Though the impact may have been felt by all Australians, Bobbi Sykes emphasises the fact that "the Embassy was a *black* affair; it wasn't blacks being guided by whites", and that it was the first truly national Aboriginal political protest: "the first *national* announcement that the pushing back was going to stop".[24] It is ironic that a demonstration which was initially named in jest[25] could attract such media attention and academic praise for its brilliance, while the Yirrkala bark petition—originally suggested by distinguished whites visiting the area—fell upon relatively deaf ears.

The Embassy episode deserves more attention. While it is clear that the timing and the siting of the demonstration were both extremely clever, one must ask, "Did the Embassy really represent a pan-Aboriginal protest?". In addition, "Why was the tent permitted to remain for as long as it did if its presence was such an acute embarrassment to the government?". In Coe's opinion, the federal government initially tried to ignore the Embassy, but the fact that international publicity increasingly became centred upon the protest eventually forced its hand.[26] This explanation is plausible as far as it goes, but it may not go far enough. The theory which Middleton advances is an intriguing one: that the McMahon government purposely left the demonstrators alone long enough for them to hang themselves on the noose of public opinion.

Clearly, most Australians, even if they were sympathetic to the Aboriginal cause, would have baulked at the excessiveness of the Aborigines' demands, which included claims for large areas of reserve and Crown land throughout the country, financial compensation totalling six billion dollars, and an annual percentage of the gross national income. Even Kevin Gilbert, one of the original organisers of the protest, has written, "I regret that the land claim put out by the Embassy was not a little more realistic".[27] It is arguable that the scale of their demands actually lessened the demonstrators' effectiveness and made them appear more like extravagant idealists than authoritative national Aboriginal spokespeople. Second, it is also possible that, the longer the Embassy remained, the more its impact wore off. One of the major strengths of the concept was its novelty but, once begun, it was difficult to end with dignity. Instead, by resisting the forces of law and order (which had been held in abeyance for so long) the demonstrators may well have harmed the image of the Embassy even further by opposing its removal as violently as they did.

Middleton makes a valid point here: "Once the policy of discrediting the land rights campaign had been achieved—not on the Canberra lawns but on television screens and in peoples' minds—the Government sent the police to remove the Embassy".[28] There appears to be little doubt that the media's revelation of the fact that the Embassy had been initially funded by the Communist Party of Australia demeaned the land rights campaign in the public eye, and encouraged a popular association of urban black radicals with Communist "stirrers" even though, as Gilbert protests,

From its inception to its demise, the Aboriginal Embassy was a totally Aboriginal thing. Besides treating us with ordinary courtesy at its inception and providing the car and the funds to kick it off, the Communists had no influence over it nor did they exercise any control. [29]

The Embassy may have been a unifying and reinforcing experience for many Black Australians throughout the country but, as George Abdullah pointed out, it represented a symbolic protest rather than something which led directly to an improvement of black living conditions. In his opinion, it was not an expression of the national Aboriginal viewpoint: "The tent embassy in Canberra didn't achieve a bloody thing ... what was missing was the full support of the total Aboriginal population".[30] It is therefore ironic that many white commentators, such as Rowley, Loos and Thomson overemphasise its success in conveying Aboriginal demands to the white population. Not only were those demands fairly unrepresentative, but news coverage in fact probably alienated many Europeans. In short, the Embassy was a two-edged sword. While it focussed black attention upon Canberra and acted as a symbolic pan-Aboriginal protest (though it is difficult to gauge the level of support for the demonstration in remote areas such as the Northern Territory) it may also have dealt a blow to Aboriginal/white collaboration over the land rights issue. Similarly, the effect of the media was an ambivalent one: while international coverage undoubtedly did embarrass the Australian authorities to some extent, domestically, the media coverage of the Embassy could very well have polarised opinion against the Aboriginal cause. The Embassy probably acted as both a unifying and a divisive factor, simultaneously influencing different elements of the population.

The Labor Party's accession to power in 1972 had important consequences for government policies and programmes dealing with Aborigines. What was most immediately apparent about Labor's Aboriginal policy was its creation of new instrumentalities to serve Black Australians (e.g. the Department of Aboriginal Affairs, the Aboriginal Arts Board, and the National Aboriginal Consultative Committee) and the massive injection of funds which these new bodies received. The Whitlam era also marked a dramatic shift of government policy *vis à vis* land rights. When the Woodward Commission was established in February 1973, its mandate was to investigate and determine, not whether Northern Territory Aborigines should possess rights in land but, rather, how such rights should be implemented: "the appropriate means to recognise and establish the traditional rights of the Aborigines in and in relation to land".[31]

Woodward handed down two reports: the most important recommendation contained in the first was that two federally-funded

Aboriginal Land Councils should be created in the Northern Territory, to represent Black Australian land claims more clearly and effectively. Since their establishment, these and subsequent land councils have become centres for the airing of Aboriginal grievances and political demands, as well as for the organisation of various services: the councils have assumed far more importance than their creators ever envisaged. Woodward's second report of April 1974 was significant for a number of reasons. First, the inquiry, with its emphasis upon the Northern Territory and upon traditional and demonstrable links with land, was founded upon a concept of land rights which automatically disqualified many Aborigines who had moved from their original areas (even if under government direction) or had become fringe or urban-dwellers—a sizeable proportion of the Aboriginal population. In short, land rights was not a national concept but a Northern Territory experiment. Second, by ruling that Territory Aborigines could not block mining in their traditional areas if it was deemed to be in the "national interest", Woodward further restricted the definition of land rights to one which—in the event of disagreement—yielded to White Australian political and economic interests. Third, by recommending that town lands should be exempt from claim under the legislation, Woodward opened the door to the arbitrary extension of town boundaries by civic leaders attempting to obstruct potential land claims—as has subsequently occurred.

In all, Woodward's recommendations lived up to the letter of Labor's 1972 pre-election promise to institute Aboriginal land rights if elected, but did not fulfil the understood spirit of that guarantee. For at the national Labor party convention in Hobart in 1971 it had been agreed that, as a matter of policy, Aboriginal land rights were taken to include ownership of sub-surface minerals and the consequent control over their extraction. It is significant that, at the party's 1973 conference in Surfers Paradise, this policy was altered to negate these mineral rights. Woodward's findings were in keeping with the relatively more liberal trend of the Labor administration, but reflected an awareness of economic pragmatism which the Labor government itself came to realise upon entering office. Once many Aborigines began to perceive the extent to which Labor promises would not be fulfilled and came to see that the concept of land rights was restricted in so many important ways, their initial optimism in the wake of the Labor victory gave way to frustration. In fact, from the moment that Woodward was appointed some had misgivings, as Gilbert writes:

The government had stressed, right from the start, that consultation with blacks was central to its thinking. Yet the appointment of Justice Woodward was accomplished without any consultation whatsoever. Blacks felt that no white Australian, no matter how experienced, could recommend on land justice. Many felt that a black jurist or jurists from a neutral country should have been sought for the job and that Aborigines should serve on the Land Rights Commission as well. Clearly it was another case of blacks 'being done to'.[32]

By the time Woodward's second report had been tabled, this attitude had given way to outright indignation in many Aboriginal quarters. James Laughton's viewpoint seems typical of many Black Australians at that time:

> The Labor Party has done a lot for the Aboriginal but they still haven't done what they promised ... As far as land rights is concerned, things really stink. They allocate certain areas to our people and they say, 'That's your land.' But they keep the mineral rights. They go down there and find maybe uranium, bauxite, iron or what have you. Then they just come in and take it ... They give the Aboriginal something with one hand and take it away with the other. We're only going to put up with that shit for so long.[33]

What is significant here is, above all, the sense of betrayal. Despite the admission that the Labor administration has aided Black Australians it is the unkept promises, the guarantees given in bad faith, which cause the feeling of Aboriginal resentment. In this sense, the Woodward episode was typical of the Aboriginal affairs of the era following 1961. As was so often the case, the arousal of hopes and expectations produced Aboriginal optimism and co-operation; their dashing resulted in Black Australian cynicism and the determination to achieve autonomy from white control.

As the mining issue had revealed, Aborigines often had less power than multinational corporations when it came to exerting pressure upon the Australian government. This fact was all the more important because, for good or ill, mining became one of the primary contact points between Aborigines and Europeans during the 1970s, especially in the Northern Territory. In Vachon and Toyne's words,

> Today, overshadowing the influence of missions, pastoralists, and government agencies, mineral exploration and extraction have emerged as the major contact point between Aboriginal and European societies in remote Australia.[34]

In recognition of the sensitivity and importance of this nexus, in July 1975 the Whitlam government established the Ranger Uranium Environmental Enquiry (popularly known as the Fox Commission) to investigate the proposed uranium mine at Jabiru in the Northern Territory. The Fox Commission was given the task of assessing the potential social and environmental impact of the enormous uranium extraction complex contemplated for Jabiru, including the creation of a mining town virtually *ex nihilo*. Despite the fact that the proposed open-pit mines were in close proximity to Aboriginal sacred sites, and in spite of the documented social and psychological problems which mining had previously brought to Aborigines in other areas of the Territory—let alone the ecological dangers inherent in the open-pit technique—in 1977 the Fox Commission released its findings in favour of the proposed development.

In August of that year, the Fraser Liberal government announced that uranium mining would commence at Jabiru immediately. It also revealed that all mines would proceed simultaneously, thereby ignoring the Commission's recommendation that there should be gradual, sequential development of the region in order to minimise Aboriginal social dislocation. As Broome has noted, it is very telling that, in the entire 415-page report, only one Aboriginal opinion was quoted—and it was an anti-mining viewpoint.[35] Certain privileges were given to local blacks in an attempt to soften their opposition, but the fact remained that once the economic realities had become obvious, the Oenpelli Aborigines did not have ultimate control over the land to which they had supposedly been granted rights by the government. To quote Broome again:

> No doubt the attraction of the estimated profits ranging from $574 to $3591 million which would 'provide high rates of return on capital invested' was too powerful to allow 1000 Aborigines to stand in the way of development![36]

At the time the Ranger decision was announced, land rights legislation—the *Aboriginal Land Rights (Northern Territory) Act* of 1976—was in force in the Territory. Even with this legislative support, the Oenpelli Aborigines were unable to veto mining in their traditional area. Part of the reason was that the 1976 Act was an amended version of Land Rights legislation first introduced by the Whitlam government prior to its fall in 1975 which had, in turn, been essentially based upon the recommendations of the second Woodward Report.

Some commentators have expressed surprise at the fact that land rights legislation of any sort was passed by a conservative Liberal party administration. Broome, for one, takes heart from the situation and observes:

> Certainly it was remarkable that a conservative government, partly representing land-holders and mining companies, went as far as it did in this Act. This was evi-

dence of the growing community pressure for Aboriginal justice.[37]

This may be valid as a partial explanation of the events, but it does not fully explain them. In Ryan's view the 1976 legislation was brought down primarily because of the momentum of legislative change established by the previous Labor government.[38] Moreover, she imputes a rather sinister motive to the Liberal administration, in view of the fact that the Territory was granted self-government soon afterwards, in 1978. Her theory is that, by casting off its jurisdiction, Canberra could shed its responsibility for both the administration and the amendment of the Territory's land rights legislation. In Ryan's words:

> There is no doubt that one of the reasons why the Federal government was so anxious to give self-government to the Northern Territory was to give that government ultimate responsibility for the Aborigines in the Northern Territory and to allow it to amend the federal land rights legislation and so make it much harder for Aborigines there to get access to land.[39]

Although it is probably impossible to prove Ryan's claim, there is no doubt that the Territory administration subsequently made significant amendments to its own land rights and sacred sites legislation. In addition, it mounted an intense public relations campaign to persuade Australians that its recommended changes to the federal land rights legislation were in the best interests of all Territorians. For example, in August 1982, full-page advertisements were placed in all the major Australian newspapers under the auspices of the Northern Territory Chief Minister, exhorting readers to send away for an information package which would detail the allegedly urgent need for such changes. In a very professional and polished fashion the package—complete with misleading statistics and maps—argued that a time limit should be placed on Aboriginal land claims; that stock routes, reserves, and public purpose lands should be immune from claim; and that blocking "future applications for claims being made by the Land Council for land in which the estates and interests are held by or *on behalf of* Aboriginals was necessary".[40]

Clearly, the issue of land rights is a complex and contentious one, not only in the Northern Territory but throughout the entire nation. The matter is complicated by the lack of legislative uniformity on the issue among the various states and territories. In South Australia[41] and the Northern Territory, relevant legislation has been passed and, as has been observed, in the latter case has been subjected to considerable pressure to limit the scope of its operations. Other states, such as New South Wales and Victoria, are at differing stages of legislative preparation and enactment. Although a land rights act was passed by the New South Wales parliament in 1983, controversy has dogged Aboriginal attempts to claim under its provisions. In fact, the Liberal administration which seized power in March 1988 raised the possibility of repealing and completely re-drafting the legislation. In Victoria the situation is also in disarray, so much so that in December 1986 the state government asked Canberra to assume responsibility for the finalisation of its land rights measures.[42] Western Australia, which has a reputation for relative conservatism in the field, instituted a land rights enquiry in 1983-84. Despite the recommendations of its author, Paul Seaman, the upper house of the Western Australian parliament rejected the *Western Australian Aboriginal Land Bill (1985)* on the grounds that Black Australians should not be given even a partial right to veto mining exploration.[43] Finally, the most intransigent states in the field, Queensland and Tasmania, have dismissed the concept of land rights outright. In fact, in the past the Queensland parliament has prevented the Aboriginal Land Fund (predecessor of the Aboriginal Development Commission) from purchasing properties for Aboriginal communities, let alone contemplating the grant of any territory to Black Australians.

Throughout all of this debate, what has been the role of the federal government, constitutionally empowered with the right to override state legislation in respect of Aborigines? In the view of many Black Australians, in the latter half of the 1970s and during the early years of the 1980s, the federal Liberal government largely failed them. For example, it exerted tremendous pressure upon the Northern Land Council to ratify the Ranger uranium mining agreement in 1978. According to Collins, at the final ratification meeting:

> Alex Bishaw, the European manager of the Land Council, stood over the Land Council … and he said to them: 'I have been told by a person in Canberra who actually sits in the Cabinet room when Cabinet's making its decisions, that if you don't sign this agreement the government will not arbitrate, they will not negotiate any further, they will legislate to put the Land Council out of existence'.[44]

On other occasions, the Liberal administration maintained a non-interventionist stance, to the detriment of Aboriginal Australians. The classic example of this hands-off attitude was the Aurukun and Mornington Island case of 1978. The federal Liberal government refused pleas to intervene when the Queensland state government offered the Aboriginal residents, not leasehold or freehold tenure, but only "self-management" of their state-owned lands. Despite the fact that they are traditional owners who can demonstrate spiritual links with their territory, the people of Aurukun and Mornington Island do not possess the same "inalienable freehold title as that given to all the reserve people in the Northern Territory".[45]

The landslide victory of the Hawke Labor government in 1983 rekindled many Aboriginal hopes for uniform federal land rights legislation. However, in spite of the proclamation of the *Aboriginal and Torres Strait Islander Heritage (Interim Protection) Act* in 1984, many Black Australians feel that the government has not been moving rapidly enough to impose its overriding mandate in Aboriginal affairs on recalcitrant states. These fears were reinforced when, in February 1985, the federal Labor government reversed its published land rights policy upholding the right of Aboriginal people to withhold consent to exploration and mining on land returned to them via legislation. The so-called "preferred model" put forward by Canberra met with such staunch opposition from Black Australian groups that, in November 1986, the government abandoned its proposed national land rights legislation. Even after the return of the Hawke government for a third term in July 1987, the Commonwealth has not been able to go further than to issue an official statement "acknowledging that Aborigines and Torres Strait Islanders were the original owners of Australia". But, as Germaine Greer has pointed out, this in itself was not an acceptance of responsibility because "the federal government used a form of words implying the dispossession was done not by Australians, but the British".[46]

Throughout the 1970s and 1980s, Aboriginal Australians have organised as never before to consolidate their gains and to combat those injustices which still remain. Mention has been made of the urban response, in the form of legal and medical services, Aboriginal hostels, and other self-help organisations. Black Australians also worked to an increasing extent within the federal system and came to be represented in the most senior ranks of the bureaucracy: in the Department of Aboriginal Affairs—of which Charles Perkins was appointed Secretary in 1984—the National Aboriginal Conference (NAC), and the Aboriginal Development Commission (ADC), established in 1980. Throughout Western Australia, the Northern Territory, and Queensland, the land councils and their representatives grew in importance as political spokespersons to an even greater extent than organisations created by white administrators, such as the NAC.

More militant blacks have spurned those who have allegedly sold out to the European system by entering such organisations. In fact, following a review, the NAC was disbanded in 1987 and various replacement bodies have been mooted, including an elected national Aboriginal parliamentary assembly.[47]

In spite of the difficulty of gaining a balanced historical perspective upon such recent socio-political happenings, certain major aspects of the Black Australian response to the events of the past twenty-seven years can be isolated. The first relates to protest. Since the days of the Freedom Rides, Aborigines have voiced their dissent clearly, articulately, and often stridently. They have made increasing use of the mass media to express their grievances (and, likewise, the media have made frequent—if sometimes biased—use of Black Australians). By international standards, the protests have been singularly non-violent and—as in the case of the Brisbane demonstrations of 1982 and the huge Sydney rally on Australia Day, 1988—have therefore cultivated sympathetic overseas publicity and support. This leads to the second major aspect of the Black Australian response: its ever-increasing international format.

News of the Gurindji walk-out, of the Tent Embassy, and of the 1980 confrontation which pitted the Aborigines of Noonkanbah, Western Australia against the Amax Petroleum Corporation (and the Western Australian government) went around the airwaves of the world. In addition, Black Australians have made more immediate contact with international bodies than via the media; for example, over the past twenty-seven years a number of petitions have been sent by Aboriginal groups to the United Nations. In September 1980, in the wake of the Noonkanbah dispute, a delegation from the NAC travelled to Geneva for meetings with the United Nations Sub-Commission on the Rights of Minorities. The cultural contacts of artists, dancers, musicians and—of special significance in this context—writers, augmented and complemented these political envoys to many nations throughout the world. The result is that international bodies have been taking a far greater interest in the plight of the Aborigines than ever before. The siting in Canberra of the WCIP's Third General Assembly, and the visit of the World Council of Churches' investigative team, both of which took place in 1981, are just two of the most obvious examples of these international bridges of support and concern.

The third significant aspect of contemporary Black Australian protest relates to a pan-Aboriginal identity. It is no coincidence that all Black Australian demonstrations now incorporate the red, black, and yellow Aboriginal flag, the symbolism of which is derived from the land rights campaign: a campaign begun by the traditional Aborigines of the Northern Territory in the 1960s and now close to the hearts and minds of almost all Black Australians. There is probably no corresponding issue in White Australian society which unites the vast majority of its citizens so fervently. Aboriginal protest predated the land rights campaign as such, but that campaign is now the linch-pin of protest. It is a crusade which is bringing Aborigines of all backgrounds and situations closer together; there is an increasing pan-Aboriginal consensus born of the belief that these are rights owed to every Black Australian. Importantly, this accelerating expression of demands on a national scale now incorporates a marked ideological dimension: of respect for traditional culture, pride in Aboriginality, and awareness of the existence of a symbolic Aboriginal nation. It is in their articulation of this distinctive ideology that Aboriginal writers are making a most noteworthy contribution, both to their own people and to Australian society as a whole.

Of course, not all Aborigines—or even all Black Australian authors—are involved to the same extent in this movement. For the illiterate, poverty-stricken fringe-dweller, slogans may be far less meaningful than the certainty of basic food and shelter, but this does not negate the fact that such Black Australians would benefit greatly from the granting of land rights nationwide. Naturally, too, there are rifts in the Aboriginal movement as there are in most social groups, but these are primarily disagreements over ways and means rather than fundamental differences over ends. To require Black Australians to be unanimous in their views would be to impose an arbitrary and unrealistic expectation upon them which white society would be equally incapable of fulfilling.

Judgements made by European observers often import their own cultural preconceptions. For example, there is often the tendency for a reader dealing with Aboriginal literature to succumb to the eurocentric temptation of evaluating the works solely according to Western literary standards—another form of unreasonable expectation. It is illuminating to compare Black Australian writings with those of certain White Australian authors, but this provides only a partial understanding of the Aboriginal works. In my view, that understanding is really gained from an analysis of Aboriginal literature in its own right; from seeing it as a discrete body of Fourth World literature in which striking themes and concerns emerge. The power and

122 Black Words, White Page

impressiveness of Aboriginal writing stems from the authors' intimate knowledge of their subjects, their strong belief in what they are accomplishing through literature, and their socio-political involvement and awareness. Above all, this strength and distinctiveness derives from their exploration of what it is to be an Aboriginal Australian.

All of the writers to be discussed in the remainder of this study have written and published their work since 1961. It has been a time of rapid social change for Aborigines and of advances in many areas. As Coombs has noted:

> Who ten years ago would have believed that all the major churches in Australia would have appeared almost unanimously as the supporters of Aboriginal land and other rights? Who would have thought that all the major newspapers in Australia would in the last three months have expressed support for land rights and for a movement towards a freely negotiated treaty? These changes represent significant achievements.[48]

However true this may be, the same decade was one of abused confidences and unfulfilled promises in Aboriginal affairs. The most glaring of these centred on the issue of land rights, whether in Aurukun in Queensland, Amadeus in the Northern Territory, or Noonkanbah in Western Australia. Hence, it is not surprising that there is both confidence and pessimism in Aboriginal literature, both optimism and cynicism, as a reflection of this era of progress and frustrated expectations. Underpinning all of these views, there is an awareness that, as the next chapter will illustrate, the Aboriginal present can never be divorced from the Aboriginal past.

Notes

1   C.D. Rowley, *Outcasts in White Australia*, (Canberra, 1971), p. 263.

2   Richard Broome, *Aboriginal Australians: Black Response to White Dominance*, (Sydney, 1982), p. 176.

3   Ronald Taft *et al.*, *Attitudes and Social Conditions*, (Canberra, 1970), p. 31.

4   Hannah Middleton, *But Now We Want the Land Back*, (Sydney, 1977), p. 123.

5   Hannah Middleton, *But Now We Want*, (Sydney, 1977), p. 113.

6   Charles Perkins, *A Bastard Like Me*, (Sydney, 1975), p. 74.

7   *ibid.*, p. 76.

8   *ibid*, p. 80.

9   Frank Hardy, *The Unlucky Australians*, (Sydney, 1968).

10 C.D. Rowley, *Outcasts in White Australia*, (Canberra, 1971), p. 406.

11 Rowley,*Outcasts*, p. 384.

12 Middleton, *But Now We Want the Land Back*, p. 117.

13 Lyndall Ryan, "Federal Policies in the Seventies", in Erik Olbrei, ed., *Black Australians: The Prospects for Change*, (Townsville, 1982), p. 35.

14 Milirrpum v. Nabalco Pty. Ltd., *Federal Law Reports*, (Supreme Court of N.T., 1971), p. 252.

15 ibid., p. 243. (Here, Blackburn was quoting the Judicial Committee's ruling, on appeal from the Supreme Court of New South Wales, in the case of Cooper v. Stuart, 1889, p. 286).

16 For example, see such examinations of the historical tenacity of Aboriginal resistance as Fergus Robinson and Barry York, eds, *The Black Resistance*, (Sydney, 1975), and Henry Reynolds, *The Other Side of the Frontier*, (Ringwood, 1982). Nevertheless, it must be admitted that, in eighteenth century terms, the annexation was both legal and normal. For a discussion of this issue, see Alan Frost, "New South Wales as *Terra Nullius*: The British Denial of Aboriginal Land Rights", *Historical Studies*, vol. 19, no. 77, October 1981, pp. 513-523.

17 Milirrpum v. Nabalco, p. 244.

18 ibid., pp. 202-203.

19   Bobbi Sykes, *MumShirl: An Autobiography*, (Richmond Vic., 1981), p. 74.

20   Ann Turner, ed., *Black Power in Australia: Bobbi Sykes versus Senator Neville T. Bonner*, (South Yarra, Vic., 1975), p. 60.

21   Rowley, *A Matter of Justice*, (Canberra, 1978), p. 2.

22   Quoted in Kevin Gilbert, *"Because A White Man'll Never Do It"*, (Sydney, 1973), p. 29.

23   Noel Loos and Jane Thomson, "Black Resistance Past and Present: An Overview", in Olbrei, ed., *Black Australians: The Prospects for Change*, p. 28.

24   Quoted in Gilbert, *"Because"*, p. 29.

25   See Paul Coe's comments, quoted in *ibid.*, p. 29.

26   Gilbert, *"Because"*, p. 30.

27   Gilbert, *ibid.*, p. 28.

28   Middleton, *But Now We Want*, p. 160.

29   Gilbert, *"Because"*, p. 28.

30   Quoted in Kevin Gilbert, *Living Black: Blacks Talk to Kevin Gilbert*, (Ringwood, Vic., 1978), p. 207.

31   Broome, *Aboriginal Australians*, p. 185.

32   Gilbert, *"Because"*, p. 67.

33   Quoted in Gilbert, *Living Black*, p. 218.

34   Daniel Vachon and Phillip Toyne, "Mining and the Challenge of Land Rights", in Peterson and Langton, eds, *Aborigines, Land, and Land Rights*, (Canberra, 1983), p. 307.

35   Broome, *Aboriginal Australians*, p. 188.

36   Broome, *ibid.*, p. 188.

37   Broome, *ibid.*, p. 190.

38   Lyndall Ryan, "Federal Policies in the Seventies", in Olbrei, ed., *Black Australians: The Prospects for Change*, p. 36.

39   *ibid.*, p. 37.

40   The Northern Territory government's pamphlet, *Draft Proposals on Aboriginals and Land in the Northern Territory*, (Darwin, 1982). The emphasis is mine.

41   The *Pitjantjatjara Land Rights Act*, no. 20 of 1981.

42   Stan Pelczynski, "Land Rights Supplement", *Action for Aboriginal Rights Newsletter*, no. 22, 1987, pp. 2-5.

43   "Land Rights—The Story So Far", *Land Rights News*, September 1985, p. 9.

44   Bob Collins, "Land Rights in the Northern Territory", in Olbrei, ed., *Black*

Australians: The Prospects for Change, p. 46.

45   Harris, "*It's Coming Yet* ... ", p. 51.

46   Germaine Greer, "Time to Party, or Protest", The *Independent*, 4 January, 1988, p. 15.

47   Anne Jamieson, "The Push for an Aboriginal Parliament", The *Weekend Australian*, 6-7 February, 1988, p. 24.

48   Dr H.C. Coombs, "Commentary", in Olbrei, ed., *Black Australians: The Prospects for Change* , p. 38.

6

Views of Australian History in Aboriginal Literature

In some ways, Australians are now more preoccupied with their own past than they have been at any other stage in their history. As the recent spate of feature films dealing with Australian heroes and legends attests,[1] the history of such domestic and international endeavours caters to a wide popular audience. During 1988, the bicentennial of the British invasion, the emphasis upon Australian achievements of the past has naturally increased and there is a considerable amount of glorification of many of those events. It is ironic that this trend towards the honouring of the country's history occurs at a time when probably more Australians than ever before feel a sense of guilt and responsibility over their ancestors' treatment of Black Australians. Among this group there seems to be a wide acceptance of the viewpoint expressed by Shane Howard in his best-selling song, "Solid Rock (Sacred Ground)":

> They were standin' on the shore one day
> Saw the white sails in the sun.
> Wasn't long before they felt the sting
>   White man—White law—White gun
> Don't tell me that it's justified
>   'Cause somewhere—
>   Someone lied.[2]

If many Australians identify with this feeling of guilty responsibility, there are equally many others who not only laud their own history and heritage, but also insist that Aborigines should become more tolerant and forgiving of past injustices. This attitude naturally irks many Black Australians for, in the words of Jack Davis:

I really think the majority of Australians are just buffoons. They tell us to forgive and forget what's happened in the past. Then, every Anzac day, they glorify their own history. How are we supposed to forget what's happened to us *in Australia* when White Australians keep on remembering their own violent history elsewhere? Besides, we have a lot more to remember right here.[3]

As is the case with many other historically oppressed indigenous minority groups throughout the world, the memories of Black Australians are often very long and very bitter. Kevin Gilbert considers this to be unavoidable, and he feels that Aboriginal writers should not shy away from examining the past, even if it produces resentment:

An onus is on Aboriginal writers to present the evidence of our true situation. In attempting to present the evidence we are furiously attacked by white Australians and white converts, whatever their colour, as 'Going back 200 years … the past is finished …!' Yet, cut off a man's leg, kill his mother, rape his land, psychologically attack and keep him in a powerless position each day—does it not live on in the mind of the victim? Does it not continue to scar and affect the thinking? Deny it, but it still exists. [4]

Aboriginal writers have, for the most part, heeded Gilbert's advice. A preoccupation with the theme of past injustice and an emphasis upon the concept of a venerable, autonomous, Aboriginal history is present in almost all Black Australian literature, regardless of the genre of expression.

There are a number of reasons for this preoccupation. One of these is the desire to give an Aboriginal version of post-contact history, to rectify what blacks see as distortions by European authors and historians. As Gerry Bostock writes, in his poem "Black Children":

The white man settled this vast country;
Cleared the land;
Built a great nation democratic and free,
And they looked after you, their friends,
Our brothers, the Aborigine.

They had to protect you, care for you,
They gave you a home
Or you would have died of disease
Or starved if they left you to roam …

These are the lies
Of our white Judas brother;
He has taught us deceit

And contempt for one another
And watched amused
As we grovelled for fresh air
Under his racist care;
Derelict and abused.[5]

However, Black Australian views of history are not always as confrontationist or as polemical as in this example. The theme of the precontact past can be invoked in order to emphasise other factors, such as the longevity and continuity of Aboriginal residence in Australia. In this vein, Oodgeroo Noonuccal writes:

Let no one say the past is dead.
The past is all about us and within.
Haunted by tribal memories, I know
This little now, this accidental present
Is not the all of me, whose long making
Is so much of the past ...

A thousand thousand camp fires in the forest
Are in my blood.
Let none tell me the past is wholly gone.
Now is so small a part of time, so small a part
of all the race years that have moulded me.[6]

Moreover, in her poem "Stone Age", Noonuccal uses the concept of past eons as a symbol of the potential reconciliation of Black and White Australians:

White superior race, only time is between us—
As some are grown up and others yet children.
We are the last of the Stone Age tribes,
Waiting for time to help us
As time helped you.[7]

Another approach which Aboriginal writers employ is to focus upon Black Australian history, in order to establish Aboriginal pride in indigenous heroes and heroines of former generations. As Gilbert illustrates, the problem is one of both historical ignorance and purposeful neglect:

Ask white or black Australian kids to name a heroic Red Indian chief or a famous Indian tribe and most will be able to do so because of comics and films. Ask them to name an Aboriginal hero or a famous Aboriginal tribe and they will not be able to do so because Aboriginal history is either unknown or negative. [8]

Thus, what Aboriginal writers like Colin Johnson are attempting to do in novels such as *Long Live Sandawara* is to fill this cultural void with positive historical images of Black Australians. Again, this desire to counteract the negative image with which Aborigines have been associated in most European histories—if they have been described in any detail at all—finds expression in other genres of Black Australian writing. For example, Maureen Watson writes:

> "Aboriginaland", yes, your birthright,
> No matter what some name it;
> So dig your fingers deep in the soil,
> And feel it, and hold it, and claim it.
> Your people fought and died for this,
> Tho' history books distort it all,
> But in your veins runs that same Aboriginal blood,
> So walk tall, my child, walk tall ... [9]

Finally, in some of their most recent writing, certain Aboriginal writers are expressing their race's past in the present by drawing on distinctive and sometimes traditional modes of black oral narration in their works.

In this chapter, a number of Black Australian literary approaches to the past will be examined: the usage of singular and venerable black narrative structures, the attempt to explore the lives of heroic Aboriginal figures of the past, and the revisionist view of Australian history which conveys, for the first time, an Aboriginal interpretation of past events. Black Australian literary views of history are primarily concerned with an illustration of the lives of Aborigines, but it is inescapable that, in an alternative assessment of the Australian post-contact past, these writers should engage themselves with white historical figures and European "myths" as well. This does not result in objectivity or dispassionate writing. It does mean that, in their eagerness to counterbalance the bias of previous white interpretations of the continent's black/white interracial history, Black Australians sometimes run the risk of over-compensating by positing equally biased and contentious versions of past events.[10] This is to be expected, for the literary search for a viable black history signifies an Aboriginal effort to establish racial facts and fictions at least equal in stature to those of White Australia.

Since 1788, Aborigines have frequently been engulfed in a cloud of historical ignorance born of the eurocentric bias of most Australian historians, a bias which did not begin to be counteracted until the past twenty years. Only during the past decade have historians such as Henry Reynolds, in his *Aborigines and Settlers* and *The Other Side of the Frontier*,[11] shown the wealth of knowledge which can be gained from an attempt to understand the Australian past from an Aboriginal standpoint. As W.E.H. Stanner put it in his fifth Boyer Lecture of the *After the Dreaming* series in 1968:

> It has seemed to me for some years that two aspects of the Aboriginal struggle have been under-valued. One is their continued will to survive, the other their continued effort to come to terms with us ... There are many, perhaps too many, theories about *our* troubles with the aborigines. We can spare a moment to consider *their* theory about *their* troubles with us. [12]

One of the damaging results of the "cult of forgetfulness" which Stanner describes was that Aborigines became little more than "a melancholy footnote"[13] to Australian history. Another was that what was done to Black Australians by Europeans was often conveniently ignored or glossed over—and much of this was, as we now know, extremely brutal. Of course, in many ways Australia was founded by the British upon the principle of organised, systematic brutality in the form of convictism; a form of institutionalised violence which has been penetrated very effectively by Australian authors as diverse as Marcus Clarke and Thomas Keneally. I will return to the theme of violence as it pertains to Aborigines and Australian society in the next chapter. What is significant here is that the near-invisibility of blacks in Australian historiography masked for so long the fact that Aborigines and Europeans held radically different views of what actually happened in Australian black/white interracial history. Only very recently has this Aboriginal version of historical events come to the fore.

It has not done so in a conventional way, for even today there are very few Aboriginal historians, and those such as Phillip Pepper and Robert Bropho have written books which can be considered not only as family histories but as socio-political analyses of oppression.[14] The number of Aboriginal histories written by Black Australians will definitely increase in the future, as writers like Wayne Atkinson produce further work. But the question remains, "What other sources exist for the tapping of Aboriginal history?". The oral history approach is often fruitful, and there is no doubt that much work remains to be done in this field, despite the completion of projects such as Read's oral history of the Wiradjuri people of New South Wales. As Kevin Gilbert's eclectic *Living Black* has proven, this is a very fertile area for Aboriginal involvement.

However, even in the case of Aboriginal oral history gathered by

Black Australians, there are inherent limitations to the accuracy and comprehensiveness of the technique. In spite of Gilbert's ground-breaking contribution to the oral method, which showed just how much could be revealed by Black Australians responding to the questions of other Black Australians, the author was perceptive enough to realise that his information-gathering approach was restricted in a fundamental way. One of Gilbert's interviewees, Kate Lansborough, explained that: "there were some other things I could tell you, but I don't think I'd better put them on this tape. Personal things that happened when I was little".[15] Even when being interviewed by another Aborigine, Lansborough felt inhibited by the technology of tape recording and by the awareness of possible publication of her words. This sort of reticence is almost certainly further compounded when relatively unknown white researchers attempt to secure personal interviews with Aboriginal people. This is not to deny the worth of oral historical projects; in the search for the Black Australian viewpoint, these projects are in many ways superior to a reliance upon official governmental and institutional records of Aboriginal affairs. Nevertheless, it must be recognised that the technique does have inbuilt restrictions.

Then it still must be asked, "Is there any other source of knowledge into the post-contact Aboriginal past?". The answer is an affirmative one, and in it lies one of the most significant aspects of Aboriginal literature: its historical dimension. It is not surprising to discover that Aboriginal autobiographies and political treatises have a marked historical perspective. They often illustrate the effects of coercive government policies upon the individual narrator and, by extension, upon the Black Australians of the time. It is perhaps more unexpected to find how significant and revealing Aboriginal creative writing dealing with historical themes can be.

Even with an increase in histories written by Black Australians (both those of a more conventional type and those derived from oral information), this will continue to be the case. For, when compared with white historical literature, Aboriginal historical novels and plays frequently offer strikingly different interpretations of past events—and do this in a stylistically unique fashion. In addition, oral material can be incorporated into Aboriginal creative writing at least as effectively as it can be into histories written by Black Australians. Aboriginal authors can thereby tap the huge wellspring of the oral tradition—a source which is as rich as it is foreign to European culture—and the use of such sources renders Aboriginal writing even more culturally independent from White Australian literature.

Much seems to depend upon the genre which a Black Australian author chooses to explore. For example, Aboriginal short stories have tended to be modelled upon the European format and, despite their frequent Black Australian themes and concerns, have not demonstrated links with traditional black oral literature—which is one of the main reasons why they are not examined here. On the other hand, while no Aboriginal novelist has yet fully succeeded in incorporating the rhythms and atmosphere of such oral material into his or her work, Colin Johnson has made progress in this direction in his most recent novel, *Doctor Wooreddy's Prescription for Enduring the Ending of the World*. It is in the genres of poetry and drama that some black authors have truly made this oral connection. These are the works in which Aboriginal literature breaks truly new ground in terms of both style and content: in a very real sense, this is an expression of the historical in the contemporary. I will return to an examination of the overall distinctiveness of Black Australian poetry in Chapter Eight. In this chapter, I emphasise the historical theme in several prominent Aboriginal plays and novels, some of which demonstrate this identifiable link with the black oral tradition.

The link is clearest in some Aboriginal drama, such as Jack Davis's play *The Dreamers*. Unlike some of Davis's other plays, such as *Kullark* and *No Sugar*, *The Dreamers* is not set in the past. Nevertheless, while not obviously historical in the temporal sense, it is strongly imbued with the sense of a specifically Aboriginal history. This is as a result of the *Nyoongah* language used throughout, the reminiscences of the old Aboriginal, Worru, and the strong Black Australian atmosphere established by the dream dances and didgeridoo music which bracket various scenes. However, the play is also consciously and overtly Black Australian in the contemporary sense, depicting the lifestyle of a typical Aboriginal urban household in the 1980s. Moreover, the almost entirely Aboriginal cast, setting and recollections, and the ever-present *Nyoongah* represent a challenge to the white theatre-goer and provide a unifying, contemporary sense of identification for Black Australians in the audience. Thus, in order to understand *The Dreamers*, it is important to realise that it portrays the Aboriginal past *preserved in* the present in a distinctive, memorable and entertaining fashion.

The play makes it clear that the current social problems and demoralisation of the Wallitch family have long historical roots. The past and present are intermingled very skilfully in the character of

Worru, as are memories both happy and sad. In short, Davis blends the two times through the play's structure, atmosphere and language; throughout, that language is rhythmically and colloquially Black Australian:

WORRU: Yeah, big mob, all go to Mogumber, big mob, 'ad to walk. Toodjay, Yarawindi, New Norcia. Summertime too. Can't go back to Northam, no *Nyoongahs. Kia.* I runned away with Melba. [*Laughing.*] Jumped the train at Gillingarra. Went back to Northam [*miming handcuffs*] *manadtj* got me at the Northam Show. Put me in gaol, Fremantle, for a long time. When I went back to settlement Roy was born, [*gesturing*] this big, *kia* [*laughing*] little fella.16

As this extract reveals, elements of personal memories, the *Nyoongah* language and Aboriginal history are cleverly integrated in a mutually supportive, yet unobtrusive, fashion. Davis has many natural talents which he applies through his plays to an exploration of his own heritage. For example, in interview he explained the source of his theatrical technique:

It's not too long since we were introduced to television and all that type of thing and when we lived in the Bush we had our own way of doing these things ourselves, so, that's why it's not too difficult for me to find an Aboriginal theme.17

What makes Davis's drama so distinctive and so important in historical terms is the unique Aboriginal lens through which he views these events. The legacy of the Black Australian past emerges in the way the speech is constructed as much as it does through the content of that speech. In short, *The Dreamers* is steeped in Black Australian history, even when Davis is not writing about the past.

Perhaps the best way to illustrate the singular characteristics of Davis's dramatic technique is to briefly compare his plays with Robert Merritt's, *The Cake Man*, an example of Aboriginal drama with a precise historical setting. It is noteworthy that the historical atmosphere of Merritt's play is established by its locale and action far more than by its dialogue. *The Cake Man* is a very impressive play in many respects, and represents a strong indictment of the New South Wales Aboriginal reserves (popularly called missions) as they were thirty years ago. One of the most important themes in *The Cake Man* is a religious one. The Aboriginal father, Sweet William, declaims bitterly against Christianity, which is totally foreign to him:

Rube, my missus, she's always thankin' Christ for everythin' ... anythin' ... nothin' Her an' that fuckin' book. [*With a laugh*] She heard me say that, I'd be in strife

Christian she is, my old lady, a mission Chrishyun, the worst kind. [18]

The play is patently anti-missionary and, therefore, against forced conversion. In Merritt's view, the Church has buttressed the efforts of government to remove all the authority of Aboriginal men: together the two have, in figurative terms, emasculated them. Laments the [not so] Sweet William:

> But, Rube, there ain't nothin' now I know to do. Just hopeless, and no price I can pay because there ain't no price I've got to give that anyone wants. *I've got nothing they want!* [19]

This is a vital historical comment. The wife and mother, Ruby, is the one who literally holds the family together—not her husband. Her greater strength of purpose is due to her religious devotion; Christianity is an essential prop or solace. But, as Merritt sees it, this interpretation is false, for he feels that the Bible enjoins her to be passive—to accept God's lot unquestioningly—and this ensures that she will never escape the mission system. He feels very strongly that Christianity has been:

> the most destructive force that has ever hit the Aboriginal people. And, to be quite truthful—I mean it's sad to say this— ... I think that if religion *has* enabled them to survive for 200 years they probably would have been better off ... being killed, wiped out, annihilated ... You can't even say it's Christian charity; it's a sick interpretation of a sad political philosophy. [20]

The Cake Man is an historical play which makes pointed comments about black/white interracial history in Australia. The key point is that, unlike Davis, Merritt does not use the black oral tradition to convey this sense of the Aboriginal past. For example, in the overtly historical opening scene of the play, the author relies upon caricature—the symbolic stereotyping of the Priest, Soldier and Civilian and the Aboriginal Man, Woman, and Child—to satirise rather heavy-handedly the combined forces of "God and Gun". There is no Aboriginal dialogue at all here (the black characters are either dumbfounded or dead in this scene). The music is not Aboriginal but is, instead, a re-working of the Bing Crosby tune "There's A Happy Land Somewhere". In short, the first scene is predominantly white in speech, content, and action.

Merritt's technique of surrounding the main section of the play with two monologues delivered by Sweet William is also one derived from the European theatre (although he does incorporate a re-telling of the legend of the "Emu and the Curlew" in the first of these, and a

description of the "Eurie woman" in the second). In *The Cake Mar*
Merritt has skilfully appropriated the techniques of Western theatre
in his first dramatic work. Unlike Davis's drama, the language of
Merritt's play never presents a challenge to white members of the
audience. It caters more to European theatrical conventions and is
generally more accessible to non-Aborigines as a result. Admittedly
Davis also bows to some of these conventions but he pushes his
drama further from European expectations, into a realm of greater
overall originality.

Of course, there is a certain amount of tension between the socio-
economic constraints of the Australian theatre—part of the Western
dramatic tradition—and all Aboriginal drama. Not only is there often
a gap between the largely affluent white audience and the black
poverty depicted on stage, but the high price of admission to most
venues makes it impossible for the majority of Aborigines to view
these works, at least in major centres. On the other hand, live theatre
can be taken on tour to small towns and Aboriginal settlements, and
has the potential for conversion into public "street" performances,
which would reach even poor, illiterate Black Australians
Unfortunately, the same cannot be said of Aboriginal novels in
English: the genre dictates, if anything, an even more restricted
Aboriginal audience. It is therefore clear that if Black Australian novelists had to rely for sales solely upon Aboriginal purchasers of their
works, publishers would rarely, if ever, accept their manuscripts. At
least at this juncture, it can be taken as given that Aboriginal novelists
must rely to a great extent upon white funding bodies, publishers
and readers in order to make their way into print.

It is therefore interesting to observe that in his second and third
novels, *Long Live Sandawara* and *Doctor Wooreddy's Prescription for
Enduring the Ending of the World*, Colin Johnson claims to be making a
conscious attempt to write in a style which is more accessible to
Aborigines. With reference to the genesis of Aboriginal literature in
English, these are both very significant texts which merit detailed
analysis in a number of areas. The novels include historical treatments of pivotal episodes in the Aboriginal post-contact past. In
Sandawara and *Wooreddy* Johnson endeavours to counterbalance years
of white bias in the interpretation of these historical events. A close
examination of the books reveals that he only partially succeeds in
this aim: a careful comparison of the two with historical novels by
White Australians reveals that his stated aims of accessibility to fel-
low-blacks and autonomy from white literary influence are, at least in

the case of *Sandawara*, partially subverted by his historical and literary method.

In order to understand what Johnson was trying to emphasise in *Sandawara*, it is necessary to briefly consider the historiography of Aboriginal resistance to the European incursion into Australia. In writing the novel, the author was attempting to overturn the dominant notion, widely held in Australian society until very recently, that the Aboriginal people offered no meaningful resistance to the white invasion of their continent. According to this popular view, such opposition as did arise was not only sporadic and short-lived but also disorganised and decidedly ineffective. Only during the past decade have Australian historians begun to re-examine, and to challenge, the myth of Aboriginal passivity. As one of the foremost of these revisionist historians—Henry Reynolds—has stated:

> Recent confrontations at Noonkanbah and Arukun [sic] are not isolated incidents but outcrops of a long range of experience reaching back to the beginnings of European settlement ... The much noted actions of rebel colonists are trifling in comparison. The Kellys and their kind, even the Eureka diggers and Vinegar Hill convicts, are diminished when measured against the hundreds of clans who fought frontier settlers for well over a century.21

One of the most striking episodes of Black Australian resistance took place in the Kimberley district of Western Australia where, for three years, a former police tracker named Sandamara22 led a concerted rebellion against white pastoral expansion. Sandamara carefully organised his resistance movement: taking advantage of European firearms and supplies, he adopted guerilla tactics which, on a number of occasions, were more than a match for his white opponents.

The exploits of Sandamara and his men have, until very recently, been largely ignored by white historians. To this day, the only published and readily available treatment of the insurrection by a White Australian is an historical novel, *Outlaws of the Leopolds*, by Ion L. Idriess.23 This fact was made abundantly clear when, in his Honours thesis dealing with Sandamara, Howard Pedersen observed that the rebel was almost entirely neglected in studies of Western Australian Aboriginal history. Pedersen concluded, "a novel, written in 1952 by Ion Idriess, is the only major piece of writing devoted to the subject".24 This statement is ironic, because Pedersen was either total unaware of, or chose to ignore, Johnson's *Long Live Sandawara*, which was published in 1979, one year before the appearance of his thesis. Whether this omission was intentional or not, it is ironic that the contemporary achievement of an Aboriginal Australian was thrown into the shadow of neglect in a study which was casting light on an historical Aboriginal achievement eclipsed by the same shadow.

In view of this historical vacuum concerning Sandawara, the importance of both Idriess's and Johnson's novels becomes very clear. At the outset, one would expect the two novels to be very different. They are separated by a quarter-century of socio-political changes; the two authors come from vastly dissimilar cultural backgrounds; and they emphasise quite different aspects of the clash between Sandamara and his followers and the white authorities. Idriess, naturally aiming his book at a white reading audience, emphasises not only the threat which the wily and dangerous Aboriginal leader presented but also, in particular, the courage, tenacity and cleverness of the police patrols which hunted him down. In a prefatory note he commented, "But for the ceaseless work of the hard-riding police patrols he would have caused a lot of white tragedy in our Australian Kimberleys",[25] with a noteworthy emphasis on the word "our". Indeed, his final line in this introduction was a somewhat wistful *adieu*: "And so, farewell to the 'Days of the Big Patrols' "(p. 8).

Colin Johnson obviously had another aim in mind when he wrote his novel, for he has stated that it was directed at an Aboriginal readership far more than his first book, *Wild Cat Falling*. In his words, "This was a conscious decision. Even the style is as non-intellectual as possible. I didn't want words getting in the way of the action and the argumentation". *Long Live Sandawara* is also a far more stylistically experimental book, one half being written in the contemporary inner-city slang of the Perth slums, and the other in far more grand and imagistic language. Johnson explained the reason for this dual structure as follows:

> It was two stories right from the beginning, in order to relieve the tedium of the modern novel. Also, it is very difficult in Western Australia not to write about modern times when you're writing about the past.[26]

Whereas Idriess is lauding, above all, the valour of the Kimberley law enforcers, Johnson's emphasis is patently upon the heroism of Sandamara, and the style of his historical segment was deliberately adopted with this consideration in mind. As he put it, "Very few Aboriginals know of this Aboriginal hero. That is why this part of the book is written in an epic style".[27] Whether or not this consciously-chosen style accurately reflects the meaning which Johnson hoped to convey is a more thorny question.

From the first word, the two books are at variance structurally and stylistically. As was noted in Chapter Two, Idriess, the inveterate outback raconteur, utilises hyperbole, hyperbolic punctuation (exclamation marks are ubiquitous) and animal imagery, to achieve the desired atmosphere of drama commensurate with the clash of civilised and loyal white man against primitive and depraved Aboriginal man. Near the beginning of the novel, Constable Richardson—who is later murdered by Sandamara when he commences his rebellion—inspects his black prisoners, suspecting that they are concocting a plan to break loose from their chains. The language is very revealing:

> His mind now obsessed by a file, he stepped down from the verandah to again examine the chain, grimly conscious that his "tigers" knew more of local conditions and happenings than he did, now that he was alone and Pigeon and Captain were away. Stone Age men! but cunning as a bagful of monkeys (p. 10).

The equation of the animal and Aboriginal worlds is repeatedly emphasised throughout the novel. The black men are devious, stealthy, and treacherous, but all the while somehow less than human—or so the imagery implies. For example, one chapter is typically entitled, "Caught Like Rats In A Trap", and when Sandamara discovers a means of escape from the cave whose mouth the police are guarding, his "eyes gleamed exultantly, his mouth widened in a long-drawn, animal-like whimper of joy"(p. 160). His men start digging their escape route "with deep hisses and low, guttural growls"(p. 161) while outside a constable berates a black "boy" with the words, "You've got less brains than a porcupine" ... "And stop that hyena laughter" ... "or I'll chuck you down the cave"(p. 156). There appears to be little doubt that Idriess was, at heart, a white supremacist. To add insult to Aboriginal injury, the tone of his entire novel conveys the impression that it is historically accurate adventure reportage. The impression of historical scholarship is conveyed by the the author's preface, which quotes references to numerous Police Department reports, the inclusion of a score of photographs of an anthropological nature intermittently throughout the text, and the author's assertion that he had consulted "aboriginal friends" who obliged with "big-feller talk"(p. *vi*) concerning the days of Sandamara and his guerilla fighters. Considering that Idriess travelled through the area and completed his research on Sandamara half a century after the events took place, he surely does not have a monopoly on historical veracity.

By the same token, neither does Colin Johnson, but what is beyond doubt is that his view of the significance of Sandamara's deeds is vastly different from that of Idriess. In his case the imagery is indicative of the goal which Johnson hoped to achieve by writing the novel. Idriess discovered in the Sandamara episode the potential for a fast-paced adventure story which was thoroughly Australian, and then proceeded to write one; a pattern of discovery and description which he repeated more than twenty times throughout his career. He continually subverts the potential heroism of Sandawara in the novel by emphasising the element of the chase: while the fox receives our sympathy during the hunt, he is not meant to win any more than grudging admiration. On the other hand, Johnson had a cogent personal and social aim in mind when he wrote *Long Live Sandawara*. The former goal was the attempt to rediscover his own roots in Western Australia after a seven-year absence from the country. The latter aim was an attempt to inculcate a sense of Aboriginal pride in those Black Australians who read the book: to cultivate the awareness of an Aboriginal history which included indigenous heroes and leaders, who had fought and died for their cause. The imagery, especially of the historical portion of the novel, is indicative of these aspirations. It is powerful, resonant, and fluid:

> All the land moves, whirling like a cyclone, and the eye of the storm is this man, Sandawara, who sits apart from the others, his mind weighing the odds and thinking only of the final victory.[28]

In the Idriess version of the events, Sandamara is calculating, cunning and warlike, but he is still a mere mortal. However, Johnson describes him as a quasi-supernatural figure, a *maban* or shaman with magical powers:

> The men collect at the water's edge and nearby they see a soft rainbow light pulsating without strength from a dark figure. It is Sandawara. The men creep towards their leader and the strange roar dies away leaving only the sound of the rain and wind and thunder. Beyond them, the fires sizzle out. A lightning flash strikes a tree right next to where Sandawara is sitting and the fire runs down the trunk. In amazement and fear they seem to see a huge serpent wrapped about the body of their leader. It writhes about his body (p. 82).

Above all, Sandamara is what Kevin Gilbert has termed a black "patriot",[29] who feels at one even with the Aboriginal trackers who pursue him and ultimately chase him to earth. He dies, not bitterly gasping and cursing the trackers, as in the Idriess novel(p. 239), but poignantly and serenely:

> At last the trackers gingerly approach the fallen figure and circle it. They edge in and

stand looking down. The white men are far off. The black men stare at their fallen brother and watch as he stirs and gets into a sitting position. 'Brothers, the white man can never take what I have', he gently murmurs, then falls back into freedom (p. 166).

The alteration in the character of Sandamara, and the new exhortatory and educative role he is given are both equally clear.

It must be remembered that only one half of *Sandawara* is an historical novel. The other half is terse in style, urban in environment, often humorous in characterisation, and frequently sexual in pre-occupation. It is also very much concerned with the concept of Aboriginal patriotism. Sandawara as an historical figure is ever-present: as a role model for Alan, the sixteen year-old leader of the group, as an inspirational poster on the wall, and as a memory in the mind of the old, downtrodden Aboriginal elder, Noorak, who becomes Alan's link with his past and with his heritage. The parallel structure of revolution which is established, serious in the historical episode and comical—until the final gruesome chapter—in the contemporary segment, is very successful. According to the author, despite the blood-bath at the end of the modern segment (which indicates the futility of armed rebellion in Australia), the salient aspect is that Alan—the new "Sandawara"—survives, to become a fully-initiated Aboriginal patriot and himself an inspiration for the future.[30]

Therefore, both halves of Johnson's *Sandawara* differ stylistically from Idriess's *Outlaws*. The contemporary section of Johnson's book portrays very accurately the dialogue, speech patterns and environment of urban Aborigines, and it is this segment of the novel which is most evidently directed at an empathic Aboriginal readership. However, despite Johnson's claim that the style of the historical half of *Sandawara* is intentionally of epic proportions, Stephen Muecke correctly points out that his adoption of a mode of description appropriate to a romantic novel of the Western tradition could alienate potential Black Australian readers. In short, if Johnson is intending his book first and foremost as an inspiration for other Aborigines, he may in this way be defeating his own purpose. As Muecke puts it, in this section "Pigeon the historical figure disappears, to be replaced by a romantic hero. The position of the reader shifts once more. We (as readers) need no longer be white or Aboriginal".[31]

It is hardly surprising to find differences in the approach of Idriess and Johnson. What *is* surprising, and is perhaps a cause for some critical concern, is the similarity in content which becomes apparent upon a close reading of the two texts. It must be emphasised again that although the version Idriess provides of Sandamara's exploits is only one interpretation of history (based largely upon Police Department records in Western Australia) other historical sources can be unearthed and other interpretations can be put forward, as Pedersen has shown. Yet, it is patently clear that, like many others, Johnson has used Idriess as his primary historical source. It is ironic that an Aboriginal author, who popularises a Black Australian resistance fighter and advocates close ties with traditional Aboriginal society, has allowed the work of a racially prejudiced White Australian writer to be his major factual wellspring.

It is true that Johnson and Idriess highlight different aspects of the Sandamara legend. For example, in the earlier novel, Sandamara's close ties with his mother and with his woman, Cangamvara, are repeatedly emphasised. Johnson does not note the first relationship at all and gives only glancing emphasis to the second. In the Idriess book, Sandamara's death spells the end of the rebellion, which is viewed as a disturbing aberration from the norm, presumably, of Aboriginal passivity. In the later novel, the hero's death is part of a continuum of Aboriginal resistance against white invasion. However, similarities of plot present themselves repeatedly in the two books. In both novels, Sandamara and his accomplice, Captain, are incited to revolt by their prisoner, Ellemara, who allegedly has a supernatural power of suggestion. In both, after killing the settlers Burke and Gibbs and taking over their supplies, Sandamara permits his men to open and consume the white men's casks of liquor (and an orgy of violence ensues) and the battle of Windjina Gorge is described in very similar terms in both books. In fact, on one occasion, Johnson seems to have come very close to plagiarising from the earlier novel, as the following two extracts reveal, the first from Idriess:

'Ah!' Pigeon would chuckle, 'it is because they love me so. They are always chasing me, they want me to be always with them—in a little hole in the ground. They will plant you too like that when they catch you, so that you can never get away again. So take care and cover your tracks, always remember that your tracks are leading you to a little hole in the ground. Never take a chance, always cover your tracks. Otherwise they might track you while you sleep. And you will wake up with lead in your guts!'(p. 168).

Johnson's language is almost identical:

He listens to his men and chuckles and says: 'Those white fellows really love me. They run after me all the time and how can I say "no" to them. They love me so much that they want me to be with them for ever—in a little hole in the ground with no way out. You better watch out that they don't start loving you and come chasing after you. They want you just a little now, and once they catch you, you'll never be free of them.' His voice hisses, then echoes on: 'So take care and always cover your tracks. Always be on your guard and be sure that no tracks lead towards your refuge in the earth. Never leave a mark for them to follow; never sleep with both eyes closed, or one day you'll sleep on with lead in your guts' (p. 144).

Aside from any ethical considerations which the above extracts might raise, does it matter that the historical segment of Johnson's novel is derivative? In a number of ways, it does. First, the fact that a Black Australian appears to confirm the accuracy of a significant portion of the Idriess novel has important consequences. Not only is one far less likely to question the veracity of the description in *Outlaws of the Leopolds*, but the reliability of the sources Idriess has used remain equally unchallenged. In short, no alternative historical sources are contemplated. Yet as Pedersen relates, Aboriginal oral history paints a very different picture of Sandamara's defection from the police to a life of armed rebellion. According to oral tradition, the hero was himself a magic man, or *maban* (as Johnson notes) but he was not suddenly swayed to revolt against white authority by the persuasive, quasi-hypnotic influence of Ellemara. Rather, Sandamara killed Constable Richardson and liberated his prisoners because of tribal obligation: he had slept with many of the men's wives and had to make reparations; the discharge of those obligations necessitated the murder.[32]

This is a far cry from the spontaneous conversion spawned by Ellemara, which Idriess suggests and Johnson accepts. After all, if Ellemara had possessed that kind of sway over Sandamara, it is logical to assume that the former—not the latter—would have been the leader of the insurrection. At the very least, the rapidity with which contacts were made with tribes throughout the Kimberleys, the speed with which action was taken by Sandamara and his newly-liberated men, and the organised, military style of the leader's tactics, all suggest, as Pedersen has pointed out, a premeditated plan of attack, whatever the motive.[33]

Even if Pedersen's theory is accepted, it may not seem obvious what this has to do with Aboriginal literature. The answer lies in the fact that, in the field of black/white race relations writing in Australia, literature and history are very closely related. Mention has been made of the slowly emerging trend of white historians to examine Aboriginal history in its own right. In the absence of such study, literary works such as those of Idriess are often assumed to be a motherlode of accurate historical material. Such an assumption is quite misleading; such fiction is never factual, nor is there any requirement for it to be so. Yet by the same token, it is arguable that some degree of historical accuracy does matter in such cases, for otherwise readers absorb ideas and prejudices in good faith without realising that the book they have put their trust in is only one version of the truth. No historical novel is value-free, and those of Idriess are no exception. The derogatory attitudes towards Aborigines which are evident in *Outlaws of the Leopolds* are echoed in statements which Idriess made about Black Australians on other occasions. At best, his attitude is highly ambivalent:

> Never become too familiar with the Abo, but treat him in a friendly way, and leave him with the impression that you are a friend of him, and he of you. Then, should an opportunity occur later, he will do anything for you.[34]

What of Johnson's novel? It has numerous strengths: the clarity of its characterisation, its realistic dialogue, its satire and the wedding of the historical and contemporary segments of the book. But after reading *Outlaws*, it is difficult not to have a lower estimation of the historical section of Johnson's novel. Hugh Webb has stated that *Sandawara* is "black words on a white page",[35] in symbolic terms. Unfortunately, as has been demonstrated here, this is not entirely the case. Johnson is a talented novelist but, in order to do justice to his convictions, he will have to seek out sources and inspirations other than those provided by a writer like Ion L. Idriess.

Muecke has suggested that Aboriginal oral history of the type investigated by Pedersen may be one such source. It is fascinating to speculate about the novel that would have resulted had Johnson discovered this oral tradition. For example, Daisy Utemorrah of Mowanjum, Western Australia, has related a story of Sandamara's capture which differs in a number of striking respects from the Idriess/Johnson tale of his death by shooting. According to Utemorrah, the police and black trackers managed to locate the magical stone in which Sandamara's powers inhered:

Utemorrah:	I think they find that stone then that he was weakened. And they waited for him at the steps and he came down.
Interviewer:	And they just shot him, did they?
Utemorrah:	No, they waited for him because he was so weak. His other wife gave him away.
Interviewer:	Ah really … she betrayed him?

Utemorrah:	Yes, she betrayed him. She came down the steps and when they caught her they said, 'Call Pigeon'. She said, 'Oh Pigeon! I'm being attacked, come on!' She said, 'Pigeon!, Pigeon!' And he came down—and they caught him ... [Laughing] I would have cracked that woman's head; yes! Well, then, they caught him then. And they said they gave him this stone. And he said, 'No, it's too late; I don't want that one'. And he didn't want to run away and escape. He gave himself up ... bravely too.
Interviewer:	Idriess says he was shot, but you say he was hung?
Utemorrah:	Yeah, behind the rocks. Behind the place where he was camping. We went up there and we saw them gallows ... They said, 'You know what that for?'. He said, 'Yes; for me. I'm not frightened for it.'36

It is certainly tenable that Johnson's novel would have been far more distinctive, original, and independent of White Australian literary influence had it been based upon such a resource.

The author has admitted that his sources for *Sandawara* were limited: one was actually Dame Mary Durack, who told him of the supposed sway which Ellemara had over Sandamara. Others were police records in Perth, "a deliberate use of Idriess to establish a parallel and contrast", and "some tales I heard". It is significant that almost all of these sources are European, and it is equally significant that Johnson makes no apologies for this fact. The main reason is that, in the author's words:

> My novel is really more mythical than historical ... a novel is essentially 'gammon', fiction, and is not a factual work. It is not history, or even psych-history ... I must emphasize that Sandawara though based on the historical person, is not Pidgin. At an early stage of writing the novel I might have entertained the idea of historical accuracy, but in the later stages I left any such idea, hence the name change to Sandawara and Eaglehawk.37

In fairness, Johnson cannot be taken to task for not writing a purely historical novel—this would be as foolhardy as the condemnation of an allegorist for not being adequately literal. The mythic power of *Sandawara*, derived from sources as diverse as the Ramayana, the Mahabharata, and the Bible, is one of the outstanding attributes of the novel. The point is that, despite the author's protestations, the historical segment of *Sandawara*, because of its indebtedness to *non-mythical* white influences, does have an aura of factual legitimacy about it, as if it has been based upon events which actually occurred. The derivative aspect of *Sandawara* is strong enough to undermine the mythical strength of the novel; in short, Johnson partly subverts his own aims by relying upon white interpretations.

There is evidence that the author realises this contradiction. For example, with reference to *Sandawara*, he has admitted that 'Plagiarization in historical writing is to some extent unavoidable'.[38] The converse may be that in literary "myth-making", plagiarism and an over-reliance upon "foreign" sources can be very detrimental, if not self-defeating. It is also noteworthy that, subsequently, Johnson emphasised the crucial role of the oral tradition in the development and expression of contemporary Aboriginal literature:

> The Aboriginal writer defines and portrays Aboriginal people ... An art or literature divorced from its roots is pure dilettantism ... Our literary tradition as oral literature has existed since time began. The love song cycles of Arnhem Land are of utmost importance as the inspiration for future literature both in content and form ... Oral literature continues to form the basis for much Aboriginal literature.[39]

In other words, Johnson has become more convinced of the necessity to express his own cultural roots—not the devices of White Australian culture—in the production of culturally independent Aboriginal writing.

This places him, as a Black Australian novelist, in a difficult dilemma: what is to be done when no such oral sources exist? For example, with reference to his most recent novel, *Wooreddy*, he has written:

> *Wooreddy* may be a more historical novel than *Sandawara*, but much of it is conjecture. There are no oral sources for it, otherwise I would have used them.

Consequently, he has been forced once again to rely upon a white interpretation of Aboriginal history to a significant degree:

> In *Wooreddy*, I use the journals of G.A. Robinson, as one of my main sources of information on the events in Tasmania. Parallels can be seen at once, and one of my intentions is to allow these to be seen rather than to be heavily disguised.[40]

In other words, a comparison of the writings of Robinson and Johnson could potentially offer intriguing and contrasting black and white interpretations of Aboriginal history. A comparison of *Wooreddy* with two contemporary fictional treatments of the same episode of Australian history is perhaps more just and is even more rewarding. Despite Johnson's injunction that, as "a literature of the Fourth World", Aboriginal writing "should not be compared to the majority literature",[41] the fact of common European source material means that a comparison of *Wooreddy* with Vivienne Rae Ellis and Nancy Cato's *Queen Trucanini: The Last of the Tasmanians* and Robert

Drewe's *The Savage Crows* is a particularly interesting and fruitful one.

Queen Trucanini and *The Savage Crows* were first published in 1976, and the authors of both novels examine the complex of collective and individual guilt which has enveloped Tasmania's black/white inter-racial history. In both cases, the core of the historical action is derived from the journals of Robinson: these are paraphrased, extrapolated from, and are occasionally quoted directly. Finally, both books—and especially the former—treat the relationship between Truganini and the so-called "Great Conciliator" in detail; they are easily the two most developed and interesting historical figures in the novels. On the other hand, in Johnson's book the focus shifts (as the title indicates) to highlight the exploits and philosophies of Truganini's husband, Wooreddy. The man who plays no more than a supporting part in the two works written by White Australians is elevated into a starring role in Johnson's book, where he becomes an Aboriginal prophet and visionary.

The change is far more than one of gender or emphasis (although it is generally true that Johnson is more at home, and more successful, with his depiction of male characters). Unlike Cato, Ellis and Drewe, Johnson does not trade in an exploration of the theme of guilt in historical and contemporary Australian society. Instead, he develops an often symbolic consideration of good and evil in the Black Australian world, examines how the two can be reconciled, and shows how the Aboriginal past and present co-exist. In short the three novels offer, through varying styles, techniques and thematic emphases, very different interpretations of the same or similar historical events.

Cato and Ellis's *Queen Trucanini* is the most conventionally structured and, in a number of ways, the simplest and least successful of the three books. It replicates the chronological pattern of a typical biography, literally from the moment of Truganini's conception to the time of her burial, and in so doing follows very closely the life and letters of Robinson. The novel is competently, though in some respects rather archaically, written. The final impression remains that in their attempt to remain detached chroniclers of the events, the authors have sacrificed the reader's interest for the sake of historical thoroughness and accuracy. For example, their tendency to include minute details of personal habits and garments is an unnecessary brake on the pace of the novel,[42] as in the following extract:

The native men in their Sunday trousers and checked shirts with kerchiefs at the neck, were drawn up in ragged lines on the beach. As the portly, impressive figure of Sir John stepped ashore, in naval uniform of blue double-breasted frock coat and

white trousers, his brown, kindly face beaming under his cocked hat, the natives
gave a concerted yell and began capering in delight ... Lady Franklin ... had a pretty
smile and eyes as blue as the straits, but her dress was sober in the extreme, a brown
worsted travelling gown without adornments of any kind, and a shady straw bon-
net.[43]

Ironically, elsewhere in the book it is the authors' lack of explicit
detail which gives a rather quaint, juvenile atmosphere to the text,
perhaps due to the fact that the novel was written with a school-age
audience in mind. This is particularly true when Cato and Ellis are
referring to the sexual relationship between Robinson and Truganini.
The unevenness of the book is further emphasised by the fact that,
while this sexual dimension is repeatedly cited, it is always described
with an incongruous and coy daintiness. For example, "seeing
Truganini emerge sleek and shining from a river", Robinson "turns
hastily away to hide the stirring in his loins at the sight of her" (p. 66)
and when he finally succumbs to Truganini's wiles, the "seduction"
is described as follows: "She flung herself backward, so that he fell
top of her. Nothing but a shred of wet shirt between them. And that
not for long." (p. 82). Finally, Robinson's reaction to her love-making
is to lie back and give "himself up to a new sensation" (p. 83) and
later, when he thinks of the event, "fear and desire were once more
contending for the mastery" (p. 86). This euphemistic treatment of
sexuality is one which contrasts very markedly with Black Australian
novelists' exploration of the same theme, as will be observed in the
next chapter.

Understated as it may be, the sexual sparring between Truganini
and Robinson represents one of the most interesting aspects of *Queen
Trucanini*. Another is the emphasis upon guilt in the novel, which operates on a number of levels. There is the guilt of the white
"Vandemonians" over their attempt to exterminate the Aborigines so
ruthlessly, and that of Robinson, for leading many of them to the island of their banishment and death, and for later turning his back
upon the few survivors. Finally, there is the remorse of Truganini
over having been involved—and in many cases having been more instrumental than Robinson—in coaxing her countrymen from their
traditional areas to join the doomed "Friendly Mission". One of the
more successful images in the novel is that of Robinson's guilty
nightmare in which he dreams of:

a ghastly procession of natives passing by his bed, with their curly hair and
their deepset eyes; but all their faces were white. He was calling the roll and
they answered:

'Tunninerpeevay Jack Napoleon. How say you? Dead or alive?'
'Dead.'
'Robert Timmy Jemmy Smallboy?'
'Hanged by the neck; dead.'
'Isaac Problattener?'
'Dead.'
'Thomas Bruny?'
'Dead.'
'Rebecca Pyterrunner?'
'Dead.'
'Count Alpha Woorrady?'
' … Dying.' (p. 212).

This sense of heartfelt, disturbing guilt is one with which Stephen Crisp, the protagonist of Robert Drewe's *The Savage Crows*, readily identifies. Culpability is the essence of the novel. Repeatedly, Crisp trades in remorse in a mildly masochistic and slightly sadistic fashion. When he gets his girlfriend pregnant six months before his mother's death, his sense of guilt over both events—and the possible relationship of the second to the first—is amplified. Yet, as a child, he had purposely tried to inculcate guilt in his mother for not realising that the symptoms of his prolonged illness were those of meningitis. Crisp's childhood embarrassments and inadequacies became the beacons which lit the way to the neuroticism and dissatisfaction of his adult life. For example, his failed attempt to rescue his friend Harley Onslow from drowning (especially after the two had just argued) elicited:

> Certain guilts on different levels as well as sadness. His culpability quotient had in fact risen ever since. It unfortunately showed no sign of levelling off as people around him were hurt in varying degrees.[44]

Even as an adult, the criticism of a private investigator concerning his impending divorce has the same effect:

> "I'm a fond father myself". Nevertheless, the old guilt juices flowed anew. Even a three a.m. homily from this avuncular idiot started them off (p. 134).

It is the concept of guilt and responsibility which links the historical and contemporary sections of the novel and gives the Black Australian past a cogent meaning in the White Australian present. Crisp, a metaphorical self-flagellator, feels so intensely about his ancestors' attempted extirpation of the Tasmanian Aborigines that he becomes totally preoccupied with his thesis on the subject, in an attempt to achieve some form of catharsis. This, by reflection, indicates

Drewe's belief that a larger sense of shared regret over these atrocities is surfacing in contemporary Australia. It is noteworthy that when Crisp finally travels to the Tasmanian mutton-birding islands to find that the state's Aborigines are not in fact extinct, he asks their leader:

> "But what's the Blue Plum deal in?" But Crisp, above anyone, already knew. "Guilt, of course. Fuckin' guilt. There's money in it boy, and a new tractor or abalone boat when you need it"(p. 262).

As the text reveals, and as the author summarises:

> Guilt is the constant theme throughout. I mean a country's guilt paralleling the protagonist's guilt—Stephen Crisp's personal guilt ... I wanted to write about the sort of person who was looking for a sense of expiation rather than performing that act in the book.[45]

Drewe's comments are revealing, and go a long way towards explaining why the work is brave, in places brilliantly evocative, but ultimately flawed. One reason for this is the novel's bipartite structure. While the parallels drawn via the technique of counterpoint often do succeed—as when the news of Crisp's father's death is juxtaposed with an historical letter from Archibald McLachlan, concerning the morbidity of the Aborigines relocated to Swan Island—it is very difficult to balance the reader's interest between the historical and contemporary segments of the novel. Due to the mordantly cynical style of much of the book's modern section, and the far more reserved, descriptive style of the historical portion, the reader tends to resent wading through the latter in order to return to Crisp's contemporary dilemma. Ironically, this is largely a result of Drewe's desire to maintain even-handedness and detachment in the historical segment, especially when dealing with the Robinson/Truganini relationship:

> I did think I had treated her [Truganini] with dignity, first of all as a *woman*, and I mean I was interested in her as a woman firstly ... I scrupulously kept to historical facts ... I resisted the temptation of having her romantically inclined with ... George Robinson; when in fact I am positive that they did ... He [Robinson] being a lower middle-class English ... artisan, wasn't going to put it in his memoirs that he'd slept with a black woman. And so I didn't feel it honourable or honest to sort of have them ... going to bed at every opportunity ... Given the lee-way that I had, I think that that was actually fairly scrupulous.[46]

The tension between Drewe's desire to remain "scrupulous" and his natural inclination to cast Robinson and Truganini as lovers is a liability in the novel. Similarly, there is a disjointed atmosphere in the book created by the author's attempt to divorce art from overt political commentary. The irony is that, while he attempts to take refuge in the mythical concept of uncommitted, impartial historical "fact" in *The Savage Crows*, the thrust of the novel as a whole is inescapably political. The intensity of the contemporary segment of the novel reflects not only the working-out of Crisp's own guilt through the discovery of Aboriginal survival and resourcefulness in Tasmania, but also Drewe's own deeply-felt convictions. There is a passionate tone to Crisp's fictional dilemma, as there is to Drewe's own feelings about Black Australia. When asked in interview, "What goes on in your mind when you are writing a book like this?" he replied, "I wanted to annoy white racists; I wanted to bore it up the white racists—right across the country … I wanted to annoy *them* more than I wanted to bring pleasure to Aborigines". At the same time, Drewe tried to restrain this intensity for aesthetic reasons:

> I am personally deeply committed to the [Aboriginal] question, but I wanted it to be the *core* of my book; the core of my book of *fiction*, rather than to override everything else … I don't know how subtle you can be—I mean the balance of subtlety and passion— … it's the two things coming together that might make the art *work*. One without the other is … just sheer polemics; it loses me I'm afraid, even though it's a cause I believe in intensely. It loses me as art. [47]

The author is treading a thin, ambivalent line between commitment and detachment, and this is reflected by the novel's contemporary and historical segments respectively. Robert Drewe is a skilled author: the sardonic, pithy and sometimes distasteful images he employs have made Stephen Crisp memorably irresolute. Drewe's dilemma is shared by many sensitive White Australian authors who firmly believe in the Aboriginal cause. They support such issues so strongly that they feel compelled to fictionalise them, but when they enter the fictional universe, they feel constrained by literary conventions and a perception of the inviolability of "art"—and the result is a disconcerting sense of tension. *The Savage Crows* is far more accomplished than *Queen Trucanini*. However it is ultimately flawed by the disjointed tone of the book's two time streams, stemming from Drewe's inability to achieve a satisfactory "balance of subtlety and passion" in the novel.

This raises the contentious issue of literature as propaganda, which will be considered with reference to poetry in Chapter Eight. It is significant that in his novel *Wooreddy*, Colin Johnson makes no claim to "academic even-handedness". In this book, which is, unlike *Queen Trucanini* and *The Savage Crows*, directed equally at Black and White

Australians, the author endeavours to write "with a 'passionate control' about the history of his race"[48] and through his subtle and far-reaching symbolism, he succeeds in doing so. *Wooreddy* is evidence of the fact that politically-informed and relevant literature does not necessarily have to be overtly polemical: it is a very accomplished example of Aboriginal writing.

The work—Johnson's first entirely historical novel—pivots on dualities: those of fire and water, black and white, good and evil. In *Wooreddy* the author informs known Australian history with symbolism and mythology drawn from Aboriginal and Eastern cultures. The symbol of resolution and enlightenment in the novel owes as much to Buddhism as it does to Black Australian religion. All of this is accomplished through the device of the visionary or seer, the relatively unknown Tasmanian Aboriginal historical figure, Wooreddy. In the opening pages, which depict Wooreddy's initiation, Johnson establishes his symbolic universe and Wooreddy's position in it:

> His uncles held him down while a stranger thrust a firebrand into his face. Another man chanted the origin of fire and why it was sacred for him. Fire was life; fire was the continuation of life—fire endured to the end. He came from fire and would return to fire ... Fire was a gift from Great Ancestor and Wooreddy had been selected as one descended from that gift. Now while he lived he had to ensure that fire lived.

In *Wooreddy*, the potency of fire's conqueror—water—is even more pronounced: "The salt-smell caused him to think of that thing, neither male nor female, which heaved a chaos threatening the steadiness of the earth" (p. 1). In short, fire is representative of Aboriginal cultural continuity—of goodness—while water reflects the generalised evil power of *Ria Warrawah*. By extension, water also images the white men who sailed upon its surface, who raped and plundered the Aborigines, and who eventually—with the aid of Truganini and Wooreddy—removed some of the battered remnants of their race to an off-shore island to pine away and perish:

> The creature touched the land. It carried pale souls which *Ria Warrawah* had captured. They could not bear being away from the sea, and had to protect their bodies with strange skins ... Clouds of fog would rise from the sea to hide what was taking place from Great Ancestor. Then the pieces holding the last survivors of the human race would be towed out to sea where they would either drown or starve (p. 4).

The phrase "It is the times" becomes a refrain which underlines the inevitability of the defeat of the Tasmanian Aborigines by the European invaders. From the outset, an atmosphere of predestination is created by the author. It is because Wooreddy as visionary can perceive that the "world is ending" for the Tasmanian blacks that he can clothe himself with the numbness and detachment which enable him to observe that process. Then, with considerable levity and irony, Johnson proceeds to detail these events, primarily as they affect the three main characters—Wooreddy, "Trugernanna" and Robinson.

Aside from its symbolic aspects, one of the most distinctive elements of the novel is the author's usage of traditional song rhythms to evoke the atmosphere of special tribal occasions. This is the first Aboriginal novel in which such traditional Arnhem Land oral literature is recognised and emulated in poetic fashion:

> The women sit thinking of their men folk:
> They stand thinking of their men—
> While we dance thinking of our women,
> Thinking of our beautiful women—
> While they dance thinking of their
> Handsome men, handsome men—
> Handsome men thinking of beautiful women.
>
> The eyelashes flutter together—
> Breast to breast together—
> Heart to heart together—
> Fluttering, seeking, finding—
> Dance, men, dance you to me—
> Sing, women, sing me to you:
> We come, we are coming—
> You come, you are coming—
> Hallahoo, hallahoo hoho:
> Hallahoo, hallahoo,hoho! (pp. 163-164).

Hence, though there are no Aboriginal oral sources for the Wooreddy story as such, Johnson has skilfully managed to incorporate a poetic legacy of the black oral tradition into his work. In addition, although *Wooreddy* details many of the same events that are chronicled in *Queen Trucanini* and *The Savage Crows*, there are significant divergences in plot. For example, the rebellious Tasmanian amazon, Walyer, and her band of renegade male warriors are a striking inversion of the traditional Aboriginal leadership model, and they appear only in *Wooreddy*. Stylistically, Johnson's book is also set apart by its consistent and effective caricature of Robinson, which is taken much further than in either of the books by White Australians. However, what is most important is the symbolic context of

Wooreddy; above all, the illumination of the book's protagonist just before his death.

After a night in which Wooreddy dreams of his spirit ancestors holding out their beckoning hands to him, Wooreddy's mainland companion, Waau, leads him to the sacred cave of his ancestors while he discusses the potency of evil:

> *"Puliliyan is our Ria Warrawah,* but unlike you and your people we face him and gain powers," Waau said matter-of-factly.

> "And some of us too have faced *Ria Warrawah* and gained powers", Wooreddy asserted. *"Puliliyan* and Our Father are close relatives," Waau stated. "Everything comes in twos, but behind them stands only one" (pp. 195–196).

This leads Wooreddy to the revelations which represent the climax of the novel—and of his life. After having believed since his birth that evil always resided in, and was manifested by, the ocean, he comes to realise that this conception is only partially correct:

> Wooreddy began to feel a terrible dread rising in him. It seemed that all he had believed, the scheme that had supported his life, had been but part of the truth. Things were not the simple black and white he had imagined them to be (p. 196).

Instead, behind the dualities which had marked eons of Tasmanian Aboriginal existence lay a new awareness of unity:

> He trembled all over and kept in the light falling through the cave mouth. Great spears fell from the roof. Great Ancestor casting down his spears to keep *Ria Warrawah* at bay—but other spears rose from the floor to join them in a oneness. They met and there was no conflict as he had always thought there should be—that there had to be! And his skin did not itch at the proximity of *Ria Warrawah,* and he did not feel threatened by the new truth, though he felt beyond his old life. *Ria Warrawah* and Great Ancestor came from a single source and somewhere was that source he had been seeking in his dream. He moved further into the dripping darkness of the cave and it did not panic him. It was the origin of all things (p. 197).

This is a crucial and symbolic phase in the novel, in the life of Wooreddy, and in Johnson's analysis of the span of the black Tasmanians' traditional world. It is at this stage that the reader is made aware of the fact that all three will and must soon end.

What, specifically, does the symbolism mean, especially with reference to Aboriginal history? To begin with, it is only through contact with a foreign tribe that Wooreddy discovers this universal truth. This seems to imply the necessity for pan-Aboriginal communication in order to arrive at the unity behind diversity in contemporary Aboriginal affairs. Second, if evil and good, fire and water, black and white, all emanate from the same source, violence done to the other is equally violence done to the self. This would appear to indicate that blood-letting on both sides was clearly barbarous and was no solution to historical interracial conflicts in Tasmania, just as Johnson believes such brutality is futile today. Third, this image seems to suggest, not stoic detachment, but Aboriginal adaptability and resilience. There is also an implied awareness that not all whites are evil, just as in the days of Wooreddy, there were also compassionate Europeans, such as those who rescued Truganini's father, Mangana, from drowning in the ocean.

Above all, the image emphasises the spiritual wholeness of Aboriginal culture and the desire for a black solidarity in contemporary Australia, especially in light of the symbolic final paragraph of the novel. The body of Wooreddy is found dead in the ship which is returning Truganini and Dray to Flinders Island. But "the real Doctor Wooreddy"—his spirit of pride and survival—lives on and informs modern Aboriginal commitment and action. There can be no doubt that the following passage was very carefully and deliberately written:

> The yellow setting sun broke through the black clouds to streak rays of light upon the beach. It coloured the sea red (p. 207).

Therefore, the spark of light which then rockets up from Wooreddy's shallow grave to the sky travels through a firmament which is coloured in the hues of the Aboriginal land rights flag, a symbol which, while not immediately obvious to all readers, is strong and distinctively Black Australian.

The historical theme, one of the most important of all those developed in contemporary Aboriginal literature, is conveyed in many ways: through usage of the techniques of the venerable Aboriginal oral tradition; through the endeavour to foster a sense of contemporary Aboriginal pride in leaders and heroes of the Black Australian past; and through a reinterpretation—often vividly symbolic—of Australian interracial history. These are just some of the most important ways in which contemporary Aboriginal writers articulate their racial heritage. Throughout, as the closing lines of Johnson's *Wooreddy* attest, the present is perpetually infused with the past.

Notes

1   *Breaker Morant, Gallipoli, The Man From Snowy River*(both the original and its sequel) and *Phar Lap* all come under this category.

2   Shane Howard, "Solid Rock (Sacred Ground)", on the album "Spirit of Place" by *Goanna*, W.E.A. 600127, (Sydney, 1982).

3   Personal interview with Jack Davis, Canberra, November, 1981.

4   Kevin Gilbert, "Black Policies", in Jack Davis and Bob Hodge, eds, *Aboriginal Writing Today*, (Canberra, 1985), p. 41.

5   Gerald L. Bostock, "Black Children", in *Black Man Coming*, (Sydney, 1981), p. 14.

6   Oodgeroo Noonuccal (Kath Walker), "The Past", in *My People*, (Milton, 1981), p. 92.

7   Noonuccal, "Stone Age", in *ibid.*, p. 21.

8   Gilbert, *Living Black: Blacks Talk to Kevin Gilbert*, (Ringwood, 1978), p. 3.

9   Maureen Watson, "Walk Tall", in *Black Reflections*, (Wattle Park, 1982), p. 15.

10 Biskup makes this point in his article, "Aboriginal History", in Mandle and Osborne, eds, *New History Today—Studying Australian Society*, (Sydney, 1982), p. 30.

11 Henry Reynolds, *Aborigines and Settlers: The Australian Experience 1788-1939*, (North Melbourne, 1972); *The Other Side of the Frontier; Aboriginal Resistance to the European Invasion of Australia*, (Ringwood, 1982).

12 W.E.H. Stanner, *After the Dreaming*, (Sydney, 1969), pp. 55, 57.

13 *ibid.*, p. 25.

14 Phillip Pepper, *You Are What You Make Yourself to Be*, (Melbourne, 1981); Robert Bropho, *Fringedweller*, (Sydney, 1980).

15 Kevin Gilbert, *Living Black: Blacks Talk To Kevin Gilbert*, (Melbourne, 1978), p. 2.

16 Jack Davis, *The Dreamers*, in *Kullark/The Dreamers*, (Sydney, 1982), p. 134.

17 Quoted in Adam Shoemaker, "An Interview With Jack Davis", *Westerly*, vol. 27., no. 4, December, 1982, p. 114.

18 Robert J. Merritt, *The Cake Man*, (Sydney, 1978), p. 12.

19 *ibid.*, p. 30.

20   Personal interview with Robert Merritt, Sydney, July, 1982.

21   Henry Reynolds, *The Other Side of the Frontier*, pp. 200-201.

22   Also referred to as "Sandawara" and "Pigeon".

23   Stephen Hawke has prepared a revisionist history of the Kimberleys based upon Aboriginal oral testimony, cross-referenced with government records. Scheduled for publication in 1988, excerpts of the book—including the story of "Jandamarra"—were published under the title, "Our Black Past", "The Great Weekend" Supplement, The Brisbane *Courier-Mail*, 5 March, 1988, pp. Weekend 1-2.

24   Howard Pedersen, "Pigeon: An Aboriginal Rebel. A Study of Aboriginal-European Conflict in the West Kimberley, North Western Australia During the 1890s", Unpublished Honours Thesis, (Murdoch, 1980), p. 2.

25   Ion L. Idriess, *Outlaws of the Leopolds*, (Sydney, 1952), p. iv. All following quotations will be taken from this edition and page references will be given in parentheses in the body of the text, immediately after each citation.

26   Personal interview with Colin Johnson, Brisbane, July, 1980.

27   ibid.

28   Colin Johnson, *Long Live Sandawara*, (Melbourne, 1979), p. 72. All following quotations will be taken from this edition and page references will be given in the body of the text, immediately after each citation.

29   Gilbert, *"Because a White Man'll Never Do It"*, p. 203.

30   Personal interview with Colin Johnson, Brisbane, July, 1980.

31   Stephen Muecke, "Discourse, History, Fiction: Language and Aboriginal History", *Australian Journal of Cultural Studies*, vol. 1, no. 1, May, 1983, p. 77.

32   Pedersen, "Pigeon: An Aboriginal Rebel", pp. 52-53.

33   See ibid., p. 57. In Pedersen's words, "It is difficult to believe that such well orchestrated action and a planned military offensive could have arisen in a space of little more than a week. It invites speculation that Pigeon was thinking of such a move well before he killed Richardson".

34   Idriess, "Give 'Em A Go", *SALT*, vol. 5, no. 9, 1943, p. 18.

35   Hugh Webb, "Black Words on a White Page: Colin Johnson's *Long Live Sandawara*", Seminar paper, Murdoch University, September, 1981.

36   Personal interview with Daisy Utemorrah, Perth, February, 1983.

37   Personal letter from Colin Johnson, August, 1982.

38   ibid.

39   Colin Johnson's speech at the "Aboriginal Literature" section of the National Word Festival, Canberra, March, 1983.

40   Personal letter from Colin Johnson, August, 1982.

41 Johnson, "White Forms; Aboriginal Content", in Jack Davis and Bob Hodge, eds, *Aboriginal Writing Today*, (Canberra, 1985), p. 28.

42 This may be partly because of Ellis's thorough familiarity with the history of Truganini. Her penchant for detail may retard the pace of this fictional treatment but her biography, *Trucanini: Queen or Traitor?*, (Canberra, 1981), is stronger as a result of this comprehensive approach.

43 Nancy Cato and Vivienne Rae Ellis, *Queen Trucanini: The Last of the Tasmanians*, (Sydney, 1976), p. 158. All further quotations will be taken from this edition, and page numbers will be included immediately after each citation in the body of the text.

44 Robert Drewe, *The Savage Crows*, (Sydney, 1976), p. 90. All further quotations will be taken from this edition, and page numbers will be included immediately after each citation in the body of the text.

45 Personal interview with Robert Drewe, Adelaide, March, 1982.

46 ibid.

47 ibid.

48 Quoted from the front dustcover of *Wooreddy*.

49 Johnson, *Wooreddy*, p. 5. All further quotations will be taken from this edition, and page numbers will be given in parentheses immediately after each citation, in the body of the text.

7

Sex and Violence in the Black Australian Novel

There is, I believe, a fundamental ambivalence towards sexuality in modern Western culture, an ambivalence which is exemplified by the often brutally invasive nature of its language describing love-making. As numerous commentators have observed, sexual relations—theoretically in the realm of love—have often been perverted into forms of violence.[1] In contemporary Australian society, this destructive ambivalence persists both linguistically and actively, as belligerent and violent slang terms for intercourse, and rising rape and incest statistics both attest. Put crudely, in White Australian culture, to achieve victory in the so-called "battle" between the sexes males far too often feel they must both complete and control the sexual act.

What of the original, indigenous Australian society: that of the Aborigines? Some anthropologists and ethnographers, such as Geza Roheim, have maintained that sexual relations in traditional Aboriginal society were equivalent to the habitual rape of women by men:

> Marriage and rape have become almost identical concepts among the Central Australians ... In the unconscious, the penis is a spear, a weapon. Coitus is therefore rape and the symbol of marriage is a spear.[2]

If this were true, then it could be argued that Aboriginal contact with Western civilisation has at least partly improved the situation. However, there is strong evidence to the contrary, and clear indications that Roheim's description is inaccurate. For example, despite the powerfully patriarchal nature of traditional Aboriginal society, a number of anthropologists have concluded that sexual relations were treated with considerable reverence and respect, as an integral component of ceremony and ritual. Significantly, in Robert Brain's words,

"In Black Australia sexuality, not marriage, has been ennobled with elaborate preliminaries of courtship, songs and the visual poetry of rituals and ceremonies".3

From a eurocentric perspective, some traditional love song cycles compare favourably with the greatest examples of amorous poetry ever written in English. On a more practical level, in traditional Aboriginal culture, one of the most common positions for sexual intercourse involved the male lying on the ground while the female squatted on his penis—hardly a posture conducive to rape. Finally, with reference to the common tribal custom of subincision:

> The ethnographical evidence seems to suggest that the subincised penis is considered an imitation vulva ... The wounded penis in some parts of Australia is actually called 'vulva' and the bleeding that occurs when the operation is repeated during ceremonies is likened to women's menstruation ... Black Australian rites recognize that men feel a need to express their femininity amd women their masculinity ... White Australians on the other hand theoretically follow a 'myth' of the pure male and the pure female, a myth based on a misguided belief in exaggerated sexual differentiation ... This refusal to accept a degree of bisexuality is so extreme that it results in bitter sexual antagonism and a neurotic belief in the superiority of one or the other sex.4

There was a significant amount of violent ritual in traditional Aboriginal society that had at least a partly sexual base; however, by its nature, it was restricted to special ceremonies. It is therefore possible that there was less *overall* potential for sexual violence in pre-contact Black Australia than there is in contemporary White Australia.

Of course, traditional Aboriginal culture is now retained only very locally, primarily in central and northern Australia. Nowhere are there Australian Aborigines untouched by modern White Australian culture, whether via its doctors and community advisors or by its miners and liquor salesmen. As a significant proportion—arguably, the majority—of Aborigines are now urbanised, it is therefore not surprising to find that the five novels under discussion in this chapter are written by urban-dwelling Black Australians. All of these books have been published during the past twenty-five years and all exhibit a distinctive world-view which, though not Aboriginal in traditional terms, does incorporate elements of the Black Australian cultural past and present into a unique contemporary synthesis. An important connective thread in all five of these novels is the theme of a special Black Australian identity, forged as a result of both historical and contemporary attacks on the Aboriginal way of life. All three novelists are to some extent "integrated", in the sense that they have been influenced by White Australian teachers, authors, editors and publishers, let alone by the media and the political system. But Johnson, Bandler, and Weller are all aware of the extent of their integration: this self-knowledge has enabled them to succeed in a culturally foreign form of creative expression, and has steeled their resolve to preserve and celebrate that distinctive Black Australian identity which they retain.

In their works, these authors portray sexual relations as a mirror of violence in a way which exemplifies how attuned to this form of contemporary brutality they have become. This approach shows how incisively all three writers have examined the White Australian world, as well as their own. Two of them, Colin Johnson and Faith Bandler, project the image of that violence back into history to illustrate how self-sufficient peoples were removed from their homes, killed, violated, and transplanted to foreign and unwelcome shores. It is noteworthy that, in Johnson's *Doctor Wooreddy's Prescription for Enduring the Ending of the World*, a clear parallel is established between the rape of the Tasmanian Aboriginal women and the metaphorical rape of their land, sacred sites and heritage. Johnson and Bandler emphasise that in the traditional social and spiritual context sexual intercourse was highly revered, and that the arrival of Europeans in Australia cheapened, degraded, and perverted its beauty and purpose.

Sexual and cultural violence is dealt with in historical novels such as *Wooreddy* and *Wacvie*, but the treatment of the subject is relatively muted when compared with the direct, searing sexual and physical brutality of Aboriginal novels set in the contemporary urban environment, particularly Johnson's *Long Live Sandawara* and Weller's *The Day of the Dog*. It is ironic that, though they were the instigators and perpetrators of much of that violence, few White Australians have had the bravery and insight to recognise and describe it accurately until very recently. Thus, Aboriginal novelists, in their best work, play the important role of illustrating the sometimes base, raw reality of Australian social violence. Sexual relations as the reflection of that violence are so pre-eminent in these novels primarily because they are stories of cultural clash in which white mores are dominant. Were they stories of traditional Aboriginal culture, the theme would likely not be present, nor would it be necessary. These novelists directly, perceptively, and disconcertingly hold a mirror up to European violence, sexual jealousy, physical brutality, and authoritarianism.

This is not to say that Aborigines were devoid of violent passions and were perpetually peace-loving before the advent of whites in Australia. But I contend that the behaviour which novelists such as Johnson and Weller describe: the excesses of violence and liquor, and the degrading of sexual relations—allegedly "deviant" or "anti-social" behaviour according to white sociologists—is actually a response largely in European terms to an untenable situation created by White Australians. In this sense, it is sadly ironic that Aborigines are now satirised and harshly punished for emulating too enthusiastically the "deviant" behaviour of their white mentors. In order to illustrate the development of this theme of sexual and larger cultural violence, the historical novels written by Black Australians—Faith Bandler's *Wacvie* and Colin Johnson's *Wooreddy*—will be discussed before the unrelenting brutality of the contemporary scene, imaged most clearly in Archie Weller's *The Day of the Dog*, is examined.

Wacvie is a fictionalised biography of Bandler's father, Wacvie Mussingkon, who was transported from the Pacific island of Ambrym in the New Hebrides to the Mackay area of Queensland, in 1883.[5] Stylistically, *Wacvie* is the most simple and most reserved of the Black Australian novels. One of the book's strengths lies in Bandler's keen eye for detail and colour, but her work is flawed by an over-emphasis upon culinary and housekeeping minutiae in the houses of the Queensland plantation managers. At times it appears that she is more concerned with her fictional menu than with the squalid living and harsh working conditions endured by the kanakas outside the owner's mansion. There is also a rather too ready idealisation of traditional Ambrymese life, described in Utopian terms which strain credibility:

> In the main they knew no sickness. Childbirth was without pain. Their teeth did not decay. Their days were an endlessly repeated cycle only broken by their desire for food. They fished, cooked and ate; they danced, sang and made love.[6]

Whatever the possible attractions of life in Melanesia before the arrival of Europeans, one has difficulty believing that it was as perfect as Bandler's description suggests.[7]

Bandler has stated in interview that she was keen to illustrate the institutional violence of the labour trade, both through its impact upon the Pacific islands and upon the transported individuals themselves.[8] She does so effectively, as when she describes the white over-seer in the fields:

> Unmercifully, with all his strength, he flicked the whip across the sweating, flannel-covered backs, and vehemently cursed them in the new language, repeating over and over the two words: "Black Bastards! Black Bastards!" (p. 25).

Bandler also gives examples of individualised cruelty and shows very clearly how such violence can breed a like response:

> Suddenly the overseer was standing over her. Cursing, he ordered her back to work. Then, with his highly polished boot, he kicked her.

> Emcon gently put her baby back in its cane trash cradle. Then she picked up a knife and with all the strength she could muster, she plunged it into the field master, at the same time calling to the other women for help (p. 40).

Sexual exploitation of one race by the other also takes place in Wacvie's world. The whites use their black servants as sexual chattels and transform sexual relations into a crude form of bartering. The whites—both male and female—offer minor privileges or concessions in return for sexual favours. There are a number of dimensions to this relationship of manipulation and exploitation. First, as Bandler aptly illustrates, the European women on the cane plantations could wield as much sexual power as could the men, especially as there were many more available black men than women working in the fields. Her description of the owner's wife's post-coital bliss effectively reveals how meaningless sexual relations between the races had become:

> Maggie waited for her husband's snores but they didn't come. She was feigning sleep, afraid that he might take from her the pleasure still lingering from having successfully seduced one of the black men that afternoon. She was unaware that none of them were happy about taking pleasure with her, that they considered she didn't really know how to excite a man. She didn't know that each man had come to her thinking he might as well take his share, since others would have her if he didn't. Even if the piles of red flesh, flabby thighs and blue veins were repulsive, it was free and he was usually rewarded with some of Russell's tobacco or a bottle of his rum (pp. 52-53).

The second major aspect of the sexual power play described in *Wacvie* is that Black Australians themselves began to perceive the potential of intercourse as a tool for gain, a means of advancement. For example, Emcon, who earlier murdered the overseer in the fields, reacts to the advances of the sugar refining company chairman in the following way:

'Well?' Fox whispered. His hands twisted in hers and she tightened her grasp. But he was listening. She would use this man like a tool, like her kitchen tools; she could use him to make things better for her people (p. 75).

Thus, sexual relations between owner and servant can be seen as a reflection of their imbalanced power relations. The sexual act is transformed by the whites into a means of asserting their authority; by the blacks, into a means of attempting to make relations between the races more equitable. The European debasement of Black Australians' sexuality accompanied the exploitation of their labour, the restrictions on their freedom, and the introduction of alcohol and gambling, all of which had the effect of maintaining white supremacy. Wacvie is perceptive enough to realise that the dangers of drunkenness and gambling are far greater than physical ones. He pleads with his fellow-workers not to attend the horse races: "If we come to this place, the money the white man gives us for working, he will now take back—then we can't start to work for our own ground—and our freedom"(p. 109). However, *Wacvie* is at base an optimistic novel, for it shows how, with persistence and bravery, that freedom was achieved.

Colin Johnson's *Wooreddy* is a very different novel, which details the progressive enslavement and virtual annihilation of the Tasmanian Aborigines. Both *Wacvie* and *Wooreddy* end with the death of the eponymous character but Wacvie's death signifies the sacrifice which has made liberty possible; Wooreddy's, the awareness of the ending of the traditional world for the Tasmanian blacks. Yet the matter is more complex than this for, as I noted in Chapter Six, the spirit of Doctor Wooreddy lives on and makes it possible for Johnson to write with a distinctive Aboriginal pride and world-view. The corpse of Wooreddy may be buried in a shallow grave but a symbolic spark of light representing his spirit or soul shoots "up from the beach" and flashes "through the dark sky towards the evening star".[9] As this example illustrates, the structure and informing ideas of Johnson's book are far more symbolic and intricate than are those of Bandler's novel.

In *Wooreddy* the violence wrought upon traditional Aboriginal life is said to be the result of a generalised malevolence inspired by *Ria Warrawah*, the evil and dangerous spirit most wickedly manifested in the ocean. The *num*, (that is, the "ghosts", or white men) are thought to be agents of this malevolent force, given their spectre-like appearance and their ability to traverse the ocean with ease. Hence, initially, the Tasmanian blacks of Johnson's novel accept the sexual violence done to their women as being a result of the unavoidable dictates of fate:

> Mangana's wife had been raped and then murdered by *num* (ghosts), that came from the settlement across the strait. What had happened had had nothing to do with her, her husband or her children. It had been an act of *Ria Warrawah*—unprovoked, but fatal as a spear cast without reason or warning (p. 10).

Mangana laments because a supernatural being cannot be killed by a human, because all his people are under the curse of an evil deity:

> They were under the dominion of the Evil One, *Ria Warrawah*. They killed needlessly. They were quick to anger and quick to kill with thunder flashing out from a stick they carried. They kill many, and many die by the sickness they bring ... A sickness demon takes those that the ghosts leave alone (p. 11).

As the novel progresses, Johnson relates how Wooreddy gradually comes to realise that the *num* are human as well—often violent, cruel and rapacious—but still human. He gains this knowledge largely through an observation of the Europeans' treatment of Aboriginal women, who were initially less afraid of the *num* as they were protected by their femaleness from the forces of *Ria Warrawah* in the ocean. In many cases, these black women were fatally mistaken to be unafraid, for the whites viewed them as valuable only in sexual terms. In the following passage describing the rape of Truganini, Johnson illustrates both European sexual greed and Wooreddy's gradual enlightenment concerning the corporality of the whites:

> On the soft, wet beach-sand a naked brown-skinned woman was being assaulted by four ghosts. One held both her arms over her head causing her breasts to jut into the low-lying clouds; two more each clung to a powerful leg, and the fourth thudded away in the vee ... The doctor noted with interest the whiteness of the ghost's penis. He had accepted the fact of their having a penis—after all they were known to attack women—but he had never thought it would be white ...
>
> He was beginning to find the rape a little tedious. What was the use of knowing that the *num* were overgreedy for women just as they were overgreedy for everything? He could have deduced this from the record of their previous actions and they did appear fixed and immutable in their ways (pp. 20-21).

Significantly, Truganini does not resist these rapists; like Emcon in *Wacvie* she learns the material value of sexual availability. But she pays an important price in so doing. Though she does not realise it, Truganini's agreement to debase her own sexuality—to make prostitution a virtue because it is a necessity—renders her incapable of sexual tenderness even with other Aborigines whom she loves. When

Wooreddy finally successfully woos and marries her:

> The woman accepted her fate with a numbness worthy of Wooreddy. In the past she had found sex to be a weapon useful for survival and felt little pleasure in it. She gave her body in exchange for things and that was where the importance lay. Her husband's love-making meant less than the rape that had been inflicted on her. She hated the men for doing that, and was indifferent to what Wooreddy could or would do (p. 47).

Wooreddy, for his part, is confused and distressed by his wife's frigidity, and cannot fully appreciate the psychological trauma she has undergone:

> Wooreddy did not know that Trugernanna had only endured the rough embraces of ghosts, and so many older women had died that she had remained ignorant of the different sexual positions. The man, almost twice her age and having already had one woman go to the fire, wondered at her lack of knowledge and movement (pp. 46–47).

Significantly, though disappointed, he does not reject her for her sexual coldness:

> Each day Wooreddy made love to his wife, but her lack of response began to bore him. After all, he was a doctor with a knowledge of love-making and he had already been married. Now it all seemed for nought. Finally, he accepted the fact that they were together, not for love, but for survival (p. 48).

A number of conclusions follow from Johnson's treatment of the theme of sex as it relates to violence. First, the author clearly implies that Black Australians were traditionally experts in the art of love-making and only the invasion of the Europeans extinguished this talent. Second, the whites rape not only women but, in symbolic terms, practically everything else with which they come in contact. They appropriate terrain as easily and as completely as they conquer individuals:

> Bruny Island belonged to the ghosts. The land rang with their axes, marking it anew just as Great Ancestor had done in the distant past ... The ghosts had twisted and upturned everything (p. 25).

Third, even well-meaning whites were unable to give real help to the Tasmanian blacks because of their persistent but paradoxical belief in the child-like intellect, yet licentious nature, of the Aborigines. One of the real strengths of Johnson's novel is his satirical treatment of George Augustus Robinson (officially the Protector of Aborigines), whose policies ultimately ensured the sterility and near genocide of the race he was allegedly preserving. One of Robinson's most enthusiastic converts was, of course, Truganini, who readily accepted the juvenile role Robinson assigned her: "the word 'fader' constantly fell from her lips when Robinson was within hearing"(p. 33). But Meeter Ro-bin-un, as Wooreddy calls him, is no saint: his reaction to Truganini is constantly and comically sensual, as when she and other women emerge from an oyster harvest in the ocean:

> Robinson's mouth went dry and his ruddy face paled as the women rose like succubi from hell to tempt him with all the dripping nakedness of firm brown flesh ... 'Very good,' the *num* replied, meaning not the harvest of the woman, but her body (p. 43).

As Johnson makes explicit, the whites are no less licentious, and may well be more so than the blacks to whom they impute this "sinful" trait.

There are many examples of brutality in the novel: axe murders of Aboriginal mothers and children; retaliations against white shepherds by Wooreddy and other remaining blacks; and the final scene, in which Unmarrah is publicly hanged. In all cases, Johnson maintains careful control over his material, and sexual relations are an accurate reflection of both the invasion of the whites and, occasionally, of the dwindling havens remaining to the blacks: "Wooreddy enjoyed Walyer's firm body as much as she enjoyed his. Somehow, both found a tenderness which they had thought lost"(p.121). Thus, even in the face of the ending of their world, Aborigines who remain sexually undefiled by the whites can still find solace in each other's sensuality.

What is noteworthy about Johnson's first, and in a number of ways least successful novel, *Wild Cat Falling*, published in 1965, is that such a sexual haven does not exist. The nameless part-Aboriginal protagonist, recently released from jail, seems to have internalised all the brutality of his surrounding society and the institutional violence of life in boys' homes and prison, so that he rejects any opportunity for tender intimacy with women. This rejection applies equally to black and white females. In all cases he feels, not love, but anger, bitterness and disgust in his sexual relationships. In fact, his aversion to sex—accentuated by its constant association with drunkenness—is so severe that it produces acute feelings of nausea:

> Some of the men came in with a few more bottles and the women gathered round like flies. A big full-blood gin cottoned onto me.

> 'Give us a drink, yeller feller. Just a little one and I'll be nice to you ... Come on ... Jesus, that was good. Just one more. Come on ... '

Shrieks of laughter, sound of breaking bottles, angry argument and drunken couplings ... Warm brown breasts and heavy nipples rising and falling in drunken sleep ... I staggered out, vomited and stumbled to a tap ... 10

When a drunken white girl tries to seduce him at a university party, his repugnance is just as strong:

She pushes open a door and I feel for a switch. 'Don't need any light,' she says.

I understand her now. She pulls me down with her onto a bed and sighs as her arms twist round my neck. My body is as warm as hers but my mind is detached and cold. This time I don't feel anything like hate or love. Only feel sick. I throw off her stranglehold and fling myself out the door (p. 93).

The most disturbing aspect of the protagonist's attitude towards sex is his transformation of sexual overtures into aggression, of intercourse into attack, of love into hate. The clearest evocation of the synthesis between sex and violence occurs when he is in bed with a part-Aboriginal woman, Denise:

God, I feel awful and I want to be alone, but she's here and I suppose I have to sleep with her—oh damn ...

The bottle falls to the floor and she leans back against the wall. Her breasts jut under her jumper and desire floods into me. I want her and hate her for making me want her. I pull off her clothes and take her violently, like it was rape. Hate her. Hate her. Love her. It is finished. I fling away from her and she lies like a discarded doll. There's no more wine blast it! When I get drunk I usually end up with a chick, but why should this girl mean something to me? I want to be unmoved by everything—like a god (p. 59).

This scene is one of the most lucid and distressing examples of the blending of sexual and violent impulses in contemporary Australian literature.

In *Wild Cat Falling*, violent sex is always triggered by over-indulgence in alcohol; throughout all of Johnson's work, intoxication is always linked with cruel, excessive or pitiful behaviour—often sexual abuse or attempts at seduction. It is significant that this alcoholic trigger for sexual violence is, in *Wild Cat Falling*, described very much as a Black Australian problem. In his later novels, liquor is described as a curse introduced by White Australians, which sapped the strength and purpose of the blacks. In both *Sandawara* and *Wooreddy*, it is therefore considered to be at least as much an historical White Australian problem and, therefore, a contemporary white responsibility. This is not to say that there is an implied advocacy of, for example, repressive drinking laws for blacks. Rather, the implication is that White Australia must bear the onus for the wasted life of an alcoholic ex-convict like the character Tom in *Sandawara*, and that it should provide financial support for his rehabilitation.

Fifteen years elapsed between the appearance of *Wild Cat Falling*—the first published Aboriginal novel—and Johnson's second book, *Long Live Sandawara*. In the former, Johnson's style is, for the most part, spare and direct, although his Beatnik idiom has dated very rapidly. As has been noted, in the latter he ranges from urban Aboriginal slang in the contemporary segments to near-epic prose in the historical sections of the book. It is in some ways unfair to consider the two halves of *Sandawara* separately, for the historical and contemporary segments provide such a successful counterpoint, but for the sake of this argument such an artificial division will be made. It is striking that, in the historical portion of the book, sexual relations are hardly mentioned, although—as was discussed in Chapter Six—the violence of the liberation struggle against the white settlers and police outriders is described in great detail. In addition, the theme of alcohol as a weapon in the invasion arsenal of the Europeans is emphasised. Drunkenness can be seen as a form of disease which, like other diseases, removed Aborigines from their own territory. Johnson makes this obvious in the historical segment of his book, in which the guerilla leader Sandawara permits his followers to drink the liquor captured from a raided party of settlers:

> He lets the liquor be passed around among his people, unaccustomed to any sort of drug. He should stop it, but hell exists deep within his mind. He has known the viciousness of the white man—thus comes despair and the desire to experience to the full a moment or two of heightened life before death.

> He drinks deeply of the whisky, feeling the warmth spreading like a fever through his numb body. The ways of the white men begin to prevail in the gorge. The natural disciplines, the obedience to the Law, passed down from the very dawn of humanity, disappears from the river flat.

> Scenes as riotous as in old England erupt in shrieks and cries of alcohol pain kicking out in spasmodic violence ... This is his earth, his people and the white man's hell.[11]

Unlike the historical segment, the contemporary section of *Sandawara* contains, in Blanche d'Alpuget's words, "lashings of casual sex",[12] and a considerable amount of violence as well—especially during the novel's climactic bank robbery but, unlike in *Wild Cat Falling*, the two are disparate. It is adolescent, exploratory sex described in minute detail, virtually sex for its own sake.

Furthermore, Johnson's descriptions of sexual relations in *Sandawara* are often intentionally humorous, both because of their frequency and the choice of location for the love-making. For example, Rob and Rita have an insatiable appetite for each other which is amusingly paralleled with their constant cooking. They make love incessantly, but it almost always seems to be in the kitchen:

> The couple are in their territory, the kitchen, where Rob's trying his hand at kangaroo stew and dumplings. He wants to try something simple, something Rita can't spoil. Often he wishes that she wouldn't offer to help him every time. She's always brushing against him, and the kitchen table's becoming rickety from their constant screwing.(p. 29).

At one stage in the novel it appears that Johnson is writing a primer of adolescent sex, as two girls, Sally and Jane—neither more than thirteen years of age—become initiated into the sexual activity of the so-called "crashpad". What is noteworthy is not only the explicitness of the author's description, but also the matter-of-fact attitude which the girls have adopted towards sex. Intercourse is, initially, hardly more interesting for them than watching television:

> The youth manages to get the girl on to her back. He gets off her jeans with a lot of help, then plunges ahead. He bangs away and Jane lies beneath him wondering why this activity is supposed to be wonderful. Sally stares at her friend jealously. No ever takes any notice of her. Why haven't they got a telly in this place? She doesn't want to sit there watching them do it all night. She wants it done to her too ...

> Sally hasn't really got past the fumbling stage before. Well, once or twice and then she hadn't found it much fun. It was something to endure and part of life (p. 86).

Some have argued that Johnson over-emphasises the character and frequency of the sexual encounters in such Aboriginal urban communes, and that the reader is occasionally made to feel like a voyeur. Interestingly, such arguments have actually been voiced by Black Australian readers. In Johnson's words, "Aboriginal criticism of *Sandawara* is often about the amount of sex in it ... Aborigines criticize it from what they know or what they want to see themselves as, rather than from historical fact".[13] However, in interview, he has maintained the accuracy of his depiction: "That's the way it often is with young people today. It's realistic; it's like that". He adds, "most of the characters are based upon real-life individuals",[14] even Ron, the humorously grotesque derelict of the novel.

If sex in *Sandawara* is not a mirror, or a concomitant of violence—as in the other Black Australian novels—what is its purpose? To begin with, the Aboriginal concept of sex as a refuge from a hostile white world is again emphasised: when the police raid the crashpad, it is the under-age girls whom they take into custody. When Alan, the leader of the group, rescues Sally and Jane at the holding centre, he symbolically and audaciously makes love to each in the dormitory before helping them escape. Alan is important to Johnson in another sense as well. As the new Sandawara, or liberation fighter, he is far more in touch with his Aboriginal heritage than are the other urban blacks. As a consequence of this traditional connection, he is described as being by far the most accomplished lover, despite his young age. When Sally climaxes with Alan, it is far more than a level of television excitement that she achieves, although the description risks becoming a cliche: "Suddenly the ceiling and floor seem to meet. She gives a scream and her mind goes blank for an instant"(p. 92). The third use of sex in the novel is a more sociological one: though it often appears gratuitous and, therefore, meaningless, in Johnson's fictional world intercourse is always harmless and always a means of escaping from the boredom, poverty, and depression of urban Aboriginal life. Not only is sex free, but it is described as a far more wholesome and unifying "high" than alcohol or drugs. The social implication clearly is that in the pre-AIDS era in which the novel is set, unrestricted, casual sex is fortifying in a rebellious commune such as this one, and helps to form a sense of group identity and solidarity.

One of the chapters in Johnson's novel is entitled "Love and Guns". It is a convenient epithet for the second half of the novel, which moves from sexual exploration to a brutal slaughter in gunfire at the end. All of the members of Alan's group are mown down by the police in a gory massacre as they try to rob a bank. Only Alan—the modern Sandawara—survives this baptism of fire and thereby grows to maturity. In Johnson's words:

> Alan didn't really know what violence was like until it hit him in the face. His youth dies then and this is paralleled by Sandawara's death: all his loving world is wiped out by their gunfire.[15]

The violence at the close of *Sandawara* is brutal, excessive, and graphically described. But because the book is replete with satire and irony, the tone of the novel as a whole is not overly harsh. In fact, the blood-bath at its end has a distinct air of unreality, of attempting to push an ideological line too far. Johnson obviously feels that these mass deaths are essential for Alan's illumination, but there is no logical sense in which they can be considered inevitable or even likely, and this strains the credibility of the end of his book.

Archie Weller's first novel, *The Day of the Dog*, does not suffer from any such internal inconsistency or strain. It has a searing, pressing inner momentum and a stylistic force which carries it inexorably forward. There is no other Aboriginal novel in which a sense of being foredoomed is so clearly conveyed. Whereas Johnson's contemporary characters in *Sandawara* choose their future in an undramatic, easy-going way, Weller's protagonist, Doug Dooligan, is relentlessly pressured back into the criminal world by ties of family, friends, and the dictates of his own false pride. The most apt metaphor for *The Day of the Dog* must be a spider-web. It is an image which surfaces repeatedly in this extremely violent, disconcerting and linguistically precise novel. Of Doug and his mates Weller writes:

> No-one owns them. They are their own bosses. They have cobwebs in their hair and minds and, spiderlike, they dream up new dastardly deeds for their initiation. They paint on lies and blood from fights, to make themselves look elegant with patterns from their new Dreaming. They dance to their gods of flashing lights and hopes.16

From the day he is released from Fremantle jail, Doug is far more a vulnerable insect than a spider. He is open to exploitation from all quarters, as his girlfriend laments: "Them boys just use ya up; ya people use ya up, ya think I don't see that?"(p. 116).

If Doug is the pawn of others, the women in the novel are even more so the physical and sexual property of men. Valerie Yarrup, for example, endures the drunkenness, the violent rages, and the infidelity of "Pretty Boy" Floyd:

> Floyd pretends to sulk, which is the closest he will get to telling Valerie: sorry about hitting you and running out on you and stealing all the time. But just try to see the good things about me.

> Valerie, who knows her man, accepts and coils up beside him, wrapping an arm around his elegant neck (p. 96).

The Day of the Dog is a novel which illustrates, not violent sex as in *Wild Cat Falling*, but sex in the midst of an overwhelmingly violent life. This means that the love which Weller implies should accompany the sexual act is normally absent in this novel, for those such as Floyd just do not have the vocabulary or the basic ability to convey their affection. As Doug muses: "Poor Floyd, so young and unable to express himself in any way except through violence—even to express love, the tenderest yet cruellest of emotions"(p. 78). Hence, one night

Floyd sleeps peacefully with Valerie, the following night he beats her, and the next night he is forgiven: the world which Weller describes is an extremely brutal, cruel and male-dominated one.

The only character in the book for whom sex and love actually coalesce is the protagonist, Doug Dooligan. He and his girlfriend, Polly, have a very passionate relationship and their sexual experiences are described as being on a different plane from those of their friends:

> They both think it is the best lovemaking they have ever experienced; not out loud, like a rooster crowing at the death of gentle night and all her warm secrets, but soaring silently in circles of inner joy like a godly eagle, swift and high above earthly matters (p. 66).

Furthermore, in a book in which men treat their women as expendable sexual objects, Doug surprisingly shows that his love is more than just the afterglow of intercourse, as he confides in Polly: "If ya love a girl, then ya don't 'ave to make love all the time. If you do, that's not proper love, ya know"(p. 52). This may not be a particularly profound concept, but in Doug Dooligan's world such an attitude borders upon the heretical.

Violence is ubiquitous in *The Day of the Dog*. Gangs feud with gangs, individual blacks take on others to prove their masculinity, and the police harass the Aborigines constantly. They hound Doug and make it clear that their aim is to get him back behind bars as soon as possible. On one occasion, after belting him by an old railway bridge, one of the special constables hisses, "I hate your guts, you little mixed-blood misfit, ... If it's the last thing I do I'm putting you back in Freo, where snivelling gutless snakes like you belong"(p. 87). Weller emphasises this theme in the novel and writes of it so persuasively because it is a type of abuse which he has personally observed and endured. When asked in interview about the special police squad in the book, nicknamed "The Boys from Brazil", he replied:

> Yes, there were some police called the three stooges ... and ... they used to be the 'Larrikin Squad' when I was younger, and they used to give people a really hard time. They even called my foster brother in one time and they said, 'Come 'ere, David', and he came down; and they wound up the window of the car with his head in it, and ... took off. He put his foot flat on the floor—this was just for fun.[17]

The police harassment in the novel is so severe that even when Polly and Doug are peacefully sleeping in each other's arms in his bedroom—another example of Aboriginal sexuality as a temporary refuge from the persecution of the outside white world—detectives burst into the room without a warrant to interrogate them both about a car theft. The symbol is patently clear: even the most private and intimate Black Australian relationships are open to police abuse and authoritarianism. Even their sexuality is degraded by the detectives, as Weller illustrates:

> Carnal knowledge. There they were, making what they thought was beautiful love, and all along it was just 'carnal knowledge'. People have to spoil everything (p. 100).

In this novel, sex is not just a symbol of exploitation or of Doug's attempt to find peace and solitude in the face of the white world of authority and the black world of crime. As in *Wooreddy*, the image of rape is associated with the wanton destruction of nature, in order to satisfy White Australians' innate aggressiveness. Weller's description of land-clearing is very revealing:

> The youths revel in the hard work and in each other's company. They have not been together just by themselves for a long time. Amidst the tortured screams of the dying trees, as the chainsaw's teeth bite into their virgin bodies, and the rumbling of the old faded red dozer smashing into the trees, knocking them senseless, and pushing them into broken piles, their raw yellow roots jagging obscenely into the air, and the thudding of the cruel axe,—amidst all this Doug no longer needs the friendship of the bush. In all its silent dignity it draws away from the youth who so badly needed a proper friend. Now he laughs as he slaughters the trees with his companions (pp. 151-152).

Finally, sex is also used by Weller as a potent image of temptation and rejection, which sets in motion the events leading to the blood and destruction with which the novel ends. Doug finds comfort and fleeting happiness in his sexual relationships with other Aborigines, but in his seduction of the white waitress at the Halfway House, he degrades himself, demeans the woman, and makes the sexual act totally meaningless and damaging. Angelina's attitude towards sex is made painfully clear by the author—it is no more than exploitative physical stimulation: "She will go with anyone if he has the money. A quick hello, a bit of fun, then a clean goodbye; it's quick and clean love that can be used over and over again with no worries"(p. 140). But the absence of worries in this case necessitates the absence of any affection and commitment, so that what Doug and Angelina experience is little more than mutual masturbation:

> Naked, they struggle into the back seat, giggling from the whisky and the difficulties encountered. On the plush sheepskin covers, he reaps the reward that his money and patience sowed and grew. They love and drink and love and sleep; at least, they make what they think is love (p. 143).

This mutual exploitation provides a fine example of the degradation of sexuality through its transformation into a commercial undertaking—a theme which one can trace throughout the Black Australian novels under consideration in this chapter. The passage illustrates another major, related theme, which is the frequent association of alcohol with repellent sexual contact, in which one partner designedly takes advantage of, or inflicts violence upon, the other. Third, sex is often a mirror of power relations, be they of owner and servant, rapist and victim, or prostitute and customer. Most of the Aboriginal novels show how such relations were introduced into Australia by Europeans, were originally inimical to Aborigines, but have now been adopted as part of black adaptation to White Australian society. Fourth, temptations of liquor, of cars, of wealth, all play a major part in motivating both crime and materialistic sexuality in these books: the man steals the car or money to impress the woman, and assumes that the expected sexual reward will be forthcoming. Hence, the White Australian consumer culture helps to entrap Black Australians in illegal modes of behaviour, in order to live up to the image of success which it portrays. Fifth, the theme of symbolic or actual rape surfaces in all the Aboriginal novels and, again, the initial aggressive impulse is described as coming from the Europeans. Finally, authority structures such as the prison system and the police force are frequently perceived by Aborigines as potent forms of institutionalised, systemic violence, which severely circumscribe Black Australian freedom.

The relationship between sex and violence is a ancient one. Despite, and perhaps because of, the durability of the connection between the two, Western cultures still suffer from disturbing rates of rape, child molestation, incest and physical abuse related to sexual conflict. Black Australians are by no means immune from the perversion of sex into violence. On the contrary, as these authors have shown, the post-contact world of the Aboriginal people has been marked by these forms of cruelty to an alarming degree. Today, crimes of a sexual nature—almost all related to alcohol and drug abuse—are rife in a number of Aboriginal communities, as they are in the larger Australian society. Therefore, what is noteworthy is that White Australians now have the opportunity of observing the impact of their mores upon a rapidly adjusting foreign culture in their midst. It can only be hoped that the sex-related violence which these novels mirror will be recognised as being a White Australian problem, just as much as it is considered to be a Black Australian one. If, by their candour and directness, these authors can help to raise awareness of the extremely damaging nexus between sex and violence while they entertain the reader, they will have performed a valuable service. It is a testament to the artistic skill of Johnson; and, in particular,Weller, that such an important theme has been handled so effectively in these books. Through their work the Black Australian novel is evolving as a significant alternative form of literature in contemporary Australia.

Notes

1 See, for example, Germaine Greer, *The Female Eunuch*, (London, 1971), and Kate Millett, *Sexual Politics*, (London, 1971).

2 Geza Roheim, *Children of the Desert*, ed. Werner Muensterberger, (New York, 1974), pp. 232-233.

3 Brain, *Rites Black and White*, (Ringwood, 1980), p. 177. Further support for this observation is provided in R.M. Berndt's *Love Songs of Arnhem Land*, (Melbourne, 1976). See, in particular, the Preface (pp. xi-xx) and Chapter One, "A Perspective of Aboriginal Sexuality", pp. 3-15.

4 *ibid.*, pp. 144, 146.

5 Although Bandler is not an Aborigine, her work merits discussion here because she descends from another dark-skinned Australian minority group, the Pacific Islanders. I am therefore examining *Wacvie* in the context of *Black Australian* literature, as defined in the Introduction. Bandler's second novel, *Welou, My Brother*, (Adelaide, 1984), traces the same fictionalised episode of history as *Wacvie*. For this reason, and as it does not add any material relevant to the theme of sex and violence, it has not been included in this discussion.

6 Faith Bandler, *Wacvie*, (Adelaide, 1977), p. 7. All further quotations will be taken from this edition, and page numbers will be included in parentheses in the body of the text, immediately after each citation.

7 In fact, in terms of historical accuracy, Bandler's description of Pacific Islander life in nineteenth century Australia is also completely misleading. See, for example, Patricia Mercer's review of the book in *Aboriginal History*, vol. 2, part 2, 1978, pp. 181-182.

8 Telephone interview with Faith Bandler, Sydney, July, 1980.

9 Colin Johnson, *Doctor Wooreddy's Prescription for Enduring the Ending of the World*, (Melbourne, 1983), p. 207. All further quotations will be taken from this edition, and page numbers will be given in parentheses immediately following each citation, in the body of the text.

10 Colin Johnson, *Wild Cat Falling*, (Sydney, 1979), p. 74. All further quotations will be taken from this edition, and page numbers will be included in parentheses immediately following each citation, in the body of the text.

11 Colin Johnson, *Long Live Sandawara*, (Melbourne, 1979), pp. 81-82. All further quotations will be taken from this edition, and page numbers will be included in parentheses immediately after each citation, in the body of the text.

12   Blanche d'Alpuget's review of *Long Live Sandawara* in *24 Hours*, quoted on the back dustcover of *Wooreddy*, (Melbourne, 1983).

13   Personal correspondence with Colin Johnson, 24 August, 1982.

14   Personal interview with Colin Johnson, Brisbane, August 1980.

15   Personal interview with Colin Johnson, Brisbane, August, 1980.

16   Archie Weller, *The Day of the Dog*, (Melbourne, 1981), p. 44. All further quotations will be taken from this edition, and page numbers will be included in parentheses immediately after each citation, in the body of the text.

17   Personal interview with Archie Weller, Perth, February, 1983.

8

The Poetry of Politics:
Australian Aboriginal Verse

I would rather see Aborigines write a book called *Kargun* than pick up a shotgun.[1]

I always believe that the old axiom, 'the pen is mightier than the sword' is really true. And I always like to modernize that phrase by saying, 'the biro is far far better than the gun'![2]

Black Australian authors are not unified in their aims and approaches to writing. The diversity of Aboriginal literary perspectives is perhaps best illustrated by Black Australian poetry in English. Whether it is published in popular Australian periodicals such as the *Bulletin* or in local and regional Aboriginal community publications like the North Queensland *Message Stick* or the *Kimberley Land Council Newsletter*, poetry has attracted more Black Australian authors than any other mode of creative writing. Whether its orientation is towards Aboriginal health, education, legal matters, or government policy, almost every Aboriginal newspaper or magazine contains poetry on a regular basis. Verse is not only the most popular genre of Aboriginal creative expression in English; it also clearly illustrates the wide spectrum of Black Australian attitudes to the practice of writing and to the social purpose and utility of literature.

Some Aboriginal poets consider themselves to be mouthpieces for their people, expressing grievances and concerns felt collectively by the entire Aboriginal community. Others emphasise this political aspect of verse even further, believing that the act of composing poetry is an inherently political one which is itself an invaluable form of activism. Others view poetry as a means of preserving impressions and appreciations of nature and the beauty of life, and eschew any political involvement. Still others consider that writing verse is an essential emotional release and a salve for bitter experiences. Finally, some Aboriginal poets hope to become successful individual role models for their people who, through international as well as domestic recognition, can bring the Black Australian situation to the attention of the world.

It is against this complex background that Aboriginal verse must be assessed. It is clear that, despite differing individual aims and aspirations, most Aboriginal poets reject the art for art's sake argument and feel that their work has at least some social utility, whether to reinforce Aboriginal pride in identity, attack government policies, or criticise social ills within the Aboriginal community. Even when Black Australian nature poetry does not have an overt socio-political dimension, as an illustration of the singular Aboriginal poetic appreciation of the Australian landscape it can be politically significant. For example, as Stanner has commented, the Black Australian sense of oneness with the soil—which is the essence of the land rights campaign—is a relationship which requires a poetic understanding:

> No English words are good enough to give a sense of the links between an aboriginal group and its homeland. Our word "home", warm and suggestive though it be, does not match the aboriginal word that may mean "camp", "hearth", "country", "everlasting home", "totem place", "life source", "spirit centre" and much else all in one. Our word "land" is too spare and meagre. We can now scarcely use it except with economic overtones unless we happen to be poets.[3]

Given the range of Aboriginal approaches to writing, any dismissal of Aboriginal poetry as simply propaganda is inaccurate and unfair. Some Black Australian verse is blatantly polemical and impassioned; other examples of Aboriginal poetry are restrained and consciously apolitical. Ranging from overt political commitment to celebrations of nature, there is talented and impressive work from an ever-growing number of capable poets. No matter how obvious or how covert the socio-political dimension of this verse, it all expresses and reinforces a distinctive Black Australian world-view, highlighting pride, dignity and survival in the face of loss. Perhaps most important, in recent years a number of Aboriginal poets have articulated that world-view in verse which has an inherently oral, colloquial and/or phonetic character—a trend which represents a unique Black Australian contribution to Australian literature.

In this chapter, examples of the entire range of Aboriginal verse will be examined in order to illustrate the diversity and talent of contemporary Black Australian poets. I will consider the political involvement and stance of these writers as well as the particular social conditions in which they live—and which they often address in their work. In order to throw into relief some of the distinctive elements of the Aboriginal authors' approach, their work will be briefly compared with that of selected White Australian poets with an apparent understanding of Aboriginal culture, such as Les Murray and Bruce Dawe. Finally, in order to emphasise the Fourth World dimension and increasingly oral predisposition of Australian Aboriginal verse, I will contrast it with the poetry of contemporary Canadian Indian writers.

Any assessment of current Black Australian verse has to begin with the woman whom her publishers have claimed is the most-purchased Australian poet next to C.J. Dennis: Oodgeroo Noonuccal.[4] There is no doubt that Noonuccal is the doyenne of Aboriginal writers: her works, both poetry and prose, have been widely translated and are currently used as educational texts as far afield as Germany, Poland, and Japan. She is, along with Jack Davis, MumShirl, Pat O'Shane, Neville Bonner, Margaret Valadian and Charles Perkins, one of the best-known and most respected Aborigines, both in Australia and overseas. It came as no surprise that Noonuccal was chosen to script the Australian Pavilion's major presentation at World Expo 88, a striking holographic version of the Rainbow Serpent legend.

In this sense, her international fame enables her to act as a positive and successful role model for Black Australians and also makes it possible for her to wield a certain amount of political influence. For example, Colin Johnson claims that the Queensland government's last-minute decision to permit one officially illegal black protest march during the 1982 Brisbane Commonwealth Games was a direct result of the fact that it was learned Noonuccal would be one of the demonstrators. He maintains the Bjelke-Petersen government wished to avoid the embarrassment which would attend the arrest of such a prominent Aboriginal Australian.[5] A further example of her political influence is the fact that her candidacy for a Queensland senate seat in the 1983 federal election was taken seriously, both by other Black Australians and by the national media, as was her decision to withdraw in support of Neville Bonner's campaign. [6]

Noonuccal's direct involvement in Aboriginal affairs has continued since her experience as Queensland state secretary of FCAATSI in the 1960s. It is hardly coincidental that her first volume of poetry, *We Are Going*, was published in 1964, at the height of her political involvement. This is not to say that the poetry merely presented political slogans in slightly-disguised verse form, but that the heightening of Aboriginal pride, resolve and socio-political involvement which characterised the 1960s helped to provide the impetus for cultural expressions of Aboriginality, as well as for public campaigns on behalf of Black Australians. Throughout Australia, Aboriginal opposition to the official assimilation policy manifested itself in many ways. One of these was in the assertion of Aboriginal individuality, protest and pride which Noonuccal's poetry represents.

What of the verse itself? Some of the initial critical reaction to *We Are Going* was very harsh. The anonymous author of one typical review of Noonuccal's book contended that what she was writing was simply not poetic:

> This is bad verse ... jingles, cliches, laborious rhymes all piled up, plus the incessant, unvarying thud of a single message ... This may be useful propagandist writing ... It may well be the most powerful social-protest material so far produced in the struggle for aboriginal advancement ... But this has nothing to do with poetry. The authentic voice of the song-man [sic] using the English language still remains to be heard.[7]

This reaction is interesting, for the critic suggests rather myopically that protest poetry of the type in *We Are Going* is essentially a contradiction in terms. In short, poetry which was critical of White Australian society was invalidated because it did not conform to a limited conception of the "permissible" forms of that society's literature. The author's own expectations are revealing, as indicated by the final sentence of the review, which implies that the only "authentic" and legitimate Aboriginal poet will be one who is able to transform the literature of the black "song-man" (presumably traditional, male, oral literature in translation) into English verse. This is as inaccurate as the suggestion that the art of Namatjira and his followers was not authentic Aboriginal painting because it was influenced by certain European techniques, which fails to perceive that it was guided by a distinctively Aboriginal sensibility. Is it too much to suggest that this sort of reaction indicated a prevailing belief amongst those involved in Australian literature (a belief espoused by many in the anthropological school during the 1940s and 1950s) that the only true Aboriginal culture was traditional in nature?

Other evaluations of *We Are Going* displayed more enthusiasm. In Jill Hellyer's consideration of the book in *Hemisphere*, she quite correctly praised the strong elements of Noonuccal's verse:

> Kath Walker's poetry possesses the very definite merit of coming to life when spo-

ken aloud ... Her free verse, too, has great fluidity ... There is no doubt that Mrs Walker possesses an innate lyricism. It is her craftsmanship that needs to be worked upon if it is to match the depths of her feeling ... When Kath Walker learns the difference between wisdom and propaganda she could well become a significant voice in Australian poetry.[8]

It is true that Noonuccal's poetry is uneven, as a result of metre which occasionally jars, and rhyme which is sometimes forced. The point is that these are technical failings which have no bearing on the question of whether or not the poetry is allegedly propagandistic (which is an implicitly pejorative term in the first place). What can be said is that some of Noonuccal's most successful verse has a clear and strong socio-political message:

> No more woomera, no more boomerang,
> No more playabout, no more the old ways.
> Children of nature we were then,
> No clocks hurrying crowds to toil.
> Now I am civilized and work in the white way,
> Now I have dress, now I have shoes:
> 'Isn't she lucky to have a good job!'
> Better when I had only a dillybag.
> Better when I had nothing but happiness.[9]

In addition, I contend that, despite the technical weaknesses in much of Noonuccal's rhymed poetry in *We Are Going*, her free verse is often impressive in its directness and poignancy.

This observation is even more true of her second volume of poetry, *The Dawn Is At Hand*, first published in 1966. In such poems as "Nona" and "Gifts" the poet displays not only a keen eye for colour and signatures of detail but a subtle and endearing sense of humour which, for the most part, critics have failed to note. Above all, these are simple and direct imaginings of Aboriginal life before the invasion of the Europeans, as in "Gifts":

> 'I will bring you love', said the young lover,
> 'A glad light to dance in your dark eye.
> Pendants I will bring of the white bone,
> And gay parrot feathers to deck your hair.'
>
> But she only shook her head.
>
> 'I will put a child in your arms,' he said,
> 'Will be a great headman, great rain-maker.
> I will make remembered songs about you

That all the tribes in all the wandering camps
Will sing forever.'

But she was not impressed.

I will bring you the still moonlight on the lagoon,
And steal for you the singing of all the birds;
I will bring the stars of heaven to you,
And put the bright rainbow into your hand.'

'No', she said, 'bring me tree-grubs.[10]

The imagery in "Nona" is equally effective:

At the happy chattering evening meal
Nona the lithe and lovely,
Liked by all,
Came out of her mother's gunya,
Naked like the rest, and like the rest
Unconscious of her body
As the dingo pup rolling about in play.
All eyes turned, men and women, all
Had smiles for Nona.
And what did the women see? They saw
The white head-band above her forehead,
The gay little feather-tuft in her hair
Fixed with gum, and how she wore it.
They saw the necklet of red berries
And the plaited and painted reed arm-band
Jarri had made her.
And what did the men see? Ah, the men.
They did not see armlet or band
Or the bright little feather-tuft in her hair.
They had no eye for the red berries,
They did not look at these things at all.[11]

Admittedly, not all of Noonuccal's verse is of this standard. The tone of the "Verses" which end *The Dawn Is at Hand* is more suited to juvenile nursery rhymes than it is to adult poetry. These vignettes are too obviously an attempt at cleverness:

Man's endless quest is to be happy,
Ever since Cain wet his first nappy;
Yet crime-waves now and A-bomb plans,
And Yanks turned Schickelgruber fans.[12]

It is one thing to say that Oodgeroo Noonuccal's poetry varies quite markedly in atmosphere and accomplishment. It is another to denounce her as merely a "rhymer" or a "versifier", as Leon Cantrell did in his 1967 review of *The Dawn Is At Hand*:

> According to my system of pigeon-holes and prejudices she is not a poet. She has absolutely no feeling for words: it's almost as if they use her rather than she use [sic] them, with the result that one can gain no notion of the individual qualities of the person behind the verse.[13]

So, too, Andrew Taylor commented in the *Australian Book Review*:

> She is no poet, and her verse is not poetry in any true sense. It hasn't the serious commitment to formal rightness, that concern for making speech true under all circumstances, which distinguishes Buckley and Wright at their best.[14]

This denial that Noonuccal is a poet amounts to a disturbingly limited critical position. Hellyer is right to criticise Noonuccal's occasional lapses into an "attitude of preaching" and her tendency towards "clumsy inversions" in certain poems.[15] But to claim that none of Noonuccal's work is poetry smacks of a closed-mindedness which she and many of the other Aboriginal poets inveigh against in their verse. Given the markedly derivative character of much twentieth-century Australian poetry, Noonuccal's best work is quite a welcome departure from the "serious commitment to formal rightness" of which Taylor speaks. In the words of the *Times Literary Supplement*'s reviewer of *We Are Going*:

> Kath Walker has no need of metaphorical paraphernalia. She has a subject ... Much of the best poetry here is effective propaganda ... When so many poets are trying to write who fundamentally have nothing to say (the jottings of casual thoughts never made poetry) *We Are Going* is on the whole a refreshing book.[16]

I do not intend to engage in a revisionist appraisal of all the White Australian critics of Aboriginal poetry, but the case of Oodgeroo Noonuccal, as the first published Black Australian poet, is an instructive one. The initial critical reception of her work was hostile partly because it was something new and different on the Australian literary scene, something which did not conform to canons of poetic acceptability as they had been devised by the White Australian intelligentsia. Despite technical flaws, it is verse which is intended to be read out loud and always gains added power when it is delivered in this way. Second, Noonuccal's work has had an undoubted impact, through healthy sales, usage in the classroom and international exposure; such an impact was in fact its raison d'etre. Most important,

Oodgeroo Noonuccal introduced an Aboriginal perspective into contemporary Australian literature for the first time. She celebrated Aboriginal survival in the face of adversity, lamented prejudice and oppression, and offered an optimistic view of the potential for inter-racial harmony in the country. She is not the most impressive or the most accomplished Aboriginal poet: others have transformed Australian English into Aboriginal English in more innovative and exciting ways. Despite her early critics, Noonuccal was a pioneer in a new form of Australian poetry, embracing directness, environmental values and an overriding Aboriginal world-view. As Doobov concludes:

> Her importance lies in showing the potentialities of the Aboriginal influence rather than in fully exploring it. Yet the importance of what she attempts to achieve should not be underestimated. She has written poetry based on the Aboriginal philosophy that art is not the province of an intellectual elite, abandoning the esoteric fashion which some believe is strangling modern European poetry. She has produced liter-ary works out of a culture which is neither traditional Aboriginal nor European, but an emerging symbiosis of both.[17]

Perhaps the most significant aspect of Noonuccal's poetry is the fact that she intended it to be a distillation of the feelings and con-cerns of all Aboriginal people in Australia. In interview, she has re-peatedly emphasised her role as a mouthpiece for the Australian Aboriginal nation: "I see my books as the voice of the Aboriginal people, not my own personal voice. They dictate what I write". When asked why she began writing poems rather than short stories or nov-els, Noonuccal replied:

> I felt poetry would be the breakthrough for the Aboriginal people because they were storytellers and song-makers, and I thought poetry would appeal to them more than anything else. It was more of a book of their voices that I was trying to bring out, and I think I succeeded in doing this ... I'm putting their voices on paper, writing their things. I listen to the Aboriginal people, to their cry for help—it was more or less a cry for help in that first book, *We Are Going*. I didn't consider it my book, it was the people.[18]

Noonuccal thus established what might be termed the "representative" school of Aboriginal poetry, an approach which has attracted other notable Black Australian poets, such as Kevin Gilbert.

There are strong pressures in Australian society which militate against this view of the writing of poetry; inherent difficulties in any attempt to mirror the collective Aboriginal voice. First, Australian society often presumes a unanimous Black Australian position on many issues, which is seldom the case. The second drawback is that poets in Aboriginal society are not chosen by their peers to pursue their craft, even if there is an emerging trend amongst Black Australian poets to acknowledge community responsibility and control over their work. The persona of the individual author inevitably pervades the writing, and no matter how impervious to the critics an Aboriginal author may claim to be, she or he almost always has personal goals or aims. In a fascinating interview with Cliff Watego, Noonuccal demonstrated—almost unwittingly—the tensions which Aboriginal poets writing in a dominant white society must endure. When asked if she had to accept Western critics' judgements of her works because she was writing in English, Noonuccal answered:

Most critics are wrong anyway in the Western world. So black writers shouldn't worry about it. That should be beneath their dignity or contempt.

However, immediately afterwards she conceded:

The only thing that worries [Aboriginal writers] about critics is whether they're going to get their books sold or whether the critic's gonna squash it.[19]

So while attempting to write for and please Aborigines, many Black Australian poets are aware that critical judgements can have an effect upon the impact of their works, at least in terms of book sales. Since the Aboriginal reading public represents only a tiny fraction of the Australian book market, poets—like all Aboriginal writers—are constrained at least in part by the knowledge that they are not entirely free of white expectations if they want their work to be printed, distributed, and read widely. This factor can produce an almost schizophrenic reaction in black authors. As Jack Davis put it:

You've got to remember, too, that Aboriginal writers are not like non-Aboriginal writers, inasmuch as they've got the political scene to contend with. And, they've got their own thoughts to put down on paper, regardless of what's political, in terms of writing something which they want to *sell*. So, it's sort of like splitting their mind. You know, if you haven't got any political hang-ups, I should imagine you can sit down and go ahead and write with your mind fairly free. But, most Aboriginal writers were involved within the Black movement ... We all started off as political people.[20]

Davis's comments go to the heart of the matter. While the majority of Black Australian authors wish to retain that political consciousness which they have developed, often through years of involvement in Aboriginal affairs, they do not wish to deny themselves the crucial opportunity to be heard, both in Australia and internationally. In the words of Cheryl Buchanan, the Aboriginal woman who almost singlehandedly published Lionel Fogarty's first volume of verse, *Kargun*, no publisher wanted to touch such "heavy political material"[21] as was contained in his second collection, *Yoogum Yoogum*— until Penguin Books answered her plea to take up the project. Yet books like Fogarty's have expanded the range and achievement of Aboriginal poetry in English. How many other Lionel Fogartys are there in Australia who have never broken into print due to the negative response of many commercially oriented publishers? It is for this reason that one of the priorities of the National Aboriginal and Islander Writers', Oral Literature, and Dramatists' Association (NAIWOLDA) is to establish an independent national Black Australian publishing house.[22]

A further aspect of the politics of Aboriginal poetry is excellently illustrated by the case of Oodgeroo Noonuccal. Though not all Aboriginal writers would agree with her, Noonuccal is fervently determined to reach, and be evaluated by, world literary standards:

> In one way I think it's a draw-back because we're trying to express ourselves in the Aboriginal way of expression and it doesn't meet with the world standard ... It should be written not for the Aboriginals but ... for a *world* audience ... a universal theme.

She continues:

> When I'm written up in the papers or the media or whatever, they always call me an 'Aboriginal poet'; they always tag me with that. And I don't see myself as an 'Aboriginal poet' ... I see myself as a poet who is proud to be of Aboriginal descent.[23]

The internal tension becomes obvious once again. While she is a committed spokesperson for the Aboriginal people and extremely proud of her heritage, Noonuccal also wants to be thought of as a successful individual writer—regardless of race. Above all, black writers like Noonuccal want to be treated and evaluated as Aboriginal human beings. However, as this study has demonstrated, White Australian administrators, politicians, anthropologists and writers have experienced profound difficulties in proceeding from a conception of Black Australians as indigenous symbols to an appreciation of Aborigines as people.

Contemporary Aboriginal poets thus face numerous obstacles above and beyond those which other Australian authors encounter. Those who wish to represent widely-held Black Australian views are often criticised for attempting to be unauthorised national spokespeople. Some lesser-known Aboriginal poets who write verse to underline their distinctive appreciation of the Australian natural landscape are made to feel vaguely uncomfortable, because their poetry is not obvious social criticism or advocacy. In the same way, those who have achieved renown have often been accused of not being adequately political or radical. Others who have written talented protesting literature have had it dismissed by unsympathetic publishers and critics as solely "protest" literature, a genre which is largely avoided in the Australian publishing industry. As Bobbi Sykes points out, this dismissal of the merits of Aboriginal creative literature of social comment and analysis is often unjust:

> Have you ever heard any white person in the so-called free world calling Alexander Solzhenitsyn a protest writer? The protest literature title that whites try and lay on Black Writers is no more than an attempt to try and negate the value of what Black writers are saying.[24]

In addition to all of these pressures, Aboriginal poets face one other drawback which confronts the members of many other indigenous minority (and majority) groups writing in the world today. Simply, it is that of dealing with the English language and making it their own. This challenge underlies the writing of poetry throughout many areas of the British Commonwealth. In the words of Professor J.E. Chamberlin:

> Certainly many of the best poets, especially Northern Irish, West Indian, and African, write with a profound sense of anxiety about the language they use, which is often much more like a foster parent than a mother tongue to them and is unmistakably associated with a colonial authority (and a corresponding literary inheritance) that is both a curse and a blessing. Purifying the dialect of the tribe has always been one of poetry's central responsibilities; how to do it when you are not sure which tribe you belong to—as a writer and a shaper of reality with the imagination—is another matter and a disconcerting one.[25]

For Aboriginal writers, who very often have had minimal formal schooling, the challenge is a daunting one. Even though many Black Australian poets do have a positive and proud sense of their own identity, this dilemma of what might be termed the "imperialism of English" is very real. It is a dilemma to which they have reacted in a variety of ways.

One response is illustrated by the poetry of Jack Davis who, in his first volume of verse, *The First-born and Other Poems* adopts a conventional European metrical approach to his work. Davis's early verse is customarily composed in evenly measured end-rhyming lines of four stresses or less; there is very little experimentation with run-on lines, caesura, or internal rhyme. Beston has commented, "lacking confidence as they enter a field previously monopolised by whites, and handicapped by a limited education, they [the Aboriginal poets] seem to find a measure of security in the short line lyric with its established metrical and structural pattern",[26] and this observation is probably most accurate with reference to Davis. Despite the regularity of his poetic form, Davis is, like Noonuccal, not always in complete control of his verse. For example, in "The Boomerang", the shift in end-stressed syllables is somewhat jarring:

> But for me this is not so,
> Because I throw and throw.
> My eyes are bleary,
> I am arm-and-leg weary,
> Right to the marrow.[27]

But there is no denying the sincerity and honesty of Davis's impressions. As is the case with many of the most powerful poems written by Black Australians, a number of Davis's are occasional—composed in the immediate aftermath of socio-political events bearing upon Aborigines. For example, his "Laverton Incident" was written in the wake of the police shooting of a young Aborigine, Raymond Watson, after a dispute outside the pub in Laverton, Western Australia. The author arrived on the scene soon afterwards and the sight of Watson's blood on the ground remained etched in his mind:[28]

> The two worlds collided
> In anger and fear
> As it has always been—
> Gun against spear.
>
> Aboriginal earth,
> Hungry and dry,
> Took back the life again,
> Wondering why.
>
> Echo the gun-blast
> Throughout the land
> Before more blood seeps
> Into the sand.[29]

Beston has called Davis the "gentlest and most contained" [30] of the

Aboriginal poets, but the best examples of his earlier work are the most impassioned, such as "The First-born", "Prejudice", "Lost", "The Drifters" and "Desolation". In the last of these, the poet writes:

> We are tired of the benches, our beds in the park,
> We welcome the sundown that heralds the dark.
> White Lady Methylate!
> Keep us warm and from crying.
> Hold back the hate
> And hasten the dying.
>
> *The tribes are all gone,*
> *The spears are all broken:*
> *Once we had bread here,*
> *You gave us stone.*[31]

Like many other Black Australian poets, Davis has made a long and significant contribution to Aboriginal socio-political affairs, through his work for the Aboriginal Advancement Council and his six-and-a-half years as editor of *Identity* magazine.[32] Despite Noonuccal's desire for universality, it is actually Davis who, especially in his second collection of verse, *Jagardoo—Poems From Aboriginal Australia* has more frequently engaged other than specifically Aboriginal poetic themes. For example, over ninety per cent of Noonuccal's poems in *My People* deal with Black Australian themes such as white racism, Aboriginal identity, oppression, dispossession and so on, while less than one-third of Davis's poems in *Jagardoo* can be so classified.

In this volume Davis celebrates the beauties of nature—rivers, birds, trees, the seasons, and the ocean, in addition to whimsical childhood experiences. He also delves into issues such as analysis of the self, convalescence from illness, and the evils of militarism. There are poems dedicated to other Aborigines, such as Oodgeroo Noonuccal and Charles Perkins. *Jagardoo* is stylistically significant too, for Davis often loosens the measured grip on metre which characterised *The First-born*, and experiments with repetition, free verse, parody and variations in pace. These are often successful. Some poems are still marred by archaisms such as "A-beckoning to me"[33] but his best work displays careful observation and reflection of people and events both in Australia and overseas. For example, in "Bombay" he neatly encapsulates the irony of cultural relativism and shows that urbanised White and Black Australians are in some ways not as dissimilar as they might think:

The taxi,
honking, weaving, swaying,
took us in our opulence
through the people-teeming streets.

An old man,
thin black,
shook the dust of night
from limbs made gaunt
by caste and Eastern ways.

A pig
sucked the street's grey mud
with slobbering jaws,
growing fat, no doubt,
as men died around him.

While we, wide-eyed,
clicked our tongues
and made decisions
arrived at, by what we saw
through Western eyes.[34]

The verse of Noonuccal and Davis is marked by its imagistic clarity. But even in their more experimental poetry, even in their overtly political work, they contribute little to Australian poetry which is—structurally or technically—uniquely Aboriginal. Their themes and concerns and world-view are undoubtedly Black Australian, but not their poetic technique.

Kevin Gilbert's poetry is also remarkable for its directness, but it is frequently more caustic than the verse of his predecessors. Gilbert's published poetry shows as much concern for Aboriginal social issues as Noonuccal's, but he brings a greater daring, a greater appreciation of Black Australian colloquial speech patterns and far more bitterness to his work. Part of the bitterness is due to a sense of profound frustration; part, in literary terms, is due to what he views as betrayal. Gilbert saw the manuscript version of his first published collection of verse, *End of Dreamtime*, radically altered by a white editor—without his permission—prior to publication. The episode presents one of the worst cases of European editorial intrusion in the field of Aboriginal literature, and offers an opportunity for textual criticism of Gilbert's corpus of poetry far beyond the scope of this study. One poem can serve as an example of just how important these unauthorised changes were. In "People *Are* Legends", the poem which gave its title to Gilbert's "authorised" 1978 volume of verse, the original manuscript version (composed in the late 1960s while he was still in prison) is as follows:

Kill the legend
Butcher it
With your acute cyncicisms
Your paternal superfluities
With your unwise wisdom
Kill the legend
Obliterate it
With your atheism
Your fraternal hypocrisies
With your primal urge of miscegenation
Kill the legend
Devaluate it
With your sophistry
Your baseless rhetoric
Your lusting material concepts
Your groundless condescension
Kill it
Vitiate the seed
Crush the root-plant
All this
And more you must needs do
In order
To form a husk of a man
To the level and in your own image
Whiteman.[35]

The poem was printed exactly in this form in the 1978 volume[36] whereas in 1971, the following, significantly condensed, version was published without Gilbert's approval:

Kill the legend
butcher it
with your acute cynicism
your paternalist wisdom

Kill the legend
scrub it out
with your hypocrisy
your malice and mockery

Kill the legend
rubbish it
with materialistic rhetoric
and grasping lust

Go on
kill it
crush the seed
hack at the root
make me a husk
make me like you
whiteman.37

It could be claimed that these are minor revisions since they do not alter the basic intent or meaning of the poem. According to standards of simplicity and effect, it is possible to argue that the edited version is poetically superior. However, this is not the issue: it is one of trust and ethical integrity. The decision to revise Gilbert's work without his sanction implies that the editor of Island Press not only considered Gilbert's writing as it stood to be unfit for publication (an opinion contradicted by the University of Queensland Press seven years later) but that he also felt he had the right to "improve" it according to his own particular standards. It is no surprise that Gilbert has repeatedly and publicly disowned the version of his poems which appeared in *End of Dreamtime* and, for this reason, that volume will not be discussed any further here in relation to his verse.

Gilbert's poetry has been enthusiastically received in some quarters and viewed with disfavour in others. For example, one critic enthused that *People Are Legends* "consists of metrical poems that flash and sparkle like polished gemstones"38 while another complained that "often the language is stiff and mannered, and nowhere more so than in the title poem, whose good deal of truth does not cover up its verbal shallowness, facile twists of bitter wit, self-defeating bluntness, and carelessness of prosody". In a sense, such a wide range of opinion is to be expected concerning poetry which is so accusatory and disconcertingly direct. As the same reviewer continued, "The poems are embarrassing, and the more we sympathise, the more disarmed and unhelpful we feel in the face of an angry, bitter tone".39 Gilbert certainly does not mince his words, as some of his more striking openings attest:

I've had a cunt of a life

> I suppose
> As a woman.[40]

and:

> I'll sell me moot for half a note
> And a bottle of wine if you need.[41]

and finally:

> Then the white man took his bloodied boot
> From the neck of the buggered black
> Did you expect some gratitude
> His smile "Good on you Jack?"[42]

Elsewhere, he just as forthrightly takes the (presumably white) reader to task:

> But I reckon the worstest shame is yours
> You deny us human rights.[43]

While Gilbert can stir feelings of culpability in sensitive White Australian readers, many would dismiss his stance as anti-white racism. But a careful reading of Gilbert's verse makes it impossible to maintain this view. For he is just as critical of Black Australians who allegedly sell out their people by accepting European accolades or well-paid government employment, or by passive complacency. Some of the author's most trenchant verse is aimed at these supposed betrayers of the Aboriginal movement. For example, the clipped line length and powerful rhyme scheme in "The 'Better Blacks' " is most effective:

> Watch for the traitors
> Dressed in black
> Watch for those jackies
> Up you Jack!
> Watch for the puppet
> Watch for the brute
> Living like a whiteman
> Grey serge suit
>
> "Tommin' " for his pay now
> "Tommin' " for his job.
> Watch him watch him brothers
> Watch his sleek black hide
> Selling out our people
> While our people die.[44]

There is no clearer example of Gilbert's ability to rankle others than the aftermath of his caustic poem, "To My Cousin, Evonne Cawley", given pride of place in The *Bulletin Literary Supplement* of September, 1980:

> I wonder, Evonne, when you're playing
>   straight sets
> And you "haste" your opponent so well,
> Do you ever look back at your
> grandmother, black
> And catch glimpses of her in her hell?[45]

The publishers of the *Bulletin*, Consolidated Press, were put in an awkward position when the poem they had highlighted in their advertising for this issue prompted Cawley to undertake ultimately successful legal action against them. Not only did this demonstrate Gilbert's ability to raise indignation through his verse; it was also an excellent example of the potential social impact of Aboriginal literature, of the convergence of poetry and political considerations.

Like Noonuccal, Gilbert subscribes to a "representative" notion of his work:

> I've adopted writing as a means of voicing the Aboriginal situation ... I try to present as truly as possible the Aboriginal situation and the Aboriginal response.

But he is also motivated by didacticism:

> There is the need to educate White Australians to the present situation of Aboriginal people ... I'm presenting it as honestly as possible—it's not a pretty picture.

Gilbert draws much of his conviction from his time behind bars:

> I spent fourteen-and-a-half years in prison. I saw human rights contravened every day. Despite the debasing conditions there, it still wasn't as unjust as the system oppressing Aborigines. [46]

Though there is a strong, militant side to Gilbert's often sarcastic poetry, there is another side of which most Australians are not aware. Even in *People Are Legends*, a sense of sardonic humour emerges in such poems as "Granny Koori", in which Gilbert portrays the symbolic emasculation of Aboriginal men:

> Dear Director of Aboriginal Grants
> My association needs $55,000 bucks
> To purchase silky black ladies pants
> A quota to cover each area, the Territories-
> State by state

> To conceal from the prying eyes of the world
> The Aborigines poor buggered fate.[47]

Gilbert's vibrant humour is often disguised in his poetry, but is particularly evident in his drama—as will be illustrated in the following chapter.

There is a further facet to Gilbert's talent which encompasses most of his unpublished material. He has written a number of very different poems, still only in manuscript form, which celebrate such themes as love and devotion. If one examines an unpublished poem such as "Extract From a Letter to a Woman Friend", one might not believe it was written by the same man who produced *People Are Legends*:

> And I would part the weeping willows
> Hold the birch firm in my hand
> Gently stroke the living waters
> Whispering to the fertile land
> Beams of sunshine shot with silver
> Thriving brown and vital hue
> Resting land aglow with nature
> Dreaming of the ever you.[48]

More recently, Gilbert has written a substantial series of whimsical and light poems in the form of nursery rhymes directed at children, but again, these exist only in unpublished form:

> Once I met a mad Rosella
> He was quite a crazy fella
> Who got drunk on nectar-ferment
> From a rich old bottle-brush
> His wings he flapped and fluttered
> While foolishly he muttered
> I wish I was an eagle
> Or a fine plumed English thrush.[49]

Many of these poems deserve publication; however, the variety of Gilbert's accomplishments have been downplayed both by the media and by publishers, thereby perpetuating his image as solely a "protest" poet. This is primarily because, in Gilbert's words, "publishers didn't want my love poetry".[50] It seems to be commercially more profitable to publish a militant Aboriginal writer—as long as he or she is not too acerbic—than to print less controversial material. Therefore, Australian publishers have, in a further sense, dictated the public image with which well-known Aboriginal authors have been cloaked—a further motivation for NAIWOLDA's establishment of an independent Black Australian publishing house.

One wonders whether Les Murray's rather unjust review of *People Are Legends* might have been different if all the dimensions of Gilbert's poetic achievement had been represented in the book. Murray commented, "Worst of all, he confuses vehemence with poetic intensity. Unlike many radical versifiers, he has things to be vehement about, but poetry will not be forced."[51] Some of Gilbert's work is awkward in terms of metre and scansion; like all poets, he is not consistently successful. But some of his most fluid verse is that which relies upon an ear for Aboriginal colloquial speech and intonations, as in "The Gurindji":

> Poor fellow
> Simple fellow
> Sweet fellow
> Strong
> Sittin' in the desert
> Singin' desert song
> Cryin' countin' chickens
> Chickens made of lan'
>
> Poor fellow
> Silly fellow
> Sad fellow
> Cry
> White fellow gibbit lan'
> To hide you when you die [52]

Other Australian poets have attempted to structure their poetry in the Aboriginal idiom, most importantly, those of the Jindyworobak group. As was noted in Chapter Three, their commitment to the idiom was formal and superficial: they frequently attempted to utilise Aboriginal concepts and phrases in a parodic and ineffectual fashion. Les Murray has been termed "the last of the Jindyworobaks" by Bruce Clunies-Ross.[53] Clunies-Ross is correct to ascribe Jindyworobak sympathies to Murray and, as the poet has explained, there are cogent personal and environmental reasons for this.[54] Probably more than any other contemporary White Australian poet, Les Murray has been aware of the "Aboriginal presence"[55] and has consciously and conscientiously attempted to incorporate it into his work. But (again like many of the original Jindyworobaks) Murray apprehends Black Australians primarily as symbols and representations of Australia's "greatest autochthonous tradition"[56]: during his childhood, they were "partly a people, partly a caste, partly a class".[57] His observation of individual Aborigines from his own experience certainly has influenced his verse. However, the treatment of Black Australians in his poetry is—however sympathetic—one of types of human beings rather than of truly individualised characters. For example, in "The Ballad of Jimmy Governor" the speaker is representative of Aboriginal fugitives, not only from white law, but from European culture. The poem abounds in references to feet, shoes and the earth: the contrast is between barefooted (or free and natural) Aborigines and shod (restricted and destructive) whites. As Jimmy relates:

> Today I take that big step
> On the bottom rung of the air....
>
> Mother, today I'll be dancing
> Your way and his way on numb feet.[58]

Murray is intrigued by, and concerned with, White Australian myths about Aborigines and with the mythology of the Black Australians themselves. He appears far less interested in portraying Aborigines as people, or in reflecting their characteristic rural or urban speech patterns. For example, his poem "Thinking About Aboriginal Land Rights, I Visit the Farm I Will Not Inherit" is a personal evocation of the pain that the dispossession of land can cause:

> By sundown it is dense dusk, all the tracks closing in.
> I go into the earth near the hay shed for thousands of years.[59]

Here it is implicit that Murray's feeling for the farm which he will be denied is akin to the sense of loss which has afflicted Black Australians confronted with the white encroachment into their continent. He feels very intensely that White Australians view their land as far more than an investment: "It's bullshit to say that 'property' is the concept that whites have for land; I couldn't live in another place from where I've come from".[60]

While it is true that White Australians have developed a real and heartfelt feeling for their sometimes unlovely land since 1788, Murray's reference to "thousands of years" pushes the parallel too far. The sense of *belonging* of which he speaks is of a different order of magnitude to the sense of being *owned by* the land, which is the traditional Aboriginal concept, with all the sanctity of religious veneration. Murray draws this parallel because of his belief in the convergence of the White and Black Australian cultures. He claims that

Europeans have absorbed—almost without realising it—a number of Aboriginal concepts, such as the appreciation of periods of seasonal work interspersed with periods of nomadism (as practised by miners, cattlemen, and shearers), the annual summertime holiday "walk-about", and the dislike of "hobby farmers" on the part of both Aborigines and country people. Murray's position, while intriguing, is simplistic and eurocentric. Despite his sincere interest in Aboriginal culture, he has restricted himself to a quasi-anthropological appreciation of that culture because of his fascination with the traditional Aboriginal world-view. This leads him to an admitted over-emphasis (like the original Jindyworobaks) upon tribes such as the Aranda, an over-reliance upon anthropologists such as Strehlow, and a lack of appreciation of contemporary Aboriginal culture. He does not see that culture as an adaptive, ongoing phenomenon which is just as viable in urban as well as in country areas.

Les Murray's poetry on Aboriginal themes is therefore one step removed from the ground level of current thought about Aboriginal culture. Unlike many other concerned White Australian authors, Murray does not recognise the concept of a collective European historical "conquest-guilt" which he thinks "may be no more than a construct of the political Left".[61] Other prominent contemporary White Australian poets, such as Bruce Dawe, would not agree. His poem, "Nemesis", is an excellent and effective example of the kind of sentiments which other poets such as Judith Wright have also expressed:

> But what is that one slaughter
> repeated many times
> to us who tread domestic grass
> and thrill to 'foreign' crimes?
> We cannot call the Turrbul back
> and guilt's a slippery thing
> if all it feeds is speeches
> and songs that poets sing...
>
> When the Kalkadoons stopped running
> and charged and charged again
> they fell as fell their tribesmen
> on earlier hill and plain.
> And we who wrote their finish
> must turn and write a start
> if *we* would turn from running
> and face our thundering heart.[62]

Les Murray and Bruce Dawe are arguably representative of the two major thematic streams of White Australian literature of the past fifty years which has dealt with Aborigines. The former is a member of the school of symbolic usage of the Aboriginal theme, which counts Katharine Susannah Prichard, Xavier Herbert, the Jindyworobaks, and even Patrick White amongst its members. The latter illustrates the stance of the school of concerned conscience (often motivated by guilt) which numbers those such as Judith Wright, Thomas Keneally and Robert Drewe amongst its adherents. The two streams are not mutually exclusive (Herbert, for instance, crosses the boundaries) but this schema makes it possible to contrast the attitudes of White Australian authors more clearly.

If there is any "school" of Black Australian poetry it is one of social protest. This is not to say that Aboriginal verse is one-dimensional. As Cliff Watego has put it:

> With protest poetry, this tradition of protest poetry, they like to say 'Oh, that's just protest poetry, and that's it. We can easily handle that.' That's what critics have a tendency to do … But it's not a limiting factor. To emphasise this protest tradition, or what they want to call protest poetry, it's unfair, because it's made up of all different aspects, different viewpoints, as the poets or writers know themselves.[63]

It is probably best to see Black Australian poetry as stemming from a long tradition of opposition to the established order—but that opposition takes many forms. In his *The Song Circle of Jacky, and Selected Poems*, Colin Johnson illustrates some of those forms while he criticises the dominant Australian culture. His thirty-five poems in the Jacky series often have an undercurrent of satirical bitterness, as in "Song Twenty-Seven":

> A youthman was found hanging in his cell
> On Nadoc day when everywhere the Aborigines
> Were dancing, everywhere the Aborigines were marching.
> 'They're just like us', was the quaint refrain,
> 'They like balls and footy and songs and beer':
> They ignored our call for Landrights!
>
> On Nadoc day a youthman strangled in a cell:
> Who killed him, who were his murderers?
> 'Not I,' said the cop, 'I only took him in.'
> 'Not I,' said the town, 'I never spoke his name,
> It's no fault of mine that he had to die—
> We treat them as we would our own,
> There's no racism in our town.'[64]

Johnson's poem assumes great power when seen in the light of the work of the Muirhead Royal Commission into Aboriginal Deaths in Custody, established in late 1987. It found that between January, 1980 and February, 1988, ninety-six young Aboriginal men died in unusual circumstances while incarcerated: the majority were found hanged, over half while they were in police custody.[65] It is this coalescence of politics and poetry which makes it impossible to divorce the social context from what black poets like Johnson are expressing.

It also makes it impossible not to see Johnson as one of the most talented Aboriginal poets, for he handles such themes with an innovative confidence. His range in *The Song Circle of Jacky* is striking:

> Born between straight lines;
> Dying between straight lines;
> Laid to rest between straight lines,
> Buried in rows as straight as supermarket goods:
> Our heaven will be straight lines;
> Our hell will be all curved lines,
> Unable to fit the straightness of our souls.[66]

As in his historical novels, Johnson emphasises that Black Australian history was a proud saga of resistance. The apparently simple rhyme scheme in "Song Five" underpins a purposely didactic tone:

> Ned Kelly was a man,
> Who rode through this land,
> An' Irishman, brave and true—
> Then the British hung him high,
> So that his feet danced in the sky—
> And Jacky says they did the same to—
> Yagan, Melville Harry, Broger, Lory Jack,
> Ellemara, Talboy, Merridio, Therramitchie,
> And many, many, too many Jacky Jackies.[67]

The familiarity of Johnson's rhythm insinuates his message in the reader's mind so effectively that the parallel which he establishes would be clear to any Australian secondary school student.

Elsewhere, his experimentation with rhythm is particularly marked. In his usage of the linked song-cycle format, Johnson has consciously reached back for inspiration to the oral poetic traditions of his forebears. In places, he also captures the stylistic wholeness of traditional Aboriginal songs, with their frequent repetition of words and sounds, and their incremental progress of story-line:

He takes young man, he takes old man, makes them shiver in fright and fear;
He takes young man, he takes old man, makes them see his visions;
Makes them shiver in fright and fear, makes them suffer from the storm;
Makes them see their spirit maker, makes them leave him all alone,
While he finds his secret things, sacred objects of his trade:
Whispers to the magic wand, sings softly to the dilly bag,
Murmurs to the emu feathers, lights the fire with a word,
Brings the whirlwind to his feet, glides off to see the world:
Jacky, Jacky, he no fool; Jacky Jacky, he kurdaitcha man![68]

Thus, Johnson's poetry of protest relies upon structure and style as much as content to make its statement about Aboriginal independence.

Of course, this protest genre is not confined to Australia. It surfaces all over the world, especially amongst indigenous groups who have only relatively recently gained a political and literary voice. The poetry of Canadian Indians is a prime example of the same phenomenon. It is striking that, in both Canada and Australia, indigenous peoples share a strong and vibrant spiritual affinity for one another as oppressed "first citizens", for their traditions and, above all, for their land. A convenient way to exemplify this affinity is to examine the Canadian Inuit and Indian and Australian Aboriginal position papers on ideology and political rights, tabled at the World Council of Indigenous Peoples' Third General Assembly, held in Canberra in April-May, 1981. The Inuit and Indians declared:

We, the indigenous peoples of Canada, know that the Creator put us on this land.

We were given our languages, our culture, and a place on the Earth which provided us with food, water, medicines, shelter.

We were created as free peoples.

We have maintained our freedom. Although in recent times we have made agreements and signed treaties so that major portions of our lands could be shared with others, we have never given up our freedom. We have conserved our languages, our traditions, and we have protected our lands. We have reserved to ourselves the right to govern our own people and our own affairs, and to determine our destiny.

Peoples of the world who have their language, culture, and lands, and who have never surrendered the right to govern themselves, are considered to be nations.

THEREFORE:

We are nations.

We have always been nations.

We have the right to govern ourselves.

We have the right to self-determination.

We have the right to control our lands and our resources.[69]

Though the wording of the National Aboriginal Conference's paper on "Aboriginal Ideology" is different, the sentiments are very similar:

The land, for us, is a vibrant spiritual landscape. It is peopled in spirit form by the ancestors in the dreaming. The ancestors travelled the country, in adventure which created
   the people
   the natural features of this land
   the code of life
The law has been passed on to us
Through the reverence and the celebration of the sites of the ancestors

           Songs and dance
           Body, sand and rock painting
           Special languages and legends
           These are the media of the law to the
           present day.

And now our social existence is in conflict with white society
But our existence is based on an unrelinquished will
   to maintain identity
   to maintain our relationship with the land
   to reject the interference of the white institutions.
And as we draw on our 'myths' to retain our existence
So must the whites draw on their 'myths' of superiority
   to secure power
   and rule in our lands.[70]

A comparison of Aboriginal and Indian poetry is particularly rewarding in view of this common ideological stance, and because of the numerous other similarities between Canada and Australia. Literature is playing an increasingly important role in the articulation of both Aboriginal and Indian cultural identity, and poetry as the genre of creative expression perhaps most amenable to previously oral cultures is, for indigenous groups in both countries, the single most popular medium of creative expression in written English. In both countries, most of those indigenous people writing verse are very politicised and active in the field of agitation for their rights. In the case of Canadian Indian poetry the symbolic, spiritual nature of indigenous existence is extensively explored; in Aboriginal poetry, what defines contemporary "Aboriginality"—the distinctive Black Australian self-definition—is a common emphasis. The poets of both nations display in their work an overriding sense of loss: the loss of happiness, of traditional laws, of togetherness and of freedom. Hence, the poetry is very often bittersweet and ambivalent.

The atmosphere of evanescence—of witnessing the fading away of the old ways—strikes one of the strongest chords in indigenous poetry, both in Canada and in Australia. Oodgeroo Noonuccal addresses this dilemma of potential identity loss, and emphasises the fragility of the entire human species, in her most famous poem, "We Are Going", which ends:

> The scrubs are gone, the hunting and the laughter.
> The eagle is gone, the emu and the kangaroo are gone from this place.
> The bora ring is gone.
> The corroboree is gone.
> And we are going.'[71]

The lamentation for lost heritage is equally fervent in Canadian Indian poetry. Jim Dumont uses the symbol of the buffalo to represent the extinction of traditional ways:

> In my youth
> I went south,
> In my dreams
> I went south.
>
> There
> I watched them hunt …
> I watched them hunt the buffalo.
> And in my heart
> I hunted with them.
>
> Now they are gone.
> The buffalo have left,
> Ashamed,
> That we had let them die,
> Mercilessly,
> At the hands of the white hunters.[72]

In his poem "The Last Crackle", Gordon Williams illustrates effectively how the rape and destruction of Indians in the past continues in the exploitation of Indians today:

All our men are dead and our young ones
Have no ambition. They took it all away,
Those bearded men, with their strange ways.
'Kneel with us' they said, 'and pray!'
Then they took our land and children.

Now they've taken their beards off and shorn their
Hair, and they smile quick as a rattler's strike:
Before you open your door, a face of stone,
Then before your door is fully open, a smile
Trying to sell an old woman beauty cosmetics.[73]

This sense of the loss of Indian traditions is a spiritual one as well; the damage done cannot be measured solely in material terms. In this regard, the loss of pride, of autonomy and of a feeling of importance have caused a severe loss of self-respect and confidence which, while not quantifiable, is equally harmful. Indian lecturer, activist, author, film-maker and poet, Duke Redbird, expresses this atmosphere of enervation very effectively in his poem, "Tobacco Burns":

Tobacco curls when touched by fire
The smoke rises—up—
Blue and grey
A fog that holds medicine
The spirit is strong.
The story is old
The smoke curls
I feel a sound—the sound
Of drums on distant hills
Of buffalo hoofs on frozen ground
A medicine chant wailing by breezes
That have not blown
For many moons; nor suns
That shine no longer on brown children
My eyes seek a vision—
For old people told of visions
That were not seen by eyes
But burned in the mind and mouth
Of our men
Who fought battles
But did not win.
My body cries for strong medicine
But my eyes water from whisky
My brain bleeds—my heart sweats
I regret

That tobacco burns
And I am not strong.[74]

In both countries the verse of the indigenous peoples also celebrates those links with the past which are still retained today. The very act of writing much of this poetry is an exercise of celebration and reinforcement of traditional ties. For example, Jim Dumont ends his "For Joe Mackinaw" with the words:

... in my old age
I will go in dreams
And I will find the buffalo again.[75]

Similarly, Oodgeroo Noonuccal underlines the fact that history lives on for many contemporary Aborigines, in her poem, "The Past":

Let no one say the past is dead.
The past is all about us and within.
Haunted by tribal memories, I know
This little now, this accidental present
Is not the all of me, whose long making
Is so much of the past ...
a thousand thousand camp fires in the forest
Are in my blood.
Let none tell me the past is wholly gone.
Now is so small a part of time, so small a part
Of all the race years that have moulded me.[76]

In her poem "Drums of My Father", the Canadian Indian author, Shirley Daniels, makes almost exactly the same point using very similar language:

A hundred thousand years have passed
Yet, I hear the distant beat of my father's drums
I hear his drums throughout the land
His beat I feel within my heart.

The drums shall beat, so my heart shall beat,
And I shall live a hundred thousand years.[77]

If the relationship between the past and present—between historical and current injustice—is one of the major themes in both Indian and Aboriginal verse, another pertains to the future, uncertain as it may be. One of the most potent images of the future is, of course, the child, and indigenous poets in both countries, such as the Black Australian, Maureen Watson, and the Canadian Indian, Eleanor

Crowe, highlight this concern in their poetry. For example, in Watson's "Black Child", the author despairs that she cannot shield her child from the harsh realities of racism:

> Then he grows older, he's off to school,
> Mother waves her babe goodbye,
> Faltering smile upon her lips,
> Determined not to cry.
> And there's anger in a black brother's fists,
> And shame in a father's heart,
> That he sees his people suffer so,
> And a black child's world falls apart.
> While he sees all the black man's truths,
> Distorted by white man's lies,
> Poor innocent, helpless, wounded babes,
> With tears in their big dark eyes.
> Oh, I'd cut out my heart to lay at your feet,
> And I'd rip the stars from the blue,
> I'd spit on the sun and put out its light,
> If I could keep all this hurt from you.
> Flesh of my flesh, and blood of my blood,
> You never hear how my tortured heart cries,
> To a people too cruel, too blind to see,
> The tears in my black child's eyes.[78]

In Crowe's poem, it is the death of the child which haunts the speaker:

> Red child died
> screaming in my head today
> only i heard him
>
> At dusk he and his brothers gather
> shadows
> in front of my windshield ...
> and there are no words to exorcise you
> from my skull, from my gut where you twist
> die again and again
> where I cannot save you ...
>
> red child
>
> your eyes   your mother's
> cries
> inhabit this land only
> well through sounds of wheels that roll

on your bones
that rattle and wail
that drive me
to find you.[79]

Watson makes it clear that it is impossible for her to protect her son from the racial persecution he will suffer in educational institutions, however much she wishes to. It is noteworthy that her direct, emphatic style is accentuated by her measured metre and regular rhyme-scheme—which has the effect of building the impact to a crescendo at the close of the poem. The Aboriginal poets' desire for a vivid, telling impact means that their verse very frequently incorporates a steady rhyme scheme and rhythm together with the repetition of key words in successive lines. The best-known Aboriginal poets—Oodgeroo Noonuccal, Jack Davis, and Kevin Gilbert —incorporate these techniques in the majority of their poems, and only in the last ten years have Aboriginal poets begun to experiment to a greater extent with blank verse, irregular metre, and phonetic spellings.

On the other hand, as Crowe's "Shadows" exemplifies, Canadian Indian poets have been more inclined to write unrhymed verse which emphasises word order, positioning, and pauses, rather than repetitive sounds. Indians have also been experimenting with written poetry for a longer period of time and with a significant amount of success. Some of Duke Redbird and Marty Dunn's ventures into the realm of concrete poetry have been very effective, particularly as they have moulded their pictorial verse into graphic illustrations which have meanings for both native and non-native Canadians. In one striking example, attributes of the White and Indian cultures are unified into a prescription for the social evolution of the North American consciousness by the year 2001. These "male", "active" (white) and "female", "passive" (Indian) characteristics coalesce into a unified circle, which is depicted as shining like the moon over a totem pole.[80]

To cite another example of Indian poetic experimentation, Sarain Stump illustrated his own extended, book-length poem, *There Is My People Sleeping*, so that the graphics become an integral component of the very lyrical text. There is no Aboriginal poet who has yet written a sustained work of either the calibre or the length of Stump's poem, nor is there a Black Australian who has illustrated her or his own publication as meaningfully. A brief, unillustrated excerpt does not adequately convey the total effect of his book, but may give some indication of its density:

> AND THERE IS MY PEOPLE SLEEPING
> SINCE A LONG TIME
> BUT AREN'T JUST DREAMS
> THE OLD CARS WITHOUT ENGINE
> PARKING IN FRONT OF THE HOUSE
> OR ANGRY WORDS ORDERING PEACE OF MIND
> OR WHO STEALS FROM YOU FOR YOUR GOOD
> AND DOESN'T WANNA REMEMBER WHAT HE OWES YOU
> SOMETIMES I'D LIKE TO FALL ASLEEP TOO,
> CLOSE MY EYES ON EVERYTHING
> BUT I CAN'T
>   I CAN'T....
>
> I WAS MIXING STARS AND SAND
> IN FRONT OF HIM
> BUT HE COULDN'T UNDERSTAND
> I WAS KEEPING THE LIGHTNING OF
> THE THUNDER IN MY PURSE
> JUST IN FRONT OF HIM
> BUT HE COULDN'T UNDERSTAND
> AND I HAD BEEN KILLED A THOUSAND TIMES
> RIGHT AT HIS FEET
> BUT HE HADN'T UNDERSTOOD[81]

The majority of Canadian Indian poets have succeeded in creating extremely visual poetry, in which word positioning on the page, artwork and design are important components. For example, the manner in which the poems of Skyros Bruce are printed on the page contributes importantly to their success:

> in
> dian
>
> we are north americans
> he said
> and made me feel
> ashamed   that i was not wearing
> beads at my throat
> small proud flowers
> growing there
> or leather
> sarain stump
> handsome faced

colour of earth rose
quietly
telling me that i am
indian now
and ending all
the identity fears[82]

In a similar fashion, Leo Yerxa's "I Searched" gains its maximum effect from the visual pauses which its layout necessitates:

i searched
the places in the
long narrow streets
and at times
i even looked between the sheets,
in the morning
all i found
was a head   full   of hurt,
a dime on the shelf
and the devil
to pay[83]

Such pauses are also essential to the impact of Wayne Keon's "Moosonee in August":

the Cree women
are laffing
& hide their faces
behind a worn blanket
every time a man
raises a camera
in front of them ...

one woman
speaks to me
in a dialect
i cannot
understand
& I feel stupid
but smile anyway

my face
gets hot
when I walk away
and take the hand

of my blonde
woman[84]

Naturally there are exceptions to this visual trend, such as the work of Gordon Williams. In his poem, "Justice in Williams Lake", he offers the reader a hard-hitting poetic critique of a judicial system which can permit the acquittal of the rapists and murderers of an Indian woman. In so doing, he uses the techniques of assonance, alliteration, and a jagged, repetitive rhythm, in order to produce a poem which is orally very effective:

the wind blows colder
and the flag snaps angrily
bells of freedom ring
thru an idealistic dominion
publication
prints
splots
of ink
splotted splatted
blotted
plotted
democratic rapists
set free
fined forgiven—
Indian maiden
raped and killed
too young
too dead to smile
her murderers
set free
this is democracy
mute flags indifferent to lamentation
manipulation of justice
in Williams lake.[85]

This is not to imply that Canadian Indian verse is superior to Australian Aboriginal poetry. The point is that, while poets of the two indigenous groups share many thematic concerns—such as the question of identity, and of "unjust justice" in a white society—they have engaged in stylistic experimentation which has generally taken them in different directions. While the Indian writers have largely written more visual, unrhymed verse, the Aboriginal authors have developed more rhymed and, particularly, more oral poetry, which has a greater impact when read aloud as a result of its increasing emphasis upon phonetic sounds and the spoken dialect.

Over the past fifteen years, a number of Black Australian poets with very distinctive voices have emerged. One of them is Tutama Tjapangati, a tribal man from the Papunya area of the Northern Territory, who has published only sparingly. His poetry breaks new ground in Australia through its unique phonetic synthesis of Pintupi/Luritja and English—as in this brief poem, which concerns a severe storm which lifted a sheet-iron roof off a dwelling:

> Ohhh,
> > too much/
> > > little bitta cheeky bug/
> kapi purlka/ walpa purlka/ ohhh! ebbrywhere!
> jitapayin WHOOF! gone. Pinished!
> /kapi kapi kapi/ cough'a cough'a cough'a
> ohhh, too much.[86]

Another of Tjapangati's poems, "Aladayi", tells the story of the local school bus:

> big one mutukayi
> kulaputja katiku
> bring em up here
>
> big one
> Tjukula, show em a you
> my country
>
> Mickini, mighty be we take em
> Mayayana, my daught
> Nolan, my brother
> Kayiyu Kayiyu, Nampitjimp
>
> Ohh, too much!
> grab em big one you
> ebbrything a tucker
> kapi too/puttem a-drum
>
> you right that's 'im
> my country, piyu
> kala!

[mutukayi—motorcar; kulaputja—schoolbus; katiku—will bring; Tjukula—a place in the eastern Gibson Desert; Nampitjimp—

shortened version of Nampitjinpa, a skin-name; kapi—water;
piyu—all's well; kala—anyway, what next?][87]

Another semi-tribal man of the same area, Nosepeg Tjupurrula,
has recited "Pangkalangka dreaming", also of this synthetic style:

I'll tell you somethink
    that Pangkalangka gotta kungka parnpa
        he gotta kungka—that's his wife
big mobba tjitji—
    Pangkalangkas son, daughter,
        same like a kungka this ones mob!
gotta lotta pamily,
    from dreamin,
        all here, no worries!
Big tall pella him
    go ebbrywhere: Amanturrngu, Kintore,
    Karrinyarra;
        anythinga they take em:
they gotta boots,
    parltja/trabil underground
just like a wind him go
    we callem 'walpa'/
        big like a city inside;
they gotta lid,
    shut em up,
        key em up,
           inside;
then they go way workin,
    vijiting more Pangkalangka,
        ebbrywhere they go!
They gotta spear,
        stone knife,
    little tomahawk (notta
        whitepella tomahawk!),
women gotta coolamon.
Ohh, too much

That Pangkalangka, him notta nguntji:
notta bullshit: him true! proper!
pilkarti! cheeky bugger! really wild!—

    sometimes a lover boy they fight!!![88]

It must be noted that these recitals have all been assembled in written
poetic form by a white Literature Production Supervisor working in

the area. Nevertheless, the potential for the writing of such verse by Aborigines as an inherently oral, bilingual and unique form is certainly vast.

There is also a discernible trend in much urban Black Australian poetry towards oral verse which emphasises, above all, the phonetic sounds of words. Oodgeroo Noonuccal discovered this poetic door; Kevin Gilbert began to open it; but it is urban poets like Bobbi Sykes, Aileen Corpus and Lionel Fogarty who are beginning to cross the threshold. One of the best-known and most active Black Australian spokepersons of the 1970s, Bobbi Sykes, has had a considerable influence upon Aboriginal Affairs as well as Black Australian literature. Sykes's more colloquial poetry replicates the Black American idiom, in a dialect similar to that chosen by poets such as LeRoi Jones:

> When that man comes home/
> I'm going to tell him/
> Right/
>
> You—the clinkhead dude/
> Who is making my life/
> A misery—
>
> Playing on my
>   e/motion/s
>   'n'
>
> Coming in late/
>   with/
> Your enigmatic smile[89]

There is little doubt that the "Black Power" and "Black is Beautiful" movements in the United States have had at least some effect upon the format and the language of Black Australian political protests. Similarly, the Black American vocabulary has also influenced the writings of some Aboriginal poets, such as Gerry Bostock, Lionel Fogarty, and Aileen Corpus. Corpus is one of the most promising of the growing number of Aboriginal people who have published one or several poems in various magazines and newspapers. Her verse, printed in journals such as *Identity* and *Meanjin*, is frequently urban in focus, quite colloquial, and often captures sounds in an onomatopoetic fashion:

bright red spurted out
in warm tiny drops
to my heart-beats,
pht. pht. pht.

fingers tensed unbending
and outstretched
as blood-springs said
tch. tch. tch.
as they drop upon
bright red spots
turning black.
blk. blk. blk.[90]

Corpus has also made some of the most effective use of consonants and phonetic sounds in Aboriginal poetry, as in "blkfern-jungal.", a poem which is clearly indebted to Black American phraseology:

wlk'n down regent street i see
blks hoo display blknez
(i min they sens of blknez)
n they say t'me...

     'ime gonna lif yoo outta
     yor blk hole n sho yoo
     how t'wlk n dress n tlk.'

n i sit in th'gutta
of regent street
(outside wair we ol meet)
n i look up n see
arown th' haylo of they hair,
a cosmetic afro ring-
a shiny haze
like it blines me man!!

so mu eyes go down t'thair
smart soot ol prest n cleen
n thair hi heel kork shooz
n i turn mu head n look at mu
soiled blknez, n i sez...

     'ime gonna lif yoo outta
     yore blk hole n sho yoo
     how t'wlk n dress n tlk'[91]

This is one of the most effective examples of the Black Australian trend towards the writing of poetry which has an inbuilt phonetic imperative quite unlike anything White Australian poets have produced. It is noteworthy that this trend is common to both urban and semi-tribal Aboriginal poets (such as Tjapangati) and that it represents the single most significant stylistic contribution of Black Australian verse to Australian literature.

This oral imperative has also affected the work of one of the most important younger Aboriginal poets: Lionel Fogarty. With only minimal education ("half of grade nine"[92]) Fogarty has had few poetic models to emulate and has instead relied upon an ear finely tuned to the spoken language of the Aboriginal fringe-dwellers. He has also been influenced by slogans, advertising jingles and popular songs, and the amalgam of all these influences is fascinating, if not always successful. In his first volume of verse, *Kargun*, one of Fogarty's weaknesses is an occasional lack of control: the vituperation sometimes spills out as suddenly and as violently as the blow-out of an inner tube:

> I get out my best knife
> cut the heart out
> then stuff it in their mouth
> until it went down the gut.
> I thought
> I must slice off the balls
> and shove
> in the eyeballs
> with blood
> spitting out of the nose.[93]

Fogarty's bitterness is probably justified. Not only was he raised on Cherbourg reserve in Queensland but he was also falsely implicated in a conspiracy trial in the mid-1970s. Nevertheless, the kind of uncontrolled rage which occasionally surfaces in *Kargun* is self-defeating and serves to alienate even the most sympathetic reader.

Elsewhere in his first book, Fogarty is far more effective. For example, his poem, "You Who May Read My Words" is a successful, self-reflective treatment of the theme of tokenism with reference to Aboriginal literature:

> Now!
> Everyone wants writings of Aboriginals
> Past, Present and Future.
> But do they want the REALITY

> Or, is it good words
> nice words
> Patronising
> pat on the back.[94]

In the same vein is his "Mr. Professor", which attacks exploitive white research into Aboriginal culture:

> Our guns are alive
> that's the reality
> alive
> like lava
> and your intellectual
> and academic criticisms
> have been your industry
> out of our oppression.[95]

The most memorable aspect of the collection is probably its fervent tone of exhortation, with a pronounced Fourth World dimension:

> Red power show me you're not lost
> Black power row me to meeting you
> Yellow power sing me a wing, tall in flight
> Brown power make me sounds, aloud
> White power, don't take me
> Aboriginal power give me power
> Now, I'll go—take.[96]

Fogarty's second collection of verse, *Yoogum Yoogum*, was published in 1982. Most of the poems were composed very rapidly and then Penguin Books rushed the typescript into print in a fortnight, so that the volume could be launched during the Brisbane Commonwealth Games. The launching of *Yoogum Yoogum* during Commonwealth Writers' Week provided one of the clearest possible examples of the conjunction of Aboriginal politics and poetry. One of the speakers at the book's launching, the well-known Black Australian activist Gary Foley, underlined the role of such literature as an integral part of the Aboriginal political movement:

> You can't divorce what Lionel has written from what is going on in the streets of Brisbane today and tomorrow and the day after. It is part of our struggle; an *important* part of our struggle, as any book that is written—as Kevin Gilbert's ... —as any book that is written by Aboriginal people ... We make no apologies for being overtly political; we see more clearly than anyone else in this country what is wrong with this country.[97]

Paradoxically, the urgency of Fogarty's own feelings is both his greatest strength and his most important failing in *Yoogum Yoogum*. The rapid, unrevised pace of his composition has given these poems candour and immediacy but it has also led to confusion and obscurity—sometimes in different parts of the same poem. As Chris Tiffin pointed out in his review of the book:

> *Yoogum Yoogum* is not the work of an unconfident writer, in fact its successes and its faults stem from a confident and courageous experimentalism.[98]

When his thoughts are apparently not focussed, Fogarty's verse can be very frustrating for the non-Aboriginal reader:

> Wise oaks crack compass broken
> wash mud
> sorrow flickering cats
> waxed glorious colour butterflied
> harmless caterpillars
> just to screen gloved 'pray to Gods'.[99]

What is beyond doubt is that Fogarty is increasingly a poet who writes the spoken Aboriginal word. Colloquial expressions and expletives are accentuated by alliteration in "Decorative Rasp, Weaved Roots":

> Couples contemplating
> followed another bunch
> of friggen portable rubbish public
> jumped up propaganda
> fair dinkum mates
> think them sick scratched pissed patients
> inmates of time.[100]

On some occasions the poetry is as vibrant as a sustained exclamation:

> Old Billy, young alive, was he denied?
> He look around
> and he frowns
> Also Billy is hairy
> Wowee...some fella call him
> YOWIE.
>
> He black
> Smell even
> Green eyes crept behind you
> and BOO! YOU![101]

An emphasis upon oral communication becomes even more apparent in Fogarty's subsequent two volumes of poetry, *Kudjela* (1983) and *Ngutji* (1984). As Cheryl Buchanan writes in her foreword to the latter, Fogarty's own "experience of oppression and frustration grew into a revolutionary style of writing that no other Aboriginal person has achieved". She continues, "Lionel regards himself as 'a speaker, not a writer', and does not like to be categorized as a 'poet' ".[102] Fogarty is, as Colin Johnson has termed him, a "guerilla poet wielding the language of the invader in an urge to destroy that imposition and recreate a new language freed of restrictions and erupting a multi-meaning of ambiguity".[103]

The assault on European language includes an attack on contemporary modes of western communication; for example, in "Ain't No Abo Way of Communication" he writes:

> Godfather, do you remember?
> Ring, ring, the phone calls for you
> come grab, it's yubba, for you
> Hello, hello, who's this?
> You know who.
> Look, yubba, me don't like your attitude or your ways
>
> me don't wanta have any to do you no more.
> Well, get fucked. Bang, down it went...
>
> Yubba, whoever you are, ring me no more
> But see me, feel one.
> Don't use their phones, be a real murrie[104]

The critique of the dominant Australian culture in Fogarty's verse often extends beyond the country's shores:

> The people, country, Pine Gap, conceals in arms race
> Victories cannot confirm goals
> Less confrontation political or philosophical
> taking greater strength
> Who's threatening?
> Whites are threatening
> are threatened ... even tomorrow[105]

Fogarty's poetry is difficult to assess, because of its experimental unconventionality. What can be said is that it necessitates being read aloud, it is confident and unique in Australian literature. As Kevin Gilbert has put it, "Coming from a tradition of oral poetry, having been forced by assimilationist policy of the government to forego traditional language and to adopt the European tongue, Lionel used the written English like a dervish wields a club."[106] It is true that Fogarty's poetry is often hard for the non-Aboriginal reader to comprehend, but that is precisely the point: it is *meant* to be. Just as Jack Davis's plays challenge the theatre-goer linguistically and make the audience work to understand the dialogue, Fogarty makes no concessions to simplicity. This is just another way in which Aboriginal authors are breaking new ground in Australian literature: it is a form of what the Jamaican poet Louise Bennett has termed "colonisation in reverse".[107] It implies that the White Australian reader will be on the outside, purposely externalised from an easy understanding of the text.

In this way, to criticise Fogarty for being obtuse or inaccessible is to adopt a limited critical stance. As Colin Johnson has expressed it:

> In modern Aboriginal writing, and by modern Aboriginal writing, I signify writings by such writers as Lionel Fogarty, there has been a shift away from what has been a simple plea, or a writing slanted towards white people and to be used as a tool for understanding. This early writing did not result in a return of understanding, but an outrage of critics directed at such writings as being puerile and essentially not as good as European writing ...

> Aboriginal writing has developed towards a spirituality interested in using and exploring the inner reality of Aboriginality in Australia. Naturally in doing this, there are problems in that there may be no readership for such a writing or that those critics who dismissed Aboriginal writing for accessibility may now dismiss it for obscurity.[108]

The underlying principle of Fogarty's "spoken" writing is undeniably a political one, supporting the Black Australian struggle for thoroughgoing autonomy. However, as Johnson indicates, he does run a risk in so doing: of making his work so difficult that non-Aborigines refuse to make the effort to comprehend it. The fact that his work is already being studied at the tertiary level indicates that there are those prepared to make that effort; to understand how the Aboriginal political movement finds expression through the creative writing of its authors.

Of course, not all Black Australian writers are comfortable openly associating their poetry with the Aboriginal movement. For example, Mona Tur (who writes under her tribal name of Ngitji Ngitji) states, "I'm not one for political things", and she adds, "I get most of my poetry through nature". Yet even she admits, "I know politics and life go together to a certain extent" and one of her best poems,

"Uluru", was written immediately after viewing a documentary on "The Rape of Ayers Rock": "I was so ropeable after I had watched that film ... that I sat up half the night writing it".[109] Tur's sincerity and heartfelt grief is communicated in her lyrical verse:

> My heart bleeds, our beloved Rock,
> To see you torn apart.
> Our dreamtime tells of your forming,
> You put forth your beauty at dawning.
> As evening comes, your haunting beauty
> Mirrors beauty beyond compare.[110]

In one sense, all Aboriginal poetry is political, in that public statements of Aboriginality or of affinity with nature can be interpreted as support for the ideology of the land rights campaign. Often, though, this is not the stated intention of the author, who may be writing a celebration of the natural world with no ulterior motive. An example is Leila Rankine's lyrical evocation of the Coorong district of South Australia:

> Land of my father's people,
> Place of my ancestors past,
> Never will forget you
> For, you are dear to my heart
>
> I've climbed your golden sand dunes,
> And walked through your native scrub,
> Swam in your sea green waters
> Watched the birds, in their evening flight ...
>
> Oh spirit of the long ago
> And guardian of the past
> As I stand beside your waters
> My soul knows peace at last.[111]

However, even Rankine admits that the attraction of poetry for Aboriginal writers is a more than "natural" one:

> You can do it in poetry form and be very *strong* in your approach without being hassled. It's an art form, which allows you to say a lot—express a lot—without getting into strife with the authorities.[112]

Clearly, this is yet another motivation for the convergence of Black Australian politics and poetry.

Ever since Oodgeroo Noonuccal's *We Are Going* was first released in 1964, Aboriginal poets have often reacted in the same immediate way to socio-political incidents which specifically affected Black Australians. Noonuccal herself wrote "Acacia Ridge"; Jack Davis composed "Laverton Incident"; Kevin Gilbert wrote "Mister Man"; Lionel Fogarty composed most of his verse; and Gerry Bostock wrote one of the most impassioned, rhythmic, and exhortatory of all the Aboriginal poems: "Black Children". In Bostock's words, "The poem just flowed the day after the Aboriginal Embassy collapsed",[113] and every time he recites "Black Children", he re-awakens the strong emotions that were aroused at that time:

Prepare Black Children
For the Land Rights fight,
Our cause is true,
Our aim's in sight,
Unite my people,
Unite!

Come on, Black Children
Rise on your feet!
Get out of the gutter
And onto the street;
United together,
Hand in hand,
Heads raised high we stand,
Then, march as one,
Surging forward and onward,
For justice
For freedom
And for our land.[114]

Above all else, Aboriginal poetry is remarkable for its striking immediacy, which is often augmented by the personal or political stance of the author. It is this factor which conveys its political, literary and, most recently, its colloquial, oral and/or phonetic strength. While Aboriginal poetry underscores the Fourth World dimension of the Black Australian situation, it highlights at the same time the distinctive Aboriginal world-view in Australia. In the introduction to his landmark anthology of Aboriginal poetry, *Inside Black Australia*, Kevin Gilbert highlights most eloquently the independent paradigm of black verse:

Black poets sing, not in odes to Euripides or Dionysus, not Keats, nor Browning, nor Shakespeare; neither do they sing a pastoral lay to a 'sunburnt country' for they know that that russet stain that Dorothea Mackellar spoke of is actually the stain of blood, our blood, covering the surface of our land so the white man could steal our land.[115]

Although many of the traditional song-poets have died, Black Australians' awareness of the lyricism and power of the spoken word lives on in the verse of its contemporary poets.

Notes

1 Personal interview with Oodgeroo Noonuccal, Stradbroke Island (Queensland), August, 1980.

2 Quoted in Adam Shoemaker, "An Interview With Jack Davis", *Westerly*, vol. 27, no. 4, December, 1982, p. 116.

3 W.E.H. Stanner, *After the Dreaming*, (Sydney, 1969), p. 44.

4 See the inside cover of Noonuccal's *My People*, (Brisbane, 1970). Noonuccal also asserts this fact in her interview with Jim Davidson in *Meanjin*, vol. 36, no. 4, (December, 1977), p. 428. It was in December, 1987 that Kath Walker officially changed her name to Oodgeroo Noonuccal, to protest the Bicentennial celebrations of 1988. In her words, "I have renounced my English name because the House of Commons and Lords in England have neglected us for 200 years. They could not spell the Aboriginal names so they gave us English ones". Quoted in "Poet Changes Name, Returns MBE in Bicentennial Protest", the Brisbane *Courier-Mail*, 15 December 1987, p. 4.

5 Personal interview with Colin Johnson, conducted by Cliff Watego and Adam Shoemaker, Brisbane, September, 1982.

6 See, for example, "It's Politics as Usual for Independent Bonner", The *Canberra Times*, 13 February, 1983, p. 1, and "Kath Walker Withdraws", The *Canberra Times*, 15 February, 1983, p. 6.

7 *Australian Book Review*, May, 1964, p. 143.

8 Jill Hellyer, "Aboriginal Poet", *Hemisphere*, vol. 8, no. 12, December, 1964, p. 18.

9 Noonuccal, "Then and Now", in *My People*, (Milton, 1981), p. 91.

10 Noonuccal, "Gifts", in *My People*, p. 39.

11 Noonuccal, "Nona" in *My People*, p. 31.

12 Noonuccal, "Verses", (Number "VII"), in *My People*, p. 83.

13 Review of *The Dawn Is At Hand*, in *Poetry Magazine*, no. 1, February, 1967, p. 31.

14 Andrew Taylor, "New Poetry", *Australian Book Review*, no. 36, Winter, 1967, p. 44.

15 Jill Hellyer, "Aboriginal Poet", p. 18.

16 "Australian Poets", The *Times Literary Supplement*, 10 September, 1964, p. 842.

17 Ruth Doobov, "The New Dreamtime: Kath Walker in Australian Literature",

Australian Literary Studies, vol. 6, no. 1, May, 1973, pp. 54-55.

18   "Interview: Kath Walker", *Meanjin*, vol. 36, no. 4, December, 1977, pp. 428-429. (Conducted by Jim Davidson).

19   Personal interview with Oodgeroo Noonuccal, Stradbroke Island, August, 1982, conducted by Cliff Watego. Quoted with permission.

20   Quoted in Adam Shoemaker, "An Interview with Jack Davis", *Westerly*, vol. 27, no. 4, December, 1982, p. 116.

21   Cheryl Buchanan's speech at the official launching of Fogarty's *Yoogum Yoogum*, Queensland Institute of Technology, September, 1982.

22   See Colin Johnson's "Report of the Proceedings of the Second Aboriginal Writers' Conference", Melbourne, November, 1983, pp. 41-42.

23   Personal interview with Oodgeroo Noonuccal, conducted by Cliff Watego, Stradbroke Island, August, 1982. Quoted with permission.

24   Quoted by L.E. Scott in his unfortunately titled article, "Writers From A Dying Race", *Pacific Moana Quarterly*, vol. 4, no. 4, October, 1979, p. 430.

25   Personal correspondence with Professor J.E. Chamberlin, January 23, 1984.

26   John Beston, "The Aboriginal Poets in English: Kath Walker, Jack Davis, and Kevin Gilbert", *Meanjin*, vol. 36, no. 4, December, 1977, p. 458.

27   "The Boomerang", in *The First-born, and Other Poems*, (Melbourne, 1983), p. 7.

28   Personal interview with Jack Davis, Canberra, November, 1981.

29   Davis, "Laverton Incident", in *The First-born*, p. 22.

30   Beston, "The Aboriginal Poets in English", p. 461.

31   Davis, "Desolation", in *The First-born*, p. 36.

32   Davis has also been involved for many years in the activities of the Australian Institute of Aboriginal Studies, as a committee and a council member, and in 198 both he and Oodgeroo Noonuccal were named as members of the Aboriginal Art Board of the Australia Council.

33   Davis, "From the Ward Window", in *Jagardoo: Poems from Aboriginal Australia* (Sydney, 1978), p. 20.

34   Davis, "Bombay", in *Jagardoo*, p. 37.

35   Kevin Gilbert, "People *Are* Legends", in "Poems 1970", Mitchell Library mss. no 2429, 1970.

36   Kevin Gilbert, *People Are Legends*, (St. Lucia, 1978), p. 54.

37   Kevin Gilbert, "People *Are* Legends", in *End of Dreamtime*, (Sydney, 1971), p. 14.

38   Gil Perrin, "Songs of Protest and Rural Poems", *Village News and NALA Journal*, September, 1978, n.p.

39 Peter Monaghan, "Fruits of Oppression", The *Canberra Times*, 27 May, 1979, p. 15.

40 Gilbert, "Riches", in *People Are Legends*, p. 17.

41 "The Other Side of the Story", in *ibid.*, p. 11.

42 "The Flowering...", in *ibid.*, p. 51.

43 "Shame", in *ibid.*, p. 13.

44 "The 'Better Blacks' ", in *ibid.*, pp. 26-27.

45 Kevin Gilbert, "To My Cousin, Evonne Cawley", The *Bulletin Literary Supplement*, September, 1980, p. 2.

46 Personal interview with Kevin Gilbert, Canberra, May, 1981.

47 Gilbert, "Granny Koori", in *People Are Legends*, p. 42.

48 Gilbert, "Extract From a Letter to a Woman Friend", in "Poems 1970", Mitchell Library mss. no. 2429, 1970.

49 Kevin Gilbert, Untitled Verse, in "Kids' Poems", National Library of Australia ms. no. 2584, 1979, n.p.

50 Personal interview with Kevin Gilbert, Canberra, May, 1981.

51 Les A. Murray, "In Search of a Poet", The *Sydney Morning Herald*, 7 October 1978, p. 16.

52 Gilbert, "The Gurindji", in *People Are Legends*, pp. 44-45.

53 Bruce Clunies-Ross, "Survival of the Jindyworobaks", *Kunapipi*, vol. III, no. 1, 1981, p. 62.

54 Les A. Murray, "The Human-Hair Thread", *Meanjin*, vol. 36, no. 4, December, 1977, pp. 550-551.

55 ibid., p. 550.

56 ibid., p. 571.

57 ibid., p. 551.

58 Murray, "The Ballad of Jimmy Governor", in *Poems Against Economics*, (Sydney, 1972), p. 15.

59 Murray, "Thinking About Aboriginal Land Rights, I Visit the Farm I Will Not Inherit", in *Lunch and Counter Lunch*, (Sydney, 1974), p. 30.

60 Personal interview with Les Murray, Canberra, June, 1981.

61 Murray, "The Human-Hair Thread", p. 551.

62 Bruce Dawe, "Nemesis", The *Bulletin Literary Supplement*, 1 November 1983, p. 81.

63 Cliff Watego, "Aboriginal Poetry and White Criticism", in Jack Davis and Bob Hodge, eds, *Aboriginal Writing Today*, (Canberra, 1985), pp. 87-88.

64 Colin Johnson, "Song Twenty-Seven", in *The Song Circle of Jacky, and Selected*

Poems, (Melbourne, 1986), p. 40.

65 Tracy Maurer, "More Deaths in Police Custody Than Prisons", The *Australian*, 5 March 1988, p. 3.

66 Johnson, "City Suburban Lines", in *The Song Circle of Jacky*, p. 84.

67 "Song Five", in *ibid.*, p. 16.

68 Johnson, "Song Two", in *ibid.*, p. 13.

69 "Declaration of the Indigenous Nations of Our Place in Canada's Constitution", tabled at the Third General Assembly of the WCIP, Canberra, April/May, 1981.

70 Adapted in brief from the NAC's "Position Paper on Indigenous Ideology and Philosophy", and published in *Identity*, vol. 4, no. 4, Winter, 1981, p. 36.

71 Oodgeroo Noonuccal, "We Are Going", in *My People*, p. 78.

72 Jim Dumont, "For Joe Mackinaw", in Day and Bowering, eds, *Many Voices: An Anthology of Contemporary Canadian Indian Poetry*, (Vancouver, 1977), p. 49.

73 Gordon Williams, "The Last Crackle", in *ibid.*, p. 61.

74 Duke Redbird, "Tobacco Burns", in *ibid.*, p. 40.

75 Dumont, "For Joe Mackinaw", in *ibid.*, p. 50.

76 Noonuccal, "The Past", in *My People*, p. 93.

77 Shirley Daniels, "Drums of My Father", in *Many Voices*, p. 47.

78 Maureen Watson, "Black Child", in *Black Reflections*, (Wattle Park, 1982), p. 13.

79 Eleanor Crowe, "Shadows", in *Many Voices*, pp. 37-38.

80 Duke Redbird and Marty Dunn, Untitled concrete poem in *Many Voices*, p. 45.

81 Sarain Stump, *There is My People Sleeping*, (Sidney, B.C., 1970), pp. 14, 116.

82 Skyros Bruce, Untitled poem, in *Many Voices*, p. 77.

83 Leo Yerxa, "I Searched", in *Many Voices*, p. 67.

84 Wayne Keon, "Moosonee in August", in *Many Voices*, pp. 69-70.

85 Gordon Williams, "Justice in Williams Lake", in *Many Voices*, p. 63.

86 Tutama Tjapangati, "Wangka Tjukutjuk", *Overland*, no. 80, July, 1980, p. 32.

87 Tutama Tjapangati, "Aladayi", The *Bulletin Literary Supplement*, 1 November 1983 p. 64.

88 Nosepeg Tjupurrula, "Pangkalangka dreaming", The *Bulletin Literary Supplement* 1 November 1983, p. 65.

89 Bobbi Sykes, "That Man", in *Love Poems and Other Revolutionary Actions* (Cammeray, 1979), p. 22.

90 Aileen Corpus, "Suicide 2", *Meanjin*, vol. 36, no. 4, December, 1977, p. 473.

91   Aileen Corpus, "blkfern-jungal", *Meanjin*, vol. 36, no. 4, December 1977, p. 470.

92   Cheryl Buchanan, Foreword to *Kargun* (North Brisbane, 1980), p. 4.

93   Lionel George Fogarty, "Capitalism—The Murderer in Disguise", in *Kargun*, p. 93.

94   Fogarty, "You Who May Read My Words", in *Kargun*, p. 78.

95   "Mr. Professor", in *ibid.*, p. 23.

96   "Please Don't Take", in *ibid.*, p. 95.

97   Gary Foley's speech at the launching of *Yoogum Yoogum*, Queensland Institute of Technology, Brisbane, September, 1982.

98   Chris Tiffin, "Language of Anger", The *Australian Book Review*, vol. 48, Feb./Mar., 1983, p. 18.

99   "Sentiment Transcends", in *Yoogum,Yoogum*, (Ringwood, 1982), p. 50.

100   "Decorative Rasp, Weaved Roots", in *ibid.*, p. 14.

101   "To a Warm Veined Yubba: Billy Gorham", in *ibid.*, p. 98.

102   Cheryl Buchanan, Foreword to *Ngutji*, (Spring Hill [Queensland], 1984), n.p.

103   Colin Johnson, "Guerilla Poetry: Lionel Fogarty's Response to Language Genocide", *Aspect*, no. 34, August, 1986, p. 78.

104   Lionel Fogarty, "Ain't No Abo Way of Communication"in *Kudjela*, (Spring Hill [Queensland], 1983), pp. 58-59.

105   "Ambitious Nuclear War Whites", in *ibid.*, p. 154.

106   Kevin Gilbert, "Introduction", in Gilbert, ed. *Inside Black Australia: An Anthology of Aboriginal Poetry*, (Ringwood, 1988), p. 156.

107   Quoted in Helen Tiffin, "Looking Back into the Future: Literature in the English Speaking Caribbean", *New Literature Review*, no. 7, p. 6.

108   Colin Johnson, "Paperbark", Unpublished lecture delivered at the University of Queensland, 23 March 1988.

109   Personal interview with Mona Tur, Perth, February, 1983.

110   Ngitji Ngitji [Mona Tur], "Uluru". Unpublished *ms.* provided by the author in February 1983.

111   Leila Rankine, "The Coorong", *Social Alternatives*, vol. 2, no. 4, June, 1982, p. 9.

112   Personal interview with Leila Rankine, Adelaide, February, 1982.

113   Personal interview with Gerry Bostock, Sydney, July, 1980.

114   Gerald L. Bostock, "Black Children", in *Black Man Coming*, (Sydney, 1980), p. 18.

115   Gilbert, *Inside Black Australia* , p. xxiv.

9

Aboriginality and Black Australian Drama

In 1971, a new quarterly magazine began in Australia. *Identity* was destined to become the single most important and influential Aboriginal periodical in the country. The magazine's name was very appropriate for, especially during the six-and-a-half years that Jack Davis was its editor, the magazine explored the evolving Aboriginal view of what it meant to be a "First Australian" living in the 1970s and 1980s. This theme of Aboriginality is probably the most important of all those dealt with in contemporary Black Australian writing. It underlies the Aboriginal preoccupation with history, and is closely related to issues of black politics, health, education and cultural achievement.

There is no single definition of Aboriginality. One approach is to explore the range of experience encompassed by the term, as Kevin Gilbert does in *Living Black*:

> But what is Aboriginality? Is it being tribal? Who is an Aboriginal? Is he or she someone who feels that other Aboriginals are somehow dirty, lazy, drunken, bludging? Is an Aboriginal anyone who has some degree of Aboriginal blood in his or her veins and who has demonstrably been disadvantaged by that? Or is an Aboriginal someone who has had the reserve experience? Is Aboriginality institutionalized gutlessness, an acceptance of the label 'the most powerless people on earth'? Or is Aboriginality, when all the definitions have been exhausted, a yearning for a different way of being, a wholeness that was presumed to have existed [before 1788]?[1]

These questions underline many of the negative characteristics which may form part of the Black Australian self-definition. However, as many of the women and men whom Gilbert interviewed revealed, Aboriginality was for them as much a positive state of mind as any catalogue of observable attributes. In the words of Keith Smith:

> I don't mean that we have to go back with our spears and our boomerangs and nulla
> nullas and hunt our tucker and do this type of thing. What I mean is that we've got
> to regain the spirit of our Aboriginality so that we can go on to greater things
> according to whatever a community wants ... The spirit, the soul, the Aboriginality
> of it. You're an Aboriginal, you've got to be proud, you've got to know something of
> your background, know where you come from, where you're going and what you're
> doing, but at the same time you've got to take that Aboriginality with you. You're a
> black, you know and you've got to respect the black. Nobody can change it. [2]

Aboriginality is the legacy of traditional Black Australian culture. It implies movement towards the future while safeguarding the pride and dignity of the past. But Aboriginality is also counter-cultural in European terms: a reaction against the dictates of White Australian society. This can lead to a black self-image which is potentially very rebellious and outside the law. In interview, Robert Merritt explained this alternative form of the search for identity:

> It suits society's purpose to give government mandates to build filthy institutions
> that keep Aborigines in prison. If you want an identity today ... if you're sick you'll
> get a band-aid, and you're an Aborigine—and everyone knows about ya. And if
> you're a drunk, or if you're a crook, you'll get a two-bob lawyer that's been out of
> law school for five years. You've got an identity. If you want to be a normal person
> there's no incentive in life whatsoever for ya ... To break the law now—it's a
> substitute initiation. [3]

Thus, Aboriginality is both an inheritance from Black Australian history and an immediate, sometimes violent reaction to the Black Australian present.

More than ever before, Aborigines from all parts of the country are mounting a unified response to major events. The 1982 Brisbane Commonwealth Games protests and the anti-Bicentennial protests of 1988 in Sydney, Brisbane and Canberra are the most obvious examples of this trend. The national scale of these causes and effects shows that, despite past divisions and disagreements, pan-Aboriginalism is an increasingly important part of the Black Australian self-definition. One of the most prominent Aboriginal national representatives, Charles Perkins (Secretary of the Department of Aboriginal Affairs) describes the emergent feeling as a "growing appreciation" of Black Australians for one another:

> Aborigines are starting to realise right throughout Australia that there's a thing
> that's binding them together: that's the psychology of being an Aboriginal, that's
> culture, that's blood-line, everything. [4]

It is ironic that greater Aboriginal self-confidence and the oppression that still persists in some areas of Australian society have both helped to articulate the idea of Aboriginality. The concept of Aboriginality encompasses many things: respect for the Aboriginal past and for traditional Black Australian ties to the land, a sense of pride and dignity, and sometimes one of dismay and outrage. An impetus towards action in both the social and political spheres is also involved, ranging from petitions and demonstrations to the establishment of Aboriginal-controlled health, legal, and housing services. The pan-Aboriginal trend is reinforcing all of these factors and is enabling spokespeople of the Black Australian movement—be they politicians, artists, social workers or writers—to gain a voice and a supportive public.

When Aboriginal people define themselves in literature, they emphasise not just the shared experience of oppression but also the shared enjoyment of life. In spite of all that has been endured by Aborigines, they have managed to retain a distinctive sense of humour which acts to combat depression and to promote the cohesion of the Black Australian group. The mimicry and mockery of whites and the humorous celebration of their own lifestyle has been one way in which blacks have opposed the encroachments of European society, and have asserted their own independence and capacity for endurance. Jack Davis has succinctly stated that, historically, Aborigines "learnt to keep themselves alive by laughing".[5] Those who have carried out extensive field work in Aboriginal communities corroborate this statement. The White Australian anthropologist Anna Haebich has commented:

> Aboriginal people keep on laughing to stay afloat. In interviews they emphasise the good times and it's very hard indeed to get them to talk about the bad times.[6]

This reliance upon laughter in the midst of adversity is an important element in the Aboriginal self-image. It is one which emerges very clearly in Aboriginal literature, particularly in Black Australian drama.

The historical dimension of black drama was examined in Chapter Six of this study. In this chapter, other equally distinctive elements of Aboriginal drama will be explored. These will be briefly contrasted with the work of selected White Australian playwrights, in order to highlight the contribution of Black Australian dramatists to the Aboriginal movement, to the formulation of the concept of Aboriginality, and to the enrichment of Australian literature as a whole. Aboriginality has many facets: endurance, pride, protest, poverty, sorrow, anger and humour. All of these important aspects will be discussed, but the distinctive Black Australian approach to humour will be given particular attention.

Black Australian playwrights have all used humour extensively in their works, though none of their plays could properly be termed a comedy. All the Aboriginal plays written so far describe scenes of hardship, misery, poverty, discrimination and even death, but none of them is unrelievedly sombre in tone. Humour tempers the seriousness of these plays and concurrently enhances their impact; it rescues them from any danger of being oppressive in tone. As Jack Davis has observed, black drama usually displays a wide range of emotions:

> Don't just show them [the audience] the comic side of life right through ... show them sadness, pathos, gladness, happiness, sorrow, and all the in-between ... all those emotions.[7]

Since the elements of Black Australian humour are so relevant to the concept of Aboriginality, it is worthwhile to examine the general characteristics of that humour before observing its specific applications in Black Australian plays. In an excellent article on the subject, Stanner noted both the general and particular aspects of the phenomenon. There are, of course, situations and events which both White and Black Australians find amusing:

> the hammer on the thumb, the slip on banana peel, the sudden loss of dignity—all these 'reversals', the basis of a universal class of humour, evoke much the same responses among the Aborigines as among Europeans.[8]

However, as Stanner notes, there is a further class of humour which seems particular to Aboriginal people. Although it is difficult to define in a precise way, Black Australians have indicated some of its characteristics:

> The humour of western culture, because western culture is competitive, is itself competitive ... You'll find that amongst traditional Aboriginal people ... "put down" humour is not seen as all that funny. [They have] the humour that is often one of endearment, often one of familiarity ... it equates people with other people, people with animals and what have you ... you'll find that even in urban situations Aboriginal people can recognise somebody way down the street by the way they walk. Because they know peoples' walks and mannerisms. And those things are more noticed by, and more remembered by, Aborigines than they are by white people.[9]

The humour seen in many Black Australian plays derives from the traditions and particular skills of Aborigines, especially those of mime and impersonation. Jack Davis has given a vivid example of these talents in the fringe-dwelling situation, and has shown how they can inspire Black Australian drama:

You see, we've always been acting. Aboriginal people are the greatest actors in the world ... We've acted up before magistrates, we've acted up before the police, we've acted up before social workers; we've always done our own mime ... Like the man who burns his feet and he doesn't even know his feet are alight. He's standing on the fire and he says [imitating voice] 'By Crikey, I can smell somethin' burnin' there! You fellas burn an old bag there somewhere? Or you burnin' kangaroo skin?' [New voice] 'Uncle! You're standing in the fire. Get out of the fire there!' He never wore boots for forty years and he's got callouses on his feet that thick, and he was standing in the fire. His feet were burning and he didn't even know it! And laughed—you know that,[claps] ... that went around the camp for a week. Well, little incidents like that, you know, that carry on all the time—it's not very hard to put 'em down on paper. I'm sure the Aboriginal playwrights have seen that.[10]

In interview, Robert Merritt highlighted the same point when asked about the levity in his play *The Cake Man*: "Well, there's humour in the people ... no one's looked at it before ... it's beautiful".[11]

While the distinctive Aboriginal approach to humour is visible in contemporary black theatre, its roots are in the tribal/traditional sphere. Stanner noted this phenomenon amongst the traditional and semi-traditional Aborigines with whom he lived and worked for many years. He relates the reaction of an old man, one of the last remaining members of his tribe, to his question, "In a few years you will all be dead; there will be no blackfellows left; but you laugh about it. Why do you laugh? I see nothing amusing":

He would not be drawn for some time. Finally he said, 'Bye-and-bye, altogether blackfellow dead. Plenty white man sit-down this country. White man walkabout longa bush. Him losim himself longa bush. Altogether white man try findim. Altogether white man losim himself longa bush. No blackfeller. Can't findim. Whitefeller dead. Blackfeller dead.' And he smiled sardonically.[12]

Stanner also emphasises the longevity of humorous tales derived from real-life experiences amongst Black Australians. In one noteworthy case, he and an Aboriginal friend, Charlie Dargie, shot a barramundi wallowing in a pond—which someone else had already caught:

We had touched the depths. To *shoot* a *caught* fish *tied up* to the bank by a *string*. Jarawak saw that the tale spread. The blacks never forgot it. To this day, half a lifetime later, they still laugh. When I go fishing with them, someone is sure to say in an innocent tone, 'You got plenty bullet?'[13]

The kind of humour which Stanner describes still persists and is given effective expression in Black Australian drama.

Until now, Aboriginal dramatists have taken their inspiration almost entirely from the direct observation and recollection of personal experiences. To a great extent, characters are based upon individuals the playwright has known, or are at the least dramatic impressions of men and women coping with situations which are typically (if not always exclusively) Aboriginal. To the extent that Black Australian dramatists are writing for their own people, the degree of faithfulness to their perceived reality is the criterion by which many blacks judge the works. In fact, sometimes the arbitrary division between stage and personal experience breaks down entirely. Gerry Bostock has related how, during the performance of one scene of his play *Here Comes the Nigger*—in which a group of Aborigines are set upon by two white thugs—some Black Australians from Elcho Island became incensed and tried to climb on to the stage to offer their assistance, yelling "I'll help ya, brother!" and "I'll come and save ya, cousin!"[14] This is relevant to the concept of Aboriginality. Not only was the reaction of the visiting blacks—while understandable—very amusing, but Bostock takes obvious pleasure in relating the story as proof of the power and immediacy of his drama. In other words, the same episode in Bostock's play produced a violent reaction and a humorous response; both arose out of the *verisimilitude* of the drama.

The Aboriginal playwrights' goal of faithfulness to perceived black reality is clearly an important one. Black Australian dramatists have endeavoured to illustrate the Aboriginal past and present, however sorrowful it may be, with honesty and directness. For example, Kevin Gilbert explores the psychology of deprivation, subservience and loss in his first play, *The Cherry Pickers*. Gilbert's play was performed at the Mews Theatre in Sydney in August, 1971, during the Captain Cook Bicentenary celebrations, an ironic time for the debut of the first Aboriginal play. No less ironic was the fact that it took nearly eighteen years for *The Cherry Pickers* to be published, in the Australian bicentennial year of 1988.[15]

The Cherry Pickers focusses upon a group of itinerant Aboriginal fruit-pickers who return each year to the same white-owned cherry orchard. The fruit season represents the climax of the year for these fringe-dwellers, not only because the "Cherry tree means money—*and* food"[16] but also because of the convivial atmosphere which is created in their camp. As the play opens, they are waiting to begin work at the orchard and are also awaiting the arrival of Johnollo, a hero for the children and an inspiration in more ways than one for the women: "that Johnollo! 'leven babies he made las' season an' only one miss!"(p. 12).

However, this year there is something amiss. Despite the slapstick atmosphere of the play's opening, there are almost immediate indications that all is not right in the orchard. First, the young boy Phonso runs on stage with a dead rosella in his hand yelling "Johnollo has come!" (p. 3), which is not only a false alarm but also foreshadows the end of the play. Then Subina, the last remaining member of the "old tribe", reports that she has witnessed a bad omen—the "Wahwee Bhugeene" or [spirit] bat—which is believed by the group to be the "Messenger of the Dead"(p. 6). Soon afterwards, she breaks down in tears recalling the wooing of her now dead husband: "All dead!—all ... gone!"(p. 7) she laments. This is followed by the arrival of their European boss, Gegga, who brings the ominous news that "King Eagle" (the name the Aborigines have given to the oldest and largest of the cherry trees) is "a little slower and dying a little I think"(p. 13).

As the play progresses, the audience realises how much the Aboriginal characters have lost: gone is their traditional livelihood, gone is their self-determination (after all, it is a white man's orchard, however much of a "White blackfellah"[p. 6] he might be), and gone is their tribal culture. The sense of loss produces a strong feeling of pessimism at the end of *The Cherry Pickers*, when it is revealed that Johnollo has died in a car accident on his way to the orchard. The curtain closes on the group wailing a dirge while they burn King Eagle in a funeral pyre. Yet in spite of all this privation and bereavement, the fringe-dwellers have not lost their Aboriginality. This is articulated most clearly in the play through the vibrancy and humour of Gilbert's dialogue, a quality which endears the characters to the audience while it celebrates their endurance.

This jocular dialogue has definite characteristics: it customarily has sexual overtones, often deals with such themes as religion, alcohol and gambling, and frequently deflates pretensions, especially those of White Australians and of "white-thinking" Aborigines. A clear example of this last approach occurs when an Aboriginal army private visits the camp of the black fruit-pickers and introduces himself ostentatiously as "Jeremiah Ivan James Chickenmar Edward

Vance Goolagong from Myameelareena Station, West Weethaliban".
Another Aboriginal character, Emma, replies mockingly:

> *You* ain't *no one* but just old Jerry Goolly an' you never *had* no King nor no Country
> 'cause you is a blackfeller like us—now git! (p. 11).

Sexual innuendo consistently weaves its way through much of
Gilbert's entertaining dialogue, especially during that part of the play
which is an interlude of pure fun and mocking, termed "geenjing
time". Punning, slang expressions, mimicry and quick repartee are
the hallmarks of this lively scene, and the undertone is consistently
sexual:

FANNY:	How's yer bunions?
REGGIE:	A bunion grows on a foot—I haven't made the grade yet!
FANNY:	How's yer ditty?
REGGIE:	Not so pretty—but it's well and able!
FANNY:	How's yer knackers?
REGGIE:	They drive me crackers beneath me sweeties table!(p. 28).

Gilbert's ear for the poetic potential of the patois in his local region
is obvious. One has little doubt that the *double entendres* are taken
from real life exchanges, and they are just as believable as the
"misunderstandings" of English which he includes:

OLD TOODLES: Heh—heh—heh. Say, were you on Mrs Gegg's "clinic" inspection
this morning?—no?—well she goes 'round checkin' everyone's
teeth an' that an' she come to old Biblar an' asks, 'how's yer pulse
this mornin' Biblar? Old Biblar sez, 'Oh, missus they're hanging
very low!' (p. 29).

This is not just punning for its own sake. The episode of "geenjing
time" is, linguistically and dramatically, one of the most energetic
and successful scenes in *The Cherry Pickers*. It is also integrated into
the structure of the play as a whole, so that immediately after the
hilarious lampooning of policemen and motorcyclist which takes
place, a real motorcycle policeman arrives on the scene bearing the
news of Johnollo's death. The transition is very effective, and the
mourning with which the play closes is accentuated by the frivolity
which precedes it. Yet, though Gilbert demonstrates an acute ear for
colloquial dialogue in some parts of the play, elsewhere he sacrifices
naturalism and plausibility to make a socio-political point about
Aboriginality. The language of Zeena (one of the cherry-pickers) is so
elevated as to strain credibility, in a play which seems to be striving
for linguistic credibility:

Oh—I'm not complaining. I am merely trying to tell you that we can't live, nor find a new life by embracing a stone-age identity in this Nuclear Age. We should be rightfully proud of our old culture for what it was—the expression, the cry, the search for beauty by primitive man. This *truth* we should hold, and advance by, not revert to that cultural age. Man must advance, must mature, and must never, never revert back for life is a constant process of growth (p. 23).

A number of related themes run through *The Cherry Pickers*: the affinity between Aboriginal people and nature; the despoiling of the natural world by Europeans; the inability of Black Australians to return to the past, despite the retention of tradition and superstition; and the incapacity of even "good whites" to fully comprehend and appreciate the Aboriginal ethos. But the most important achievement of the play is its assertion of the vitality of Aboriginality in the face of all odds and this is accomplished, above all, through the vibrancy of Gilbert's dialogue. He is a far less successful dramatist when he pontificates. His real talent emerges in his entertaining dialogue—especially when that dialogue is humorous.

Gilbert's second play, the unpublished *Ghosts in Cell Ten*, is further evidence of the author's keen ear for black speech patterns. Like many of the Black Australian plays, it is set in an environment typically, if not exclusively, Aboriginal: in a prison. It is interesting that Gilbert's stated aim in writing the play was to expose the "actual debasement, the punishment and psychological attacks"[17] which he maintains take place daily in the prisons of New South Wales. It is a subject on which Gilbert can justly claim to be an expert from his own experience: "The ritualised prison routine, the body searches, the mental and medical attitudes which I portray in the play are based on actual observation"(p. 2).

Ghosts in Cell Ten is ostensibly about the mental and physical torments of a white character called Preacher, whom the reader observes progressively hardening throughout his prison term. At the outset he is a raw novice in the violent prison world and is treated as such by the "screws"; by the close of the play he is a seasoned veteran who is being accused of the murder of his cell-mate. However, the play is really about all sorts of prejudice and exploitation: personal, psychological, sexual and racial. In fact, it is not until the Aboriginal character, Clarry, is thrust into the cell with Preacher that the drama gains focus and real power—and this is three-quarters of the way through the work. Up to that point, Gilbert details more or less plausible events of daily prison life, which alternate with highly implausible dream sequences in which Preacher sees angels of salvation and corruption tormenting his sleep: the "ghosts" of the title.

The dialogue between Preacher and Clarry is the focal point of the play. It enables Gilbert not only to criticise the judicial and punitive system, but also to illustrate perceived failings in his own Black Australian society. Clarry reveals that he has been unjustly imprisoned for a rape which he never committed, but scorns the help of the Aboriginal Legal Service:

> Too much work involved for them. They're all too busy fightin' each other or too busy seeing who can git the most out of the set-up by putting in the least work effort to worry about *me* (p. 32).

This is definitely a contentious viewpoint for an Aboriginal playwright to express. The critique is, significantly, not limited to Aboriginal issues. Gilbert casts the net wider so that he addresses larger questions of human rights and prison reform; in the words of Preacher: "They call it 'rehabilitation and correction' mate, the system at Grafton is as corrupt as any 'crim' I've ever known"(p. 33).

Clarry's harangue concerning the oppression of Aborigines is extremely strong and sustained: the socio-political criticism in *Ghosts in Cell Ten* is far more overt than in *The Cherry Pickers*. But Gilbert rescues the play from unbroken didacticism by again interspersing humour with seriousness. After Preacher rolls Clarry a "joint" the latter exclaims:

CLARRY:	Christ it's savage on the old lungs. Tastes like dried horseshit.
PREACHER:	Dunno, I've never tried horseshit before.
CLARRY:	You missed out on a very important stage in your childhood then. I've smoked cane, grass, tea-leaves, horseshit, everything that could be rolled, including goatshit. This tastes like horseshit (p. 36).

As in all the Aboriginal plays the humour is direct, unabashed and frequently sexual. It also rings true, as when Preacher asks Clarry if the "grass" has taken effect:

PREACHER:	Say Clarry are you feeling it yet?
CLARRY	Too bloody right I am. I've got me two hands around it to stop it wriggling up and poking me eyeballs out! (p. 37).

This is not egregious vulgarity. It serves a dramatic purpose, which is to act as a foil for Clarry's socio-political commentary and, thereby, to enhance the effectiveness of his pointed censure:

It's a good country with whites in it? The Pub crawl bragging, the Poky playing, the bet on the gee-gees, Melbourne Cup, 'Footy', and the bloody R.S.L. club mind? If you can even call it a mind. The whites in this country are only fit for Gun-fodder in times of war. *That's* why the Yanks *use* Australia (p. 39).

This is heady political commentary. But is it viable as theatre? Until now, no Australian company has tackled a production of *Ghosts in Cell Ten* nor has any publisher printed the script. In a number of ways this is regrettable. The play is not entirely successful, for its "dream" sequences are not skilfully presented, and do not harmonise with the hard-edged atmosphere of the remainder of the work. Nevertheless, *Ghosts in Cell Ten* is sociological drama of an important and often entertaining kind. It serves to illustrate the bitterness and resentment which is often as much a component of Aboriginality as the attitude towards sex, violence, and humour. Many Australians were shocked by the initial plays of Buzo, Hibberd and Williamson, but now it is appreciated—both inside and outside their country—just how much they have done to produce a distinctive Australian voice in theatre. Many Australians would find *Ghosts in Cell Ten* disturbing and shocking today but again, that could potentially be a salutary experience, not only for White Australian audiences, but also for Black Australian writers trying to gain more literary autonomy.

Robert Merritt has spoken of imprisonment as a "substitute initiation" for Aboriginal people, and it is an initiation which many Black Australians have undergone. The dilemma of the high imprisonment rate of Aborigines has received considerable publicity and the problem is recognised as being, to a significant extent, the result of bias built into the law enforcement and judicial apparatus of White Australia. For example, in a speech in Canberra in February 1983, Pat O'Shane (the permanent head of the New South Wales ministry of Aboriginal Affairs) noted that the rate of imprisonment of Black Australians in the state was approximately 600 per 100,000 people: "many times higher than the rate of incarceration of other indigenous groups throughout the world".[18] In 1971, the rate of Aboriginal imprisonment in Australia as a whole was 1,000/100,000, which was over fourteen times higher than the national average for all groups of 70/100,000.[19] O'Shane concluded that "there is something very seriously wrong with the Australian criminal justice system".[20] The fact that so many Aboriginal authors have been in jail at some stage of their lives is one indication of how widespread this institutionalised anti-Aboriginal bias has been. Ironically, some of the most significant Aboriginal writers, such as Gilbert and Merritt, received a better education behind bars than they ever did as free men. In short, some of the finest examples of Aboriginal literature are born of incarceration.

The Cake Man, written during 1973-74 when Merritt was held in Bathurst jail, is one of these. The historical relevance of *The Cake Man* was discussed in Chapter Six; the emphasis upon Black Australian history displayed in Merritt's play is a vital component of the concept of Aboriginality. But the author captures many other elements of the Black Australian self-image in *The Cake Man*. Like Gilbert in *The Cherry Pickers*, he portrays the contemporary search for Aboriginal identity, the loss of traditional authority structures, and the figurative emasculation of Aboriginal people which has resulted. *The Cake Man*, too, is set in a location which is characteristically Black Australian: a government settlement or, in New South Wales, a "mission". Merritt depicts this environment as it was for many New South Wales Aborigines in their childhood. Merritt's play is very popular amongst the Aboriginal people because of its verisimilitude. Song-writer Candy Williams's sentiments are typical: "It really freaked me out. The first production was really tops. It moved me no end, because on every mission there's a Cake Man story." [21]

Despite these similarities with *The Cherry Pickers*, *The Cake Man* is more subtle and complex drama. It is a play built upon often bitter illusions. While Ruby's religious devotion does give her the strength to keep her family together in the face of the despondence and near-alcoholism of her husband—the ironically named Sweet William—it also enjoins her to accept the will of God without question. In John Newfong's view:

> She is only strong because she believes more devoutly in her own fantasy. So whether you call that strength or an illusion of strength, I don't know. Sweet William at least believes in his own potential. And Ruby, because of her Christian beliefs, undermines his beliefs in himself because she doesn't dare believe in herself. [22]

However, Sweet William also lives in a fantasy world. He manages to convince himself and, significantly, his son Pumpkinhead, that his major decisive action of going to Sydney will be the salvation of the family:

> Rube, I'll just go down to that Sydney, I'm gonna be lucky and get a job and find somewhere that's gonna be ours, and soon buy a big red house like Pumpkinhead wants and clothes and a 'lectric iron for you, 'lectric light, too, and plenty of tucker for the kids that we could buy out of my good job I'll get. I can work, Rube, you

know I can. Job, that's all it needs.[23]

This dream is an important one: not only is it expressed in Western, materialistic terms (which shows the degree of Sweet William's acculturation) but Merritt makes it obvious that the character has no chance of realising his goal. Through no fault of his own, Sweet William is arrested because he is standing near a pub door when the police arrive to quell a brawl. According to Brian Syron, who has directed and acted in a number of productions of *The Cake Man*, what is important is not the arrest of the father but the instilling of hope and pride in the son. In his view, the key is Sweet William's decision to try and break out of the institutionalised degradation of the mission system: "The sons of the father will be perceptive even if the father is not".[24]

Somewhat like Alan at the close of *Long Live Sandawara*, Pumpkinhead is to be the hope and the "instrument of change"[25] for the future. Newfong would add that Sweet William's victory was not merely a vicarious one, but primarily consisted in his action to break free from what he terms the "black matriarchy", which had contributed to his powerlessness. As he explains it:

> When one society is dominated by another society and the dominating matrix of society is male-dominated, the men of the *dominated* society will be emasculated. And it's almost a subconscious thing, you see. You notice that in *The Cake Man* the mission superintendent and Inspector ... defer to Ruby—this is to further undermine William's standing, simply by not addressing themselves to him. And this is what is always done.[26]

Newfong's theory is, to say the least, contentious, in that it suggests a profound psychological and political ploy to suppress Aboriginal men.[27] The theory is particularly intriguing in view of the female leadership of numerous Black Australian lobby groups and services, as well as some government departments. But Newfong goes too far to ascribe to these women positions of power by default. There is no doubt that Aboriginal women, from Oodgeroo Noonuccal and MumShirl to Margaret Valadian and Pat O'Shane, have been innovators and leaders because of their own talents, determination and commitment. It is difficult to maintain, as Newfong does, that politicians "find it easier to deal with black women because 'they're only women anyhow'. They find intelligent black men much more of a threat."[28] While it is valid for him to note the way in which sexism can reinforce racism, his implication that the only effective Black Australian spokespeople are males is contradicted by the achievements of numerous Aboriginal women. It is arguable that the real reasons for the frail self-image of Aboriginal men like Sweet William are that he has been prevented as a father from providing for his wife and children by unemployment, the institutional bias of Aboriginal reserve managers and the prejudice of White Australians.

The Cake Man raises numerous socio-political issues which bear upon Aboriginal male/female relationships, activism, and the Black Australian self-image. Merritt highlights many aspects of Aboriginality in his play: of despondency, family closeness, the threat of alcohol and the retention of pride—or at least the capacity to be proud. The potential for an unremmittingly pessimistic atmosphere is skilfully offset by the author, again through the use of levity. The humour of Robert Merritt is less brash and overt than that of Kevin Gilbert, but it is derived from similar sources: it is primarily the humour of "sacrilege", of the bottle and of sexual innuendo. Sweet William repeatedly takes organised religion to task:

> What's that bit again? 'For y'travel over land and sea to make one convert ... an' when ya finished with 'im, why, that feller's twice as fit for hell as you are y'self'(pp. 12-13).

The double meanings contained in Merritt's humorous dialogue have usually been enthusiastically received by Black and White Australians alike. For example, Sweet William's lament, "I been stewin' all my life. Ain't made me no better, Rube" is answered by his wife with a smile and the words "You always tasted good to me" (p. 32)—a line which exemplifies the subtle and affectionate sense of levity in the play. Merritt also has a keen ear for the colloquial speech, not only of adults but of children as well. His gentle humour is very successful, as when Ruby admonishes Pumpkinhead for being gullible enough to believe in "birriks" (or invisible spirit devils). He replies:

> Me and Collie and Noelie seen 'em. Two of 'em, all dressed in black down the church and we were scairt and we run all the way to the mission and we told Uncle Foley and he said they was so! He said they *holy* birriks and he knows 'cos he's wise! (p. 23).

Aboriginality, as depicted in *The Cake Man*, is equivalent to the discovery of pleasure in the midst of much pain. In the author's own words, "I was on a suicidal trip of trying to find beauty where beauty is not expected to be found".[29] The playwright does succeed in his aim, for the Black Australian family relationship he portrays is both moving and persuasive. In short, Merritt challenges the European reader or theatre-goer to try to see and appreciate the Aboriginality which *The Cake Man* displays.

Gerald Bostock offers much the same sort of challenge in his *Here Comes the Nigger*, a play which deals above all with the theme of blindness. Bostock engages this theme on a number of different levels: he portrays not only sightlessness, but also the figurative blindness resulting from racism and the colour blindness which enables one to overcome racial prejudice. This is made explicit by the excerpt of his poetry with which the play was advertised:

> What is colour
> What is blue and what is white
> Can colour be distinguished In the darkness of night?[30]

Bostock's play is a fast-paced, modern and violent examination of the disabilities—both physical and mental—which afflict urban Aborigines in contemporary Australia. It is an extremely powerful and pointed piece of work which, unlike all the other Black Australian plays, mounts to an intense climax at the very end. As a result, its atmosphere is episodic and cinematographic.

The two major characters in the play are a blind Aboriginal poet named Sam Matthews and a white woman, Odette O'Brien, who is tutoring him for his HSC examinations. They gradually develop an affectionate relationship and (though the playwright is careful never to portray a sexual dimension) those round the pair are convinced that each is sexually taking advantage of the other. Bostock is very strong in his lucid illustration of racist and sexual stereotypes employed on both sides of the colour line. As Sam's brother Billy says, "You know what these gubbah [European] women are like. They can screw you right up"[31] and his girlfriend Verna adds, "You know what they say: if ya start mixin' with that white stuff too much it might rub off on ya!"(p. 18). Similarly, Odette's brother Neil warns, "You know what they say about white women who muck around with black men. They say they've got a sweet tooth; that they're partial to the taste of licorice sticks"(p. 87). These racist and sexual misconceptions can be very destructive, Bostock suggests, and the near-tragic ending of the play is a direct result of their operation.

Though the two main characters do largely succeed in achieving "colour blindness", they become victims of an environment which is all too attuned to racial differences. It is significant that this environment is the city, for *Here Comes the Nigger* is the first Black Australian play to be set in an urban milieu. As a result, police harassment is ubiquitous, the Aboriginal dialogue is often enlivened by the patois of the urban sub-culture and the pace of the action is rapid. It is equally significant that Bostock's poetry is highlighted in the play and is integrated quite plausibly into the production. As the author admits, one of his reasons for writing *Here Comes the Nigger* was to "give people a dose of my poetry"[32] and this he does, especially when Billy recites Sam's [Bostock's] poem "Black Children" to the wild acclaim of a group of Aborigines gathered for a party. Both his themes and his poetic technique enable Bostock to introduce a pan-Aboriginal element into the work, for the Black Australian urban experience is a similar one throughout the country.

The urban black concept of Aboriginality which Bostock explores in *Here Comes the Nigger* involves almost daily violence, but also underlines the solidarity of the city-dwelling blacks. Like all of the Aboriginal dramatists, Bostock has captured realistic situations and naturalistic dialogue. There is such power and immediacy in his work that, according to the author, both black and white members of the audience were sometimes physically affected by viewing the play:

> The only way to get the message across was to show people what it was really like in Redfern. White people would write in saying they couldn't sleep after the performance. White girls would say to me, 'We're not like that! We're not like that!', and others were getting so harassed they'd leave the show.[33]

Significantly for Bostock, one of the most important criteria of dramatic success is immediate and observable impact upon the audience. This largely explains why he has devoted his energies to film and television script-work since the performance of *Here Comes the Nigger* in 1976. What is also important is that his sometimes frank polemicism is mitigated by a buoyant vein of largely sexual humour, which permeates the entire play. For example, Sam and Verna trade suggestiveness throughout almost an entire scene:

VERNA: Gettin' any lately, big brother? ...
SAM: I know love's suppose t'be blind ... but I ain't found anyone that blind enough yet!
VERNA: *[giving him a sexy hug]* Nemmine. Ah still loves ya, honey! *[He gives her a playful slap on the backside]*
SAM: *[smiles]* Garn, ya gin. I bet ya say that t'all us handsome blackfellas!
VERNA: *[She snaps her fingers and wriggles her hips]* Whell ... white may be right, but black is beautiful! Anyway, I'd rather be a slack black than an uptight white! ...
VERNA: I know what's wrong with him. He's sex-starved, the bastard!
SAM: This could be true!

VERNA:	Too bloody right, it's true! But then, so am I.
SAM:	You gins are all the same, hey?
VERNA:	I don't see any of you black-fellas knockin' us back.[34]

This type of repartee is noteworthy for a number of reasons. First, Bostock obviously displays an indebtedness to the Black American idiom as well as to the urban dialect of his own people—an indication of the international influences in his drama. Second, the lecherous tone is intentional and no offence is taken. Third, such banter takes place in the play only between Aborigines and is therefore a type of cultural signifier. Fourth, the laughter is characteristically interspersed with seriousness; for example, this exchange is immediately followed by Verna's angry outburst concerning the major health problems of rural Aborigines in South Australia. This social criticism is then immediately followed by a return to "sexual" dialogue:

| VERNA: | Ya know what they say about the Old Red Ned ... puts lead in ya pencil! |
| SAM: | S'no good having lead in your pencil if you got no bastard to write to.[35] |

Bostock's technique of intermittent levity—common to all the Aboriginal drama produced so far—releases the pressure of vitriol and resentment. In addition, the humour reflects, both linguistically and symbolically, a unified urban Aboriginal group. Therefore, it not only creates light relief but also signifies membership in the Black Australian sub-culture and subscription to its mores. Thus Aboriginality, as Bostock reflects it, is besieged but defiant, and as vibrant as the humour in *Here Comes the Nigger*.

Aboriginality, as some White Australian dramatists have attempted to portray it, has amounted to many things. Katharine Susannah Prichard made it a symbol of the sexual life-force in *Brumby Innes*, David Ireland largely equated it with depression and depravity in his *Image in the Clay*, and it became the representation of the outcast in Dymphna Cusack's wartime drama, *Shoulder the Sky*. In Bill Reed's *Truganinni* Aboriginality was the image of tragic extinction; it was tantamount to degradation and sexual temptation in Dorothy Hewett's *The Man from Mukinupin* and a serious liability in the workplace in Jill Shearer's brave attempt to mirror the impact of contemporary urban prejudice, *The Foreman*. There are few White Australian playwrights who have celebrated aspects of Black

Australian culture as thoroughly as the Aboriginal dramatists; even fewer who have managed to depict Aborigines as plausible individuals rather than as symbolic representations. Hardly any European playwrights have even approximated the distinctive Black Australian approach to humour.

There is a brief glimmering of resemblance in George Landen Dann's *Fountains Beyond*, in the exchanges between the characters Wally and Peggy:

WALLY: Hello, beautiful one!
PEGGY: Wally! … I should of guess it was you—making all that noise. I got
               a good mind I stick this fork into you.
WALLY: I couldn't take it … too tough!36

Despite Dann's undoubted sympathy for Black Australians and his careful construction of an Aboriginal fringe-dwelling locale, the dialogue of the black characters is generally stylised and posed—as is the erudite diction of the visiting British author, Miss Harnett. The most significant aspect of *Fountains Beyond* is that it illustrates the dominant viewpoint at the time it was written, that the fringe-dwellers were inevitably doomed to extinction. In Miss Harnett's words:

> For people like you who have lived for years on the outskirts of towns, there is no
> hope. It is too late to hold out hope. In time you shall pass away and the
> townspeople shall heave sighs of relief.37

As Dann's work shows, sympathy and fine intentions are no guarantee of naturalistic dialogue.

Even White Australian dramatists who have researched the topic have failed to reproduce Aboriginal experience. An excellent case in point is Thomas Keneally's *Bullie's House*. His play illustrates the risks of misinterpretation which befall even the best-intentioned European writers. Keneally bases his play upon an incident described by R.M. Berndt in his 1962 monograph entitled, *An Adjustment Movement in Arnhem Land*. Berndt's book details a movement amongst the Aboriginal inhabitants of the Elcho Island mission in which the tribe's *ranga*, or sacred objects, were put on public display in totemic fashion. In the original incident, two individuals—Buramara and Badanga—were primarily responsible. The former was attempting to come to terms with the fact that a willy-willy had totally destroyed his hut while by-passing all the others on the island, while the latter was simultaneously a " 'headman' for the Elcho Island people" and a Methodist "church elder".

Buramara was on the horns of a dilemma because some local leaders had informed him that the destruction of his hut was a dreaming "manifestation" ... "to punish him because he had not fulfilled all his ritual obligations", while others assured him that God had sent the willy-willy upon him "because he had been backsliding"[38] in a Christian sense. *Bullie's House* takes this incident as its starting point and explores the dilemma of Buramara (whom Keneally renames Bulumbil or Bullie), and his resultant attempts to atone for the wrongs he believes he has committed. He also introduces a love triangle in which Bullie is "sung" by Doolie, the wife of his friend Mallie, and adds a stereotyped Professor of Anthropology, a representative of the Department of Native Affairs, and a Methodist minister.

The distinctiveness of Black Australian plays is thrown into clear relief when it is contrasted with the largely unsuccessful efforts of playwrights such as Keneally to employ a Black Australian idiom. The speech the author gives his Aboriginal characters is sometimes appropriate, but is more often lacklustre and unconvincing. Of course, this is as much a function of Keneally's limitations as a dramatist as it is of his inability to penetrate the Aboriginal world-view.

As a result of ethnocentricity rather than malice, Keneally significantly misinterprets the importance of the display of the *ranga* upon which his work hinges. Through this misconception, Bullie and his cronies are reduced to little more than simple-minded lusters after European culture—and material goods. In Bullie's words,

> Why did I want to bring out the *ranga*? That's what you want to know. It's a gift, like Barraga says. There isn't any other gift as big as that. And we wanted gifts back. And we'll get them, too, because the Professor's here to see the *ranga* we brought out.[39]

The others add:

MALLIE: We want that generator they wouldn't give us.
BARRIE: And the air pump—
MALLIE: And the gear, the whole kit. And the teacher to show the young blokes how to dive for shell ... (p. 46).

According to the author, Bullie promoted the unveiling of the *ranga* not only to expiate the sin that caused the destruction of his house but also, because he wished to receive in return "the spiritual genius of the Europeans summed up in a few visible symbols ... in some potent and magical and easily presentable symbols".[40] But there is an inherent difficulty (if not an impossibility) involved in this formula: that which is "magical" is not normally "easily presentable" and is, moreover, degraded by its expression in material terms. Hence, though Keneally has attempted to depict the display of the *ranga* as a symbolic olive branch—a means of detente between Christianity and traditional Aboriginal religion—the impression one is left with upon reading the work is that Bullie wants, above all, to learn how to live his life according to the European pattern.

However, Berndt's monograph—the stated source for the play—illustrates that the fundamental reason for the unveiling of the sacred objects was the Aborigines' desire to demonstrate the richness of their culture and thereby, to assert their independence and autonomy. In Berndt's words,

> These eastern Arnhem Landers, generally speaking, see no virtue in being 'like' Europeans. Indeed, they are sometimes told they never can be ... What they desire is merely a greater amount of control over their own affairs, politically and religiously, and in relation to education and employment.[41]

Finally, though Keneally did attempt to base his play upon an event which "actually happened",[42] he had no idea that two of the protagonists were still alive. These Aboriginal men actually viewed a production of *Bullie's House* and it comes as no surprise that "at a meeting back in their country they voted unanimously against the play".[43] It is unfortunate that the research which Keneally did undertake was both insufficient and misconceived. To his credit, he at least had the courage to admit the difficulties he encountered:

> It's very hard for a novelist or a playwright to stick to the facts. I think he ought to make sure that his *creative* distortions are in line with what the meaning of the event was ... There are a number of things that happened when I began writing the play *Bullie's House* which taught me great lessons ... I had no idea that the man who had presented the *ranga* ... was still alive, and in fact had not received a full detente from the Europeans as a result of his act of enormous generosity—had in fact suffered a more subtle punishment: he'd become an MBE.[44]

As *Bullie's House* illustrates, Aboriginality is a very difficult theme for a White Australian dramatist to express in a persuasive way, especially when the author's talent falls short of his or her ambitiousness.

In the work of Jack Davis, his talent as a dramatist and his ambition to express Aboriginality in literature are extremely well balanced. Davis has had to rely for his historical sources upon documentary material almost entirely amassed by whites and housed in White Australian institutions. Yet he avoids some of the pitfalls which Keneally encountered because his facts *are*, in the latter's words, "*creative* distortions in line with what the meaning of the event was". *Kullark* is an occasional, admittedly partisan play which was created by the impetus to "set the record straight" in Western Australia. It achieves this—and more—partly by integrating relevant facts and figures into the production, but primarily by offering the reader careful characterisation and precise dialogue. This gives the drama a veracity which no catalogue of statistics could provide. Davis has an uncomplicated, poetic apprehension of colloquial Black Australian speech and he has also had a life-long exposure to the dialogue of White Australians. For both reasons, *Kullark* displays a tone of simple and honest naturalism.

In addition to being the Aboriginal dramatist most indebted to traditional black oral literature, he is also the playwright who has some of the most insightful observations to make upon contemporary Black Australian society. In *Kullark* Davis perceptively illustrates the range in Aboriginal socio-political attitudes, and the fact that there is a genuine ambivalence on the part of many Black Australians confronted with what they believe is radicalism. The Aboriginal mother and father, Alec and Rosie, exemplify these misgivings:

ROSIE: You know, I'm startin' to worry about Jamie.
ALEC: Why, 'e looks alright to me.
ROSIE: I dunno, 'e don't seem happy to me.
ALEC: All them land rights an' that. 'E's too much mixed up with them white students, if you ask me.
ROSIE: Well, what's wrong with land rights and that? Young people stick together more these days, that's all.
ALEC: Yeah, but those *Wetjalas*'ll lead him on, an' when the chips are down he'll be out on 'is ear.[45]

Davis, more than any other Aboriginal dramatist, has captured the feel of the gap in attitudes and beliefs between Black Australian generations. He is also an extremely astute observer of personal inconsistencies and foibles. This enables him to develop one of his strengths, which is the genial highlighting of the ironies and self-contradictions which are part of Aboriginal life in a predominantly White Australian society. For example, Alec displays his own version of the motto, "there is an exception to every rule" when he is discussing whom Jamie should marry:

ALEC:	That ain't got nothing to do with it, I don't want im marryin' no *Wetjala yok* [white woman].
ROSIE:	You're just plain bloody racist.
ALEC:	No I'm not, but 'e's a *Nyoongah* like you and me, and 'e should marry a *Nyoongah*.
ROSIE:	What about your sister Mary? She's married to a *Wetjala*.
ALEC:	Aw, that's different. Ol' Bill, 'e's all right.
ROSIE:	Yeah, specially when 'e brings you a flagon around now an' again (p. 17).

The play is in three sections, and in all of them Davis develops the theme of independent and sustained Aboriginal resistance. All the way through, whites figure as invaders and/or intruders, whether fought against, served under, or grudgingly invited home. The keynote of the entire play is the sentiment of the poem with which Davis ends it:

> With murder, with rape, you marred her skin,
> But you cannot whiten her mind.
> They will remain my children forever,
> The black and the beautiful kind.
> The black and the beautiful kind (p. 66).

Significantly, according to Davis, one of the most visible ways Aborigines have survived the white onslaught is through reliance upon each other, upon their traditions, and upon their distinctive mores; in short, through Aboriginality itself. Again, humour is an integral part of the equation. For example, organised religion comes in for some light-hearted ridicule in *Kullark* when Alec describes the local missionary as a "bookie's clerk":

> You know, 'e can't lose—it's like an each way bet: If 'e can't get ya to 'is church that don't matter, 'e'll still get to 'eaven 'cause 'e tried. It's even better than an each way bet, because 'e bets on the whole bloody field (p. 9).

Alec and Rosie fortify their lively relationship by feuding repeatedly over his drinking. As he pours himself a glass of wine he admits, "You know, in the twenty five years we've been together I never won an argument yet", and Rosie replies, "And if you drink that you won't win this one either"(p. 17). The sexual innuendo is more subtle than in *Here Comes the Nigger*, but it is present nonetheless:

| ALEC: | Yeah, you went to a lot of trouble, borrowin' that bed an' mattress orf that flamin' do-gooder Lyn what's-'er-name. |

ROSIE:	Here you go again. Any *Wetjala* does you a favour you call 'em a do-gooder.
ALEC:	Just because she lent you a bed an' mattress you think the sun shines out of her *kwon*. Wouldn't mind betting she'll be around to share the bed with 'im before too long.
ROSIE:	You dirty-minded ol' bastard.
ALEC:	[*laughing*] Watch your language, love, watch your language. [*Suddenly disgruntled*] We never needed the flamin' bed, anyway (p. 16).

In the play published in tandem with *Kullark—The Dreamers*—it is Davis's attention to even minute details of scene and language which establishes the Aboriginal atmosphere of the play consistently, plausibly and entertainingly. It is a far more personal play than *Kullark*, not only because Davis wrote it envisaging himself in the lead role of Worru, but because one sees the many sides of the Wallitch family: their happiness and sorrow, their quarrels and togetherness, their drunkenness and sobriety. The play is written without artifice, without embarrassment and frequently, with lyrical sensitivity.

The *Nyoongah* language, the repeated framing of scenes with traditional Aboriginal music and dance, and the awareness of otherness which the young black children of the Wallitch family possess, all clearly indicate the continued strength of a separate sense of Aboriginality. Twelve-year-old Shane knows few *Nyoongah* words, but he can still remark to his white friend Darren: "I know what *Wetjala* is, that's you".[46] Similarly, when his fourteen-year-old sister, Meena, is preparing to go out with her boyfriend he counsels her to "watch it", not for reasons we might expect, but because "he might be a relation, you know we got hundreds of 'em"(p. 113).

In many respects, *The Dreamers* is a marvellous work. Linguistically, its consistent usage of *Nyoongah* challenges the White Australian reader or member of the audience. For one of the few times in Australian literature, it makes her or him feel a stranger in the continent which, after all, has been occupied by Europeans for only two hundred years. As a result of this, and because of the strong awareness of Aboriginal history and traditional oral literature in which is steeped, *The Dreamers* is one of the most culturally independent and autonomous Black Australian theatrical statements to date. It truly breaks new ground in the field of Australian drama. As Robert Hodge has observed:

Aboriginal words weave through the dialogue, making no concessions to White ignorance, so that Whites simply have to put up with the unselfconscious exclusion of them and their language that so many Aboriginals have endured at greater length: they have less chance of understanding 'Milbert, yuarl nyinaliny gnullarah', for instance, than Shane ... has of knowing that London is the capital of England. This salutory experience for Whites of being part of a disregarded, peripheral culture is intensified if there are a large number of Aboriginals in the audience, becoming a majority as well as a dominant culture, guffawing uninhibitedly with the joy of recognition of Aboriginal life affirmed on a public stage.[47]

As Hodge illustrates, though the European reader might be daunted by the seeming inaccessibility of some of the language of the play, the effort which is required to come to terms with it is a valuable cultural experience. The challenge to the audience is also insignificant when compared with the effort which Davis has invested in *The Dreamers* to make it one of the most lucid statements of Aboriginality in Black Australian literature.

Both *Kullark* and the *Dreamers* are, in quite different ways, celebrations. The former shows the reverse side of the Western Australian commemoration of its sesquicentenary, which also represented 150 years of oppression and exploitation of Aborigines. The latter is a celebration of what it is to be an urban Aboriginal, despite hypocrisy, untruths, and the constant pressure of the surrounding European world. There is no clearer sense in which *The Dreamers* becomes an oasis of Aboriginality in the Australian theatre than through its engaging and distinctive humour. One scene crystallises the conflicting dictates of traditional Aboriginal religion and modern Christianity very amusingly. The Wallitch family is sitting down to a meal of roast kangaroo:

SHANE: Do we only say grace when we are eating kangaroo?
ROY: [*putting his spoon back on his plate and swallowing*] We thank you, Lord, for what—
WORRU: You put bacon in this?
ROY: We thank you—
WORRU: Bacon, *wah*?
SHANE: Ssh, ssh, Popeye, close your eyes.
ROY: We thank you, Lord.
WORRU: What for? Can't eat with me eyes closed.
ROY: We thank you, Lord, for what we have got.
WORRU: [*to* SHANE, *pointing upwards*] I forgot about that fella up there.
ROY: Oh Gawd! (pp. 102-103).

The humour is decidedly vibrant, especially when enlivened by drinking and verbal competition:

ELI: Look, I tell you, I played full forward for Federals in Wagin. One match I kicked ten goals, right through the big sticks. [*He demonstrates*]
ROY: Full forward. [*Laughing*] Full and forward, belly up to the bar and then you got kicked right outa the pub! (p. 125).

The irony of the typically black situations Davis brings to life is equally impressive. For example, the shiftiest and most unreliable member of the family, Eli, reports upon his day's success in begging at the shopping centre, while wearing a false eye patch:

ELI: Yeah, we were doin' all right outside the shopping centre today, yeah, gettin' fifty cents a bite. One *wetjala* bloke, hippy, he give me two dollars.
WORRU: *Kia*, two dollar.
ELI: Anyways, some of them *Nyoongahs* spotted me. There they was: 'Give me fifty cents, brother', 'Give me a dollar, nephew', 'Give me fifty cents, uncle'; and you know none of them black bastards are related to me. That's true. Pop, I never seen blackfellas like 'em, they real bloody dinkum out and out bludgers. Can't stand the bastards (p. 105).

Though it is far less emphasised than in the plays of Gilbert and Bostock, the sexual theme is again dealt with in a humorous vein by Davis. For example, when Meena defends her boyfriend from her mother's criticism, she starts out on dry land but ends up in deep water:

MEENA: What's wrong with Ross's car? He's got a V8 panel van and he's done it up real nice, got an air conditioner, stereo, bed and ... and ...
DOLLY: Yeah, I bet he has. You make sure you're home by ten o'clock (pp. 116-117).

In *The Dreamers* as in *Kullark*, humour is a vital component of the distinctive Aboriginal self-image. There is realistic violence, sorrow and suffering in both, but Davis conveys such an honest tenderness in his black characterisation and such a believable emphasis upon Aboriginal uniqueness, humour and endurance, that the sense which remains at the end is bittersweet: a feeling of stubborn faith in the face of loss. Perhaps this is the most accurate adjective to use when describing Aboriginality as well: a sense that while all can never be regained, all will never be lost.

Davis returns to an explicitly historical theme in *No Sugar*, first published in 1986. Although written three years after *The Dreamers*, *No Sugar* actually precedes it thematically and chronologically. *No Sugar* is the first part of Davis's dramatic trilogy focussing upon the past half-century of Aboriginal history in Western Australia, which *The Dreamers* continues and the as-yet unpublished *Barungin (Smell the Wind)* completes. The play highlights the oppression of institutionalised Aborigines by focussing on the story of the Millimurra family, the ancestors of the Wallitch clan of *The Dreamers*. Forcibly removed from Government Well near Northam to the Moore River Native Settlement, the Millimurras represent Aborigines throughout Australia in the 1920s and 1930s, coerced to live in areas far removed from White Australians.

No Sugar is very faithful to the historical record, so much so that documented massacres are dealt with as an integral part of the drama. Davis's treatment of Aboriginal history is, as always, intriguing. He manages to establish a simultaneous position as chronicler of, and participant in, the Black Australian past. He achieves this by alternating between European styles of historical narration—as when A.O. Neville addresses the Royal Western Australian Historical Society—and Aboriginal dialogue, in which the rhythms of colloquial speech and usage of *Nyoongah* alter the entire atmosphere of the story. Billy's recounting of the Oombulgarri [Umbali] Massacre is made much more vivid in this way:

BILLY:	Big mob politjmans, and big mob from stations, and shoot 'em everybody mens, *koories*, little *yumbah*. [*He grunts and mimes pulling a trigger.*] They chuck 'em on a big fire, chuck 'em in river. [*They sit in silence, mesmerized and shocked by* BILLY'S *gruesome story.*]
JIMMY:	Anybody left, your mob?
BILLY:	Not many, gid away, hide. But no one stop that place now, they all go 'nother country.
JOE:	Why?
BILLY:	You go there, night time you hear 'em. I bin bring cattle that way for Wyndham Meat Works. I hear 'em. Mothers cryin' and babies cryin', screamin'. *Waiwai! Wawai! Wawai!*[48]

Although it is less technically adventurous than *The Dreamers*, *No Sugar* is equally notable for its vibrant, often amusing dialogue. One of Davis's greatest skills is his ability to balance conflict—between police and prisoners, "Protectors" and their charges, Magistrates and defendants—through his usage of repartee which is as irreverent as it is appropriate:

SERGEANT:	Yeah, and you tell that bush lawyer brother of yours, if he comes here arguing I'll make him jump: straight inside. [*They turn to go. As they leave he raises his voice after them.*] You hear me?
MILLY:	[*calling*] Yeah, I hear you. Can't help hearin' you. [*They walk down the street.*]
GRAN:	[*calling*] You don't want to shout like that, Chergeant. You'll have a fit, just like a dingo when he gets bait.
MILLY:	[*calling*] Seein' you're drinkin down the Federal every night, Sergeant, you can tell old Skinny Martin to stick his stag ram right up his skinny *kwon*!
GRAN:	[*calling*] Yeah, an' the boots too (p. 23).

The humour is often critical but is never really offensive:

SERGEANT:	Look, there's nothing I can do about it except put in a reminder to the Department in Perth. Why don't youse go around to St John's and ask the vicar?
MILLY:	For blankets? He'll give us nothin', he's like that.
GRAN:	[*adopting a praying attitude*] Yeah, when he come to Gubment Well he goes like that with his eyes closed and he says the Lord will help you, and now he prays with his eyes open, 'cause time 'fore last Wow Wow bit him on the leg ... musta wanted a bit a' holy meat (p. 43).

Davis also establishes basic motifs which resurface throughout the play, such as tobacco (called "nigger twist"[p. 43]); soap (requested by the blacks and denied by the whites); and, most effectively, sugar. The Chief Protector of Aborigines, A.O. Neville, admonishes Jimmy with the words, "Munday, let me give you a piece of advice: sugar catches more flies than vinegar"(p. 39). But the truth is, as the play's title indicates, that the Aborigines have "no sugar", both literally and figuratively. As they sing on Christmas Day at Moore River, in a parody which enrages Neville:

> There is a happy land,
> Far, far away,
> No sugar in our tea,
> Bread and butter we never see.
> That's why we're gradually
> Fading away (p. 98).

The tightness and cleverness of the play's structure demonstrates that Davis has extended the range of his dramatic writing even further in *No Sugar*. *Barungin (Smell the Wind)* both completes his dramatic trilogy and establishes Davis as the most ambitious and accomplished Aboriginal playwright.[49]

Barungin is Davis's most overtly political and accusatory play, set in the context of the Bicentennial and the Royal Commission on Aboriginal Deaths in Custody. Its final scene cuts so close to the bone that newspaper headlines concerning black deaths are projected on the set as a vital component of the impassioned climax. At times, the barriers between the audience and the players break down more completely than in any of Davis's previous plays. At one stage "Uncle" Peegun and Shane actually busk for the theatre patrons and pass around the hat afterwards, saying "You look like a rich mob of people".

Once again, the distinctive naturalism of Black Australian drama is underlined—a trademark of all the of the Aboriginal plays written to date. And again, Davis's irrepressible sense of humour shines through, as the Wallitch family plays "Trivial Pursuit" together, as they discuss Captain James Cook ("Jim the Ripper") and as Christian and non-Christian Aborigines are compared:

ROBERT	[*Gesturing skywards*] I got the right fella looking after me.
PEEGUN	[*With disdain*] Jesus!
ROBERT	That's him!

In May 1988 Davis realised a long-standing dream "that during the Bicentennial year Australians would be able to see the complete trilogy under the title *The First-born*"[50] when all three plays were performed in sequence at the Fitzroy Town Hall. This was a triumph for Davis, and for what reviewer Dennis Davison termed "the hidden side of Australia":

The main impression of the trilogy is an authentic portrayal of everyday living, acted so naturally that we are absorbed ... Davis is neither sentimental nor didactic but an honest realist.[51]

It has to be added that Davis's success at weaving together observations of his people, his poetry and his wise humour have made him a world-class dramatist of whom all Australians should be proud.

The question then arises: "Just how important to Black Australians as a whole—and specifically, to the Aboriginal movement—are the black playwrights?" Davis strongly believes in the worth of writing, as opposed to some forms of political activism and demonstration:

I think they're [Aboriginal writers] the most important thing we've got ... you could put up a tent today and people would laugh at it ... now, it's time for the people with the pen to take over.[52]

Brian Syron concurs that Aboriginal writers are a cogent, articulate and representative voice:

> We are fighting through art. This is the healthy alternative to the radicals. The radicals are a "Mickey Mouse" reproduction of United States and Great Britain radicals.[53]

Leila Rankine is equally optimistic:

> I think, hopefully, through writers, through artists, and through the art form, we can be able to do more than maybe even governments to try and bring about change.[54]

However, though many Black Australians feel that Aboriginal literature—and especially drama—can help to effect social change, others are not convinced. For example, with reference to performances of *The Cake Man*, Charles Perkins makes the point that:

> Some people would probably accept it fully and sort of fit it into their mind just what is happening in Aboriginal Affairs, and it would develop their understanding as a consequence. But others would probably take it on the night ... for entertainment value and leave it at that and say, 'Oh yes, very good; great fun'—and then forget about it.[55]

Of course, it is difficult to quantify the impact of drama in this way. What can be said is that, if Black Australian plays are only performed in standard Australian theatres and are not, for example, taken to the streets and parks and Aboriginal settlements of the country, very few black people will be able to see the works. Moreover, there is a sense in which many Australian theatre-goers would not pay to view a play such as *The Dreamers* or *No Sugar* unless they already sympathised to some extent with the Aboriginal cause. In short, as currently performed, Aboriginal drama is preaching to the converted to a significant extent.

For these reasons, John Newfong is sceptical about the ability of Black Australian playwrights to effect any socio-political change through their works:

> I know there is a view being expressed ... that things are going to change through the arts ... but I don't see those things really changing all the while the arts remain elitist ... As far as the impact of theatre goes in Australia—and you're not dealing with a theatre-going public in Australia—as far as it has an influence on Australian thinking, I think plays like *The Cake Man* and Jack Davis's plays *have* had an enormous influence ... But if you're talking about direct influence, 'No'. I mean *The Cake Man* is not going to change the budget for the ADC. *The Cake Man* is not going to get land rights. *The Cake Man* will create an awareness over and above an awareness that any political spokesman can create but, you see, that's a building

block for the future.[56]

While Newfong's view is valid as far as it goes, it arguably does not tell the entire story. Aboriginal public servants and dramatists alike are bounded by the dictates of their own horizons, interests and employment. For example, the view that Aboriginal radicalism—and the capacity to achieve significant socio-political gains—has been silenced by the co-option of leading Aborigines into government departments is frequently voiced by activists as well as by authors. It is also true (and Newfong admits as much[57]) that political advances for Aboriginal people can be very transitory, while attitudinal change is often far more long-lasting. Finally, it is possible that the international and domestic impact of Aboriginal literature—and drama in particular—help to create a climate of opinion which favourably influences the Australian government to make political concessions to Black Australians. Hence, the most balanced view is that while there are few direct and observable socio-political consequences of Aboriginal drama, its importance as a means of furthering the Black Australian cause should not be underestimated.

There are two final factors which must not be overlooked, one of which is education. Theatre may be elitist but education is universal, and it is in the schools and universities of Australia that plays such as *The Cake Man*, *The Dreamers* and *No Sugar* will have their most significant effect. Already, in recognition of their literary worth and socio-political relevance, all have been accepted for inclusion in the syllabuses of major state high school systems. Lastly, Aboriginal drama has the potential for effective conversion into the media of film, video, and television,[58] all of which would greatly enhance the exposure and impact of the works themselves.

Education and the mass media are two of the most potent means by which the portrayal of Aboriginality can be disseminated throughout Australia. While the Black Australian view of Black Australians is multi-faceted, it is also one which more and more Australians of all racial backgrounds will encounter in the late 1980s and early 1990s. When they do, the seemingly irrepressible humour which is an integral part of Aboriginality will be one of the most persuasive ambassadors for Black Australian literature.

Notes

1   Kevin Gilbert, *Living Black: Blacks Talk to Kevin Gilbert*, (Ringwood, 1978), p. 184.

2   Quoted in *ibid.*, p. 193.

3   Personal interview with Robert Merritt, Sydney, July, 1982.

4   Personal interview with Charles Perkins, Canberra, January, 1983.

5   Quoted by Patti Watts in her article "Plea for Assistance", The *West Australian*, 17 July 1980, p. 58.

6   Personal interview with Anna Haebich, Canberra, November, 1980.

7   Quoted in Adam Shoemaker, "An Interview with Jack Davis", *Westerly*, vol. 27, no. 4, December, 1982, p. 112.

8   W.E.H. Stanner, "Aboriginal Humour", *Aboriginal History*, vol. 6, part 1, June, 1982, p. 41.

9   Personal interview with John Newfong, Canberra, July, 1982.

10   Quoted in Adam Shoemaker, "An Interview with Jack Davis", *Westerly*, vol. 27, no. 4, December, 1982, pp. 114-115.

11   Personal interview with Robert Merritt, Sydney, July, 1982.

12   Stanner, "Aboriginal Humour", p. 41.

13   ibid., p. 43.

14   These events were related by Bostock during a workshop session of the first National Aboriginal Writers' Conference, Murdoch University, Perth, February, 1983.

15   *The Cherry Pickers* was released by an independent Canberra press, Burrambinga Books, in May 1988. This was timed to coincide with the Aboriginal protests during the opening of the new Australian Parliament House by Queen Elizabeth.

16   Kevin Gilbert, *The Cherry Pickers*, Typescript, Canberra: National Library of Australia, mss. no. 2584, 1970, p. 22. All further quotations from *The Cherry Pickers* will be taken from this manuscript version, and page numbers will be included in parentheses in the body of the text immediately after each citation.

17   Kevin Gilbert, *Ghosts in Cell Ten*, Unpublished typescript, Canberra, National Library of Australia, ms. no. 2584, 1979, p. 1. All further quotations will be taken from this version of the play, and page references will be given in parentheses

immediately after each citation, in the body of the text.

18   Pat O'Shane's speech was delivered to students of the Australian National University, Canberra, on 26 February, 1983.

19   Richard Broome, *Aboriginal Australians*, (Sydney, 1982), p. 183.

20   Pat O'Shane's speech at the ANU, Canberra, February, 1983.

21   Personal interview with Candy Williams, Sydney, July, 1980.

22   Personal interview with John Newfong, Canberra, July, 1982.

23   Robert J. Merritt, *The Cake Man*, (Sydney, 1978), pp. 32-33. All further quotations will be taken from this edition and page references will be included in the body of the text, immediately after each citation.

24   Personal interview with Brian Syron, Canberra, May, 1981.

25   Personal interview with Robert Merritt, Sydney, July, 1982.

26   Personal interview with John Newfong, Canberra, July, 1982.

27   There is a body of American psycho-social work which lends support to Newfong's theory concerning the de facto emasculation of Black Australian men. For example, Abram Kardiner and Lionel Ovesey, in their *The Mark of Oppression: Explorations in the Personality of the American Negro*, (Cleveland, 1962) note that "The lower-class Negro female cannot be 'feminine', nor the male 'masculine'. Their roles are reversed. Since these values are just the opposite from what they are in white society, and since the values of white society are inescapable, the male fears and hates the female; the female mistrusts and has contempt for the male because he cannot validate his nominal masculinity in practice" (p. 349). However, Newfong's conclusion is flatly contradicted by more recent scholarly analyses of specifically Australian sexual oppression, such as Anne Summers's *Damned Whores and God's Police*, (Ringwood, 1975).

28   ibid.

29   Personal interview with Robert Merritt, Sydney, July, 1982.

30   The advertising poster for *Here Comes the Nigger*, reproduced in *Meanjin*, vol. 36, no. 4, December, 1977, p. 482.

31   Gerry Bostock, *Here Comes the Nigger*, Third draft of filmscript, Typescript kindly provided by the author, Sydney, 1980, p. 13. All further quotations will be taken from this version of the play except where noted, and page references will be given immediately after each citation, in the body of the text.

32   Personal interview with Gerry Bostock, Sydney, July, 1980.

33   Personal interview with Gerry Bostock, Sydney, July, 1980.

34   Gerry Bostock, "Two Scenes from *Here Comes the Nigger*", *Meanjin*, vol. 36, no. 4, December, 1977, p. 483.

35   ibid., p. 485.

36   George Landen Dann, *Fountains Beyond*, (Melbourne, 1942[?]), p. 9.

37   *ibid.*, p. 68.

38   Ronald M. Berndt, *An Adjustment Movement in Arnhem Land*, (Paris, 1962), p. 34.

39   Thomas Keneally, *Bullie's House*, (Sydney, 1981), p. 44. All further quotations will be taken from this edition, and page references will be included in parentheses in the body of the text, immediately after each citation.

40   Personal interview with Thomas Keneally, Brisbane, September, 1982.

41   Berndt, *An Adjustment Movement*, p. 87.

42   Personal interview with Thomas Keneally, Brisbane, September, 1982

43   Bob Maza, "Introduction", in *Bullie's House*, p. xv.

44   Personal interview with Thomas Keneally, Brisbane, September, 1982.

45   Jack Davis, *Kullark*, in *Kullark/The Dreamers*, (Sydney, 1982), pp. 43-44. All further quotations will be taken from this edition, and page references will be given in parentheses in the body of the text, immediately after each citation.

46   Davis, *The Dreamers*, in *Kullark/The Dreamers*, (Sydney, 1982), p. 97. All further quotations will be taken from this edition, and page references will be given in the body of the text, immediately after each citation.

47   Robert Hodge, "A Case for Aboriginal Literature", *Meridian*, vol. 3, no. 1, May, 1984, p. 85.

48   Jack Davis, *No Sugar*, (Sydney, 1986), pp. 67-68. All further quotations will be taken from this edition, and page references will be given in the body of the text, immediately after each citation.

49   In 1986, Davis also wrote his first play for children, the highly successful *Honeyspot*. Both *Honeyspot* and *Barungin* enjoyed popular seasons as part of the official "World Expo on Stage" Australian Drama Series in Brisbane in July-August 1988.

50   Wendy Blacklock, "The Marli Biyol Company", in the World Expo on stage programme for *Barungin* (Sydney, 1988).

51   Dennis Davison, "Honest Look at the Hidden Side of Society", *The Australian*, 9 May 1988, p. 10.

52   Quoted in Adam Shoemaker, "An Interview With Jack Davis", *Westerly*, vol. 27, no. 4, December, 1982, p. 116.

53   Personal interview with Brian Syron, Canberra, May, 1981.

54   Personal interview with Leila Rankine, Adelaide, March, 1982.

55   Personal interview with Charles Perkins, Canberra, January, 1983.

56   Personal interview with John Newfong, Canberra, July, 1982.

57   "You may make political gains, but you have to fight to keep them". Quoted from

personal interview with John Newfong, Canberra, July, 1982.

58   Merritt's *The Cake Man* has, in fact, already been televised. However, the condensed, one hour-long version which was broadcast on the ABC in 1977 did not do the play full justice.

Conclusion
Black Words on White Pages

Mining in Australia occupies less than one-fifth of one percent of the total surface of our continent and yet it supports 14 million people. Nothing should be sacred from mining whether it's your ground, my ground, the blackfellow's ground or anybody else's. So the question of *Aboriginal land rights* and things of this nature shouldn't exist.[1]

"I didn't know the buggers could write!"[2]

The gap between multinational mining companies and Black Australian poetry may appear vast, but both activities are very important to Aboriginal Australians today. The first brings them directly into contact with European technology, politics and mores in remote areas of Australia's north. The second brings them into contact with writing achievements which engender Black Australian pride and confidence. The two activities are related in the further sense that Aboriginal writers frequently tackle socio-political issues—such as mining—in their work. A fine example of this is Gerry Bostock's sardonic poem, "An Australian Miner":

> A young Australian Miner
> Sat in his Company's diner
> Having coffee and Yellow Cake;
> He seemed quite amused
> By the Black's land he'd abused
> In the National Interest's sake.[3]

In this study, I have highlighted the fact that Black Australian literature is attuned to, and involved with, the Aboriginal political movement. Repeatedly, Aboriginal writers emphasise this aspect of their work. In the words of Bruce McGuinness:

All our struggles I think aim towards that one area, of ultimately achieving the land back so that we can become truly economically independent, so that we can achieve our own ends, so that we achieve those things that we want to achieve. Aboriginal writers have a responsibility here, a very important responsibility, to take that message not only to white people but to Aboriginal people as well, so that we can foster within our own communities a very important concept. That concept is that if we are going to survive, we are going to have to do it as a community, we are going to have to do it as a nation and not as individuals.[4]

Speaking more generally, Colin Johnson underlines the significant role of black writers in continuing and promoting Aboriginal culture:

We are already writing of the present. It is being detailed and made a part of history almost as fast as we act it out, but the future still remains a mystery. Writers are torches lighting up that mystery. They can show us the path or paths along which to travel just as much as the song-cycles of our ancestors mapped out the waterholes. Writers through their writings make us aware of the past, the present and the future.[5]

Not only the content but also the fact of Aboriginal literature is an important focus for Aboriginal pride. Writers such as Noonuccal, Gilbert and Davis have become role models of success for their own people. As Mick Miller observed:

they are taking their place amongst the greats in this country and the further we go on, in years to come, they're going to be standing out there for everybody to see—Aboriginal people to see—that we have somebody out there who is just as good as anybody else in the country.[6]

Miller's positive optimism is echoed by Jack Davis, who has commented:

People are going to turn over one morning and say, 'Christ! Look what I've got in my library!'. You know, I really think so … I talk in terms of decades—ten years—everything I think of in terms of ten years. And I see the changes in my lifetime. And I'm going to see it in the next ten years—and I think I'll live to see that—the people are going to have, not half a dozen; they're going to have thirty or forty books on their shelves which are going to be written by Aboriginal writers. And I think they'll cover the whole field.[7]

It can be argued that as Aboriginal authors, the majority of these spokespeople have a vested interest in publicising and extolling the virtues of Black Australian writing. But those such as Mick Miller are political activists, not creative writers, and his optimistic enthusiasm matches that of the authors themselves. However, it is true that some Aboriginal representatives view the close interrelationship of socio-political concerns and Black Australian literature as a necessary but temporary phase, which will be transcended in the future. Charles Perkins notes the contemporary political utility and impact of Aboriginal literature but adds:

> The ultimate is not to dabble too long in obvious political problems ... because in three or four years' time those problems will no longer be with us. And what we should be aiming towards through art and theatre and writing is creating a society of people that can develop their intellect to the highest possible level, where they can appreciate each other, their environment, and the things that are more important than those we think at the present time are important. I mean you can find ... great satisfaction and get good appreciation from what we do at the present time, but it's only the first couple of rungs on the ladder.[8]

Implicit in Perkins's assessment is the confidence that Aboriginal literature will continue to expand in volume and popularity, as well as in range of subject and focus, and will win even more domestic and international recognition.

An examination of the performance in the market-place of the most popular examples of recent Black Australian writing shows that the process of recognition has begun in earnest. For example, Archie Weller's *The Day of the Dog* sold out its 2,000 copy, hard-cover print run in less than ten months, and the paperback version of the novel rose to number four on the *Age*'s bestseller list. In excess of 30,000 copies of the novel had been sold by mid-1984[9] and significantly, the novel is just as popular amongst Aborigines and is considered by many black spokespeople to exemplify both Aboriginal achievement and black social commentary. In the words of Bruce McGuinness:

> *The Day of the Dog* is ... an excellent account of Aboriginal urban life and of our culture as developed within urban Perth, and it's very similar to what's happening in Fitzroy in Victoria, Musgrave Park in Queensland and Redfern in New South Wales ... I believe that Archie Weller has been able to give us an insight into the very distinct cultural forms that are kept [in the cities].[10]

Jack Davis concurred, and praised the book simply and directly: "to me as an Aboriginal it had the power of harsh reality".[11]

The popularity of the *The Day of the Dog* is an index of the growing awareness amongst White Australians of the value and impressiveness of Black Australian writing. There are many others. In 1987 and 1988, both Sally Morgan's *My Place* and Glenyse Ward's *Wandering Girl* were exceptionally well-received by Australian critics and book-buyers alike. Already, eminent publishers like Virago Press have offered contracts to produce both of these autobiographical books in Europe and North America.[12] Overseas, Jack Davis has joined the select ranks of Australian playwrights whose works have been produced to popular and critical acclaim in London. In June/July, 1988 *No Sugar* enjoyed an extremely successful season at the Riverside Studios in the British capital.

In the sphere of education, the first university-level course in "Aboriginal Literature" began at Murdoch University in 1983 and Colin Johnson was the founding tutor in that course, after having been writer-in-residence at the university in 1982. In 1984, Archie Weller was named as writer-in-residence at the Australian National University and Jack Davis was contracted by the Australian Elizabethan Theatre Trust to write two new plays, which became *Honeyspot* and *No Sugar*. More and more "Aboriginal Studies" units are being introduced throughout Australia and Aboriginal literature is playing an increasingly significant role in such courses. To cite two examples, Murdoch University and the University of Queensland now offer Aboriginal literature as a degree-option course at the tertiary level. This process is not only providing exposure for Black Australian writers but is also creating opportunities for Aboriginal lecturers in the same fields. Especially since 1984, and because of the impetus provided by former Director Gary Foley, the Aboriginal Arts Board has taken a particularly strong stance encouraging the publication and distribution of Aboriginal writing. All of these trends signal an expanding and positive awareness amongst the Australian community of the talent of Aboriginal writers and the importance of their works. There is also a growing realisation that activism is often an essential—and inevitable—component of the Aboriginal writer's experience.

That realisation has been heightened during 1988 by the welter of Black Australian protests against the Bicentenary. The clearest example of this was the highly-publicised involvement of Kevin Gilbert in an Aboriginal demonstration during the official opening of the new Parliament House in Canberra. Gilbert made front-page headlines across Australia when he alleged that the new parliament was "cursed" by the Aboriginal mosaic built into the forecourt of the building.[13] Although Gilbert's claim proved to be a hoax, he actually publicised Black Australian grievances far more effectively than if he had taken part in a "conventional" protest. That same month, Gilbert's ground-breaking anthology of Aboriginal poetry, *Inside Black Australia*, was released. The timing could not have been more appropriate. The launch of the first national anthology of Black Australian poetry coincided with some of the most publicised and innovative black protest activity ever seen in the country. It is ironic that even though the Bicentennial has been strongly opposed by most Aborigines, it has undeniably provided opportunities for Black Australian voices to be heard as never before—and has created a climate of heightened public interest, and involvement in, Black Australian issues.

In the anthology itself, Gilbert has assembled and superbly edited the verse of over forty Black Australian poets in a collection which will be an invaluable tool for any student of Aboriginal literature. What is particularly impressive is the range of Aboriginal poetry which Gilbert presents; from simple blank verse to clever satire, from parody to heartfelt lamentation. There is a real sense of discovery in *Inside Black Australia*. For example, in his parody of Sir Joh Bjelke-Petersen, W. Les Russell demonstrates that the traditional Aboriginal skill of mime can be transformed into verse in English:

> But here in Queensland we don't let the Federal Government
> down there in Canberra tell us what to do
> —and why should we?
> If they come up here we soon give them short shrift and short
>   change.
> We send them running back down south with their tails
>   between their legs
> and their hats behind their backs like little school boys.
> That's the way to do it—you've got to show them who's boss.
> And so I would tell Mr Cain not to worry about those
>   conservationists,
> just run right over them:
> cut right through the lot of them as if they weren't there.
> Golly, that's the way we do it in Queensland.[14]

Maureen Watson has always approached contentious issues bravely and forthrightly; she does so in "Memo to J.C." with an undertone of bitterness:

> But they don't call us religious, mate.
> Tho' we got the same basic values that you lived by,
> Sharin' and carin' about each other,
> And the bread and wine that you passed around,
> Well, we're still doing that, brother.
> Yeah, we share our food and drink and shelter,
> Our grief, our happiness, our hopes and plans,
> But they don't call us 'Followers of Jesus',
> They call us black fellas, man.[15]

But the most impassioned plea for understanding and change in *Inside Black Australia* comes from Robert Walker, who later became one of the victims in the incredible succession of black deaths in custody:

> Have you ever heard screams in the middle of
>   the night,
> Or the sobbings of a stir-crazy prisoner,
> Echo over and over again in the darkness—
> Threatening to draw you into its madness?
>
> Have you ever rolled up into a human ball
> And prayed for sleep to come?
> Have you ever laid awake for hours
> Waiting for morning to mark yet another day of
>   being alone?
>
> If you've ever experienced even one of these,
> Then bow your head and thank God.
> For it's a strange thing indeed—
> This rehabilitation system![16]

Some of the most apparently simple poems in Gilbert's collection carry the greatest weight: one of Ernie Dingo's quatrains can be taken as a symbol for Black Australian talent—and frustration—throughout the entire country:

> Aboriginal achievement
> Is like the dark side of the moon,
> For it is there
> But so little is known.[17]

Thanks to the compiling and editing skills of Gilbert, that achievement in the area of Aboriginal poetry is becoming more and more appreciated. In July, 1988 *Inside Black Australia* became one of the highest-selling paperbacks in the nation, giving rise to optimism that Aboriginal voices will be heard even more clearly in the future.

However, not all the signs are optimistic ones. In recent years there has been increasing evidence of a White Australian backlash against minorities which may seriously affect the Aboriginal movement in the late 1980s and early 1990s. An increase in Asian immigration and the allowance of land rights in parts of the nation have both prompted shrill and reactionary responses from some vocal Australian minority groups. To cite one example, Geoff McDonald reasons from inaccuracy to racist absurdity in his book, *Red Over*

Black: Behind the Aboriginal Land Rights:

> In the phoney debate about Aboriginal "land rights", it is generally overlooked that irrespective of what happened in the past, there would be no debate at all if young white Australians had not died on the Kakoda [sic] trail and other parts of South-East Asia in stemming the Japanese assault during the Pacific War. A Japanese victory would have eliminated any Aboriginal problem—by the simple process of liquidating the Aborigines![18]

Not only does McDonald totally ignore the Aboriginal contribution to the war effort, but he also argues that sacrifice of life in the defence of the nation gives White Australians the right to ownership of the country. If one were to accept this form of reasoning, the Aboriginal people who died in defence of their homeland between 1788 and 1929 would therefore be entitled to far more territory than is embraced by any land rights claim.

McDonald's book is so prejudiced and devoid of logic that, were it not for the fact that it has gone through six printings and was enthusiastically received by such notables as the former Queensland premier, Sir Joh Bjelke-Petersen, and the president of the Victorian branch of the RSL, Bruce Ruxton, it would not merit discussion. But the unfortunate fact is that the brazenly bigoted viewpoint which McDonald presents is still espoused by many Australians. McDonald tars the policy of multiculturalism and the concept of land rights with the same biased brush:

> If they [the returned soldiers from he First World War] were around today Mr. Al Grassby would have been sacked long ago and there would be no nonsense about multi-culturalism and the wrecking of Australia by the setting up of a separate nation, allegedly for the benefit of the Aboriginals. [19]

Such attitudes threaten a return to the illiberal racial intolerance of an earlier period. Unfortunately, as federal Opposition leader John Howard has indicated in 1988, the debate over racially-based policies such as immigration is still on the political agenda. It seems that numerous Australians still retain a profound antipathy towards the rights of minorities, whether they are Chinese, Vietnamese, or Aboriginal. What is important in this connection is that the land rights issue is an emotive and contentious one which is a prime indicator of racial tolerance—and intolerance—in the nation. There is no doubt that it can incite nearly hysterical defamations. In 1984 Hugh Morgan, an executive of the Western Mining Corporation, maligned the concepts of land claims and the protection of sacred sites as being:

a symbolic step back to the world of paganism, superstition, fear and darkness ... On what grounds can a minister or a parliament say on the one hand we respect, recognise and give legal support to the spiritual claims you [Aboriginal people] have to a very substantial portion of this country, but on the other hand we cannot sanction infanticide, cannibalism and the cruel initiation rites which you regard either as customary or as a matter of religious obligation.[20]

Such statements cannot be ignored, especially when they are uttered by an executive of a major Australian mining and exploration company and when they are generally sanctioned by the then federal Minister of Energy and Resources. These are crude and emotive arguments as much as they are inaccurate and illogical. According to the scenario which Morgan has sketched, the citizens of Salem, Massachusetts could not morally or legally own houses in their town in the twentieth century because they had practised exorcism and witch-burning two hundred years earlier.

The question remains: "how do such issues pertain to Aboriginal literature?" The connection is very significant: Black Australian writing and Aboriginal/white race relations are so closely interrelated that a denigration of Aboriginal culture demeans the productions of that culture, while it also potentially threatens Australian intercultural harmony. As I have shown, much Aboriginal literature is overtly and unashamedly socio-political; much of it examines Aboriginal/European conflict; much is based upon an observation and analysis of actual events. Not all Aboriginal writers are activists and spokespeople and some eschew that role. But their work—Black Australian writing—is inescapably socio-political, for two main reasons. The first is that it expresses a culture which has survived in a tangible and ongoing sense despite nearly two centuries of oppression. It is therefore frequently self-analytical, self-referential and self-defining. The second reason is that Aboriginal writing is consciously produced to express and investigate relationships with the dominant White Australian society. In short, to echo Healy, it is both black on black and black on white[21]—and both elements are often clearly socio-political.

I have illustrated the fact that some of this writing is extremely personal, while other examples of Black Australian literature reach towards a pan-Aboriginal, national framework. In the words of Charles Perkins:

I think, for example, the play *The Cake Man* has national expression. Some things that Kevin Gilbert has said can be projected on the national scene ... And ... Jack Davis's play: I think that that has national expression too ... I think that we're getting there.[22]

This leads to a very important point. Many Aboriginal spokespeople are now articulating their grievances and demands on the basis that their people are the first citizens of the country; that Aboriginal society represents the first Australian nation. Numerous Aboriginal writers have lent their creative support to this notion. For example, it underlies Kevin Gilbert's conception of the Aboriginal "patriot":

> The Aboriginal nation, as a nation of the spirit ... a nation without land or hope, a nation of underprivilege, has existed, probably, from about a generation after Captain Cook landed. Occasionally you meet one of its patriots, one of those people, who, whatever their intermediate likes and loyalties, can be seen to cast their ultimate sympathy, the core of their feelings with this Aboriginal nation ... one does not meet many Aboriginal patriots because it takes a special kind of vision to be one. And it takes courage.[23]

Similarly, much of the poetry of Gerry Bostock, Lionel Fogarty, and Maureen Watson is imbued with the sense of an Aboriginal nation. It is clearly a concept which is given expression is Colin Johnson's novels, *Sandawara* and *Wooreddy*. The very fact that Johnson—as a West Australian Aborigine—has written in such a penetrating way about Tasmanian Aboriginal history is, in itself, evidence of the developing pan-Aboriginal sense of nationhood.

Aboriginal politicians, too, have voiced their aspirations using terms derived from discussions of the nation-state. For example, Neville Bonner has said:

> I hope to see the Aboriginal race firmly established as a nation, an individual nation, with a strident voice which will be a force in government, and one which will establish social justice and equality for all of us, whether tribal, semi-tribal or urban, through sensible, well-planned programmes.
>
> This is my dream for the 1990s, to see our race gain its rightful place within Australian society, at the same time preserving the richness of our proud culture and customs.[24]

The deliberate choice of this terminology is noteworthy. First, it emulates the western rhetoric of the nation-state, normally defined as a geo-political and military entity. It is therefore no surprise that the Black Australian use of the term "nation" conjures up a welter of fears of insurrection in the minds of many Australians, who view the concept as a direct threat to the security and/or the viability of the country. To those who have formulated slogans such as "One Nation,

One Future" for use in the propaganda of Australia Day and "Celebration of a Nation" for the Bicentennial, the claims of Aboriginal spokespeople and writers to citizenship in a prior or separate nation border upon heresy. It is little wonder, then, that McDonald seized upon the notion of "a separate nation"[25] in order to excite indignation in the White Australian reader and in so doing, discredit the land rights movement. A second relevant point is that the term is one which has been taken up in the wake of claims for indigenous rights in other sectors of the globe. North American Indians have asserted that they are members of "first nations" consistently and effectively over the past fifteen years. In the United States, reference to the existence of, for example, the Cherokee Nation has been in common parlance for many years; the term therefore does not excite as vociferous and indignant a reaction amongst White Americans when it is used to buttress native land claims.[26]

This introduces a third major point. It is that the negative reaction of White Australians to the vocal Aboriginal assertions of nationhood is unwarranted and excessive. The Aboriginal nation is a *symbolic* nation but it is unlikely that it will ever be expressed in conventional geo-political terms. It is important to realise, though, that this does not lessen the importance of the concept in terms of fostering Black Australian solidarity. In recognition of this fact, the realm of symbols is one which is given serious consideration by political scientists. As Hugh Collins has observed:

> Any account of the domestic dimensions of Aborigines and Australian foreign policy cannot fail to notice that the three most prominent symbolic representations of Aboriginal politics borrow directly from the symbols of international politics and state sovereignty: the Aboriginal Flag, the Aboriginal Embassy, and the Aboriginal Treaty (or Makaratta).[27]

It is ironic that Black Australian promotion of the concept of nationhood—which has such a potentially unifying attractiveness for Aboriginal people—will almost certainly ensure that they never will be citizens of a separate geo-political nation in the Australian continent. To the extent that any threat of separation or "secession" is taken seriously by White Australians, propaganda against Aboriginal rights will intensify. Even those sympathetic to the Aboriginal cause may react strongly against their own interpretation of what an Aboriginal nation implies. For example, Bernard Smith observes:

> Is Australia two nations: a white, intrusive majority and a black, original minority? That might be a fair summary, in a nutshell, of our past. But it would be absolutely

disastrous to attempt to erect a cultural policy upon it. For if we take the notion of two nations seriously, that posits a division in law, in territory, in diplomatic representation, and much more. It sounds remarkably like apartheid to me.[28]

Smith is arguably unaware of other possible definitions of nationhood—involving such concepts as concurrent and contingent sovereignty—which do not imply such arbitrary and far-reaching divisions.[29] Furthermore, it is tenable that Black Australian spokespeople do not intend the rhetoric of nationhood to be interpreted in the conventional political and diplomatic fashion which Smith has outlined. Finally, his reference to apartheid is both alarmist and inaccurate for, in the words of Ruby Hammond, "Apartheid is practised by dominant groups; not by oppressed minorities."[30]

Paradoxically, Aboriginal people may have more to gain by de-emphasising their claims to nationhood when making public demands. They will probably achieve more success by highlighting moral and legal obligations which could motivate White Australians to grant compensation and land rights. But this does not negate the fact that their belief in the symbolic existence of a separate Black Australian nation can have a significant socio-cultural impact upon Aboriginal attitudes. For example, Collins observes how the ambiguity of the Aboriginal flag can actually be a source of strength:

> Is it a distinctive identity within the Australian nation? Or is it an incipient nationhood of an Aboriginal people? That ambiguity reflects a tension within Aboriginal politics, but the effectiveness of the symbol derives largely from its capacity to represent either notion and thus to unite both. [31]

Aboriginal literature also belongs largely to the realm of symbolic politics. However, it is far more complex than a flag or a tent on the lawns of Parliament House. While their symbolism is overt and striking, that of Black Australian writing is usually more subtle and covert. Aboriginal authors can persuade and educate the reader without the potentially alienating intensity of a march or a demonstration, even though the aims of both may be identical. In that sense, Aboriginal literature may, in the long run, have an even more important role to play in advancing the Black Australian cause than public exhibitions of grievances, which can be misconstrued by the average White Australian as intimations of so-called "Black Power".

I have underlined the fact that distinctive and talented black voices have begun to be heard in this country, and will continue to make a very noteworthy contribution to Australian, and indeed, to world literature. Black Australian authors agree that no white writer can fully appreciate what it is to be a "First Australian" and that Europeans' work in this area is, therefore, limited and often distorted. Colin Johnson puts the matter succinctly when he says "Only Aborigines can really write about Aborigines".[32] Similarly, Oodgeroo Noonuccal feels that "Only Aborigines can understand what is happening to themselves at this moment"[33] and Gerry Bostock adds, "White writers have their own terms of reference".[34] The point is that Aboriginal writers feel that they are singularly qualified to explain a unique racial experience to their fellow Australians.

The corollary of the viewpoint which Johnson, Noonuccal, and Bostock express is that no Europeans can claim to have "expert" knowledge of Aboriginal Australians. As Jim Everett put it, "The real experts are out there—we are the real experts of our own cultural beliefs".[35] While Everett's view is a reasonable one, Gary Foley carries this concept of exclusivity too far when he states categorically to white audiences that "I don't feel that any of you could write about racism any more than I could write about sexism."[36] While one can understand and sympathise with Everett's position, Foley's is ultimately an untenable one. As Smail has noted with reference to Southeast Asian history,[37] when extended to its logical limit, this view precludes all non-Aborigines from making valid criticisms of, and observations on, Black Australian literature. In turn, it implies that blacks cannot pass accurate and justified judgements on White Australian literature, let alone its society and politics. Black Australians have special insights into Australian society and a unique understanding of both Aboriginality and White Australian culture. Everett has every right to criticise self-proclaimed white "experts" on Aborigines. But to contend that whites cannot write in any valid way about racism and the Aboriginal experience—as Foley does—distorts reality and, ironically, also undermines the legitimacy of the socio-political critique made by Black Australians.

There is little doubt that Aboriginal experience dictates, to a significant extent, the form and content of Aboriginal creativity. As this study has shown, it is the experientially based nature of Black Australian literature which gives the writing so much of its power and impact. As Johnson, Noonuccal, and Bostock have stated, this experience is one which is foreign to the vast majority of Australians. However, these sorts of experiences are not foreign to other indigenous minority groups. As David Callaghan has observed:

The culture of Australia's indigenous people is more akin to those of the American

Indian, the tribespeople of the Kalahari, the Ainu of Japan, the Eskimo and many other gatherer-hunter cultures ... These cultures have been the subject of enormous misunderstanding by those girdled by what is called civilization, by the beneficiaries (and victims) of post-industrial high-tech societies.[38]

It is for this reason that the Fourth World connection has provided Aboriginal Australians with important terms of reference which they have marshalled in support of their campaign for compensation and for the recognition of rights to land. Such organisations as the World Council of Indigenous Peoples reinforce and develop Fourth World ties as well as the possibilities for mutual inspiration and support. In exploring the Fourth World dimension of their experience, Black Australian writers display an awareness of the parallels which unite them with other oppressed, indigenous minorities. This awareness encourages, rather than hinders, the developing sense of "first nationhood" which Aboriginal literature presents.

Aboriginal literature deals, above all, with identity—with that complex of attitudes, beliefs and mores which constitute Aboriginality. Aspects of Black Australians' view of themselves and of other Australians have been examined at length here: the preoccupation with history and dispossession, the emphasis upon sex and violence, the possible transformation of literature into socio-political propaganda highlighting the campaign for land and other rights, and the use of humour as a figurative lifeline in the midst of sorrow and oppression. These are some of the most striking elements of the Aboriginal self-definition in literature; others will be isolated in the future. What is significant is that throughout this process of self-assessment, Aboriginal people frequently walk a tight-rope, attempting to balance their self-perception and society's perception of them. It is not an easy task. Their identity is continually placed under stress by the dominant European culture of Australia, especially in the urban context. Bruce McGuinness aptly describes this dilemma:

It's important that people understand that Aboriginal lifestyles don't change a great degree when they are removed from a rural situation to an urban situation. It's just that they need to become less visible, because Aboriginal people are very visible within an urban situation. One Aboriginal person gets drunk and walks up the street and all Aboriginal people are drunk. Whereas if it's a white person who gets drunk and walks along the street of course, it's just another white guy walking along the street ... So while being visible in terms of maintaining their rights to exist as an Aboriginal nation, they must also remain invisible so as to escape the stereotyping and stigmatising that goes on when Aboriginal people do things that other people do.[39]

Aboriginal literature reflects these sorts of dilemmas and, in so doing, portrays the essential dissimilarities between Black and White Australians. For, despite co-operation on many fronts, these differences do exist and persist. As Jack Davis has commented, the assimilation policy never could have worked because, "There will always be differences. I don't care where it is: there will always be differences between black and white".[40] Aboriginal literature explores the positive side of this fact: the resilience and vitality of the Black Australian experience. It also examines one of the most dramatic results of the polarisation of black and white world-views in Australia: the alienation of individual Aborigines that can result from being, in figurative terms, assailed by a vast white cultural wave. Perhaps no Aboriginal author has expressed this sentiment more lucidly than Maureen Watson. In interview she detailed the distress of being an Aboriginal child in Australia so eloquently that it would be unjust not to quote her comments in their entirety:

> Black reflections aren't in white mirrors, you know. We live in our land. We are, we have all around us people who are not *of* us. We have on our land—there are people all over our land—who are not *of* our land. Aboriginal people might as well be in a foreign country, you know? Who built those buildings? Not Aboriginal people. The electric lines out there? Not Aboriginal people. That tape recorder you've got—who do you associate with that? ... The pen in your hand, the pad you're holding? The clothes you're wearing, the clothes *I'm* wearing—the watch on my hand? You know, the ribbons in my hair? Aboriginal people didn't make these things. Everywhere around us are the reflections of a foreign race; a foreign people. And they are making us foreigners in our own country.

> And the Aboriginal child in the school room ... where is there *anything* she can relate to? Now a child *must* have the right to grow up feeling good about herself and her parents and the way she lives. And, for Aboriginal people it doesn't happen. Where do they see the reflections to make them hold up their heads? ... I mean, where *are* the reflections of black people? You hold up the mirror and it's like you're invisible. You see everything else except yourself ... How does a child develop any sort of self-confidence, or pride, or dignity, without these things? And here in the city, we must be aware of that. And we've *got* to put up those images for our children. And, it's happening slowly, like the T-shirts that say, 'I'm proud to be an Aborigine', or 'I didn't get my tan on Bondi Beach'; 'I walk on Aboriginal Land'; 'I'm a Koori Kid' ... So those images *are* coming. You know, we are holding up black mirrors for black reflections.[41]

Above all, Aboriginal literature is centrally involved with the maintenance and extension of Aboriginal confidence and the feeling of self-worth. Many Black Australian authors highlight positive examples of black success in their work, and many are demonstrating that success through the fact of their own literary achievements. It could be said that three major elements coalesce in Black Australian literature—cultural nationalism, literary talent, and Aboriginal pride. Throughout, the Fourth World dimension of the work is significant, but its locus is singularly Black Australian. There is no doubt that the important first chapters in the book of Aboriginal literature have now been written. That volume will continue to grow in size and impressiveness in coming years as Australia and the world become increasingly aware of this country's black words on white pages.

Notes

1   Lang Hancock, quoted in Michael Coyne and Leigh Edwards, *The Oz Factor: Who's Doing What in Australia*, (East Malvern, 1980), p. 68.

2   Quoted from a conversation with a Canberra bank manager, Canberra, February, 1980.

3   Gerald L. Bostock, "An Australian Miner", in *Black Man Coming* ; , (Sydney, 1981), p. 11.

4   Quoted from Bruce McGuinness's paper, "The Politics of Aboriginal Literature", in Jack Davis and Bob Hodge, eds, *Aboriginal Writing Today*, (Canberra, 1985), pp. 49-50.

5   Quoted from Colin Johnson's paper, "White Forms, Aboriginal Content", in *ibid.*, p. 29.

6   Quoted from Mick Miller's speech at the launching of Lionel Fogarty's *Yoogum Yoogum*, Queensland Institute of Technology, Brisbane, September, 1982.

7   Quoted in Adam Shoemaker, "An Interview with Jack Davis", *Westerly*, vol. 27, no. 4, December, 1982, p. 116.

8   Personal interview with Charles Perkins, Canberra, January, 1983.

9   This information kindly provided by Archie Weller during a personal interview in Canberra, May 1984.

10   Quoted from Bruce McGuinness's paper "The Politics of Aboriginal Literature" in Davis and Hodge, eds, *Aboriginal Writing Today*, pp. 46-47.

11   Quoted from Jack Davis's speech at the biennial conference of the Australian Institute of Aboriginal Studies, Canberra, May 1984.

12   Information supplied by Colin Johnson and Glenyse Ward in personal discussions in Brisbane, May 1988.

13   See, for example, "Parliament Mosaic 'Puts a Curse on Whites' ", The *Australian*, 10 May, 1988, p. 1.

14   W. Les Russell, "God Gave Us Trees to Cut Down" in Kevin Gilbert, ed., *Inside Black Australia*, (Ringwood, 1988), p. 6.

15   Maureen Watson, "Memo to J.C.", in *ibid.*, p. 50.

16   Robert Walker, "Solitary Confinement", in *ibid.*, p. 129.

17   Ernie Dingo, "Aboriginal Achievement", in *ibid.*, p. 29

18   Geoff McDonald, *Red Over Black: Behind the Aboriginal Land Rights*, (Bullsbrook, 1982), pp. 141-142.

19   *ibid.*, p. 142.

20   Quoted in Robert Bowden, "Walsh Backs Morgan on NT Land Rights", The *Australian*, 13 May 1984, p. 2.

21   J.J. Healy, *Literature and the Aborigine in Australia*, (St. Lucia, 1978), p. 3.

22   Personal interview with Charles Perkins, Canberra, January, 1983.

23   Kevin Gilbert, *"Because a White Man'll Never Do It"*, (Sydney, 1973), p. 193.

24   Quoted by Colin Johnson in his paper, "White Forms, Aboriginal Content", in Davis and Hodge, eds, *Aboriginal Writing Today*, (Canberra, 1985), p. 30.

25   McDonald, *Red Over Black*, p. 142.

26   Admittedly, this usage of the term has an anthropological connotation, which partly explains its more ready acceptance in North America.

27   Hugh Collins, "Aborigines and Australian Foreign Policy: Some Underlying Issues", in Coral Bell, *et al.*, eds, *Ethnic Minorities and Australian Foreign Policy*, (Canberra, 1983), p. 69.

28   Bernard Smith, "Five Choices of Culture", The *Age Monthly Review*, vol. 2, no. 7, November, 1982, pp. 9-10.

29   Professor J.E. Chamberlin has pointed out the fact that North American lawyers representing Indian clients in land claims cases have successfully argued more fluid definitions of the concept of nationhood before the courts. This point was made during personal discussions in Sydney, July, 1984.

30   Quotation taken from Ruby Hammond's comments concerning Jeremy Beckett's paper, "Aborigines and Welfare Colonialism", delivered in "The State and Ethnic Minorities" section of the ANZAAS Conference, Canberra, May, 1984.

31   Collins, "Aborigines and Australian Foreign Policy", p. 69.

32   Personal interview with Colin Johnson, Brisbane, August, 1980.

33   Personal interview with Oodgeroo Noonuccal, Brisbane, August, 1980.

34   Personal interview with Gerry Bostock, Sydney, July, 1980.

35   Quoted from Jim Everett's speech at the biennial conference of the Australian Institute of Aboriginal Studies, Canberra, May, 1984.

36   Quoted from Gary Foley's speech at the Australian National Playwrights' Conference, ANU, Canberra, May, 1984. Foley's view is revealing. If one examines his statement, one notes the admission of ignorance concerning sexism—yet sexual prejudice often reinforces racial prejudice in relationships between Black and White Australians. Much work remains to be done regarding the connection between sexism and racism in Australia for, as Pat O'Shane has observed, "Quite

frequently in our dealings in Australia—Aboriginal and non-Aboriginal—racism and sexism are so entangled that they cannot be disentangled"(Quoted from Pat O'Shane's speech at the ANU, February, 1983).

37   John R.W. Smail, "On the Possibility of an Autonomous History of Modern Southeast Asia", *Journal of Southeast Asian History*, vol. 2, 1961, pp. 72-102.

38   David Callaghan, "What Future the Aborigine?", in *TIME Australia*, vol. 3, no. 32, 8 August, 1988, p. 13.

39   Quoted from Bruce McGuinness's paper, "The Politics of Aboriginal Literature" in *Aboriginal Writing Today*, p. 47.

40   Quoted in Adam Shoemaker, "An Interview With Jack Davis", *Westerly* , December, 1982, p. 114.

41   Personal interview with Maureen Watson, Perth, February, 1983.

List of Abbreviations

Aboriginal Arts Board	AAB
Aboriginal Development Commission	ADC
Aboriginal Legal Service	ALS
Aboriginal Medical Service	AMS
Aborigines' Advancement League	AAL
Aborigines' Friends' Association	AFA
Aborigines' Progressive Association	APA
Association for the Protection of Native Races	APNR
Alternative Publishing Co-Operative, Ltd.	APCOL
Angus & Robertson, Publishers	A & R
Australian Book Review	ABR
Australian Government Publishing Service	AGPS
Australian Institute of Aboriginal Studies	AIAS
Australian Literary Studies	ALS
Australian National University	ANU
Australian National University Press	ANUP
Bulletin Literary Supplement	BLS
Department of Aboriginal Affairs	DAA
Federal Council for the Advancement of Aborigines and Torres Strait Islanders	FCAATSI
Fremantle Arts Centre Press	FACP
National Aboriginal Conference	NAC
National Aboriginal Consultative Committee	NACC
National Aboriginal and Islander Writers', Oral Literature, and Dramatists' Association	NAIWOLDA

National Library of Australia	NLA
Oxford University Press	OUP
Times Literary Supplement	*TLS*
United Nations	UN
University of Melbourne Press	MUP
University of Queensland Press	UQP
World Council of Indigenous Peoples	WCIP

Bibliography

Literary Works

i) Drama

*Bostock, Gerald. *Here Comes the Nigger*. Excerpts from first draft, *Meanjin*, vol. 36, no. 4, Dec. 1977, pp. 479-493.
— *Here Comes the Nigger*. Ts., Third draft of film-script, Sydney: Jul. 1980.
Cusack, Dymphna. *Shoulder the Sky*. In *Three Australian Three-Act Plays*. Sydney: Australasian Publishing Co., 1950, pp. 89-177.
Dann, George Landen. *Fountains Beyond*. Sydney: Australasian Publishing Company, 1942[?].
*Davis, Jack. *The Biter Bit*. Ts., Perth: 1975.
— *Kullark*. In *Kullark/The Dreamers*, Sydney: Currency Press, 1982.
— *The Dreamers*. In *Kullark/The Dreamers*, Sydney: Currency Press, 1982.
— *No Sugar*. Sydney: Currency Press, 1986.
— *Barungin (Smell the Wind)*. Programme for World Expo on Stage Performance, Brisbane: August, 1988.
*Gilbert, Kevin J. *The Cherry Pickers*. Ts., Canberra: NLA, 1970, ms. 2584.
— *The Gods Look Down* and other sketches. Ts., Canberra: NLA, 1970, ms. 2584.
— *Ghosts in Cell Ten*. Ms. and ts., Canberra: NLA, 1979, ms. 2584.
— *The Cherry Pickers*. Canberra: Burrambinga Books, 1988.

---

* Indicates a Black Australian

Hewett, Dorothy. *The Man from Mukinupin: A Musical Play in Two Acts*. Perth: Fremantle Arts Centre Press and Sydney: Currency Press, 1979.

Ireland, David. *Image in the Clay*. St. Lucia: UQP, 1964.

Keneally, Thomas. *Bullie's House*. Sydney: Currency Press, 1981.

*Merritt, Robert J. *The Cake Man*. Sydney: Currency Press, 1978.

Prichard, Katharine Susannah. *Brumby Innes*. Perth: Paterson's Printing Press, 1940.

— *Brumby Innes*. In *Brumby Innes* and *Bid Me to Love*, ed. Katharine Brisbane, Sydney: Currency Press, 1974.

Reed, Bill. *Truganinni*. Richmond: Heinemann Educational, 1977.

Shearer, Jill. *The Foreman*. With Mary Gage, *The New Life*, Currency Double Bill Series, Gen. ed. Frank Bladwell, Sydney: Currency Press, 1977.

*Utemorrah, Daisy. *Mugugu*. *Identity*, vol. 2, no. 3, Jan. 1975, p. 11.

*Walker, Kath. *Tail of Platypus*. *Identity*, vol. 2, no. 2, Sep. 1974, pp. 31-32.

ii) Poetry

Berndt, Ronald M., trans. and ed. "The Wonguri-Mandijigai Song Cycle of the Moon-Bone". *Oceania*, vol. 19, Sep. 1948, pp. 16-50.

— *Love Songs of Arnhem Land*. Melbourne: Thomas Nelson, 1976.

— *Three Faces of Love: Traditional Aboriginal Song-Poetry*. Melbourne: Thomas Nelson, 1976.

*Bostock, Gerald L. *Black Man Coming*. Fitzroy: Gerald L. Bostock, 1980.

von Brandenstein, C.G. and A.P. Thomas, eds. *Taruru: Aboriginal Song Poetry from the Pilbara*. Adelaide: Rigby, 1974.

*Corpus, Aileen. "Different Shades". *Identity*, vol. 2, no. 7, Jan. 1976, p. 25.

— "Another Black Bird". *Identity*, vol. 2, no. 8, Apr. 1976, p. 23.

— "Five Poems". *Meanjin*, vol. 36, no. 4, Dec. 1977, pp. 470-473.

*Davis, Jack. *The First-born and Other Poems*. Sydney: A & R, 1970. Rpt. Melbourne: J.M. Dent, 1983.

— *Jagardoo: Poems From Aboriginal Australia*. Sydney: Methuen, 1978.

Dawe, Bruce. "Nemesis". *BLS*, Nov. 1, 1983, p. 81.

Day, David and Marilyn Bowering. *Many Voices: An Anthology of Contemporary Canadian Indian Poetry*. Vancouver: J.J. Douglas, 1977.

*Dingo, Ernie, "Five Poems". In Ulli Beier, Guest ed., *Long Water: Aboriginal Art and Literature, Aspect*, no. 34, Aug. 1986, p. 67.

— "Aboriginal Achievement". In Kevin Gilbert, ed., *Inside Black Australia*. Ringwood: Penguin Books, 1988, p. 29.

Erickson, Sheila. *Notice: This is an Indian Reserve*. Ed. Kent Gooderham, Toronto: Griffin House, 1972.

*Fisher, Vanessa. "My Country", "This Land". *Social Alternatives*, vol. 7, no. 1, Mar. 1988, pp. 46, Back cover.

*Fogarty, Lionel George. *Kargun*. North Brisbane: Cheryl Buchanan, 1980.

— *Yoogum Yoogum*. Ringwood: Penguin Books, 1982.

— *Murrie Coo-ee*. Spring Hill (Brisbane): Cheryl Buchanan, 1983.

— *Kudjela*. Spring Hill (Brisbane): Cheryl Buchanan, 1983.

— *Ngutji*. Spring Hill (Brisbane): Cheryl Buchanan, 1984.

*Gilbert, Kevin J. "Drafts of Literary Works". Ts., Canberra: NLA, 1969-1970, ms. 2584. Another copy held under the title "Poems 1970". Ts., Sydney: The Mitchell Library, 1970, ms. no. 2429.

— *End of Dreamtime*. Sydney: Island Press, 1971.

— *People Are Legends*. St. Lucia: UQP, 1978.

— "Kids' Poems". Ts., Canberra: NLA, 1979, ms. 2584.

— "To My Cousin, Evonne Cawley". *BLS*, Sep. 18, 1980, p. 2.

— "Accessories After the Fact", "Baal Belbora", "Tree". *Social Alternatives*, vol. 2, no. 2, Aug. 1981, pp. 10, 47, 71.

— ed. *Inside Black Australia: An Anthology of Aboriginal Poetry*, Ringwood: Penguin Books, 1988.

Hall, Rodney, ed. *The Collins Book of Australian Poetry*. Sydney: William Collins, 1981.

*Johnson, Colin. "The Song Circle of Jacky". Ts., Perth: 1982.

— "Colin Johnson Replies to Adam Shoemaker", *Westerly*, vol. 27, no. 4, December, 1982, p. 80.

— *The Song Circle of Jacky, and Selected Poems*. Melbourne: Hyland House, 1986.

— "Three Poems From India". In Ulli Beier, Guest ed., *Long Water: Aboriginal Art and Literature, Aspect*, no. 34, Aug. 1986, pp. 88-89.

Kelly, Howard, et al., eds. *Aboriginal Voices*. Social Education Materials Project, Richmond: Heinemann Educational, 1978.

Murray Les A. "The Bulahdelah-Taree Holiday Song Cycle". In Chris Wallace-Crabbe, ed., *The Golden Apples of the Sun: Twentieth Century Australian Poetry*, Melbourne: MUP, 1980, pp. 189-199.

*Narogin, Mudrooroo [Colin Johnson]. *Dalwurra*. Perth: The Centre for Studies in Australian Literature, 1988.

*Njitji Njitji [Mona Tur]. "This My Land". *Identity*, vol. 2, no. 7, Jan. 1976, p. 25.

— "Spring Rain". *Identity*, vol. 3, no. 4, Jan. 1978, p. 23.

— "What Now Aborigine?". *Identity* , vol. 3, no. 6, Apr. 1978, p. 23.

— "Uluru", Ts., Adelaide: 1983.

— "Uluru (Ayers Rock)". *BLS*, Nov. 1, 1983, p. 62.

*Rankine, Leila. "The Coorong". *Social Alternatives*, vol. 2, no. 4, Jun. 1982, p. 9.

*Russell, W. Les. "God Gave Us Trees to Cut Down". In Kevin Gilbert, ed., *Inside Black Australia*. Ringwood: Penguin Books, p. 6.

Stump, Sarain. *There Is My People Sleeping*, Sidney, British Columbia: Gray's Publishing, 1970.

*Sykes, Bobbi. "Prayer to the Spirit of the New Year". In Rosemary Dobson, ed., *Australian Voices*, Canberra: ANUP, 1975, p. 129.

— *Love Poems and Other Revolutionary Actions*. Cammeray: The Saturday Centre, 1979. Rpt. St. Lucia: UQP, 1988.

*Tjapangati, Tutama. "Wangka Tjukutjuk". *Overland*, no. 80, Jul. 1980, p. 32.

— "Aladayi". *BLS*, Nov. 1, 1983, p. 64.

— "Tjanake Pite". *BLS*, Nov. 1, 1983, p. 65.

*Tjupurrula, Nosepeg. "Pangkalangka Dreaming". *BLS*, Nov. 1, 1983, p. 65.

*Utemorrah, Daisy. "Mary's Plea". *Identity*, vol. 2, no. 3, Jan. 1975, p. 27.

*Walker, Kath. *We Are Going*. Brisbane: Jacaranda Press, 1964.

— *The Dawn Is At Hand*. Brisbane: Jacaranda Press, 1966.

— "Minjerriba", "Credit and Loss", "Blue Crane". *Meanjin*, vol. 36, no. 4, Dec. 1977, pp. 443-445.

— *My People: A Kath Walker Collection*. Milton: Jacaranda Press, 1970. Rev. edn. Milton: Jacaranda Wiley, 1981.

— "China… Woman". In Ulli Beier, Guest ed., *Long Water: Aboriginal Art and Literature, Aspect*, no. 34, Aug. 1986, p. 90.

*Walker, Robbie. *Up, Not Down, Mate! Thoughts From a Prison Cell*. Kuralta Park: Catholic Chaplaincy to Aborigines, 1981.

—"Solitary Confinement". In Kevin Gilbert, ed., *Inside Black Australia*. Ringwood: Penguin Books, 1988, p. 129.

*Watson, Maureen. "Black Child", "I, Too, Am Human". *Meanjin*, vol. 36, no. 4, Dec. 1977, pp. 545-547.

— *Black Reflections*. Wattle Park: The Education Information Retrieval Service, 1982.

— "Memo to J.C.". In Kevin Gilbert, ed., *Inside Black Australia*. Penguin Books, 1988, p. 50.

Wright, Judith. *The Moving Image*. Melbourne: Meanjin Press, 1946.

— *Collected Poems, 1942-1970*. Sydney: A & R, 1971.

iii) Novels

*Bandler,Faith. *Wacvie*. Adelaide: Rigby, 1977.

— and Len Fox. *Marani in Australia*. Adelaide: Rigby/Opal, 1980.

— *Welou, My Brother*. Sydney: A & R, 1984.

Beilby, Richard. *The Brown Land Crying*. Sydney: A & R, 1975.

Casey, Gavin. *Snowball*. Sydney: A & R, 1958.

Cato, Nancy and Vivienne Rae Ellis. *Queen Trucanini: The Last of the Tasmanians*. Sydney: A.& R, 1976.

*Clare, Monica. *Karobran: The Story of an Aboriginal Girl*. Sydney: APCOL, 1978.

Drewe, Robert. *The Savage Crows*. Sydney: William Collins, 1976. Rpt. Fontana Books, 1981.

Durack, Mary. *Keep Him My Country*. London: Constable, 1955.

Gare, Nene. *The Fringe Dwellers*. London: Heinemann, 1961. South Melbourne: Sun Books, 1966, Rpt. 1973.

Herbert, Xavier. *Capricornia*. Sydney: Publicist Publishing Co., 1938. Sydney: A & R, 1938, Rpt. 1979.

Idriess, Ion L. *Lasseter's Last Ride: An Epic of Central Australian Gold Discovery*. Sydney: A & R, 1931, Rpt. 1959.

— *Drums of Mer*. Sydney: A & R, 1933, Rpt. 1962.

— *Nemarluk: King of the Wilds*. Sydney: A & R, 1941, Rpt. 1958.

— *Outlaws of the Leopolds*. Sydney: A & R, 1952.

*Johnson, Colin. *Wild Cat Falling*. Sydney: A & R, 1965, Rpt. 1979.

— "Long Live Pigeon". [Excerpts from preliminary draft of *Long Live Sandawara* in *Meanjin*, vol. 36, no. 4, Dec. 1977, pp. 494-507.]

— *Long Live Sandawara*. Melbourne: Quartet Books, 1979.

— *Doctor Wooreddy's Prescription for Enduring the Ending of the World*. Melbourne: Hyland House, 1983.

— *Struggling*. Ts., Perth, 1983.

— *Doin' Wildcat*. Ts., Brisbane, 1988.

Keneally, Thomas. *The Chant of Jimmie Blacksmith*. Sydney: A & R, 1972.

Lockwood, Douglas. *I, the Aboriginal*. Adelaide: Rigby, 1962.

— *Fair Dinkum*. Adelaide: Rigby, 1969, Rpt. 1977.

Prichard, Katharine Susannah. *Coonardoo*. London: Cape, 1929. Rpt. Sydney: A & R, 1982.

Stow, Randolph. *To the Islands*. London: Macdonald, 1958. Rpt. Adelaide: Rigby, 1978.

Stuart, Donald. *Yandy*. Melbourne: Georgian House, 1959.

— *The Driven*. Melbourne: Georgian House, 1961.

Upfield, Arthur W. *The Bone is Pointed*. Sydney: A & R, 1938, Rpt. 1980.

Vickers, Frederick B. *The Mirage*. Melbourne: Australasian Book Society, 1955.

*Weller, Archie. *The Day of the Dog*. Sydney: Allen and Unwin, 1981. Rpt. Sydney: Pan Books, 1982.

White, Patrick. *Voss*. Harmondsworth: Penguin Books, 1960.

— *Riders in the Chariot*. London: Eyre and Spottiswoode, 1961.

iv) Autobiographies and Miscellaneous Stories

*Bropho, Robert. *Fringedweller*. Sydney: APCOL, 1980.

*Dhoulagarle, Koorie [Roy Simon]. *There's More to Life*. Sydney: APCOL, 1979.

*Lamilami, Lazarus. *Lamilami Speaks*. Sydney: Ure Smith, 1974.

*Mirritji, Jack. *My People's Life: An Aboriginal's Own Story*. Sydney: Millingimbi Literature Board and AAB, 1978.

*Morgan, Sally. *My Place*. Fremantle: FACP, 1987.

*Noonuccal, Oodgeroo and *Kabul Oodgeroo Noonuccal. *The Rainbow Serpent*. Canberra: AGPS, 1988.

*Perkins, Charles. *A Bastard Like Me*. Sydney: Ure Smith, 1975.

Prichard, Katharine Susannah. *N'goola and Other Stories*. Melbourne: Australasian Book Society, 1959.

*Raggett, Obed. *The Stories of Obed Raggett*. Sydney: APCOL, 1980.

*Roe, Paddy (ed. Stephen Muecke). *Gularabulu*. Fremantle: FACP, 1983.

*Roughsey, Dick. *Moon and Rainbow: The Autobiography of an Aboriginal*. Sydney: A.H. and A.W. Reed, 1971. Rpt. Adelaide: Rigby, 1977.

Shaw, Bruce. *My Country of the Pelican Dreaming—the Life of an Australian Aborigine of the Gadjerong, Grant Ngabidj (1904-1977)*. Canberra: AIAS, 1981.

*Simon, Ella. *Through My Eyes*. Adelaide: Rigby, 1978. Repub. Sydney: Collins/Dove, 1987.

*Smith, Shirley C.[MumShirl] and *Bobbi Sykes. *MumShirl: An Autobiography*. Richmond: Heinemann Educational, 1981. Rpt. 1985.

*Tucker, Margaret. *If Everyone Cared*. Sydney: Ure Smith, 1977.

*Unaipon, David. "Legendary Tales of the Australian Aborigines". Ms. and ts., Sydney: The Mitchell Library, 1924-1925, ms. nos A1929-A1930.

— "The Story of the Mungingee". *The Home*, Feb. 1925, pp. 42-43.

— *Aboriginal Legends*. No. 1, Adelaide: Hunkin, Ellis and King, n.d., [1927?].

— *Native Legends*. Adelaide: Hunkin, Ellis and King, n.d., [1929?].

— *My Life Story*. Adelaide: Aborigines' Friends' Association, n.d., [1951?].

— "How the Tortoise Got His Shell". *Dawn*, vol. 3, no. 11, 1954, p. 9.

— "Why All the Animals Peck at the Selfish Owl". *Dawn*, vol. 4, no. 4, 1955, pp. 16-17.

— "Why Frogs Jump Into the Water". *Dawn*, vol. 8, no. 7, 1959, p. 17.

— "The Voice of the Great Spirit". *Dawn*, vol. 8, no. 7, 1959, p. 19.

— "Love Story of the Two Sisters". *Dawn*, vol. 8, no. 9, 1959, p. 9.

*Utemorrah, Daisy, et al. *Visions of Mowanjum: Aboriginal Writings from the Kimberleys*. Adelaide: Rigby, 1980.

*Walker, Kath. *Stradbroke Dreamtime*. Sydney: A & R., 1972. Rpt., rev. edn., 1982.

— "Hijack". In Ulli Beier, Guest ed., *Long Water: Aboriginal Art and Literature, Aspect*, no. 34, Aug. 1986, pp. 83-86.

*Ward, Glenyse. *Wandering Girl*. Broome: Magabala Books, 1988.

*Weller, Archie. *Going Home*. Sydney: Allen and Unwin, 1985.

Commentaries

i) Published

"The Address Given by His Holiness Pope John Paul II at the Meeting with Aboriginal and Torres Strait Islander People at Alice Springs on 20 November 1986". Canberra: 1986, p.4.

d'Alpuget, Blanche. Rev. of *Long Live Sandawara* in *24 Hours*. Quoted on back dustcover of *Doctor Wooreddy's Prescription for Enduring the Ending of the World*.

"Another Birthday"[Biographical Note on *David Unaipon]. *Australian Aborigines: The AFA Annual Report*. Adelaide: AFA, 1954, pp. 31-32. Melbourne: Hyland House, 1983.

Atkinson, Don. "Aboriginal Project". *Arena*, no. 30, 1972, pp. 3-6.

Arthur, Kateryna. "Fiction and the Rewriting of History: A Reading of Colin Johnson". *Westerly*, vol. 30, no. 1, March, 1985, pp. 55-60.

Australian Institute of Aboriginal Studies. *40,000 Years of Technology*. Canberra: AIAS, 1982.

"Australian Poets". Rev. of Kath Walker's *We Are Going*. *TLS*, Sep. 10, 1964, p. 842.

*Bandler, Faith. "The Role of Research". In Jack Davis and Bob Hodge, eds, *Aboriginal Writing Today*, Canberra: AIAS, 1985, pp. 55-62.

Bannister, S. " '...Out of the Valley of Darkness': A Review of *Living Black*". *Northern Perspective*, vol. 2, no. 2, Apr. 1979, pp. 27-28.

Barbu, Zev. "Popular Culture: A Sociological Approach". In C.W.E. Bigsby, ed., *Approaches to Popular Culture*, London: Edward Arnold, 1976, pp. 39-68.

Bates, Daisy. *The Passing of the Aborigines: A Lifetime Spent Among the Natives of Australia*. London: John Murray, 1938. Rpt., rev. edn., 1972.

Batty, Joyce D. *Namatjira: Wanderer Between Two Worlds*. Melbourne: Hodder and Stoughton, 1963. Rpt. Adelaide: Rigby, 1976.

Bauman, Toni and Linda White. "White Folks With Plastic Smiles" [Interview with *Bobbi Sykes]. *Passing Show*, vol. 6, no. 21, pt. 1, Nov. 1978, pp. 9-12.

Beckett, Jeremy. "Aborigines Make Music". *Quadrant*, vol. 2, no. 4, Spring 1958, pp. 32-42.

Bell, James H. "The Economic Life of Mixed-Blood Aborigines on the South Coast of New South Wales". *Oceania*, vol. 26, no. 3, Mar. 1956, pp. 181-199.

*Bell, Jeanie. "Cheryl Buchanan Talks About the Bicentennial and Expo 88"[Interview with *Cheryl Buchanan]. *Social Alternatives*, vol. 7, no. 1, Mar. 1988, pp. 7-11.

Bennett, Bruce and Laurie Lockwood. "Colin Johnson: An Interview". *Westerly*, no. 3, 1975, pp. 33-37.

Benterrak, Krim, Stephen Muecke and *Paddy Roe. *Reading the Country: Introduction to Nomadology*. Fremantle: FACP, 1984.

Berndt, Ronald M. and Catherine H. *Arnhem Land: Its History and Its People*. Melbourne: Cheshire, 1954.

Berndt, Ronald M. *An Adjustment Movement in Arnhem Land*. Paris: Mouton, 1962.

Berndt, Ronald M. and Catherine H. *Aboriginal Man in Australia: Essays in Honour of Emeritus Professor A.P. Elkin*. Sydney: A & R, 1965.

— *Aborigines of the West: Their Past and Their Present*. Perth: Univ. of Western Australia Press, 1979. Rev. edn., 1981.

— "Aboriginal Australia: Literature in an Oral Tradition". In L.A.C. Dobrez, ed., *Australia*. Review of National Literatures Series, Gen. ed. Anne Paolucci, New York: Council on National Literatures, 1982, pp. 39-63.

Beston, John. "Who Are the Aboriginal Writers in Australia?". *Identity*, vol. 2, no. 9, Jul. 1976, pp. 13-15.

— "The Aboriginal Poets in English: Kath Walker, Jack Davis and Kevin Gilbert". *Meanjin*, vol. 36, no. 4, Dec. 1977, pp. 446-462.

— "Aboriginals in Australian Literature: A Bibliography". *Meanjin*, vol. 36, no. 4, Dec. 1977, pp. 463-469.

— "David Unaipon: The First Aboriginal Writer (1873-1967)". *Southerly*, no. 3, 1979, pp. 334-350.

Biskup, Peter. *Not Slaves, Not Citizens: The Aboriginal Problem in Western Australia 1898-1954*. St. Lucia: UQP, 1973.

— "Aboriginal History". In W.F. Mandle and G. Osborne, eds, *New History—Studying Australia Today*. Sydney: Allen and Unwin, 1982, pp. 11-31.

*Bostock, Gerry. "Black Theatre". In Jack Davis and Bob Hodge, eds, *Aboriginal Writing Today*, Canberra: AIAS, 1985, pp. 63-73.

*Bostock, Lester. "Black Theatre in New South Wales". *New Dawn*, vol. 4, no. 4, 1973, pp. 13-14.

Bowden, Robert. "Walsh Backs Morgan on NT Land Rights". The *Australian*, May 13, 1984, p. 2.

Brennan, G.A. "The Aborigine in the Works of Judith Wright". *Westerly*, no. 4, Dec. 1972, pp. 46-50.

Broome, Richard. *Aboriginal Australians: Black Response to White Dominance, 1788-1980*. Sydney: Allen and Unwin, 1982.

— "Professional Aboriginal Boxers in Eastern Australia 1930-1979". *Aboriginal History*, vol. 4, 1980, pp. 48-71.

*Buchanan, Cheryl. *We Have Bugger All—The Kulaluk Story*. Carlton: Australian Union of Students, 1974.

Buckley, Vincent. *"Capricornia"*. *Meanjin*, vol. 19, no. 1, 1960, pp. 13-30.

Butlin, N.G. *Our Original Aggression: Aboriginal Populations of Southeastern Australia 1788-1850*. Sydney: Allen and Unwin, 1983.

"Cakeman Returns to Critics' Praise: First Professional Performance of Aboriginal Play". *Artforce*, no. 12, Apr.-Jun. 1977, p. 9.

Callaghan, David. "What Future the Aborigine?".*TIME Australia*, vol. 3, no. 32, Aug. 8, 1988, pp. 12-15.

Calley, Malcolm. "Economic Life of Mixed-Blood Communities in Northern New South Wales". *Oceania*, vol. 26, no. 3, Mar. 1956, pp. 200-213.

Chase, Athol. "Empty Vessels and Loud Noises: Views About Aboriginality Today". *Social Alternatives*, vol. 2, no. 2, 1981, pp. 23-27.

Clunies-Ross, Bruce. "Survival of the Jindyworobaks". *Kunapipi*, vol. 3, no 1, 1981. pp. 56-63.

Cole, Keith. *The Aborigines of Arnhem Land*. Adelaide: Rigby, 1979.

Collins, Hugh. "Aborigines and Australian Foreign Policy: Some Underlying Issues". In Coral Bell, et al., eds, *Ethnic Minorities and Australian Foreign Policy*, Canberra Studies in World Affairs, no. 11, Canberra: ANU Department of International Relations, 1983, pp. 50-77.

Colmer, John. *Riders in the Chariot, Patrick White*. Port Melbourne: Edward Arnold, 1978.

Commonwealth of Australia. "Aboriginal Welfare—Initial Conference of Commonwealth and State Aboriginal Authorities". Canberra: L.F. Johnston, Government Printer, 1937.

— Department of Aboriginal Affairs, *Aboriginal Newsletter*. No. 130, Nov. 1983.

Cooper v. Stuart. Ruling of the Judicial Committee of the Privy Council, 1889.

Corris, Peter. *Lords of the Ring: A History of Prize-fighting in Australia*. Sydney: Cassell Australia, 1980.

Cotter, Michael. "The Image of the Aboriginal in Three Modern Australian Novels". *Meanjin*, vol. 36, no. 4, Dec. 1977, pp. 582-591.

Coyne, Michael and Leigh Edwards, eds. *The Oz Factor: Who's Doing What in Australia*. Melbourne: Dove Communications, 1980.

C.R. Untitled Tribute to Ion L. Idriess. *Fragment*, May 1954, n.p., [Contained in the Mitchell Library's file of news clippings pertaining to Idriess].

Crick, Donald. "Aboriginal New Writing". *Australian Author*, Winter, Jul. 1975, pp. 9-13.

Croft, Julian. "Ion Llewellyn Idriess". *The Australian Dictionary of Biography*, vol. 9, Melbourne: MUP, 1979, p. 426.

Daniel, Helen. "The Aborigine in Australian Fiction: Stereotype to Archetype". *Modern Fiction Studies*, vol. 27, no. 1, 1981, pp. 45-60.

Davidson, Jim. "Interview: Kath Walker". *Meanjin*, vol. 36, no. 4, Dec. 1977, pp. 428-441.

*Davis, Jack. "The Black Scene: Yesterday and Today". *Identity*, vol. 3, no. 5, Jan. 1978, pp. 34-35.

— "Aboriginal Writers". *Australian Author*, vol. 10, Jul. 1978, pp. 22-23. Rpt. *Identity*, vol. 3, no. 8, Oct. 1978, pp. 16-17.

— "Aboriginal Total Need". *Identity*, vol. 3, no. 7, Jul. 1978, pp. 10-17.

— "Aboriginal Writing: A Personal View". In Jack Davis and Bob Hodge, eds, *Aboriginal Writing Today*. Canberra: AIAS, 1985, pp. 11-19.

— and Adam Shoemaker. "Aboriginal Literature: Written". In Laurie Hergenhan, Gen. ed., *The Penguin New Literary History of Australia*, Ringwood: Penguin Books, 1988, pp. 35-46.

Davison, Dennis. "Honest Look at the Hidden Side of Society". The *Australian*, May 9 1988, p. 10.

Donaldson, Tamsin. "Translating Oral Literature: Aboriginal Song Texts". *Aboriginal History*, vol. 3, pt. 1, 1979, pp. 62-83.

Doobov, Ruth. "The New Dreamtime: Kath Walker in Australian Literature". *ALS*, vol. 6, no. 1, May 1973, pp. 46-55.

Dugon, Margaret. "Black Voices, White World". The *National Times*, Jan. 16-21 1978, p. 38.

Durack, Mary. "The Outlaws of Windginna Gorge". *Walkabout*, Jun. 1, 1941, pp. 14-16.

Dutton, Geoffrey. *White on Black: The Australian Aborigine Portrayed in Art*. South Melbourne: Macmillan, 1974.

— Untitled rev. of Healy's *Literature and the Aborigine in Australia*. *Historical Studies*, vol. 18, no. 73, Oct. 1979, pp. 624-626.

"Editorial". *Oceania*, vol. 1, no. 1, Apr. 1930, pp. 1-4.

Elliott, Brian, ed. *The Jindyworobaks*. Portable Australian Authors Series, St. Lucia: UQP, 1979.

Ellis, Vivienne Rae. *Trucanini: Queen or Traitor?*. Hobart: OBM, 1976. Rev. edn., Canberra: AIAS, 1981.

"Empty Stomach Turned Bushman Into Great Author". The *Sydney Daily Mirror*, Aug. 22, 1979, p. 73.

Field, Michele. "Writing Subsidies for Aboriginals". *ABR*, Nov. 16, 1979, pp. 17-18.

*Foley, Gary. "Blacks on Film in the Seventies". *Identity*, vol. 3, no. 11, Nov./Dec. 1979, pp. 8-10.

*Forrest, Vic. "Reflecting the Sesqui-Centenary". [Interview with *Jack Davis]. *Wikaru*, no. 8, Aug. 1980, pp. 5-10.

Fox, R.W., Kelleher, G.G. and Kerr, C.B. *Ranger Uranium Environment Inquiry*. Second Report, Canberra: AGPS, 1977.

"French Hold Forum on Aborigines". The *Age*, Jun. 26, 1980, p. 5.

Frost, Allan. "New South Wales as *Terra Nullius*: The British Denial of Aboriginal Land Rights". *Historical Studies*, vol. 19, no. 77, Oct. 1981, pp. 513-523.

Gifford, Kenneth. *Jindyworobak: Towards an Australian Culture*. Melbourne: Jindyworobak Publications, 1944.

*Gilbert, Kevin. *"Because A White Man'll Never Do It"*. Sydney: A & R, 1973.

— *Living Black: Blacks Talk to Kevin Gilbert*. Melbourne: Allen Lane, 1977. Rpt. Ringwood: Penguin Books, 1978.

— "The Aboriginal Question". *Social Alternatives*, vol. 2, no. 2, 1981, pp. 34-35.

— "Black Policies". In Jack Davis and Bob Hodge, eds, *Aboriginal Writing Today*. Canberra: AIAS, 1985, pp. 35-41.

Goddard, Roy H. "Aboriginal Poets as Historians". *Mankind*, vol. 1, no. 10, 1934, pp. 243-246.

Goodwin, Ken. "The Uniqueness of Recent Writing—Aboriginal Writers". In *A History of Australian Literature*, London: Macmillan, 1986, pp. 263-267.

Gordon, Harry C. *The Embarrassing Australian: The Story of an Aboriginal Warrior*. Melbourne: Landsdowne Press, 1962.

Greenfield, Kathy and Peter Williams, "Bicentennial Preliminaries: Aboriginal Women, Newspapers and the Politics of Culture". *Hecate*, vol. 13, no. 2, 1987/88, pp. 76-106.

Greer, Germaine. "Time to Party, or Protest". The *Independent*, Jan. 4 1988, p. 15.

Grimshaw, Patricia. "Aboriginal Women: A Study of Culture Contact". In Norma Grieve and Patricia Grimshaw, eds, *Australian Women: Feminist Perspectives*. Melbourne: OUP, 1984, pp. 86-94.

Hardy, Frank. *The Unlucky Australians*. Sydney: Thomas Nelson, 1968. Rpt., London: Pan Books, 1978.

Harris, Stewart. *"It's Coming Yet...": An Aboriginal Treaty Within Australia Between Australians*. Canberra: The Aboriginal Treaty Committee, 1979.

Hasluck, Paul. *Black Australians: A Survey of Native Policy in Western Australia, 1829-1897*. Second edn., Carlton: MUP, 1970.

Hawke, Stephen. "Our Black Past". "The Great Weekend"Supplement, The Brisbane *Courier-Mail*, Mar. 5, 1988, pp. Weekend 1-2.

Headon, David. "The Coming of the Dingoes—Black/White Interaction in the Literature of the Northern Territory". In Emmanuel S. Nelson, ed., *Connections: Essays on Black Literatures*, Canberra: Aboriginal Studies Press, 1988, pp. 25-40.

Healy, J.J. *Literature and the Aborigine in Australia, 1770-1975*. St. Lucia: UQP, 1978.

Hewett, Tony and David Monaghan. "Blacks Boo Royal Pair on Barge". The *Sydney Morning Herald* , Jan. 27 1988, p. 2.

Hill, Marji and Alex Barlow. *Black Australia: An Annotated Bibliography and Teacher's Guide to Resources on Aborigines and Torres Strait Islanders*. Canberra: AIAS, 1978.

Hodge, Robert. "A Case For Aboriginal Literature". *Meridian*, vol. 3, no. 1, May, 1984, pp. 83-88.

*Holt, Lillian. "Oh, But We Don't Mean You—You're Different". The *National Times Magazine*, Apr. 1, 1974, pp. 19-20.

Horner, Jack. *Vote Ferguson for Aboriginal Freedom*. Sydney: Australia and New Zealand Book Co., 1974.

Howard, Shane. "Solid Rock (Sacred Ground)". In "Spirit of Place", *Goanna*, W.E.A. 600127, Sydney: W.E.A. Records, 1982.

Idriess, Ion L. "Give 'Em a Go". *SALT*, vol. 5, no. 9, 1943, pp. 18-20.

Ingamells, Rex and Ian Tilbrook. *Conditional Culture*. Adelaide: F.W. Preece, 1938.

"It's Politics as Usual for Independent Bonner". The *Canberra Times*, Feb. 13, 1983, p. 1.

Jamieson, Anne. "The Push for an Aboriginal Parliament". The *Weekend Australian*, Feb. 6-7 1988, p. 24.

*Johnson, Colin. "White Forms, Aboriginal Content". In Jack Davis and Bob Hodge, eds, *Aboriginal Writing Today*, Canberra: AIAS, 1985, pp. 21-33.

— "Guerilla Poetry: Lionel Fogarty's Response to Language Genocide". In Ulli Beier, Guest ed., *Long Water: Aboriginal Art and Literature*, *Aspect*, no. 34, Aug. 1986, pp. 72-81.

— "The Growth of Aboriginal Literature". *Social Alternatives*, vol. 7, no. 1, Mar. 1988, pp. 53-54.

"Judges' Report". The *Bulletin*, vol. 49, no. 2532, Aug. 22, 1928, p. 9.

Kardiner, Abram and Lionel Ovesey. *The Mark of Oppression: Explorations in the Personality of the American Negro*. Cleveland: The World Publishing Co., 1951, Rpt. 1962.

"Kath Walker Withdraws". The *Canberra Times*, Feb. 15, 1983, p. 6.

Kiernan, Brian. *Patrick White*. London: Macmillan, 1980.

Kohler, Anne and Janette Kohn, eds. *From Many Lands: Australians of the Past*. Richmond: Heinemann Educational, 1980.

"*Kullark*—A Play". *Aboriginal and Islander Forum*. Sep. 1978, p. 7.

"Land Rights—The Story So Far". *Land Rights News*, Sep. 1985, p. 9.

*Langton, Marcia and Brownlee Kirkpatrick. "A Listing of Aboriginal Periodicals". *Aboriginal History*, vol. 3, pt. 2, 1979, pp. 120-127.

*Langton, Marcia. "Urbanizing Aborigines: The Social Scientists' Great Deception". *Social Alternatives*, vol. 2, no. 2, 1981, pp. 16-22.

Lee, S.E. "Writer and Reader". *Southerly*, no. 3, 1971, pp. 232-233.

McCallum, John. "Black Theatre: Robert Merritt's *The Cake Man*". *Meanjin*, vol. 36, no. 4, Dec. 1977, pp. 474-478.

McDonald, Geoff. *Red Over Black: Behind the Aboriginal Land Rights*. Bullsbrook: Veritas Publishing, 1982.

*McGuinness, Bruce. "*Not Slaves, Not Citizens*, by Peter Biskup". *Identity*, vol. 1, no. 9, Jan. 1974, pp. 10-11.

— and Denis Walker. "The Politics of Aboriginal Literature". In Jack Davis and Bob Hodge, eds, *Aboriginal Writing Today*, Canberra: AIAS, 1985, pp. 43-54.

McLaren, John. "New Insights On Our Writers". *ABR*, no. 12, Jul. 1979, p. 16.

— *Xavier Herbert's* Capricornia *and* Poor Fellow My Country. Essays in Australian Literature, Gen. ed. John Barnes, Melbourne: Shillington House, 1981.

Markus, Andrew. "Through a Glass Darkly: Aspects of Contact History". *Aboriginal History*, vol. 1, pt. 2, 1977, pp. 170-180.

Matthews, Janet. *The Two Worlds of Jimmie Barker: The Life of An Australian Aboriginal 1800-1972*. Canberra: AIAS, 1977.

Maurer, Tracy. "More Deaths in Police Custody Than Prisons". The *Australian*, Mar. 5 1988, p. 3.

Mercer, Patricia. Rev. of *Wacvie. Aboriginal History*, vol. 2, pt. 2, 1978, pp. 181-182.

Middleton, Hannah. *But Now We Want the Land Back: A History of the Australian Aboriginal People*. Sydney: New Age Publishers, 1977.

Milirrpum v. Nabalco Pty. Ltd. *Federal Law Reports*, Darwin: Supreme Court of the Northern Territory, 1971.

Millett, Kate. *Sexual Politics*. London: Hart-Davis, 1971.

Monaghan, Peter. "Fruits of Oppression". The *Canberra Times*, May 27, 1979, p. 15.

Moore, Catriona and Stephen Muecke. "Racism and the Representation of Aborigines in Australian Film". *Australian Journal of Cultural Studies*, vol. 2, no. 1, May 1984.

Muecke, Stephen. "Ideology Reiterated. The Uses of Aboriginal Oral Narrative". *Southern Review*, vol. 16, no. 1, 1983.

— "Discourse, History, Fiction: Language and Aboriginal History". *Australian Journal of Cultural Studies*, vol. 1, no. 1, May, 1983, pp. 71-79.

— "On Not Comparing: Towards an Aboriginal Aesthetic". The *Age Monthly Review*, vol. 5, no. 7, Nov. 1985, pp. 8-10.

— "Body, Inscription, Epistemology: Knowing Aboriginal Texts". In Emmanuel S. Nelson, ed., *Connections: Essays on Black Literatures*, Canberra: Aboriginal Studies Press, 1988, pp. 41-52.

— "Aboriginal Literature: Oral". In Laurie Hergenhan, Gen. ed., *The Penguin New Literary History of Australia*. Ringwood: Penguin Books, 1988, pp. 27-35.

Mullard, Chris. *Aborigines in Australia Today*. Canberra: National Aboriginal Forum, 1975.

Mulvaney, D.J. "The Australian Aborigines 1606-1929: Opinion and Fieldwork". *Historical Studies: Selected Articles*, pt. 2, Melbourne: MUP, 1964.

Murray, Les A. *Poems Against Economics*. Sydney: A & R, 1972.

— *Lunch and Counter Lunch*. Sydney: A & R, 1974.

— "The Human-Hair Thread". *Meanjin*, vol. 36, no. 4, Dec. 1977, pp. 550-571.

— "In Search of a Poet". The *Sydney Morning Herald*, Oct. 7, 1978, p. 16.

*Nangan, Joe and Hugh Edwards. *Joe Nangan's Dreaming*. Melbourne: Thomas Nelson, 1976.

National Aboriginal Conference. "Position Paper on Indigenous Ideology and Philosophy". *Identity*, vol. 4, Winter 1981, p. 36.

Nelson, Emmanuel S. "Black America and the Aboriginal Literary Consciousness". *Westerly*, vol. 30, no. 4, Dec. 1985, pp. 43-54.

*Newfong, John. "The Black Diaspora". *Kulinma-Kodowokai*, no. 2, Oct.-Nov. 1982, p. 6.

"New Novels". *TLS*, no. 1433, Jul. 18, 1929, p. 574.

New South Wales. *Aboriginal Land Rights*. Bill no. 42 of 1983, Sydney: Government Printer, 1983.

Northern Territory. *Draft Proposals on Aboriginals and Land in the Northern Territory*. Darwin: Government Printer, 1982.

Nugent, Ann. "Colin Johnson's Political Poems" (rev. of *The Song Circle of Jacky, and Other Poems*). The *Age Monthly Review*, vol. 7, no. 5, Sep. 1987.

Olbrei, Erik ed. *Black Australians: The Prospects for Change*. Townsville: James Cook Univ. of North Queensland Union, 1982.

*O'Shane, Pat. "Is There Any Relevance in the Womens' Movement for Aboriginal Women?". *Refractory Girl*, no. 12, 1976, pp. 31-34.

Oxford, Gillian. "The Purple Everlasting: The Aboriginal Cultural Heritage in Australia". *Theatre Quarterly*, vol. 7, no. 26, 1977, pp. 88-98.

Palmer, Kingsley and *Clancy McKenna. *Somewhere Between Black and White: The Story of an Aboriginal Australian*. Melbourne: Macmillan, 1978.

"Parliament Mosaic 'Puts a Curse on Whites' ". The *Australian*, May 10 1988, p. 1.

Pelczynski, Stan. "Land Rights Supplement". *Action for Aboriginal Rights Newsletter*, no. 22, 1987, pp. 2-5.

*Pepper, Phillip. *You Are What You Make Yourself To Be: The Story of a Victorian Aboriginal Family 1842-1980*. Melbourne: Hyland House, 1980.

*Perkins, Charles. "Resolving the Clash of Cultures". *24 Hours*, Apr. 1981, pp. 78-79.

Perrin, Gil. "Songs of Protest and Rural Poems". *Village News and NALA Journal*, Sep. 6, 1978, n.p.

Petelin, George. "Painting and the Manufacture of Myth; Aspects of Australian Figurative Painting 1942-1962: Dreams, Fears and Desires". *Meanjin*, vol. 43, no. 4, Dec. 1984, pp. 544-549.

"Poet Changes Name, Returns MBE in Bicentennial Protest". The Brisbane *Courier-Mail*, Dec. 15, 1987, p. 4.

Read, Peter. "A Double Headed Coin: Protection and Assimilation in Yass 1900-1960". In Bill Gammage and Andrew Markus, eds, *All That Dirt: Aborigines 1938*. Canberra: History Project Incorporated, 1982, pp. 9-28.

— *The Stolen Generations: The Removal of Aboriginal Children in N.S.W. 1883-1969*. Occasional Paper no. 1, Sydney: N.S.W. Ministry of Aboriginal Affairs, 1982.

Reay, Marie. "A Half-caste Aboriginal Community in North-Western New South Wales". *Oceania*, vol. 15, no. 4, Jun. 1945, pp. 298-323.

Redbird, Duke. *We Are Metis: A Metis View of the Development of a Native Canadian People*. Toronto: Ontario Metis & Non Status Indian Association, 1980.

"The Red Page". The *Bulletin*, vol. 49, no. 2533, Aug. 29, 1928, p. 5.

Rees, Leslie. *A History of Australian Drama*. Vol. 2, *Australian Drama in the 1970s*. Sydney: A & R 1978.

Reiss, Spencer and Carl Robinson. "Aborigines vs Queensland". *Newsweek*, Oct. 11, 1982, p. 13.

Reynolds, Henry. *Aborigines and Settlers: The Australian Experience 1788-1939*. Stanmore: Cassell Australia, 1972.

— *The Other Side of the Frontier: Aboriginal Resistance to the European Invasion of Australia*. Townsville: James Cook Univ. of North Queensland, 1981. Rev. edn., Ringwood: Penguin Books, 1982.

Robinson, Fergus and Barry York, eds. *The Black Resistance*. Camberwell: Widescope, 1975.

Roheim, Geza. *Children of the Desert: The Western Tribes of Central Australia*. Ed. Werner Muensterberger, Vol. 1, New York: Basic Books, 1974.

*Rosser, Bill. *This is Palm Island*. Canberra: AIAS, 1978.

Rowe, Gordon. *Sketches of Outstanding Aborigines*. Adelaide: Aborigines' Friends' Association, 1956.

Rowley, C.D. *The Destruction of Aboriginal Society*. Canberra: ANUP, 1970.

— *The Remote Aborigines*. Canberra: ANUP, 1971.

— *Outcasts in White Australia*. Ringwood: Penguin Books, 1972.

— *A Matter of Justice*. Canberra: ANUP, 1978.

Schwerdt, Dianne. "A Changing Black Image in Australian Fiction", in W. Menary, ed., *Aborigines and Schooling: Essays in Honour of Max Hart*. Adelaide: Adelaide C.A.E., 1981, pp. 83-96.

Scott, L.E. "Writers From a Dying Race". *Pacific Moana Quarterly*, vol. 4, no. 4, Oct. 1979, pp. 424-431.

Shapcott, Thomas. *"Long Live Sandawara"*. *Westerly*, no. 2, Jun. 1980, pp. 120-121.

Shoemaker, Adam. "Aboriginal Drama: A New Voice in Australian Theatre". In Joost Daalder and Michele Fryar, eds, *Aspects of Australian Culture*. Adelaide: Abel Tasman Press, 1982, pp. 28-33.

— "Fact and Historical Fiction: Colin Johnson and Ion L. Idriess". *Westerly*, vol. 27, no. 4, Dec. 1982, pp. 73-79.

— "An Interview With Jack Davis". *Westerly*, vol. 27, no. 4, Dec. 1982, pp. 111-116.

— "Aboriginal Creative Writing: A Survey to 1981". *Aboriginal History*, vol. 6, pt. 2, 1982, pp. 111-129.

— "The Year of Black Drama". *ABR*, no. 50, May 1983, p. 20.

— "Who Should Control Aboriginal Writing?". *ABR*, no. 50, May 1983, p. 21.

— "Aboriginal Play Not For ACT". The *Canberra Times*, Oct. 17, 1983, p. 12.

— "A Checklist of Black Australian Literature". *ALS*, vol. 11, no. 2, Oct. 1983, pp. 255-263.

— "Sex and Violence in the Black Australian Novel". *Westerly*, vol. 29, no. 1, Mar. 1984, pp. 45-57.

— "Can the Prescription Be Filled?". CRNLE *Reviews Journal*, no. 1, 1984, pp. 7-9.

— " 'Fiction or Assumed Fiction': The Short Stories of Colin Johnson, Jack Davis and Archie Weller". In Emmanuel S. Nelson, ed., *Connections: Essays on Black Literatures*, Canberra: Aboriginal Studies Press, 1988, pp. 53-59.

Smail, John R.W. "On the Possibility of an Autonomous History of Modern Southeast Asia". *Journal of Southeast Asian History*, vol. 2, 1961, pp. 72-102.

Smith, Bernard William. *European Vision and the South Pacific, 1768-1850: A Study in the History of Art and Ideas*. Oxford: Clarendon Press, 1960.

— *The Spectre of Truganini*. 1980 Boyer Lectures, Sydney: The Australian Broadcasting Commission, 1980.

— "Five Choices of Culture: In the Court of the Good, the True and the Beautiful". The *Age Monthly Review*, vol. 2, no. 7, Nov. 1982, pp. 9-10.

Smith, L.R. "New Black Town or Black New Town: The Urbanization of Aborigines". In I.H. Burnley et al., eds, *Mobility and Community Change in Australia*, St. Lucia: UQP, 1980. pp. 193-208.

South Australia. *The Pitjantjatjara Land Rights Act*. Act no. 20 of 1981, Adelaide: Government Printer, 1981.

Stanner, W.E.H. *After the Dreaming*. The 1968 Boyer Lectures, Sydney: The Australian Broadcasting Commission, 1969.

— "Introduction: Australia and Racialism". In F.S. Stevens, ed. *Racism: The Australian Experience*, vol. 1, *Prejudice and Xenophobia*, Second edn., Sydney: Australia and New Zealand Book Co., 1974, pp. 7-14.

— *White Man Got No Dreaming*. Canberra: ANUP, 1979.

— "Aboriginal Humour". *Aboriginal History*, vol. 6, pt. 1, Jun. 1982, pp. 39-48.

Stevens, F.S. *Aborigines in the Northern Territory Cattle Industry*. Canberra: ANUP, 1974.

— *Black Australia*. Sydney: APCOL, 1981.

Stone, Sharman, ed. *Aborigines in White Australia: A History of the Attitudes Affecting Official Policy and the Australian Aborigine 1697-1973*. South Yarra: Heinemann Educational, 1974.

Stow, Randolph. "Negritude for the White Man". In Marie Reay, ed., *Aborigines Now: New Perspectives in the Study of Aboriginal Communities*. Sydney: A & R, 1964, pp. 1-7.

— "Transfigured Histories: Patrick White and Robert Drewe". *ALS*, vol. 9, no. 1, May 1979, pp. 26-38.

Strehlow, T.G.H. *Aranda Traditions*. Carlton: MUP, 1947.

— *Songs of Central Australia*. Sydney: A & R, 1971.

Summers, Anne. *Damned Whores and God's Police: The Colonisation of Women in Australia*. Ringwood: Penguin Books, 1975.

*Sykes, Bobbi. "Black Women in Australia: A History". In Jan Mercer, ed., *The Other Half: Women in Australian Society*, Ringwood: Pelican, 1975, pp. 313-321.

— "The New White Colonialism". *Meanjin*, vol. 36, no. 4, Dec. 1977, pp. 421-427.

*Sykes, Roberta B. "Appendix: Keynote Address to the Conference on Black Literatures". In Emmanuel S. Nelson, ed., *Connections: Essays on Black Literatures*, Canberra: Aboriginal Studies Press, 1988, pp. 111-118.

Taft, Ronald, et al. *Attitudes and Social Conditions*. Aborigines In Australian Society Series, Canberra: ANUP, 1970, Rpt. 1975.

Taylor, Andrew. "New Poetry". *ABR*, no. 36, Winter 1967, p. 44.

*Thaiday, Willie. *Under the Act*. Townsville: North Queensland Publishing Co., 1981.

Throssell, Ric. *Wild Weeds and Wind Flowers: The Life and Letters of Katharine Susannah Prichard*. Sydney: A & R, 1975.

Tiffin, Chris. "Language of Anger". *ABR*, vol. 48, Feb./Mar. 1983, p. 18.

— "Look to the New-Found Dreaming". *Journal of Commonwealth Literature*, vol. 20, 1985.

Tiffin, Helen. "Looking Back Into the Future: Literature in the English Speaking Caribbean". Sydney: *New Literature Review*, no. 7, p. 6.

Turner, Ann, ed. *Black Power in Australia: Bobbi Sykes versus Senator Neville T. Bonner*. South Yarra: Heinemann, 1975.

*Unaipon, David. *Australian Aborigines: Photographs of Natives and Address*. Adelaide: Hunkin, Ellis, and King, n.d. [1928?].

Untitled rev. of *Kath Walker's *We Are Going*. *ABR*, May 1964, p. 143.

Untitled rev. of *Kath Walker's *The Dawn Is At Hand*. *Poetry Magazine*, no. 1, Feb. 1967, p. 31.

Vachon, Daniel and Phillip Toyne. "Mining and the Challenge of Land Rights". In Nicolas Peterson and *Marcia Langton, eds, *Aborigines, Land, and Land Rights*. Canberra: AIAS, 1983, pp. 307-326.

Wagner, Lucy. "The Cakeman A US Hit". The *Sydney Morning Herald*, Jul. 31, 1982, p. 14.

*Walker, Kath. "Aboriginal Literature". *Identity*, vol. 2, no. 3, Jan. 1975, pp. 39-40.

— "A Look at the Seventies". *Identity*, vol. 3, no. 11, Nov./Dec. 1979, pp. 39-40. Rpt. in *My People: A Kath Walker Collection*. Milton: Jacaranda Wiley, 1981, pp. 42-48.

Walker, Shirley. *The Poetry of Judith Wright: A Search for Unity*. Melbourne: Edward Arnold, 1980.

Wallis, John. "Kath Walker: Poetry or Propaganda". *Checkpoint*, no. 10, Mar. 1972, pp. 22-24.

Walsh, William. *Patrick White: Voss*. Studies in English Literature, no. 62, Gen. ed. David Daiches, London: Edward Arnold, 1976.

Walton, Alastair. "This'll Get 'Em For Sure!—An Interview With Bob Merritt". *Aboriginal Law Bulletin*, no. 17, Dec. 1985.

*Watego, Cliff. "Aboriginal Poetry and White Criticism". In Jack Davis and Bob Hodge, eds, *Aboriginal Writing Today*, Canberra: AIAS, 1985, pp. 75-90.

— "Backgrounds to Aboriginal Literature". In Emmanuel S. Nelson, ed., *Connections: Essays on Black Literatures*, Canberra: Aboriginal Studies Press, 1988, pp. 11-23.

— "Being Done To Again". *Social Alternatives*, vol. 7, no. 1, Mar. 1988, pp. 32-34.

*Watson, Len. *From the Very Depths: A Black View of White Racism*. Surrey Hills: Quaker Race Relations Committee, 1973.

— "1945: Enter the Black Radical". The *National Times Magazine*, Apr. 1, 1974, pp. 4-5, 7-8, 10, 12-13.

Watts, Patti. "Plea for Assistance". The *West Australian*, Jul. 17, 1980, p. 58.

Webb, Hugh. "Black Words on a White Page". In Sneja Gunew and Ian Reid, eds, *Not the Whole Story*, Sydney, 1984.

*Weller, Archie. "Portrayal of Aboriginal Men in Literature". *Social Alternatives*, vol. 7, no. 1, Mar. 1988, pp. 55-57.

Whaley, George. "A City's Place of Dreaming: Black Theatre in Sydney'". *Theatre Quarterly*, vol. 7, no. 26, 1977, pp. 98-100.

Wickens, Charles H. *Official Yearbook of the Commonwealth of Australia*. Ed. John Stonham. No. 23, Canberra: H.J. Green, Commonwealth Government Printer, 1930.

Wilson, Katrin. "Pindan: A Preliminary Comment". In A.R. Pilling and R.A. Waterman, eds, *Diprotodon to Detribalization: Studies of Change Among Australian Aborigines*. East Lansing: Michigan State Univ. Press, 1970, pp. 333-346.

Winks, R.W., ed., *The Historiography of the British Empire-Commonwealth: Trends, Interpretations, and Resources*. Durham, N.C.: Duke Univ. Press, 1966.

Wright, Judith. *The Generations of Men*. Melbourne: OUP, 1959.

— "The Koori Voice: A New Literature". *Australian Author*, vol. 5, no. 4, Oct. 1973, pp. 38-44.

— *Because I Was Invited*. Melbourne: OUP, 1975.
— "The Writer as Social Conscience". *Overland*, no. 89, Oct. 1982, pp. 29-31.

ii) Unpublished

a) Analysis

Beckett, Jeremy. "Aborigines and Welfare Colonialism". Paper delivered in "The State and Ethnic Minorities" section of the ANZAAS Conference, Canberra: ANU, May 1984.

Carter, Julie. "The Body: Source of Mediation and Metaphor in Aboriginal Identity". Ts., Canberra: ANU, 1983.

*Davis, Jack. Speech at the Biennial Conference of the AIAS Canberra: Australian National Gallery, May 1984.

"Declaration of the Indigenous Nations of Our Place in Canada's Constitution". Document tabled at the Third General Assembly of the World Council of Indigenous Peoples, Canberra: Apr./May, 1981.

Dugon, Margaret. "Aboriginal Literature: The Voice of the People". BA Thesis, Bathurst: Mitchell CAE, 1977.

*Everett, Jim. Speech at the Biennial Conference of the AIAS. Canberra: Australian National Gallery, May 1984.

*Foley, Gary. Speech at the Australian National Playwrights' Conference. Canberra: ANU, May 1984.

Gale, J.A. "The Aboriginal Short Story Viewed From a Third World Perspective". Ts., Adelaide: Salisbury CAE, 1980.

Hall, Robert A. "The Army and the Aborigines, World War II". MA(Qual.) Thesis, Canberra: ANU, 1979.

*Hampton, Ken. "The Aborigine in Australian Literature". Ts., Adelaide: DAA, 1977.

Iseman Kay. "Katharine Susannah Prichard, *Coonardoo* and the Aboriginal Presence in Australian Fiction". Ts., Paper delivered at the Women and Labour Conference, Sydney: 1980.

*Johnson, Colin. "Black Writing". Speech during "Aboriginal Literature" section of The National Word Festival, Canberra: ANU, Mar. 1983.

— "Report of the Proceedings of the Second Aboriginal Writers' Conference". Ts., Melbourne: Nov. 1983.

— "Paperbark". Ts., Unpublished lecture delivered in Brisbane: the Univ. of Queensland, Mar. 23, 1988.

Jones, Dorothy L.M. "The Treatment of the Aborigine in Australian Fiction". MA Thesis, Adelaide: Univ. of Adelaide, 1960.

Langshaw, Jessie H. "Aboriginal Literature in English". BA Thesis, Perth: Western Australian Institute of Technology, 1979.

Melendres, Patricia Meliran. "Social Criticism in the Australian Novel: The Aboriginal Theme". MA Thesis, Canberra: ANU, 1967.

*Miller, Mick. Speech at the launching of Lionel Fogarty's *Yoogum Yoogum*. Brisbane: Queensland Institute of Technology, Sep. 1982.

Miller, Rodney G. "Rhetoric of Resentment: Protest in Two Contemporary Aboriginal Writers". Ts., Canberra: NLA, 1977, Npf no. A 821.3 M649.

Muecke, Stephen. "Available Discourses on Aborigines". Ts., Adelaide: South Australian C.A.E. [Magill], 1982.

*O'Shane, Pat. "Aboriginal Sexual Politics". Public Speech, Canberra: ANU, Feb. 1983.

Palmer, Vance. "Palmer Letters". Canberra: NLA, ms. 1929.

Pedersen, Howard. "Pigeon: An Aboriginal Rebel. A Study of Aboriginal-European Conflict in the West Kimberley, North Western Australia During the 1890s". BA(Hons) Thesis, Perth: Murdoch Univ., 1980.

Read, Peter John. "A History of the Wiradjuri People of New South Wales, 1883-1969". Ph.D Thesis, Canberra: ANU, 1983.

Richardson, B.E. "Myth and Reality: An Exploration of the Development of the Aboriginal Theme in the Australian Novel". B.Litt. Thesis, Armidale: Univ. of New England, 1969.

Shoemaker, Adam. "Drama in Black and White: Race Relations Theatre in Australia Since 1970". Ts., Canberra: ANU, 1981.

— "Black Words, White Page: The Nature and History of Aboriginal Literature, 1929-1984". Ph.D Thesis, Canberra: ANU, May, 1985.

Wilson, John. "Authority and Leadership in a "New-Style" Aboriginal Community: Pindan, Western Australia". PhD. Thesis, Perth: Univ. of Western Australia, 1961.

b)Interviews and Correspondence

*Bandler, Faith. Telephone Interview. Sydney: Jul. 1980.

— Personal Interview. Perth: Feb. 1983.

*Bostock, Gerald. Personal Interview. Sydney: Jul. 1980.

*Brennan, Gloria. Personal Interview. Canberra: Nov. 1980.

Chamberlin, Prof. J.E. Personal Correspondence. Jan. 1984.

— Personal Interview. Sydney: Jul. 1984.

*Colbung, Ken. Personal Discussion. Canberra: Nov. 1983.

*Corpus, Louise [Aileen]. Personal Discussion. Canberra: Jun. 1987.

Corris, Peter. Personal Interview. Adelaide: Feb. 1982.

*Davis, Jack. Personal Interview. Canberra: Nov. 1981.

*Dingo, Ernie. Personal Discussion. Canberra: May 1984.

*Dixon, Chicka. Personal Interview. Sydney: Jul. 1980.

Drewe, Robert. Personal Interview. Adelaide: Feb. 1982.

*Foley, Gary. Personal Discussion. Canberra: May 1984.

*Gilbert, Kevin. Personal Interview. Canberra: May 1981.

Haebich, Anna. Personal Interview. Canberra: Nov. 1980.

*Hammond, Ruby. Personal Discussion. Canberra: May 1984.

Hilliger, Josie. Personal Correspondence. Sep. 1982.

*Johnson, Colin. Personal Interview. Brisbane: Jul. 1980.

— Personal Correspondence. Aug. 1982.

— Personal Interview. Conducted by Adam Shoemaker and *Cliff Watego, Brisbane: Sep. 1982.

Keneally, Thomas. Personal Interview. Brisbane: Sep. 1982.

*Langton, Marcia. Personal Discussion. Canberra: Jun. 1984.

*McGuinness, Bruce. Personal Discussion. Perth: Feb. 1983.

*Mafi-Williams, Lorraine. Personal Discussion. Canberra: May 1984.

*Maza, Bob. Personal Discussion. Canberra: May 1984.

*Merritt, Robert. Personal Interview, with *Brian Syron. Sydney: Jul. 1982.

Murray, Les. Personal Interview. Canberra: Jun. 1981.

*Newfong, John. Personal Interview. Canberra: Jul. 1982.

*Perkins, Charles. Personal Interview. Canberra: Jan. 1983.

*Rankine, Leila. Personal Interview. Adelaide: Feb. 1982.

*Saunders, Justine. Personal Discussion. Sydney: Jul. 1982.

Shankland, Robert. Telephone Interview. Sydney: Jul. 1980.

Smith, Bernard. Personal Discussion. Brisbane: Sep. 1982.

*Smith, Shirley [MumShirl]. Telephone Interview. Canberra: Nov. 1982.

Stuart, Donald. Personal Interview. Canberra: May 1981.

*Syron, Brian. Personal Interview. Canberra: May 1981.

— Personal Interview, with *Robert Merritt. Sydney: Jul. 1982.

Tregenza, John. Personal Interview. Adelaide: Jul. 1980.

*Tur, Mona [Njitji Njitji]. Personal Interview. Perth: Feb. 1983.

*Utemorrah, Daisy. Personal Interview. Perth: Feb. 1983.

*Walker, Denis. Personal Discussion. Perth: Feb. 1983.

*Walker, Kath. Personal Interview. Stradbroke Island: Aug. 1980.

— Personal Interview. Conducted by *Cliff Watego, Stradbroke Island: Aug. 1982.

*Ward, Glenyse. Personal Discussion. Brisbane: May 1988.

*Watego, Cliff. Personal Discussions. Brisbane: Sep. 1982, Canberra: Nov. 1984.

*Watson, Maureen. Personal Interview. Perth: Feb. 1983.

— Personal discussion. Canberra: Jun., 1987.

*Weller, Archie. Personal Interview. Perth: Feb. 1983.

— Personal Interview. The Oral History Unit, Canberra: NLA, May 1984.

White, Patrick. Personal Interview. Canberra: May 1983.

*Williams, Candy. Personal Interview. Sydney: Jul. 1980.

*Williams, Harry. Personal Discussion. Canberra: Jul. 1983.

Wright, Judith. Personal Interview. Canberra: Jul. 1982.

Index